THE PHOENICIANS IN HISTORY AND LEGEND

BY

ANTHONY STRONG

© 2002 by Anthony Strong. All rights reserved.

No part of this book may be reproduced, stored in a retrieval system, or transmitted by any means, electronic, mechanical, photocopying, recording, or otherwise, without written permission from the author.

ISBN: 1-4033-6689-6 (e-book)
ISBN: 1-4033-6690-X (Paperback)
ISBN: 1-4033-8034-1 (Dustjacket)

This book is printed on acid free paper.

"The Phoenicians are entitled to be commemorated in history by the side of the Hellenic and Latin nations".

Theodor Mommsen, The History of Rome,
1911 edition, English translation. New York, Scribner's Sons

Dans les caveaux des miens plongeant mes pas nocturnes,
J'ai compté mes aïeux, suivant leur vieille loi.
J'ouvris leurs parchemins, je fouillai dans leurs urnes,
Empreintes, sur le flanc, des sceaux de chaque Roi.
....
Si j' écris leur histoire, ils descendront de moi.

Alfred de Vigny, L'Esprit Pur, Mars 10, 1863.

TABLE OF CONTENTS

Introduction xvii

Chapter One   The Historical Perspective 1

Chapter Two   The Egyptian Heritage 14
    Osiris and Isis 20
    Oracles and Divination 30
    The Tale of Sinuhe 32
    The Tell-El-Amarna Period 40
    Wen-Amon Visits Zakar-Baal Of Byblos 43

Chapter Three   The Gods Of Byblos, Tyre & Sidon 53
    Adonis 62
    Astarte 75
    Ba'al 88
    Ba'alath 108
    Kadmus 113
    Eshmun 128
    Melkart 134
    Tannit 143
    Reshep 147

Chapter Four   Jezebel and Monotheism 165

Chapter Five   Gods of Ebla and Ugarit 183
    Anat 194
    Keret 203
    The God El 210

Chapter Six   The Alphabet 218
    Visitors to the Mouth of the "Dog" River 249

Chapter Seven   Merchants and Navigators 256
    Circumnavigation of Africa 275
    The Periplus of Hanno, General of Carthage 277
    Phoenicians in America 285

Chapter Eight   Mesopotamia & Assyria 295

Chapter Nine   The Persians 305

Chapter Ten   Greece And Rome In Phoenicia 343
    Helen, Paris and the Trojan War 376
    Pygmalion and Dido 381
    Berytus and the School of Law 387

Chapter Eleven   Carthage and the Punic Wars 391

Chapter Twelve   The Writers 456

Bibliography 471

Index 483

x

LIST OF ILLUSTRATIONS

1. The Abduction Of Europa By The Bull From The Beirut Museum..116
2. Reshep "Au Foudre" As Depicted In The Stone Of The Louvre Museum..154
3. The Arrows Of Zakkur And Azorba'al..............................225
4. The Inscription In The Pseudo-Hieroglyphic Script From Byblos Showing a Combination With Archaic Phoenician Signs...228
5. Sarcophagus Of Ahiram...234
6. "The Stele Of Moab" Picture From The Louvre Museum..240
7. Stele Of Yehawmilk. From The Louvre Museum 242
8. Inscription On The Sarcophagus Of Eshmun' Azzar From Sidon (Now In The Louvre Museum, 22 Lines Of Text In Phoenician, The Longest In Existence): Photo From The Louvre Museum, Paris, Year 2000. 302

PREFACE

In a summer evening a few years ago during one of several visits to Lebanon, the country of my ancestors, I was invited to a dinner gathering where everyone was either a judge, an attorney, or their spouses. Our host was the son of the former Chief Justice of the Supreme Court of that country 40 years earlier. A close relative of mine had extended to me an invitation to come to dinner with him that evening. Because of a common custom in that country I accepted and was well received by our host. My profession, being different from that of the majority of the other guests, did not appear to have been an impediment for my participation in the conversation that took place over and after dinner. This was a quite heterogenous group of people of all kinds of political persuation that remained friendly to each other despite the war that had ravaged Lebanon in the latest decades of the 20th century AD once again and had just finished. This is another characteritic trait of the people of this country where, immediately after a 15 year-war had ended, everyone forgot the events or the reasons that led to such bloody confrontation that destroyed a large part of their cities and towns. As soon as peace was made everybody returned to enjoy the pleasures of life, a quite typical behaviour of the Phoenicians of history. For reasons that I can't recall now, over dinner we found ourselves involved in a conversation dealing with the gods of Phoenicia and their influence in the great cultural developments that took place in Egypt, Anatolia and Mesopotamia, three to four millennia before present. When the hour came to leave his home that interesting evening our host suggested to me to put in writing my impressions and opinions as they had transpired during our dinner conversation. I promised to attempt to satisfy his suggestion but expressed the idea that it would take a couple of years to write them down. As it turned out I was mistaken because the process of searching the various sources took over six years from Beirut to Byblos, from Tyre to Paris and from Seville and the Carambolo to several visits to the Louvre in Paris where several inscriptions in stone and sarcophagii are extant. Finally I had to visit the new Bibliothèque National de la France, site Francois Mitterand; the Beirut National Museum, La Direction Générale des Antiquités of Lebanon and the Regenstein Library of the University of Chicago. A thorough search by returning to the literature of the Greek and Latin Classics was a need, it took a longtime and proved to be an enormous task.

I have to give my especial thanks to the Louvre Museum which granted permission to reproduce several of the artifacts dealing with the history of Phoenicia and also to Mr Frédéric Husseini, Directeur Géneral, Services d'Antiquités of Lebanon, who granted me permission for the photographic reproduction of Phoenician inscriptions in monuments now in the Beirut Museum. On a personal basis, I have to express my thanks to Kevin Robertson who gladly volunteered to find many texts in obscure places and facilitated my access to various unique documents from distant locations, such as the Regenstein Library and other sites in the USA. To John R. Dooley, I owe my gratitude for his careful reading of an earlier version of this writing and for his interesting suggestions that definitely contributed to improve the text.

Paris, September 2000

INTRODUCTION

At the beginning of recorded history the Phoenicians already appear to have had a rather advanced civilization. Their real origin extends back in time into the realm of legend. Europa, Baal, Cadmus, are characters in whom legend and history blend. Europa, a Phoenician princess, is in mythical times abducted and raped by Zeus, who takes her to Crete where she begins the dynasty of Minos. Greek historians and poets during the 5th-4th century BC would later place this event at the onset of history. A succesion of local wars took place in the Eastern Mediterranean area during the 3d and 2d millennia BC that led to a mixture of races and cultures. To the Phoenicians, the origin of hostilities was related to the abduction of Europa. To the Western historians, the motivation for the beginning of hostilities was the phoenician behaviour. Herodotus, for instance, favors this view and makes the Phoenicians responsible for the abduction of Greek women, (Io, the daughter of Inachus, is abducted and made pregnant by a phoenician captain). Whether these were facts or legend, one can not with entire certainty clearly trace the origin of the conflict in the eastern Mediterranean shores at this period to any particular event. No extant evidence exists today. Eventually, however, the net result of these contacts was the miscegenation of European and Middle Eastern inhabitants on the shores of Asia Minor.

Many facts and names of middle eastern places came to us transmitted by the Greeks. Greek knowledge of Geography outside Asia Minor appears to have been limited in the time of Herodotus because he states that Asia is uninhabited beyond India and Europe is as large as Africa and Asia put together. The name Lybia, given by the Greeks to Africa was originally that of the wife of Poseidon and mother of Agenor, king of Phoenicia. According to Herodotus most Greeks assumed that Lybia was so called after a native woman and Asia was named after the wife of Prometheus. According to the Lydians, however, Asia was originally the name of the grandson of Manes and that of a tribe called Asias in Sardis. Finally, the name Europe seems to have derived from Europa, the Phoenician princess, sister of Kadmus, abducted by Zeus, mentioned above.

Unquestionably, the most significant and everlasting Phoenician contribution to civilization is the invention of the alphabet. This discovery was first credited to them by ancient writers, among whom arguably the most prominent was Herodotus. Its introduction into Greece during mythological times is attributed to Cadmus, the phoenician brother of Europa. Following his father's orders Cadmus went searching for his sister and initiated a lineage that blends mythology and history. The finding of the earliest extant example of the most evolved form of the consonant alphabet at Byblos, on the lid of the epitaph inscription of the Ahiram Sarcophagus, is a momentous event in the history of civilization. Its possible invention in Phoenicia proper is still subject of debate. Its diffusion by the Phoenicians to the

Greeks and Romans is a fact now accepted by most scholars. The introduction into Greece by the Phoenicians, based on historical-legendary records, seems now undeniable and widely accepted. Historically it appears, despite some disagreements among scholars, that the most likely date for the introduction of the Phoenician alphabet into Greece by Cadmus was between the 12th and 11th century BC or perhaps earlier.

This event greatly facilitated the creation, development, recording and propagation of human knowledge. The alphabet, modified and adapted by the Greeks and later by the Romans, remains in use until present and has played a paramount role in the development of Western thought. The Phoenicians would also count, among their contributions to the early history of mankind, the discovery and navigation of the Indian and Atlantic Oceans and the circumnavigation of Africa. Finally the Phoenicians, in the form of their descendants, Carthagineans and Celtiberic, appear to have also traveled to America, as more recent evidence seems to suggest.

CHAPTER ONE

THE HISTORICAL PERSPECTIVE

The word Phoenician [(**p(h)oinix** in singular), (**poiniki** in plural)], comes from the Greek and was used by them (~ late 9th to 8th Century BC) to designate the people of Canaan. It is unclear why. According to some scholars this designation was used to indicate the deep brown color of the skin of this race. Others believe the word was used to indicate their relationship with the dark red purple dye extracted by them from the Murex molluscum, so common on their Mediterranean shores. As it is well-known they used the dye to stain their textiles which became one of their main industries in the ancient world. Herodotus thought the Phoenicians had come originally from the shores of the Red Sea i.e. Eritrea. Although their site of origin is still controversial, the name **poiniki**, it is now believed, most likely referred to the bronzed-skin peculiar to this race. **Phoinos** in Greek means red.

The Phoenicians are the same people who inhabited the Eastern Mediterranean shores quite early in history and were known as Canaanites. The Greeks later on called them Phoenicians. The ethnic identity of the people who became known as Canaanites was already, very likely, established by the end of the fourth millenium BC. During the period between the 29th and the 26th century BC the civilization later identified with Phoenicia and its geographic neighbors had already become quite homogenous. Byblos, mythologically considered the first city, was already occupied during the Chalcolithic period by a people who buried their dead underground, in large jars. These people were trading with Egypt at the beginning of the third millenium BC. Thus, contrary to what has been asserted in the past, the Byblians were autochthonous inhabitants of this area long before the time, assumed to be in the middle of the 24th century BC, when the name Canaanite was first applied to them. A port city known since legendary times, Byblos, seems to have been involved as middle man in the earliest recorded trade with the first pharaohs, especially Khasekhemui, the last pharaoh of the second dynasty, as attested by an inscription on an alabaster jar found at Byblos. The city also maintained connections with Ebla, Egypt and other Eastern Mediterranean people such as Greece until the end of the second millennium.

Byblos was the name used by the Greeks for papyrus, then a commonly traded product, brought from Egypt and sold by the Byblians throughout the Mediterranean area. Then a sheet of byblos basically meant a sheet of paper. Large thick ropes of papyrus were also used in their ship-building industry: the Wen-Amon papyrus, preserved in Moscow, and brought by this envoy of the pharaoh to king Zakarbaal of Byblos, describes merchandise that included about 500 ropes of papyrus. Zakarbaal refused it, as will be dealt in detail

The Phoenicians in History and Legend

later, because he did not consider it sufficient pay in exchange for the cedar wood that the pharaoh needed. Eventually he received more goods and gave Wen-Amon the needed wood.

The Greek and Roman writers never used the term **Canaan** to designate the inhabitants of the eastern strip of land of Asia Minor bordered by the Mediterranean sea in the West and the mountain ranges of Lebanon and Anti-Lebanon in the East, the Orontes Valley in the North and the Sinai peninsula in the South. The origin of the name Canaan is unknown but the word appears already in the clay texts of Ebla during the 25th century BC referring to the people from Byblos as **Ka-na-na**. The Hurrians referred to them as **knaggi** (belonging to the land of purple). And the Akkadians named them **kinakhni**. Ramesses II in a letter written in Akkadian to Hatussi III, king of the Hittites, uses the word **kinahhi**. The equivalent phoenician term was **Kena'** or **Knín**. Not only Byblos but other typically phoenician cities such as Sidon, Tyre and perhaps Beirut were already trading with Ebla in the middle of the third millennium. By the 14th century BC in the Tell-El-Amarna letters, the inhabitants of the Eastern Mediterranean coastal strip extending from the valley of the Orontes river in the North to the Sinai peninsula in the South, called themselves in Akkadian **Kinanu**, (or Kinahnu).

Philo of Byblos (about the end of 1st century or beginning of 2d century AD.) was of the opinion that **Chna** and **Phoinix** were just two names used to designate the same people. This people, as stated earlier, were occupying the coastal strip of the Eastern Mediterranean sea that extended from the Orontes valley in the north to the Sinai peninsula in the south before the Neolithic period.

During the expansion of the first two great Near Eastern civilizations of the past, Egypt and Mesopotamia, the strip of land between the continents of Africa and Asia that separated their original areas of control was the land of Canaan. This area was to suffer from the intrusion of many foreign invaders over extended periods of time between the 3d and the 1st millennia. Among them, the Amorites and the Hyksos were the most prominent at the end of the third and in the first half of the second millennium.

Amorites meant "Westerners", a name given to them by the Mesopotamians. They were a strong stock and although initially wild, soon became civilized and took control of Mesopotamia, Assyria and Northern Syria, including the kingdom of Mari towards the last third of the 19th century BC. The Amorites of the biblical writers were the descendants of pre-historic giants: legendary people of great stature and extraordinary strenght. This assertion is not confirmed by extra-biblical sources. In Phoenicia proper there appeared to be no ethnic differences between Amorites and Canaanites: the Amorites assimilated later Hurrian and Babylonian elements remaining in the mountainous regions of Lebanon while the Canaanites spread over the Phoenician littoral and acquired more Mediterranean characteristics.

Artifacts have been found in Phoenicia which indicate that another group of invaders was there by the beginning of the second millennium BC: these were the Hyksos. The word Hyksos, **hyk**

khwsht, ("rulers of foreign lands") was the name given by the Egyptians to the foreign invaders from the Middle East during the last third of the 18th century, c.1730 BC, that came first in small groups and were to eventually occupy and control the Nile Delta. It is now generally accepted that the Hyksos came to power in the Nile Delta around 1730 BC and were driven out of Egypt at about 1580 BC by Akhmose I. Thus they reigned only for about 150 years. However, it appears that the greatest pharaoh in record, Ramessess II, who was in power during the 13th century, claimed to be of Hyksos origin. It seems likely that it was Manetho, an Egyptian historian of Ptolemaic times, who first used the name Hyksos, to designate a group of people who came to Egypt in small and ethnically different groups and eventually ended controlling the country. Evidence suggests that they first infiltrated the land of Canaan in the 19th century BC and after settling there, advanced slowly into the Delta. The idea that their name meant "king-shepherds" has been abandoned and today most scholars accept the proper meaning of the word Hyksos to have been "rulers from foreign countries". This is how some of their generals called themselves on the inscriptions in their monuments. From somewhere outside or from within the territory of Canaan, the Hyksos came in hordes, groups of strangers who were experts in working with metals and pottery, and brought the horse and the chariot as well as advanced knowledge of a new type of building construction. The evidence from their work in bronze found at Byblos suggests that they may have come originally from either the Caucasus, Mesopotamia or Anatolia. Their work on crescent-shaped daggers and toggle pins suggests Mesopotamia as their origin. Their work on tin and copper suggests Armenia and Iran as possible sources. The use of the horse and chariot suggest that they may have been an Aryan race. Where did these possible Aryans come from is still a subject of controversy. The Hyksos fortifications tended to be rectangular or square in shape, with rounded corners, such as the ones found at Heliopolis (Baalbeck) in Phoenicia. The sides or corners of these structures had a tendency to be oriented according to the cardinal points of the compass. These fortifications have also been considered of Aryan origin. Although the Hyksos were initialy considered a warlike people, the more recently uncovered evidence from excavated towns indicates that they were highly civilized, with a well-organized existence in the social sense.

The excavations in tombs at Byblos established the presence of Hyksos pottery there as early as the 19th century BC but, because of the close relations of the Byblians with Egypt, it is possible that this pottery may have been obtained by trade. As stated earlier, the Hyksos do not appear to have exercised any control in Egypt before 1730 BC. Some scholars believe that the Hyksos entered the area of the Delta about 1745 BC during the reign of Neferhotep of the 14th Dynasty. Furthermore some think that the Hyksos were Amorites and Canaanites, who pushed by Indo-Europeans such as the Hittites from Central Asia, came to the fertile Delta lands, brought the wheel, the horse chariots and introduced the cult of the god Baal. The invention of the alphabet in Phoenicia, according to some scholars, seems to date from this period. The inventor(s) of the alphabet must have been aware of the existence of the other scripts current in the Eastern Mediteranean area at the time: their genius was not only to combine the contributions of the Egyptian hieroglyphic with the pseudohieroglyphic script of Byblos and cuneiform syllabic alphabet of Ugarit but to conceive the early Phoenician alphabet between the 16th and 15th centuries BC: this alphabet was already mature in the legend inscribed on the lid of the Ahiram sarcophagus, dated by some scholars as far back as the 13th century BC.

The constructions of the Hyksos seem to have been made by people that originated in areas with large plains and no mountainous terrain i.e. South Russians could have come through a land bridge in the Caucasus. However, no independent evidence exists to suppport the latter suggestion. When the Hyksos penetrated and dominated Egypt they kept and introduced their main gods, namely El, Hadad, Baal and Anat, perhaps an indication of their Middle Eastern origin.

During the period of Roman domination of the region that started with Septimius Severus (born in Leptis, a Phoenician colony in North Africa) up to the times of Constantine the Great, there were two Phoeniciae. **Phoenicia Prima**, whose capital was Tyre and whose chief towns were Acre (Ptolemais), Sidon, Berytus, Byblos, Botrys, Tripoli, Arka and Aradus. **Phoenicia Secunda** had for capital Emesa on the east side of the Orontes river and comprised Heliopolis (Baalbeck), Damascus and Palmyra. The latter town was located on the eastern confines of the desert.

According to Augustine of Hippo (by the 5th century AD.) the Punic people (peasants) of North Africa when asked who they were, still would respond in their Punic tongue, **chanani**. Thus the words Canaanite and Phoenician appear to have been used, for an extended period, to designate the same people. Dussaud and other European scholars during the first part of the 20th century, had begun to use the two words interchangeably to name the same people.

It must be recalled here that the Greeks had visited and explored during the 10th and 9th century Egypt and the Middle East and were responsible for the multiple names given by them to people and various segments of land. However, during the Middle Bronze Age in Crete (~ 19th century BC) the Greeks had an advanced civilization that traded with the East, with Egypt in the South and with the West, thrived in the arts and architecture, used hieroglyphic and Linear A scripts and was to collapse around 1100 BC at Mycenae. Its resurgence will take place two centuries later. Thus it is incorrect to believe that the Greeks remained illiterate until the 9th century BC, because the archeologic evidence now proves that they had had a very advanced culture much earlier, before entering into a Dark Age.

Upon borrowing the Phoenician alphabet, the Greeks called the letters Cadmean characters or plainly **p(h)oiniki**. They adapted them to their tongue, introduced some changes in the forms of the letters, created some of the vowels and began to use them. In the late archaic language of Crete the word for scribe was **p(h)oinikasta**. Indeed the same root and derivation seem to be shared by both words.

Traditionally this area of land was named Canaan until the 12th or 11th century BC. Phoenicia was the Greek designation that was given thereafter to the same land, although one and the same. It is now appropriate to consider the extent and limitations of the terms Canaan, Phoenician and Phoenicia. The more recent sholarship has a tendency to favor a change: give away with the limitations that the original terms entail because they were derived mainly: first, from the designations used by Homer and second, from the asumption that everyone must accept the putative arrival of the so-called "Sea People" to the land of Canaan as the main event that made the Phoenicians what they became. Towards the end of the 13th or beginning of the 12th century the eastern Mediterranean area had been invaded by the Sea People so called in the Egyptian inscriptions such as the "The Victory Stela" of Merneptah and the Great Karnak Inscription of Ramesses III. They appeared to have arrived to this area as several separate ethnic groups still poorly defined: the Shardana, the Shekelesh, the Teresh, the Lukka, the Tjeker and the Peleset. They are described as coming either from the North or from the islands. However nothing tells us with any degree of certainty their real site of origin. The Shardana after being defeated ended as mercenaries for the Egyptians. They also were found in Byblos as mercenaries serving under the king Rib-Addi in the 14th century at the time of Amenophis IV. They would later on settle in Sardinia, where they fell under the dominium of the Phoenicians several centuries later. The Phoenicians later had to recover the island from the Shardana in order to protect their mining interests in Sardinia. The Shekelesh came most probably from Sicily. The Teresh were occupiers of Western Anatolia for a while and later would become the people from whom the Etruscans originated. The Lukka from the beginning of the 14th century are recorded as having committed acts of hostility against the Egyptians, ruled at the time by Amenophis III. They were from Western Anatolia also and later on would become allied with the Carians. The Danuna, Tjeker and Peleset attacked Egypt by land and sea from Anatolia to the Nile Delta and were defeated by Ramesses III.

The Peleset, who eventually gave their name to Palestine, after their defeat by Ramesses III, established themselves between Jaffa and Gaza while the Tjeker took possesion of Dor. The Tjeker reappear in the Wen-Amon papyrus as navigators dedicated to pyracy in the eastern Mediterranean area. Between them remained the Danuna. It does not seem that any of the People of the Sea occupied or established themselves in Phoenicia. According to Roland de Vaux there is no reason to claim that the People of the Sea exerted any influence upon the Phoenicians or taught them anything concerning their ability as navigators, something they had learned from the time they were known as Canaanites. Thus the native inhabitants of this region were likely one and the same: Canaanites and Phoenicians.

The most recent view is to consider as inadequate and limited the study of the people known as Phoenicians by the Greeks independently from the Canaanites only because the Greeks of the 9th or 8th century BC thought these to be different people and gave them different names. Byblos, Sidon, Tyre and Berytus were already well-known from the middle to the end of the 3d millennium BC, thus it is time to abandon or modify the conceptions of the past. We must now adapt our ideas to the evidence coming from the archeological and epigraphic information obtained more recently. This information would extend our knowledge farther back in time and give us a more complete and satisfactory view of who the Phoenician people were more than a millennium earlier than what has been customarily accepted. It is somewhat arbitrary to retain the old designations in view of the fact that paramount human contributions such as writing were made or were developing during this period: the pseudo-hieroglyphic script of Byblos developed between the 23d century BC and the 16th; the Ugaritic, (cuneiform, syllabic or alphabetic), between the 17th and the 14th century. The Phoenician proper, found in extant inscriptions, in its most advanced form has variously been dated between the 13th and 11th centuries. Stone inscriptions have been found dating back to the 18th century BC which contain a combination of the linear pseudo-hieroglyphic script of Byblos and the archaic phoenician alphabet. Thus the earlier forms of this language most likely had started their development long before the epitaph on the Ahiram sarcophagus was written, perhaps during the 18th or 17th century BC.

The evolution of the language, customs and culture of the inhabitants of this area had been occurring for almost two millennia. Thus it seems narrow to assume that the people known or regarded as

Phoenicians should be only those living between the time when the poetry of Homer originated and the times in which the conquests of Alexander the Great took place. We know that from the 25th to the 14th century BC the archives of Ebla, Mari, Ugarit and Tell-el-Amarna, all record the existence of other advanced cultures that originated or were located outside Phoenicia proper but which maintained close relationships with Byblos, Sidon, Tyre and Berytus. These are the same people who will dominate sea trade and spread over the Mediterranean sea and beyond the pillars of Hercules during the first millennium.

It is reasonable to state that the language spoken and written by the Phoenicians at the beginning of the first millennium BC is the same that most likely originated early on in the second or even started to develop late in the third millennium.

Before the diffusion of the Phoenician alphabet, kings and priests, governors and judges, with rare exceptions, were all illiterate; only the scribes could read and write and as such represented by themselves a class apart and for the people in power, a rare commodity. Only the scribes could teach and transmit writing. However, the language that became the written script of the scribes had to be spoken by quite a number of people, otherwise it would have served no purpose to record it. Conquerors and kings took scribes in their campaings to record the everyday events of their lives. It is likely, however, that early literature was not written for public pleasure or recreation but for the **scribes** own education.

Within the last few centuries of our era, i.e. during the 18th, early 19th and first third of the 20th century AD, scholars and historians have searched in the Near East for explanations or corroboration of biblical stories. In order to better understand the new finds, they have attempted to employ a terminology that would facilitate communication between the disciplines of history, archeology and religion and the evidence contained in epigraphic material. Thus they introduced many new terms among them the words semite, northsemitic, protosemitic, as a matter of convenience to designate not a particular race, but in the biblical sense, the alleged descendants of certain figures whose historical existence has not yet been confirmed by the archeological record. The use of this otherwise widespread designations will be avoided in this writing, whenever possible.

CHAPTER TWO

THE EGYPTIAN HERITAGE

Before the end of the fourth millennium the Egyptians were already importing from Byblos cedar wood for the coffins of their nobility and pine or cedar oil for the embalment of their dead and preservation of their mummification. The resin of the cedars and pines of Lebanon was to continue in use for about two more millennia. The most enduring relationship and influence of Egypt over Phoenicia is especially evident in the constant contact between the Kings of Byblos and the Pharaohs, documented since the beginning of the third millenium BC. Excavations at Byblos have unearthed Egyptian inscriptions that date back to the pharaohs of the First and Second Dynasty (c. 2800 BC). During the reign of Senefru, a pharaoh of the 4th Dynasty, timber from Byblos was utilized in shipbuilding. The pharaohs of the Fourth and Fifth dynasties such as Cheops, Khephren and Mycerinus send constantly their gifts to queen Ba'alath. Many of these gifts were found in the ruins of her temple at Byblos. A ship build with Phoenician cedar wood has been unearthed recently, next to the pyramid of Kephren in Giza, and is now kept under protection in a especially constructed environment to avoid its deterioration. The ship can be seen today next to the middle pyramid and is a turistic attraction. During a period that spanned two millennia Ba'alath-Gebal was represented in art in a manner similar to that of Hathor-Isis. During the Middle Kingdom again the tombs of Abishemu and Ibshemuabi, Kings of Byblos, revealed gifts sent to them by the pharaohs of the Twelfth Dynasty. The pharaohs of the Eighteenth and Nineteenth Dynasties had well established relations with Phoenicia: during this period the most prominent of them was Thutmose the III, the son of Thutmose the II and a concubine. He came to power after queen Hatshepsut, who was in power as regent and pharaoh for 24 years. With enormous vigor Thutmose III carried on 17 campaings from Egypt as far as the Euphrates and the Taurus mountains and continued to improve the establishement of the temples at Karnak, where inscriptions reveal that "he built many ships of cedar from the mountains of God's land, near the Lady of Byblos". Despite his conquests as pharaoh he was remembered for his generosity and tolerance: pardoned rebels and retained the customs and religions of the conquered lands.

Dating from the reigns of Amenhotep the III and IV, it is is well documented in the Tell el-Amarna tablets, that the nature of the relationship between the Egyptians and the main city-states of the land of Canaan was very close. These pharaohs did not care much about the fate of their allies in Phoenicia, failed to help and protect their vassals against the attacks of certain kinglets from northern Phoenicia who besieged Byblos, Beirut and Sidon. Their behavior is recorded in the Tell el-Amarna correspondence, as mentioned elsewhere. Prominent among the Phoenician kinglets were Rib-Addi of Byblos, Amunira of Beirut and Zimrida of Sidon.

After many misfortunes Rib-Addi, the saddest figure of this period in Phoenicia, is left only with control of Byblos and Batrun. His sons and his wife, his sister and her children killed; his brother surrenders Byblos to Abdi-Ashirta's sons. Rib-Addi then writes to the pharaoh:

"…many are the people who love me in the city and few are the rebels…Let my lord know that I would die for him…to have the city of Byblos return to the King, my lord,…do not let the King hold back from the city…that contains great wealth with much silver and gold within its temple…". No response from Akh-en-Aton ever came.

During the Nineteenth Dynasty the towering figure of Egyptian history came to power: Ramesses the II, son of Seti I, known as the Great. Other than fathering well over fifty sons, Egypt, during Ramesses reign, attained the highest level of civilization. He internationalized religion and fused the gods of Phoenicia and Canaan with the Egyptian deities, thus leading to recognition of a certain form of monotheism, because of internationalizing their gods. He undertook a campaign against the Hittites and after an undecisive result he established an alliance with them and married a daughter of Khattusilis, his former adversary. It has been speculated that

Ramesses II and Ahiram of Byblos were contemporaries: several artifacts bearing Ramesses II name were found in the tomb of Ahiram. Because of close commercial ties between their two countries it is possible that artifacts could be found in their respective lands as a result of trade. However, it remains doubtful whether these Egyptian and Phoenician kings were contemporaries. Multiple inscriptions from Ramesses II have been found at different levels in Byblos by Maurice Dunand. It has been claimed that although great relations did exist between Egypt and Byblos at the time, the artifacts of Ahiram's tomb were just placed there at the burial site and are not hard evidence that the two men were ever friends, contemporaries or even met each other.

A sandstone bust of the Egyptian pharaoh Osorkon I (924-889 BC) was found at Byblos and is now at the Louvre Museum: it bears a legend-dedication by Eli-baal, king of Byblos, to Ba'alath-Gebal, the Lady of Byblos, in the Phoenician alphabet, in addition to a legend in hieroglyphics.

At least towards the beginning of the 3d millennium BC, if not earlier, the Egyptians had discovered the usefulness of establishing commercial relations with Byblos in Phoenicia for the purpose of buying wood, oil and various species that they used in their religious rituals and their daily life. In order to create a durable alliance and to make their commercial treaties more stable they decided to assimilate their gods to the gods of Byblos. They discovered that EL and Asherat were considered the creators of everything in Phoenicia and Ashtar and Ashtart, the protectors of the city. Because the Egyptian beliefs were solar in nature they could not conceive a god creator, father of the other gods and men other than Re. Thus they assimilated EL to Re: a bull with 4 wings and a solar disc became the image of EL at Byblos but for Asherat, the spouse of El, it became necessary to choose a mother of all gods with resemblance to the Bull EL, that is, a divine cow. Hathor had all the characteristics fitting the need: she was a great goddess creator and the great divine cow, thus she was transported to Byblos, at least in image, to serve as spouse of EL. For the younger gods Ashtar and Ashtarte, who became the children of Hathor, the woman goddess kept her image of Ba'alath-Gebal with a sceptre and a head-dress while the male god adopted a human body and the head of a lion, image which was also present at Ugarit since the 14th century BC.

Montet discovered in his excavations of Byblos what he chose to name "the Egyptian temple", while next to it later on Dunand discovered the temple of Ba'alat-Gebal and on the southern part of this, the temple of Ba'al-Gebal and Ashtar-Reshep, the so-called "Temple of the Obelisks".

A cylinder found here by Montet depicts in hieroglyphics the gods EL=Re, Ashtar=Ba'al: most likely done by the priests that worked in the temple. In the beginning Ashtar and Ashtarte, astral deities, when they became human, conserved as their attributes the lions that were originally their symbols. A cylinder found at Ugarit by Matthiae and dating from the middle of the second millennium represents Ashtar with the head of a lion, similar to the image found in the cylinder of Byblos, and Ashtarte=Astarte, in Greek, with two lions because originally she represented the godddess of the Morning and Evening Stars. The Giblite cylinder and the clay tablet from Ugarit both personify the same gods EL and Ba'al: in both cases the inscriptions are from the same period in Phoenicia. It is known that Phoenicia was considered by the Egyptians as the Land of the Gods, the god-father EL and his son Ba'al (Ashtar, Reshep). In Ugarit Anat and Baal replaced the Ashtar and Ashtarte of Byblos. A bas-relief most likely from the early period of relations between Byblos and Egypt found by Montet at Byblos depicts the image of the Pharaoh rendering his offerings to both Ashtar on one side and Ba'alat-Gebal on the other.

A documentation confirming this interpretation was found by Claude Schaeffer in the form of an ivory tablet measuring about one meter in lenght in the Royal Palace of Ugarit: three divinities are here represented: one is Astarte, as a naked goddess with a lotus flower in one hand; another depicts Ashtar, bearing a mace and a little symbolic lion; the third shows Hathor depicted with two cow's horns and four wings: two deployed and two resting: she is breast-feeding two young boys. The style is Egyptian but the details are Phoenician. The figure of Hathor has been found in other locations of the neighboring area, the young boys have similar appearance to those of Isis breast-feeeding Horus elsewhere in Phoenicia. Other traits are not Egyptian: between the cow's horns the solar disc has been replaced by a flower within a ring. This astral representation replaced by flowers was customary in Phoenicia and Anatolia.

Hathor is represented on this Phoenician sculpture as the mother of the gods, thus as another wife of EL. Most likely this monument was made at Byblos and not at Ugarit because of the characteristics shown here which were customary at Byblos and not at Ugarit. If this were made at Ugarit, Baal and Anat would have been depicted instead of the other gods then prevalent in Byblos. At the Louvre Museum there is a battle-axe in bronze found by French excavators at Byblos that confirms the fact that the Hathor of Byblos was the same goddess at Ugarit. On one side there is a representation of Hathor with her usual head-dress, her wings and long dress and standing in a position similar to that of the ivory of Ugarit. On the other side of the bronze there is a figure of Ashtarte, naked, with long hair and holding a lotus flower. This goddess has here the face of a lion and large leonine ears. A male sphinx is seen in the border, likely to be Ashtar, the male companion. It is possible, according to scholars, that this battle-axe was also made at Byblos.

OSIRIS AND ISIS

Egyptian religious texts contain numerous references to the legend on which the cult of Osiris is based. A full account, however, was not recorded in remote antiquity. Osiris probably was first the king and later a local god of Lower Egypt. Subsequently his influence spread until he became the chief god of the Nile Delta. Isis, who was considered the wife of Osiris during pyramid times, but in other legends his sister and lover, appears to have been originally a goddess of the Delta. The legend of her love and frustrations with Osiris must have been quite well known in ancient times because a detailed record was not kept, perhaps because it was not deemed necessary.

Diodorus Siculus, a Greek historian born in Agyrium, Sicily, (~80-20 BC) in his "Library of History", attributed the parenthood of Osiris to Zeus and Semele, the daugthter of Cadmus, the phoenician, then an inhabitant of the Egyptian Thebes.

"To those who say that the god was born of Semele and Zeus in Boeotian Thebes, are simply inventing a tale. For they say that Orpheus, while visiting Egypt to participate in the initiation rites and mysteries of Dionysus, adopted them and as a favor to the descendants of Cadmus, since he was kindly disposed to them,...transferred the birth of the god to Thebes; and the common people, partly out of ignorance or partly out of desire to have the god thought to be Greek, eagerly accepted the initiatory rites and mysteries."

What led Orpheus, according to Diodorus, to transfer the birth and rites of the god, occurred like this: "Cadmus, who was a citizen of Egyptian Thebes, begat several children, of whom one was Semele; she was violated by an unknown man, became pregnant and after seven months gave birth to a child whose appearance was…that of the Egyptian Osiris. Such a child was not supposed to be brought alive into the world, either because it was contrary to the will of the gods or because the laws of nature did not accept it. When Cadmus found out what had taken place, and under the advice of an oracle commanding him to observe the laws of his fathers, he both gilded the infant and paid it the proper sacrifices, believing there had been an epiphany of Osiris among men."

"The fatherhood of the child he attributed to Zeus, thus magnifying Osiris and averting slander from his violated daugthter. This is the reason why the tale was given to the Greeks, making Semele the mother of Osiris by Zeus."

At a later time Orpheus was entertained as a guest by the descendants of Cadmus and accorded unusual honors in Thebes. Since he was knowlegable about the teachings of the Egyptians gods, he transferred the birth of Osiris from the ancient to more recent times, and out of regard for Kadmus descendants, he instituted a new ritual of initiation in which the initiates were given the account that Dionysus had been born of Semele and Zeus."

The earliest complete version came to us told by Plutarch, himself a priest of Apollo in Boeotia. His version has become the standard. Osiris was murdered by his brother Seth who tricked him during a celebration in his honor into attempting to fit into a chest especially build with Osiris dimensions. Osiris stepped into the chest and found that it fit him well. The chest was then closed by friends of Seth. The coffin subsequently was carried away by Seth's accomplices, thrown into the Nile and cast adrift into the sea. Tossed by the waves the coffin landed on the shores of Byblos at the foot of a young tree. The tree grew, according to the legend, all around the coffin. It stood all straight and vigorous thus attracting the interest of the king who had it cut down and converted into a column to support the roof of his palace. Isis, upon discovering that Osiris had been murdered, and informed by divine winds, set out to search for his body, a peregrination that took her to Byblos. Once in Byblos, she sat full of sorrow beside a fountain. She spoke to no one for a while but to the maidens of the local queen and treated them with great kindness. Informed by the maidens, the queen sent for the stranger and soon befriended her. Isis became the nurse of the queen's child. At night she would set fire to the child's body that will not be consumed by the flames and appear intact the day after. She was often seen, transformed into a swallow, fluttering her wings around the column that held the body of Osiris. The queen having discovered one night her child in the flames became greatly upset. Isis then deprived the queen's son of the gift of immortality and eternal life and made herself known to the queen mother.

The goddess Isis then demanded the column holding the roof of the palace. Having taken the chest that contained the body of Osiris from it, she returned to Egypt. Isis kept the coffin in the marshes of the Delta awaiting the birth of her child Horus, apparently conceived after his father's death. Seth appears to have discovered the body of his brother. He then cut it into pieces and scattered them over various parts of Egypt. Once again Isis went in search of the pieces and buried them in each place where they were found. The only missing part was the virile member, which had been thrown by Seth into the river and devoured by fish.

Diodorus describes the event in a somewhat different manner:

"The parts of the body of Osiris which were found were honored with burial but the privates parts were thrown by Thyphon into the Nile because no one of his accomplices was willing to take them. Yet Isis thought them worthy of divine honors like the other parts...and made it the object of the highest regards and reverences in the rites and sacrifices accorded to the god. Consequently the Greeks too, because they had received from Egypt the customs dealing with celebrations of orgies and the festivals connected with Dionysus, honor this member in both, the mysteries and the initiatory rites and sacrifices of this god, giving it the name "phallus". Although some authors have maintained the origin of the cult of Dionysus to be of Egyptian origin, others believe it really originated in Phoenicia. Dionysus became Bacchus through Greece into Rome.

Yet another version of the Osiris legend, alleges that Isis after finding the body, fluttered her wings over it and restored him to life. After restoration to life Osiris became king of the dead. This is more in keeping with the tradition that makes Osiris the supreme ruler of the kingdom of the Dead.

The region of the Afterlife, known to the Egyptians as the Field of Reeds, where the gods could live in perpetual spring, was presided over by Osiris. According to one tradition that is where Isis found and buried the head of Osiris but according to another it was his entire body, with the exception of the virile member, that was buried there. The Field of Reeds is identical to the Elysean Fields where Cadmus was sent to the afterlife with his wife by Zeus.

The Osiris myth tells of the body of the dead god floating ashore at Byblos on the Phoenician coast and reviving there as a green tree. Thus he personified a dying and ever rising god: the god of the underworld. The earliest sources identify Osiris with the grain, the waters, and the soil. The god subjected to human destiny and human mortality, like the Sun-god when kings appeared in Egypt he also became a king. Osiris is the son of Nut, the Sky goddess and eventually becomes the ruler of the Nether World. The Pyramids Texts have him dying either assasinated by his brother Seth or drowning. The unhappy news take his sisters Isis and Nephthys, wandering in the form of birds, until they find the body of Osiris floating on the waters.

The sisters embalmed the body and laid him on his tomb where a sycamore grows up and envelops him. The faithful Isis drew near her dead lord, received his seed, brought up an heir and nursed the child in solitude. The youthful Horus may eventually seek the murderer of his father. After losing an eye in battle with his uncle Seth, Horus would seek his father crossing the sea in his quest for him in Byblos. The Pyramid Texts tell us that he would raise his father from the dead and offer him the eye that he had sacrificed in his behalf, a supreme act of filial devotion. The risen Osiris finally receives his kingdom by "entering the secret gates of the Nether World, beneath the Earth, in the splendor of the lords of eternity…" His son Horus succeeds him in the land of the living as King of the Upper and Lower Egypt.

In early Egypt a primitive belief existed in a subterranean kingdom of the dead which eventually claimed all living beings. This was the kingdom of Osiris. In contrast, the pharaoh first and later the noble and powerful, belonged to the solar kingdom and gave their prestige to the glorious celestial thereafter. Thus the kingdom of the dead belonged to the people while the celestial kingdom belonged to the royalty and nobility. When the growing prestige of Osiris spread to all social classes it came into competition with the realm of the Sun-god especially in the area concerning the belief in the afterlife. Nothing in the Osiris myth suggests the belief in a celestial afterlife.

However, the predominance of Osirian beliefs among the people eventually forced the king himself to adopt some of the characteristics and identity of the King of the Dead. According to some scholars these Egyptian beliefs finally influenced Christianity: the idea of the underworld with fiery gates and seas of flame became reflected in the Christian hell and the celestial realm of the Sun-god with trees of life served as the ideal image of paradise in the heavens.

Osiris was the god whose death and resurrection were celebrated every year with sorrow and joy alternatively by the Egyptians and on this ground it is reasonable to identify him with Adonis in Phoenicia. According to a different tradition, he was born from the union of the earthly god Keb and the sky-goddess Nut. When the sun-god Re realized that his wife Nut had been unfaithful to him with her lover Thoth he cursed the child to remain unborn forever. But the moon helped them by giving away a seventy second part of every day and thus Nut was able to add 5 days to the calendar year of 360 days and used the extra five days to have Osiris born on the first and then she gave birth subsequently to the elder Horus on the second, Seth on the third, Isis on the fourth and Nephthys on the last day.

Eventually Isis married Osiris and between the two they took Egypt from a primitive status into a civilized society. Isis discovered wheat and barley and Osiris fruit-trees, grapes and corn. He then traveled the world spreading his knowledge and acquired considerable wealth. Upon his return he was made into a deity because of the benefits he had given to mankind.

According to Plutarch, after the body of Osiris drifted ashore to Byblos, Isis went to retrieve him, she was befriended by the wife of the local Byblian king who gave her child to Isis to nurse him: she gave her finger to suck instead of her breast and during the nights she began to burn away all his mortal parts in order to confer on him immortality but discovered by the queen mother she had to stop her practice: the child was thus prevented from becoming immortal. The goddess then revealed her identity to the queen and demanded the return of the body of Osiris who was interred in the trunk of one of the pillars of her palace. She took the body back to Egypt. However, her tribulations did not end there. The brother Seth discovered the body, divided it into fourteen pieces and scattered them all over the country.

Isis then had to search for the pieces and buried them in the places where she found them. It is well known that the genital member of Osiris was lost eaten by the fishes. According to some Egyptian stories the sisters of Osiris with great lamentations asked the god Re to help them restore the body of Osiris. Similar lamentations were common in Phoenicia and were part of the cult of Adonis. Re then sent several gods to piece together the body and made him the Lord of the Underworld. There he presided as a judge in the trials of the souls of the departed and decided whether to reward them with eternal life or punish them for their sins. The Egyptians subsequently believed that every man would live eternally if his friends would do for him what the other gods did for the body of Osiris.

The festivals for Osiris depended upon the variations in the level of the waters of the Nile: the waters begin to rise in early June, reach a peak in July and inundate the country by the end of September. By December and January the river returns to his ordinary bed. The rising waters on earth were accompnied since ancient times by a sign in heaven: for several millennnia before our era the brightest of the fixed stars, Sirius, appeared at dawn in the east before sunrise at the time of the summer solstice when the Nile was rising: the Egyptians regarded this as the star of Isis just as the Babylonians regarded the planet Venus as the star of Ishtar.

In both instances these people regarded the phenomena as supernatural signs: the appearance of Sirius marked the beginning of the sacred year and was celebrated with festivals for Osiris. In the official calendar the Osirian festivals varied from year to year until the adoption of the Alexandrian calendar, which began on the 29th of August on the year 30 BC with the first New Year's day. Since then the festivals have followed the solar year. The death and resurrection of Osiris was celebrated to assure for humans support in this life and confirm their belief of an eternal life beyond the grave. It appears to have been essentially a festival of sowing and took place all over Egypt, practiced by every farmer independently in memory of Osiris who was said to be the first to teach men the use of the corn.

It seems that ancient Egyptians used to burn red-haired men and scattered their ashes as an offer to the dead Osiris. The legends speak of the widespread practice of dismembering the bodies of kings and magicians and burying the pieces in the hope of improving the fertility and fecundity of the fields, men and beasts. Finally it has to be stressed that the ancients believed in the identity of Osiris with Adonis and as such this was celebrated in Byblos with somewhat similar ceremonies. In addition, the rites of Osiris and Dionysus were so similar that ancient writers thought they had a common origin: such were the opinions of Herodotus and Plutarch.

Isis, after the death of Osiris took a bow never to marry another man, and passed the remainder of her life reigning over the land with complete respect for the law and surpassing all previous kings as a benefactor to her subjects. And also like her husband, when she passed among men, she received immortal honors and was buried on a special shrine near Memphis. The Egyptian historian Manetho attributed the discovery of wheat and barley to Isis. She apparently made the discovery during a sacrifice to her ancestors who were kings and gods. She then showed the ears of barley to Osiris and Thoth.

The Egyptian reapers at harvest time, after cutting the first stalks of barley would lie them down and beat their breasts, wailing and calling upon Isis. With time Isis acquired the characteristics of faithful wife, tender mother and queen of nature with moral purity and certain degree of sanctity. This was later to appeal to the gentle spirits of Greeks and Romans more than the characteristics of other middle eastern goddesses such as Anat or Astarte.

ORACLES AND DIVINATION

According to Herodotus in the HISTORIES (Book II,55-58) the Phoenicians were involved in the abduction of two sisters from

The Phoenicians in History and Legend

Thebes (now Luxor) in Egypt that were to become the oracles of Dodona (the most ancient oracle in Greece) and Ammon in Africa. Two women connected with the service of the temple were carried off by the Phoenicians and sold, one in Lybia and the other in Greece. It was these women who erected temples to Zeus and founded the oracles.

Concerning the oracles in Hellas, Herodotus gives one version heard from the Egyptians and then his own. The Egyptian version relates that the priests of the Zeus of Thebes said that two priestesses had been carried away by the Phoenicians; one of them was sold in Lybia and the other in Hellas. These women were the first founders of places of divination in those countries. The prophetesses of Dodona told the story that two black doves had come flying from Thebes in Egypt one to Lybia and one to Dodona. This last one settled under an oak tree and declared that there must be a place of divination there, sacred to Zeus; the people understood the message as divine and established the shrine to the oracle. The dove which came to Lybia told them to make an oracle of Ammon, also sacred to Zeus". And Herodotus continues

"If the Phoenicians did in truth carry away the sacred women and sold one in Lybia and one in Hellas,…the latter being there in slavery, she established a shrine to Zeus under an oak tree…so that she would remember the temple in the land from which she had come. After this she taught divination…these women were called "doves" because they spoke a strange language that the people could not understand

and thought their voice was like the voice of birds. That the dove was black probably meant that the woman was Egyptian".

In the land of Canaan oracles were sought for guidance in obtaining help from the supernatural. Clay models of liver, used for divinations, have been found in Canaan.

THE TALE OF SINUHE

The story of Si-nuhe, an attendant and servant of the royal harem of the hereditary Princess Nefru, daughther of Amen-em-het I and wife of Sesostris I, begins shortly after the death of Amen-em-het I, around 1960 BC. Sesostris I succeeded the previous king with whom he had been co-regent for about ten years and reigned between 1971-1928 BC. When the king died and ascended to heaven to be united with the Sun Disc, his father, the people were in grief and their hearts in mourning. Sesostris I was away in a campaign in the land of the Lybians and was returning on a hurry with many living captives and large amounts of cattle. The courtiers of the palace were sent to the western border to let the king's son know the events which had taken place at the court. The messengers reached him in the evening and immediately upon learning of the news Sesostris returned in a hurry, without leting his own army know about it and probably fearing a palace conspiracy or a harem conspiracy. The transition between kings was a dangerous time for an individual not entirely acquaincted with the new king, especially given the fact that Si-nuhe was a servant of the Princess. Although he may have been not guilty, facing the possibility of civil disorder and fearing for his life, Si-nuhe decided to escape and headed for Byblos in Phoenicia (**Fenkhu**).

Upon hearing the gossip in the palace he decided to disappear and headed North to Senefru Island. He spent the day hidden in the fields and the following night he caught a barge and crossed the river with the aid of the west winds. Sinuhe may have gone in a southeastern direction along the cultivated land and passed the Nile where it becomes a single stream, somewhere near present day Cairo. He then proceeded east of the Red Mountains reaching the Bitter Lakes in the morning, hungry and thirsty. He then encountered Asiatic tribes and their chief, who had been in Egypt, recognized him: he gave him water and boiled milk and took him to his tribe. He was good to him and offered help to set him off to Byblos.

Once there, he then went East from Byblos to a location in the valley between the Lebanon and Anti-Lebanon mountains, may be the Bekaa region, rich in agriculture and close to areas of communication. Si-nuhe decided to stay here and became integrated with a tribe whose chief had an Amorite name, Ammi-enshi. He asked Sinuhe for the reason of his flight. Sinuhe responded:

"the King has departed to the horizon and no one knows what might happen because of it. I had come from an expedition in the western part of Egypt, he continued equivocally, when I learned of the news. My heart was distraught and my limbs trembled. No one had gossiped about me, not a belittling word was heard about me; yet I decided to flight. I do not know what brought me to this country. It was as if a god had sent me here".

The Amorite responded:

"Well, what that land of yours might be like, without him, that magnificent god, the fear of whom pervades foreign countries?"

Si-nuhe replied:

"Well, his son has entered into the palace and has taken the inheritance of his father. He is a god without equals and a master of understanding,…he is the one who subdued the foreign countries while his father was in the palace. He is the one who will extend its frontiers……Let him know your name. Do not utter a curse against his majesty. He will not fail to do good to the country which shall be loyal to him".

The Amorite chief then reflected:

"Good for Egypt but now you are here and you may stay with us, if you so wish. What I will do for you is good".

He kept his word: he gave his eldest daughther in marriage to Si-nuhe and allowed him to choose a part of his best land.

"Figs were in it and grapes. It had more wine than water with plenty of honey and olives. Cattle, barley and fruit trees were also there…"

The Amorite chief made Si-nuhe the ruler of one of his best tribes, thus Sinuhe says:

"Bread and wine were made for me daily, cooked meat and roast fowl, beside the wild beasts of the desert for they hunted for me and laid before me milk in every cooking".

He spent there many years, his children grew up to be strong men, each in charge of his own tribe. Every traveller going either North or South will stop to visit Sinuhe. He says: "I gave water to the thirsty, put back on the road everyone who had been lost, and rescued those that had been robbed". When the inhabitants of this area were attacked by the Hyksos, he counceled them in their movements. The Amorite chief made Si-nuhe for many years the commander of his army: he was in charge of attacking his foreign enemies, plundered their cattle, carried off its inhabitants, took away their food and slew their people with his succesful strategies…and he gained his favor. Sinuhe then says: "I found favor in his heart, he loved me, he recognized my valor and he placed me at the head of his children".

However at least in one occasion his authority is finally challenged by another man who had beaten every one of his contenders. He threatened him and Sinuhe explained to his Amorite Elder "he says that he would fight me, he intends to despoil me, and plans to plunder my cattle on the advice of his tribe".

He then continues: "I do not know him…the case is that I have never opened his door or overthrown his fences. It is hostility that motivates him because he sees me carrying out my commissions. I am really like a stray bull in the midst of another herd and another bull attacks me." He thus accepts the challenge.

During the night preceding the event Sinuhe prepared his weapons to face his contender. In the morning his contender appeared with his shield, battle-axe and javelins and unsuccessfully charged against Si-nuhe, who avoided any injury and shot him with his arrow sticking it in his neck. He cried out and fell on his nose. Sinuhe said: "I felled him with his own battle-axe and raised my cry of victory over his back, while every Asiatic roared. Then I carried off his goods and plundered his cattle. What he had planned to do to me I did to him."

He continued: "The ruler Ammi-enshi took me into his embrace. I became great thereby, increased my wealth and the abundance of my cattle". Si-nuhe had become a very successful Egyptian in another country. Yet he begins to express homesickness for Egypt.

This news must have reached the King in Egypt who as The king of Upper and Lower Egypt now began to show mercy on Si-nuhe and wrote inviting him to return to the land of his birth: the king, the queen and their children offered to receive him as another prominent man of the court. When Sesostris was told about the situation of Sinuhe, he began to send messages to him offering to receive him like the ruler of any foreign country.

"Do return to Egypt, see the home in which you did grow up...For today you have begun to grow old and have decreased your virility......You should not die in a foreign country".

Si-nuhe seems to have received the message of the Pharaoh when he was standing in the midst of his tribe and after it was read to him, he felt deeply touched. He responded to the king in the pompous style of the times with various explanations in an attempt to justify his self-imposed exile and decided to return from the land of the Fenkhu, most likely Phoenicia, in the Bekaa Valley.

The messengers sent by Sesostris I came to help Sinuhe return to Egypt. He says: "I was pemitted to expend a day in my house handing over my property to my children, my eldest son being responsible for my tribe. My tribe and all my property were now his: my serfs, all my cattle, my fruits and every pleasant tree of mine".

He then went southwards and halted at the "Ways of Horus", the Egyptian frontier facing the Sinai peninsula. "The comander there sent then a message to the Pharaoh. His majesty sent then a capable overseer of peasants of the palace, with loaded ships carrying presents from the royal family for the Asiatics who had followed me, escorting me to the "Ways of Horus". I set sail until I reached the capital in the Faiyum".

"When day had broken, very early, ten men came to summon me and ten to usher me to the palace. I firt met the royal children and then the courtiers who usher into the audience hall, set me on the way to the private chambers. I found his majesty upon the Great Throne of fine gold" and I droped into his presence "stretched out upon my belly".

Then his majesty said to one of his courtiers:

"Lift him up. Let him speak to me".

And speaking to me:

"Behold, you have come. After wandering through foreign countries, elderliness has attacked you…you have reached old age. You should not be interred by bowmen. Do not, do not act thus any longer".

Si-nuhe did not know what to say:

"What is it that my lord says to me? I should answer but there is nothing that I can do: it is really the hand of a god. It is a terror that is in my belly, like the one that produced my fated flight. Behold, I am before you, Yours is my life. May your majesty do as he pleases".

The royal children were then ushered in. Then his Majesty said to the Queen: "Here is Si-nuhe, as a Bedouin, the guise of the Asiatics".

The Queen gave a great cry and the children clamored all together and said to the King "It is not really he, O Lord"……

Then his Majesty said: "It is really he. He shall not fear. He has no title to be in dread. He shall be a courtier among the nobles."

The King ordered that he be dressed properly. He then was put into the house of a royal son…"Clothing of royal linen, myrrh, prime oil of the king and the nobles whom he loves were in every room……His body was cleaned. "I was plucked and my hair was combed……I was clad in fine linen and annointed with prime oil. I slept on a bed……I was given a house with a garden…And my craftmen built it with newly restored wood work. Meals were brought to men three to four times daily and the royal children came constantly to see me."

"A pyramid-tomb was built for me by stone-masons and…my statue overlaid with gold with a skirt of fine gold. It was his majesty who had it made. I was under the favor of the king until the day of mooring had come".

Some scholars have argued that this story probably was written about a real Si-nuhe who led a life of adventure and returned home at the end of his life. The central narrative is a credible account. If this was fiction, it was based on real events. Manuscripts about this story are plentiful and run from the Twelve Dynasty (1800 BC) to the Twenty-First Dynasty (1000 BC).

THE TELL-EL-AMARNA PERIOD

The historical record from the times of Amenhotep the III (1413-1377 BC) and his son Amenhotep the IV (1377-1358 BC) was saved for posterity by pure luck. An Egyptian peasant discovered by accident in the modern village of Tell al-Amarinah the buried archives of these two pharaohs and although some of the clay cuneiform tablets were initially lost, some sold to amateurs and others to dealers, over three hundred of them have survived and are mostly stored in the British and Berlin museums. It was Amenhotep the IV who transferred the seat of government from Thebes to a new capital: Akhetaton, today a village named Tell al-Amarinah, where a copious correspondence in clay tablets, the archives of these two pharaohs, referring the vicissitudes of their time, are recorded. The letters deal with their relations with the kings of Babylonians, Mitannians, Hittites and the kinglets of the city-states in the land of Canaan [(Byblos, Sidon, Ugarit, Tyre, Aradus and Beruth.)].

Beirut, (phoenician **b'eroth**): Until now it was thought that this was the first time in history that the city of Beirut was mentioned and known to exist but additional evidence indicates that the city had been listed in his conquests by Thutmose the III. More recently, evidence from the finds in 25th century Ebla, indicate that Byblos, Sidon and Berytus sustained commercial relations with the Eblaites and it seems that Byblos was the main port used by the Eblaites to carry on their extensive commercial enterprises with Egypt, the principal source of commerce during the time of the great pharaohs Cheops, Kephren and Mycerinus, who built the great pyramides at Giza.

During the Amarna period, Phoenicia was trapped politically between the Hittites in the north and the Egyptians in the south. Abdi-Ashirta, the Amorite king of the plains of the Orontes river, Rib-Addi of Byblos, Abi-Milki of Tyre, Zimrida of Sidon and Ammunira of Beirut, are the main characters in the correspondence of the Tablets of the Tell al-Amarinah period. Most of the letters were not from the pharaohs themselves but written by their intermediaries, Egyptian officials and the local vassals. The style is assumed to be typical of the times but depicts the phoenician kinglets in a servile and abject manner in their behaviour vis-a-vis the Egyptian rulers.

The prototype of the extravagant forms used in their protocol of the times is shown in a letter of Ammunira, King of Beirut, to his pharaoh:

"To the King my lord, my sun, my god, the breath of my life,…your slave and the dust under your feet. At the feet of the King, my lord, my sun,……I have bowed down seven times and seven times. I have hearkened to the words of the tablets of the King my lord, my sun, my god, the breath of my life, and the heart of your slave and the dust under the feet of the King my lord,………is exceedingly glad that the breath of the King my lord, my sun, my god, has gone out to his slave and to the dust under his feet…"

Abdi-Ashirta also addresses the Pharaoh in a similar fashion:

"To the King, the sun, my lord, thus said Abdi-Ashirta, your slave, the dust of your feet; at the feet of the King, seven times and seven I fall down. Behold, I am the servant of the king and the dog of his house, and all Amurru people for the king, my lord, I guard".

Abdi-Ashirta, of the valley of the Orontes and Zimrida of Sidon are the villains of this period while Rib-Addi of Byblos and Abi-Milki of Tyre remain loyal to Egypt. The behavior of Zimrida was always in question and his apparent loyalty to Egypt was always doubtful. Abdi-Ashirta's area of control extended from the north all the way to Beruna (Batrun today) and he had the support of Subbiluliuma, the Hittite king. In contrast the Byblians and Tyrians, who remained loyal to Egypt, received no attention or any help from Amenhotep IV who was more concerned with his religious changes than political situations. While Abdi-Ashirta and his son Aziru constantly besieged Byblos, Beirut and Tyre, the pharaoh never responded to the concerns of Rib-Addi: as a consequence of this after more than fifty letters to the pharaoh, he seeks assistance from Ammunira of Beirut, to whom he was related by close family ties, but gets no satisfaction. Abi-Milki of Tyre wrote over ten letters to the pharaoh with somewhat similar results: no response. No help for the city states of Canaan came and eventually all their kinglets disappeared.

Abdi-Ashirta meets violent death, Rib-Addi of Byblos and the members of his family perish, the fate of Abi-Milki is unclear from the extant evidence but he seems to have abandoned Tyre. However, it is Abi-Milki who reports to the pharaoh the destruction of Ugarit by fire and the absence of the Hittites from the area. It seems that Ugarit was burned following an earthquake circa 1365 BC. Only Zimrida of Sidon appears to have had the best part of the deals with Egypt and while never showing any hostility towards the pharaoh, he was the most astute politician among the kinglets of Canaan.

WEN-AMON VISITS ZAKAR-BAAL OF BYBLOS

This story appears to have been based on actual facts but was written during the kingless period that followed the end of the twenty dynasty (about 1100 BC). In the absence of a serious ruler the power of the Egyptians had declined via-a-vis their vassals in Asia Minor. The papyrus that describes this story was originally in the private collection of W. Golenischeff who was the first to publish it. Now it is preserved at the Moscou Museum. It tells the misadventures of a highly placed member of the court of Amon named Wen-Amon sent to Byblos to get wood for the barque of Amon-Re.

On Year 5, 4th month of the third season, day 16, Wen-Amon, the Senior member of the court of the House of Amon, was sent to Phoenicia to obtain wood to build the barque of Amon-Re, King of the Gods. This year seems to correspond to the last of the Ramessids period following the twentieth dynasty when there were two **de facto** rulers, Ne-su-Ba-neb-Ded in the Delta and Heri-Hor at Thebes in Upper Egypt but with no royal titles. Wen-Amon reached Tanis, the capital of the Delta, where he presented his credentials to Ne-su-Ba-neb-Ded in request of funds to purchase the timber needed for the barque of Amon-Re. After a month in Tanis he embarked on a ship and reached Dor, where he was well received and given food and wine by the local ruler, Prince Beder. However, a robber from his ship stole all the gold and silver that he was carrying to pay for the lumber in Byblos. In response to his loss he went to the Prince and said to him:

"I have been robbed in your harbor. You are the prince of this land, and you are its investigator, you should look for my silver. This silver belongs to Amon-Re, it belongs to Ne-su-Ba-neb-Ded, it belongs to Heri-Hor, my lord,…It belongs to you…it belongs to Zakar-Baal, the Prince of Byblos".

And Prince Beder responded:

"Irrespective of whether you are important or you are eminent…I do not recognize this accusation that you have made to me. If it was a thief from my land who had stolen your treasure, I would repay it to you from my treasury. But a thief from your ship, he belongs to you. Spend a few days here visiting me, so that I may look for him".

Wen-Amon spent ten days moored in the harbor and finally decided to go back to see the Prince. "You have not found my silver with all your captains and ships at sea".

Beder's answer is not recorded in the papyrus which is broken at this point. But he must have given reassurance to Wen-Amon because at the end of the broken text we find him in Tyre. He continues:

"I went out of Tyre at the break of dawn......to see Zakar-Baal of Byblos".

Somewhere in the break of the papyrus there must have been a statement of Wen-Amon's arrival in Byblos on the northern Phoenician coast. There follows a statement of Wen-Amon in which he seems to have recovered from the Tjeker people an amount of silver equivalent to what had been stolen from him...

"So I went away and enjoyed my triumph in a tent on the shore of the sea at the harbor of Byblos".

He apparently had the recovered silver taken from the Tjkers and kept it hidden inside the statue of Amon that he had been carrying with him all along his trip.

Zakar-Baal did not, however, give a cheerful reception to Wen-Amon. On the contrary, he refused to see him and kept sending him everyday a messenger asking him to leave.

"Get out of my harbor", he was told every day for about a month.

Wen-Amon responded through his messenger: "Where should I go? Send me a ship to carry me, have me taken to Egypt again.!

So I spent 29 days in his harbor receiving his messenger every day with the same message: "Get out of my harbor".

Then while Zakar-Baal was making offerings to his god a youth of his entourage got seized by violent motions (epileptic convulsions) which made the king believe were due to the God brought by the Egyptian envoy. He then decided to receive Wen-Amon and sent for him. While the youth was having his frenzy at night, Wen-Amon had found a ship headed for Egypt and loaded everything that he had into it, with the intention to go back. "While I was watching for the darkness to load the gold, so that no other eye might see it, the harbor master came to me saying: "Wait until morning, so says the Prince".

Wen-Amon continues:

"Are you not the one who spend the time coming to me everyday to say "Get out of my harbor". Are you not the one who now says: Wait tonight!, in order to let the ship which I have found get away? The messenger then returned to Zakar-Baal with this information from the Egyptian envoy. But he was told to return to Wen-Amon with the same message: "Wait until morning, so says the Prince".

The Phoenicians in History and Legend

"When the morning came, he sent for me but I left the god (the statuette) hidden, hidden in the tent on the shore of the sea. I found Zakar-Baal sitting in his upper room, with his back turned to the window, so that the waves of the great sea, broke against the back of his head.

I said to him: "May Amon favor you".

But he said to me: "How long has it been since you came from the place where Amon is?

So I said to him: "Five months and one day".

And he said to me: "Well, you are truthful".

"Where is the letter of Amon and where the dispatch of the High Priest of Amon.? They should be in your hands".

And I told him: "I gave them to Ne-su-Ba-neb-Ded and to his wife Ta-net Amon".

He became very angry and said to me:

"Now you see, neither letters nor dispatches are in your hands. Where is the cedar ship that Ne-su-Ba-ned-Ded gave you?...Did he not turn you over to his foreign ship captain to have him kill and throw you into the sea?...

I said to him: "It was not an Egyptian ship. Now it is sailing with Egyptian crew".

And he said to me:

"There are twenty ships here in my harbor which have commercial relations with your Egyptian lord. And in Sidon there are fifty more ships trading with Egypt". Wen-Amon then remained silent, unable to give any reason to Zakar-Baal for his inability to provide appropriate credentials to him.

Then he said to me: "On what businesss have you come?"

So I told him: "I have come after the woodwork for the great and august barque of Amon-Re, King of the Gods. Your father did it, your grand-father did it and you will do it too".

Then he responded: "That is true, they did it. And if you give me their price, I will do it".

"When my people carried out this comission the Pharaoh sent six ships loaded with Egyptian goods and unloaded them into my storehouses". You, what is it that you are bringing me?". And he opened the journal rolls of his fathers that had been brought to him, and they were read to me showing how much silver and gold and all kinds of things had been brought to him from Egypt in the past.

Zakar-Baal continued: "If the ruler of Egypt were the lord of mine and I were his servant also, he would not have to send silver and gold, saying: Carry out the comission of Amon!. There would be no need to carry any gift, such as they used to do for my father. As for me, **I am not your servant! I am not the servant of him who sent you either! If I cry out to Lebanon, the heavens open up, and the logs will be here, lying on the shore of the sea**".

This proud imprecation is a proof of how weak the Egyptian power had become at this time. Zakar-Baal doubts that Wen-Amon has sufficient goods to pay for the merchandise he needs and says: "if I were to take his ropes and other goods", Wen-Amon would not be able to return safely to Egypt.

Zakar-Baal continued: "When Amon founded all lands, in founding them he founded first the land of Egypt, from which you have come; for craftmanship came out of it, to reach the place where I am, and learning came out of it to reach the place where I am. What are those 'silly trips' they have forced you to make?."

Wen-Amon responded: "What I am engaged on are not 'silly trips' at all. There is no ship upon the River which does not belong to Amon! The sea is his, and Lebanon is his, which you claim to be yours. I have come carrying this great god. (The statue of course). But you have made this god spend twenty-nine days moored in your harbor, although you did not know. Isn't he here?......You are here to carry on the commerce of Lebanon with Amon, its lord. The former kings sent silver and gold…to your fathers in place of life and health. Now as for Amon-Re, King of the Gods, he is the lord of this life and health, and he was the lord of your fathers. They spent their lifetimes making offerings to Amon. And you also, you are the servant of Amon."

"If you carry out this comission for Amon, you will live, you will be prosperous, you will be healthy, and you will be good for your entire land and for your people."

"Don't wish for yourself anything belonging to Amon-Re……Have your secretary brought to me, so that I may send him to Ne-su-Ba-neb-Ded and Ta-net Amon, whom Amon placed in the north of his land. They will have all kinds of things sent to you."

Zakar-Baal then was sufficiently satisfied and decided to advance some of the timber for the barque of Amon and had it taken to Egypt.

"And in the first month of the next season the messenger of Zakar-Baal who had gone to Egypt came back bringing 4 jars of gold, 5 jars of silver, 10 pieces of clothing in royal linen,……500 rolls of finished papyrus, 500 cowhides, 500 ropes, 20 sacks of lentils and 30 baskets of fish…"

"And the Prince was glad. He assigned 300 men with 300 heads of cattle and he put supervisors at their head, to have them cut the timber…In the following season they had all the wood cut down and brought them to the shore of the sea. And the Prince came out and stood by them. He then sent out for me……I presented myself near him and he said to me:

> "The comission which my fathers carried out formerly, I have carried out also; even though you have not done for me what your fathers would have done for me……the last of your woodwork has arrived and is lying here. Load it and take it to Egypt. Don't give anymore excuses about the winds or the weather."

Zakar-Bal implies then that he has treated him well and now he should depart. But Wen-Amon responds with a suggestion that Zakar-Baal should erect a stela for himself describing what he had done for Amon-Re, King of the Gods and obtain "fifty more years of life and prosperity over and above his fate"......Zakar-Baal then refuses to erect a stela and tells Wen-Amon that it is he who will harvest all benefits after he returns to Egypt.

Wen-Amon's story continues: "I went to the sea shore and saw eleven ships belonging to the Tjeker coming in from the sea, to get me. I sat down and wept. And the scribe of Zakar-Baal came to me an asked: What is the matter with you?......And I said to him: Don't you see those who are coming to arrest me? How long shall I be left here?

So he went and told the Prince about me and the Prince began to weep because of the painful word that described to him my problems. He then sent his scribe with two jugs of wine and one ram. He also sent an Egyptian singer saying: "Sing to him! Don't let his heart suffer. Eat and drink. Don't let his heart be afflicted, for tomorrow you shall hear whatever have to say."

When the morning came he summoned his assembly, he stood in their midst and he said to the Tjeker: "What have you come for? And they said to him: "We have come after the ships of our enemies that you are sending to Egypt with your cedar wood."

Zakar-Baal responded: "I can not arrest the messenger of Amon within my land. Let me send him away and then you may go after him and arrest him".

Zakar-Baal's behaviour has been explained on legal basis since Wen-Amon's appropriation of the Tjeker's goods apparently took place between Tyre and Byblos.

"Thus we were loaded in and left but the winds cast me on the land of Alashiya, (Cyprus). The inhabitants of the town then came against me...but I managed to reach the place where Hoteb, the Princess of the town was. I met her as she was going from one of her houses to another.

"So I greeted her and through an Egyptian interpreter I said: "Tell my lady that I have heard, as far away as Thebes, the place where Amon is, that injustice is done in every town but justice is done here. And yet I see that injustice is done here every day'. And she said: "What do you mean by saying that?"

So I told her: "If the sea is stormy and the wind casts me in the land where you are, you should not let your people kill me. For I am a messenger of Amon....As to this crew, it belongs to the Prince of Byblos which your people are bent on killing, won't its lord find ten crews of yours and also kill them?. She then had her people summoned and stand there. She said to me: "Spend the night......"

At this point the papyrus breaks off but it may be assumed that Wen-Amon's arguments were successful and that he managed to return safely to Egypt, to have this story written in the first person.

CHAPTER THREE

THE GODS OF BYBLOS, TYRE & SIDON

Late in the first or early in the second century of our era, Philo of Byblos published an account of Phoenician traditions entitled **Phoenician History**. The work is presented merely as a translation of a native writer named Sanchuniathon of Berytus. Philo of Byblos argued that his account was more reliable than anything available then in Greek sources, which depended on the accounts of Phoenician priests, who had obscured the ancient writings. He translated the Phoenician original into Greek. According to some sources Philo was born in the reign of Nero (54-68 AD) and lived at least into the reign of Hadrian (117-138 AD). Others claim the correct dates for Philo's life were 64-141 AD.

Philo's claims provoked considerable controversy between certain European scholars in the 19th century AD and some Americans during the 20th century. His reliability, denied by certain Europeans, was accepted by American scholars, the most prominent of whom was W.F. Albright.

Albright claims that

"Sanchuniathon was a refugee from Tyre who settled in Berytus about the second quarter of the 6th century BC and it is certain that the work attributed to him is a rich source of authentic Phoenician data and is not a forgery of early times".

James Barr who wrote on Philo of Byblos regarding the existence, antiquity and reliability of the sources of the **Phoenician History** says: "the stock of Philo's credibility has been rising on the market of scholarship". Evidence supporting this position has been drawn from the demonstrated authenticity of the name Sanchuniathon and from the comparison of the Phoenician History with the mythological texts of the second millennium from Ugarit and Bogazköy. Comparison of the Ugaritic texts with the Phoenician history by Charles Virolleaud led him to conclude that the facts "demanded a complete reassessment of the prevailing scepticism about Philo's source". And Albright remarked:

"the previous pesimistic assessment of Sanchuniaton's reliability, has been disproved rather completely by the discovery and decipherment of Ugaritic mythological literature", so that "we are fully justified in accepting provisionally all data preserved by Philo".

In conclusion, he majority of recent scholars, including Albright, claim to have re-habilitated Philo. They have found in the source of the **Phoenician History** a reliable witness to ancient Phoenician religion and mythology. Furthermore, most scholars agree with the proposition that Sanchuniathon was a historical person of considerable antiquity who had access to reliable sources of tradition.

Porphyry of Tyre, a philosopher of the 3d century, claims that Sanchuniathon was a figure of remote antiquity who lived prior to the time of the Trojan war, in the days of Queen Semiramis of Assyria. Porphyry claims that Sanchuniaton reworked the records of a Phoenician priest by the name of Hierombalos, who had dedicated his history to Abibalus, a phoenician kinglet of Beirut, whose cout experts had approved its accuracy.

The mythological texts of the second millennium BC discovered in Canaanite (Ugarit) and Hittite sites confirm the authenticity of Philo's sources. Thus Phoenician mythology, as suspected, took from ancient sources in Egypt and Mesopotamia, modified the information and no doubt influenced Greek mythology. The opposite, that is, Greek influencing Phoenician mythology, indeed also must have happened.

For the purpose of this writing the Phoenician characters that appear in the Phoenician History are described here following the bilingual text, Greek-English edition, by Philo of Byblos.

From the Wind **Colpia** and his wife **Baau** (i.e. Night) were born two mortal men: Aeon and Protogonos. The most common explanation of the names Colpia and Baau is that they represent the Greek translation of unknown Phoenician words. Aeon discovered the nourishment from the trees. Some scholars suggest that **Aeon** and **Protogonos** are only one person while others such as Renan goes as far as to identify them with Adam and Eve. Their offspring were called in Greek **Genos** and **Genea**. They settled Phoenicia. **Gennaios** or **Genneas** are the Greek equivalent of names of Phoenician origin. Phoenician personal names such as **gnn** have been found in Mediterranean inscriptions. The personal name **Sknytn** has been found at Hadrumetum, a Phoenician colony in the western Mediterranean sea along the northern coast of Africa. The divine name **Sakkun** first appears in Phoenician personal names during the 5th century BC.

When droughts occurred, Gennaios and Genneas raised their hands to Heaven, towards the Sun, since they considered him, the Lord of Heaven, to be the only god and named it Baal Samem, (**B'l 'smm**) which means "Lord of Heaven" in Phoenician. This is the Zeus of the Greeks.

According to Albright the association with the Sun perhaps suggests that the head of the pantheon at Tyre was identified with the Egyptian god Aten of the Tell-El-Amarna letters (Amenhotep IV).

From Genos, son of Aeon and Protogonos, were born other mortal children. They begat sons greater in size and stature, whose names were given to the mountains over which they ruled. Thus were derived the names of Mount Kassios and Mount Amanus in the north, Lebanon and Anti-Lebanon in the south. (Kassios in Greek is the mountain described in the Ugaritic texts, where Baal Hadad lived).

Years later, from the descendants of Genos were born Hypsuranios and Usoos.

In the line of Hypsuranios were born hunters, fishers, smiths and masons. One of them, **Kushor**, (In Greek Chusor), patron and god of all forms of crafstmanship, was the first sailor. Other descendants were Misor and Sydyk. From Misor was born Taautos, who discovered writing. (? hieroglyphic writing is presumed). The Egyptians called him Thouth (Thoth) and the Greeks Hermes.

From Sydyk (**sdk** in phoenician) descended the Dioscuri, the Kabeiri and the Samothracians. The sons of Sydyk became later the founders of the school of scribes, according to Eusebius. Among their contemporaries was a certain Elioun and a woman called Berouth (**b'rwt** in phoenician), who settled the area around Byblos. From them were born Uranos (Heavens) and Ge (Earth). The union of Uranos and his sister Ge produced four children: Kronos ('El), Baetylos, Dagon and Atlas. In an encounter with beasts, Elioun was killed. After his death, he became an object of worship: his children initiated the custom of celebrating this anniversary in yearly festivals with abundant libations. Libations were a common element in primitive worship. The death of Elioun, of course, has similarities with the story of the death of Adonis in Phoenicia.

Uranos had numerous children by other women as well. Furthermore, Uranos also attempted to kill his children by Ge although unsuccesfully. When Kronos reached manhood, he would punish his father Uranos for this with the help of Hermes.

The children of Kronos were Persephone and Athena. By BC 5th century tradition Kronos and his wife Rhea had as their children also Zeus and Hera. Upon reaching the end of their lives, the Phoenicians found them worthy of divine honors, called them gods, honored them with altars, sacrifices and yearly festivals.

With the help of Hermes and Athena, Kronos waged war againt his father and after defeating him took up his dominions and his kingdom. He then founded the first fortified walled city: Byblos of Phoenicia.

Afterwards however, Kronos behaviour appears to be quite primitive, to say the least, since he became sort of a little monster: he buried? alive his brother Atlas in the depths of the earth, killed his son Sadidos because of jealousy and beheaded his own daughter to the astonishment of all the gods.

While in exile Uranos would send his maiden daughter Astarte ('Attart in Ugaritic) and her sisters Rhea and Dione to kill Kronos. Kronos discovered the ruse and made them his wives. With Astarte Kronos had seven daughters (the Titanids) and two sons and with Rhea seven other sons. Furthermore he would also have two daughters by his sister Dione of Byblos.

One of the Titanids mated with Sydyk and bore Aeskulapius, the father of Medicine. The god Eshmun of Sidon would slowly be replaced by Aeskulapius.

Kronos gave in marriage the favorite mistress of his father Uranos to his brother Dagon, while she was pregnant with Uranos' son Demarous. This Demarous would become the father of Melkart, (or Melkart himself), also known as Herakles of Tyre. Is the Baal of Ugarit-Phoenicia the same Demarous? No definitive answer is available to this question.

Dagon was an important deity during the second millenium BC in the Euphrates region and much later at Palmyra. This god was associated with the fertility of the land and at Ebla he is the head of the pantheon. This is evident in the Ebla texts of the 25th century where he is designated "Lord of Canaan" and "Lord of the land". He appears repeatedly later, by the second millenium (? the 14th-13th centuries), as the father of Baal Hadad in Ugaritic mythology and remains worshipped until the 5th century in Palestine.

In the thirty-second year of his asumption to the throne, according to Philo, Kronos finally trapped his father Uranos. He overpowered and castrated him: the blood from his genitals dripped in the streams and rivers of the island where he was defeated. At the site of his death Kronos erected then a shrine dedicated to the worship of his father. The blood from Uranos genitals staining rivers and streams is reminiscent of the story underlying the legend of Adonis: his blood would stain after his death the waters of the nearby spring and give origin to a red river that bears his name in Phoenicia.

While traveling around the world Kronos gave the kingdom of Attica to his daughter Athena. A Greek-Phoenician inscription confirms the tradition that identifies **'Anat,** the virgin sister and consort of Baal, of Ugaritic importance, with Athena. At the occurrence of a plague Kronos sacrificed his son by Anobret to his father Uranos. In most early cultures humans and gods employed human sacrifice in an attempt to obtain benefits from nature or in the hope to avoid the occurrence of great calamities.

When **Mot**, the child born of Rhea, died, Kronos made him a deity. (This is most likely the original Canaanite god Muth, Mott, who appears in the Baal epic of Ugarit as the Lord of the underworld). The Canaanite root **m,wt**=death, appears to correlate with the character attributed to this god. Mot is also equated with Pluto, the Greek deity of the underworld.

Kronos (**El**) gave the city of Byblos to the goddess Ba'alath, (also known as Dione) and the city of Berytus to Poseidon. Poseidon is, of course, the great-grandson of Kronos. Berytus appears historically founded on the 2d century BC although its greatest development seems to have been during the reign of Augustus, when Heliopolis (Baalbeck) also acquired its importance. However, the inhabitants of Berytus, it should be pointed out, had engaged in commerce and

The Phoenicians in History and Legend

exploration since the 2d century BC and founded at Delos "The Poseidon Society". Recently available evidence indicates the involvement of the Berytans in longterm settlements as sugested by their temple construction at Delos, where the worship of several phoenicians deities took place: Poseidon, Roma, Astarte-Aphrodite, Eshmun-Aeskulapius and Dionysus were venerated there. A point of discrepancy exists between the myth and history of the foundation and existence of Berytus: the city is mentioned in the Tell El-Amarna correspondence which dates back to the 14th century BC, simultaneously with Byblos, Ugarit, Tyre and Sidon. Berytus then existed at the time of the Tell-el-Amarna tablets and even much earlier, as evidenced by its mention in commercial businesses with Ebla during the 25th century BC. Its prominence in historical terms, of course, occurs much later in the recorded extant evidence.

The recent excavations, now in progress in Beirut, undertaken after the devastation of the most recent war at the end of the 20th century AD, between 1976 and 1990, have revealed the existence of the ancient site of the city at least to the beginning of the first millenium BC and when completed should perhaps bring evidence about the life style of the Berytans of that period.

Kronos transferred all of Egypt to the god Taautos, so that Egypt became his kingdom. This is in keeping with the story about the invention of writing. The creation of "the letters of the Ammoneans" is attributed to Taautos. By another account, Taautos/Thoth was the scribe of Osiris.

The "Ammoneans" are probably to be understood as priests or followers of the Egyptian god Ammon. The region of the "Ammoneans" may also refer to the region of Hamon, or Amanus, mentioned earlier as the name of one of the mortal children of the Wind. The designation was, of course, also used to give a name to the Ugaritic mountain north of the Orontes valley. Dagon is also Ba'al Hamon, "The master of the Amanus", the cedar mountains.

ADONIS

In phoenician `dn.,"master". The legends that have come to us about him were originally told by several ancient writers and, in more recent times, in its most developed form by Ovid, the Latin poet. The figure of Adonis attracted the attention of many writers in antiquity: Apollodorus, Hesiod, Panyasis, Plutarch, Antoninus Liberalis, Hyginus and Ovid, all have told his story with some minor variations. The birth of Adonis, within the realm of legend, is clouded in contradiction. By most accounts, Adonis was born from a woman named Myrrha, who had been converted into a tree, after an incestuous love with her own father named Cinyras. Cinyras was himself a great-grandson of Io, the same woman kidnapped and made pregnant by the phoenician captain at the beginning of history, as we were told by Herodotus. By Apollodorus account, a victim of the wrath of Aphrodite because she failed to honor her, Myrrha conceived a passion for her own father and without his knowledge, while he was drunk, she shared his bed for twelve nights. When Cyniras became aware of it, he drew his sword and pursued her...she prayed to the gods for mercy...the gods in compassion then turned her into a tree.

And Ovid continues: after the recognition of her incest and in desperation, Myrrha summed up her wishes in a prayer...

"O gods...I do not refuse the punishment I have deserved...surviving I offend the living, and dying, I offend the dead, drive me from both realms; change me and refuse me both life and death! Some god must have listened to her prayer...for even as she spoke the earth closed over her legs, roots burst from her toes...her blood changed to sap, her arms to long branches, her fingers to twigs, her skin to hard bark...now the growing tree had closely bound her heavy womb...The misbegotten child had grown within the wood, and was now seeking a way by which it might leave its mother and come forth. The pregnant tree swells in mid-trunk, the weight within straining on its mother......Still, like a woman in agony, the tree bends off...Then the tree cracked open, the bark was rent asunder, and it gave forth its living burden, a wailing baby-boy. The Naiads laid him on soft leaves and annointed him with his mother's tears' says Ovid. And continues: "Time glides by imperceptibly and cheats us in its flight, and nothing is swifter than the years". The son of his sister and his grandfather...is now a youth, now a man...now he excites Venus' love...

The father of Adonis is thus most commonly accepted to have been Cinyras, king of Cyprus and also Ugarit. Adonis was the product of the incesteous relationship of Cinyras with his daughter Myrrha. However, according to other sources, the father of Adonis is variously considered to be either Theias, king of Assyria; or Phoinix (? the brother of Kadmus) and his mother Alphesiboea. According to Apollodorus, Cinyras founded Paphos and having there married a daughter of Pygmalion, king of Cyprus, had several children with her among whom one was Adonis. Although the most prevalent tradition, as we have seen, makes Cinyras and Myrrha the parents of Adonis, still others believe his father may have been Zeus himself. Adonis, by other accounts, is the son of Ku^sor (Greek Chusor), a phoenician king-god mentioned by Philo of Byblos.

Apollodorus relates that while Adonis was still an infant and because of his beauty, Aphrodite hid him in a chest and enthrusted it to Persephone. Because Persephone opened the chest and saw the beautiful child she then refused to give him back, and the case had to be taken for judgement before Zeus: in the dispute between Aphrodite and Persephone, Zeus decided that Adonis should spend one third of the year with Persephone, one third with Aphrodite and one third by himself. However, Adonis decided to spend his remaining time with Aphrodite.

The story of his death is also told in various ways: while still a boy and during a hunting trip Adonis is killed by a boar. In the phoenician version, as unfaithful lover, Adonis will induce Ba'alath herself to abandon her husband Hephaistos. His death will occur at the hands of the jealous husband Hephaistos. From the blood of Adonis was born a rose without perfume and every year a river is stained red in Phoenicia. The event was motive for great celebrations every year during ancient times.

Not only in the legends but until recent times it has been claimed that every year during the rainy season the waters of the river named after Adonis are stained with his blood and enter for a considerable distance into the Mediterranean sea. Ba'alath will encounter her own death near Afqa (phoenician **ëpq** i.e. fountain or little river). During her search for Adonis she would be wounded and her blood will stain a set of bushes of white roses that will turn red from her bleeding hands. Many plants (the spring flower of anemone, the wind flower), the seasons of the corn and several animals by numerous accounts bear a relationship to the death and rebirth of Adonis.

The story of the wild boar as the killer of Adonis may have some relationship with customs observed in several different eastern Mediterranean geographic areas. Some writers have expressed the view that the Cypriote Adonis was originally the swine-god, a fact that explains the refusal by some of his worshippers to eat swine's flesh. The death of Adonis killed by the wild boar might be related to the early identification of the swine with certain forms of the god in some areas. According to some scholars the prototypes of this god in places such as Babylon (Tammuz), and Turkey [(Domuz) (pig)], represent an early conception of the legend based on the original identification of Adonis with the swine. Some scholars argue that the refusal to eat pig's meat stands from the fact that in 14th century Canaan (and perhaps earlier) **hnzr** was associated with the god Mot, supreme custodian of the underworld.

Sappho, writing in the VIth century BC, left us with this poem lamenting the death of the lover:

> He expires! O Cythere! The tender Adonis
> What are we going to do?
> ! Beat your chests, young women,!
> And tear apart your tunics

The return of Adonis from the dead takes place every year in summer, or during the spring season, mid-February to mid-March. He is the prototype of the dying-resurrecting god in Phoenicia: Adonis, Melkart, Eshmun, Tammuz, Baal and Osiris all appear to share, at different times and places, similar characteristics. In Egyptian tradition, as told by Plutarch, the celebrations of Osiris coincided with the phases of the moon at the beginning of the spring, the same time observed in Phoenicia.

The festivals of Adonis originally took place in Byblos and commemorated his death with orgiastic celebrations in spring (or summer) and with participation of men and women. During these celebrations were featured the ceremonies involving the **sacred prostitution** of women. These festivals lasted eight days and would end with the resurrection of Adonis.

At his place of death in Afqa, a temple where he was worshipped, existed in ancient times. The place was also the site of an oracle. The building of this temple was attributed to Cyniras. It was destroyed at the time of spread of a new religion, Christianity, in the 4th century CE by Constantine. A semi-destroyed wall believed to represent a portion of the ancient temple still remains today and can be seen located opposite to the site where the river emerges from the mountain forming the Afqa falls.

Adonis is basically a middle eastern deity, more specifically a phoenician god, the result of a Greek interpretation of the phoenician word for Lord **('dn).** The story of Adonis relating his death and resurrection is found throughout the East in various settings: he is identified at various periods with either Osiris in Egypt or Tammuz in Babylon. Tammuz was a figure closely associated with the cult of Ishtar, whose seasonal disappearance was customary to mourn with lamentations. The latter appear to be newer assimilations of the original phoenician myth.

The **yhwh** of the Hebrews, pronounced **adoni**, "my lord" was the equivalent, at least initially, of the Adonis of Phoenicia, the storm-god Tammuz of Babylon and the Lord (Baal) of Ugarit. Like Hadad, the minor storm-god from Ebla, and the Canaanite Baal, Yahweh rode the clouds and his voice was thunder.

A yearly celebration taking place every spring (or summer) and known as the Adonyads appears to have started in Byblos, spread later to the West, persisted in the height of Carthaginian power and was celebrated until later times in the Greek (Athens and Alexandria) and Roman periods. Even in later times these celebrations are found at places as far east as Palmyra. If we believe the true deity originated in Babylon the original name must have been Tammuz (July). The name in phoenician **'adn** meant "lord" and the Greeks converted this honorific title into a proper name.

As mentioned earlier, the Adonyads were celebrated with great solemnity in Byblos and Paphos. In both places Astarte was venerated and according to the legend in both places Cinyras, the father of Adonis, was the king. Byblos was the more ancient city of the two celebrating the feasts and claimed to be the oldest city of Phoenicia, founded by the god El. The sanctuary dedicated by Cinyras to Ba'alath i. e. Astarte (the Greek Aphrodite) was most likely located at Afqa, at the source of the river Adonis, in Phoenicia. The reason for its destruction by Constantine seems to have been on account of the character of the celebrations that allegedly took place there every year. The temple occupied a terrace facing the source of the river and comanding a magnificent view. Here Adonis and Ba'alath met and in the neighbouring mountain the hero met his death. His sacred blood stained the river and his flower, the anemone, bloomed among the cedar trees of Lebanon. In Cyprus, a rich island close to Phoenicia, the naturally commerce-minded and maritime-inclined phoenicians soon installed themselves there before the Greeks and their kings reigned at Kition until the times of Alexander the Great. The colonisers brought their gods from the motherland, they worshipped Baal in Cyprus and at Paphos Aphrodite and Adonis. Their sanctuary was one of the most celebrated shrines in the ancient world. They fused two goddesses into one for motherhood and fertility, Ba'alath and Astarte, woshipped all over the Near East since very early times, with the image of a pyramid or cone of sandstone.

In Cyprus the women were obligated before their marriage by custom to prostitute themselves to strangers at the temple of the goddesss. The practice was regarded not as an orgy of lust but as a religious duty. At Babylon every woman, whether rich or poor, had to submit to the practice of making love to strangers and dedicated the earned wages to the goddess Ishtar. Herodotus (Histories, book I, 199) describes this practice in the following terms:

"There is one custom among these people which is wholly shameful: every woman who is a native of the country must once in her life go and sit in the temple of Aphrodite and there give herself to a strange man. Many of the rich women, who are too proud to mix with the rest, drive to the temple in covered carriages with a whole host of servants following behind and there wait; most, however, sit in the precint of the temple with a band of plaited string around their heads, and a great crowd they are, some sitting there, others arriving, others going away, and through them all gangways are marked off, running in every direction for the men to pass along and make their choice. Once a woman has taken her seat she is not allowed to go home until a man has thrown a silver coin into her lap and taken her outside to lie with her. As he throws the coin, the man has to say, "In the name of the goddess Mylitta", that being the Assyrian name for Aphrodite. The value of the coin is of no consequence; once thrown it becomes sacred, and the law forbids that it should ever be refused. The woman has no privilege of choice: she must go with the first man who throws her the money. When she has lain with him, her duty to the goddess is discharged and she may go home, after which it will be impossible to seduce her by any offer, however large. Tall, handsome women soon manage to get home again but the ugly ones stay a long time before they can fulfil the condition which the law demands..."

At Heliopolis in Phoenicia, it was a law of the Amorites, that any woman who was about to marry should sit by the gate of the temple and fornicate with some stranger. At Byblos during the celebrations known as the Adonyads the people, men and women, shaved their heads in mourning for Adonis. Women who refused to sacrifice their hair were supposed to give themselves up to strangers in a certain day during the festivities and devote their earnings to the goddess.

Although shameful to Herodotus, to modern geneticists this could be considered quite justified as a form of assuring that a mixture of genes would take place and thus maintain a hybrid genetic pool, most likely directed towards fostering racial vigor, a feature which constituted a well-known characteritic of the Amorite race. No pretension is implied by this fact: the Amorites may not have been aware of the beneficial effect of miscegenation and this is likely to have originated rather by hazard than through observation.

In Greece and in Armenia, the nobility gave their daughters to the service of the goddess for a long time before they were given in marriage. At Paphos, religious prostitution was instituted by King Cinyras and was practiced even by his daughters, the sisters of Adonis, because having incurred the wrath of Aphrodite, they had to mate with strangers and were later exiled to Egypt. Thus the custom of prostitution seemed to be equally applied to princesses and to women of humble birth. Aphrodite seems to have been involved in love affairs with Cinyras, Adonis and Pygmalion, the father-in-law of Cinyras. The early phoenician kings of Paphos all carried the title of Adonis and it seems that all royal males considered themselves not only human but divine because of their relationship with Aphrodite, the goddess of love. The story relating the marriage of Pygmalion of Cyprus with the image of Aphrodite (Astarte) is a tale which was applied to all descendants of the king and was likely a widespread practice even in Carthage. Furthermore, it appears that the kings of Paphos had to mate in certain festivals with more than one sacred prostitute in the temples and the resulting offspring were considered human deities, product of the unions of the king with his wives and concubines. Finally, the first king named Cinyras may have been originally a skillful musician or harper. The word **cinyra** meant in Greek "a lyre" and the phoenician equivalent **kinnor** also meant "lyre". During the Adonyads the death and resurrection of Adonis was a practice celebrated in the Near East and in Greek areas with different ceremonies: bitter wailing by women and images of the god dressed as corpses were carried to burial into the sea.

Theocritus in his Idyll, song number XV, toward the year 270 BC, described the celebrations of the Adonyads in Alexandria: according to him great feasts took place towards the end of October, although the god was dead since the month of June. He would return however in October, after having been to Heaven and because he would have only one day to stay on Earth he would spend it with his mistress Aphrodite. This was occasion for celebration in Alexandria. The morning after, the women of Alexandria would take the image of the god Adonis and throw it into the sea: a primitive way to make the god descend to the underworld where he will spend some time with his other mistress Proserpine. Because the Phoenicians would see every day the Sun and other celestial bodies dissappear into the sea in order to reach the Netherworld, the Greeks and Romans adopted a similar view. Thus the disposition of the image of the god into the sea represented for them also the best way for him to reach Hades. However a certain year the head of the papyrus image of the god became detached and taken by the waves landed in Byblos of Phoenicia. The inhabitants recognized the head and considered the fact a "true miracle". Thus they decided to perpetuate the event from then on every year in honor of the god who had shown his predilection for Byblos by sending his head into their shores. The fact is explained today because there exists a submarine current that goes at this time of the year from northern Egypt into Phoenicia and with the help of strong winds and chance, on that occasion the head of papyrus landed in Byblos thus creating and paerpetuating a legend that lasted for many years after.

At Alexandria images of Adonis and Aphrodite were displayed with all kinds of fruits and their marriage celebrated with mourners carrying the body of the god to the sea shore where he was expected to come back to life the next day. In the temple of Astarte at Byblos the death of Adonis was celebrated with weeping, lamentations and beatings of the breast but the next day the god would ascend to heaven. The believers left on earth, as mentioned earlier, would shave their heads but women who did not desire to lose their tresses had to submit to the practice of giving themselves up to strangers, collecting the wages of their work for the temple of the goddess Astarte.

The phoenician festival was marked by the discoloration of the river Adonis in the spring when the scarlet anemones bloom. The red rose is believed to have originated on the same occasion, when Ba'alath following her lover, wounded herself on a bush of white roses and her sacred blood stained the flowers forever red. In Attica and Antioch, the Adonyads were celebrated in summer time. In very ancient times it seems that Adonis was sometimes personified by a living individual who would die a violent death playing the character of the god; the "corn-spirit" was often represented by human victims killed in the harvest field. The spirits of the victims were thought to return to life in the corn ears that they had nourished with their blood.

Thus what would have been more natural for these peasants to imagine that violets and hyacinths, roses and anemones sprang from the dust stained with the victims blood.

The Adonyads were celebrated in places as far apart such as Athens and Seville, Babylon and Syria, during the month of July. In Byblos and Alexandria it seems that no definite time had been established for the celebrations. If we believe the description of Lucien on his arrival to Antioch, which occurred in the middle of July of 362, this event coincided with the apparition in the early morning of the star Sirius. This phenomenon was quite prominent in various areas of the Orient.

Lucien describes the observation of Sirius with another prodigy which happened at Byblos at the same time: "each year the river Adonis becomes bloody and red all along the shores. The Byblians attributted the red discoloration of the river to the spill of the blood of the wounded young god. This marked the beginning of the celebrations of his death."

Other explanations for the redness of the river suggested that violent winds coming from the south-east coincided with the event at this time of the year and were responsible for removing the dust, red and dry, from the earth and sending it into the river. To this is worth mentioning that torrential rains also coincided with this season. Some writers attributed the discoloration to an additional factor: the melting of the snow from the mountains of Lebanon. The confluence of various atmospheric factors was most likely responsible for the event observed by the ancient visitors to the region from time immemorial.

ASTARTE

In phoenician '^**strt**. and in Ugaritic '**ttrt**. She appears as a late re-incarnation of Ba'alath, "mistress" of Byblos. Astarte was initially identified with the Egyptian goddess Hathor and the Babylonian Ishtar and much later with the Cypriot Aphrodite. Adopted later by the Greeks, and given the name Astarte, she was incorporated into their Olympus with the twelve gods. She was known in Egypt during the kingdom of the pharaohs Amenophis II (15th century BC) and later on in times of Seti I. At Ugarit she is prominent as a huntress but also as goddess of love and war. In Sidon she shared a common temple with Eshmun and was worshipped at Tyre with Melkart/Herakles. The Hittites worshipped her as the goddess of Sidon from the beginning of the 13th century BC. She is the same Ishtar of Babylon. The famous Ishtar Gate, build by Nebuchadrezzar II in her honor, still exists. It is today the only surviving, well-preserved monument, ornamented by bulls and dragons (6th century), dedicated to this goddess in Babylon. In Babylon she was the wife of Ashtar and the Evening star. Ashtar would later, with the passage of time, tend to dissappear while Astarte would take for consorts several celestial divinities: at Hierapolis and Ba'albeck she will become the companion of Hadad and in Palmyra she will unite with Baal

Shameem. In Beirut she will be the wife of Poseidon. Recent evidence has placed her as one of the main female deities worshipped at Ebla during the 25th century BC where she was the consort of Ashtar. At Ugarit she became the wife of EL. At Paphos and later on Greece, Astarte was later to be identified with Aphrodite; in Rome she was equated with Venus and in Egypt with Isis. In Near Eastern tradition, as goddess of love, she is represented naked and her cult was associated with orgiastic ceremonies. As a celestial deity she is the equivalent of the Evening Star and her sacred animal was the lion. Astarte is the warrior-goddess, the feminine version occasionally identified in Phoenicia proper and in Cyprus with her male counterpart Reshef (c. 4th century BC). But the most ancient inscription from Cyprus came from a Phoenician temple dating to the 9th century in the quarters of Kathari in Kition. She is also often represented as a warrior-goddess dressed with the attire of the Egyptian Hathor.

While at Byblos the cult of Astarte was associated with that of Adonis, in Sidon Astarte was venerated with Eshmun, who would eventually be replaced by Aeskulapius. In Tyre, Hiram the I built a temple to the triad of Melkarth-Kerakles-Astarte. She appears here in the treaty between King Ezaar'Haddon and Baal of Tyre during the 7th century BC. Finally among the most ancient traces of Astarte is that a bronze statue found in Seville (Spain). It has been dated recently to the 8th-7th centuries BC, dedicated to **strt hr**, that probably originally came from Phoenicia or Cyprus. In southern

Spain several statues of Astarte have been found in tombs. One of them is shown with a lotus flower over her head, a long tunic dress with short sleeves and hairdress similar to that of Hathor. It shows her arms folded over her chest with a flower in the middle. The cult of Astarte was widely disseminated among the Tartessian populations and became quite popular, as suggested by the numerous representations of the goddess. The most ancient ones date back to the second half of the 8th century BC and most likely were imported from Phoenicia. The idols of Astarte were worshipped in the mountains over Seville (El Carambolo) where a sanctuary to the goddess existed bearing on its base the most ancient phoenician inscription found in the West. It is accompanied by several small satues representing Reshep or Hadad, the Phoenician gods of war. In addition, near Salamanca several images in bronze have been found that represent the goddesss of fertility with lotus flowers.

Most scholars agree that the first visitors to the Iberian peninsula were merchants from Tyre, who came to trade their merchandise with the indiginous population around the region of Cadiz (Gades,Gadir). The city was according to historical tradition, (Diodoro Siculus), founded by them about 80 years after the end of the Trojan war, that is, around 1100 BC. The Tyrians were mainly interested in obtaining metals such as silver, which was abundant in the area known today as Riotinto and which the indiginous people did not not appreciate its value. They brought in exchange most likely perishable goods such as textiles and ceramics. The archeological evidence from the early period is poor but by the middle of the 8th century BC the Phoenicians were already bringing besides ceramics and iron objects other more lasting elements such as writing as evidenced by the find of personal gods such as Astarte. A figure of the goddess was the first object found at the place known as Carambolo. In the pedestal of this statue, know preseved in the Archeological Museum of Seville, is found the first inscription in the Phoenician alphabet.

The Phoenicians also introduced the practice of cremation of human dead bodies instead of the inhumation, used by the natives of the region. The inhumation of the individuals of higher social status or their cremation were performed with their dresses and rich ornaments. The latter will be found all over the area of the Guadalquivir River. Eventually the natives will learn from the Phoenicians the technique to work the gold alone and especially in combination with other metals.Thus, the new metal industry will develop into fine models of artwork in gold.

Towards the end of the VII and all along the VI century BC this industry and artwork will reach its peak, especially in El Carambolo. This treasure was discovered in 1958, near Seville and brought back to the minds of historians the reality of the existence and the location of the ancient city of Tartessus. The search for Tartessus by the Spanish archeologists since then lead to the discovery of other finds along the littoral of the Guadalquivir.

A large gold neckless is most likely the most important piece of the treasure of El Carambolo, which consisted of 21 pieces of gold weiging in total over three kilograms. Of particular interest in the Hill of Carambolo is the fact that this location may have been the site of a temple, a testimony of which was the find of the statuette of Astarte with a Phoenician inscription that reads: "because she heard the prayer of her…priest". Astarte and Melkart were then the main deities of Tyre, where most of the colonisers certainly came from.

The most important image of Astarte from the artistic viewpoint was found near Granada. It is in alabaster and represents a lady dressed with a long tunic and flanked by two statues of sphinxes, lying down and covering her head with a double tiara in the Egyptian style. It has a veil covering her back. It dates most likely to the second half of the 7th century and appears to have come from the northern coast of Phoenicia. Phoenician culture strongly infuenced the religion of Hispania: the statue of the Lady of Baza, found near Granada, is a clear example of such infuence. Although it follows Greek models, the presence of a dove indicates that most probably is a representation of Tannit, the goddess of Sarepta and Carthage. She also wears several amulets as ornaments on her chest, typical of phoenician deities. It seems that the Lady of Elche also represents the same goddess.

In the Ugaritic literature (12th century BC) the gods exhibit a certain order of seniority: figures such as EL and Asherat are husband and wife early on while in later times, Baal and Anat become the most powerful. The historical time of the latter are of course uncertain but seems to extend between 1700-1200 BC. No one could communicate with EL unless the visitor went to "the source of the two rivers, the fountain of the two deeps", where the abode of EL was. The Canaanites gave great emphasis to the goddesses as the source of fertility: Asherat and also the virgin Anat were commonly represented naked in both the land of Canaan and in Egypt, a symbol of both their virginity and also their fertility. Both are also the prototype of the goddesses of war. Asherat was the consort of EL and her name meant in early times "The Lady of the Sea" and later on "She who gives birth to the Gods".

In the Canaanite mythology one of the most common names of Asherat was **Qudshu, Holiness**, and in contemporary Egypt **Qds**: she was then represented nude with spirally curled locks, her hands raised while holding lilies and serpents. In the Baal epic Asherat is sometimes the opponent of Baal and Anat but also sometimes comes to their help by interceding for them before the old god EL. She is also shown under various other aspects i.e. in a Hittite tablet Asherat attempts to seduce Baal but having been rejected she goes to El to complaint about Ba'al's treatment accusing him of just the opposite behaviour: EL advises her to deal with Ba'al as she pleases but Ba'al is alerted by Anat of the intentions of Asherat.

In the treaty between Ezaar'Haddon of Assyria and King Ba'al I of Tyre, circa early 7th century BC, among the phoenician gods listed we have Ba'al Shameem, "lord of Heaven" in Phoenician (known since Ugarit as the Sun-God) with Melkarth of Tyre, Eshmun of Sidon and Astarte. In the treaty Melkarth and Eshmun are supposed to lay waste the country and Astarte is invoked as goddess of war to destroy the weapons of the Tyrians in case they fail to comply with the terms agreed upon or if they rebel against Assyria.

The practice of **sacred prostitution**, connected with the worship of Astarte in Byblos, Paphos, etc. was believed by some to be a ritual obligation for all women once in life. Other authors contend that only the "temple slaves" were subject to this practice. Elsewhere, in coastal cities of Phoenicia and its environs, professionals practiced sacred prostitution in the temples, a feature itself used as a mechanism to collect funds from foreigners, navigators and traders, on behalf of the goddess. In busy port towns of strong commercial centers, cosmopolitan sanctuaries were built with lucrative purposes. According to Herodotus in Babylon and Cyprus all women had to submit to this ritual at least once in life.

During the Adonyads, the Byblian women began to perform the secret rites in the temple of Ba'alath in honor of Adonis. This essentially consisted in weeping and wailing and shaving their heads in honor of Adonis, lover of Ba'alath, expecting his resurrection. Those women who refused to have their heads shaven had to submit themselves during an entire day to the custom of selling their bodies to strangers and the collected moneys were deposited in the temple as votive offerings. Herodotus says that

"the beautiful ones had no problem in recruiting their fees but the ugly and ungracious ones had to stay in the temple, occasionally for long periods of time, until some customer decided to pay for their bodies".

As discussed elsewhere, women became prostitutes for one day, even those of highly respected families, and gave themselves to strangers; a fact interpreted by some scholars as a tribute to the mother Earth in order to receive new seed for fertilization. The practice was widespread in antiquity and it is difficult to determine where it initially originated.

Herodotus himself describes a similar ceremony taking place in the temple of Ishtar in Babylon:

"Every woman born in the country had to sit in the temple and associate with a strange man at least once in life. After giving herself she had fulfilled her duty and could go home."

The Greek historian did not try to find an explanation for this custom while other writers made it a part of a fertility rite. However, whatever the explanation, temple prostitution and the public offering of virginity was a widespread custom from the Eastern Mediterranean temples to the Indus Valley. In Jewish temples throughout the Middle East, and in other temples from Capadocia to Byblos and Tyre of Phoenicia, prostitutes exerted their profession without shame and none the next day would remember.

The virgins that came to Cyprus, one may recall, to offer their virginity during especial ceremonies and by pure chance met the Tyrians escaping from Phoenicia under the leadership of Dido, followed them to the place where Carthage would eventually be founded by Dido and her followers. Dido had left after a dispute with her brother Pygmalion, who usurped the throne of their father in Tyre. Dido took these women in her way to the foundation of Carthage. The advent of Christianity put an end to the practice of temple prostitution.

Eusebius of Cesarea, centuries later, described the practice in Afqa of Phoenicia as

"dishonest men in pursuit of luxuriousness, soft and effeminate, betrayed the honor of their sex and engaged in dishonest traffic with women, in secret obscene procedures......" Constantine the Great ordered the destruction of the temple and discontinuation of the practice of temple prostitution when Christianity was adopted by the Roman emperor as the religion of the state, during the 4th century AD. As mentioned earlier only a wall remains today in Afqa, located opposite to the spring of origin of the river Adonis, of what is believed to have been the temple where prostitution was practiced in Phoenicia.

An interesting tale is related by Herodotus concerning the Scythians who on their way to Egypt were convinced with gifts and prayers to go no further and return to their land through Phoenicia by the Egyptian king Psammetichus. When passing through Phoenicia most of them passed by the temple of Astarte, the oldest of all temples of Aphrodite in Phoenicia ("Heavenly Aphrodite") and did no harm but some Scythians remained behind and plundered the temple. As a consequence the descendants of them were afflicted by the goddess with "the female sickness", and since then those who come to Scythia can see the people afflicted with this condition which consists of "loss of virility".

In the Ugaritic texts Attarat (Astarte) appears on several occasions with variable duties and intentions i.e. to either support Ba'al in his struggle against Prince Sea and Judge River:

> "With joy Attarat cries out
> Scatter him, O mighty Ba'al,
> Scatter him, you who mount the clouds,
> for Prince Sea has held us captive,
> he has held us captive, with the support of Judge River.
> Then Ba'al goes out,
> and Ba'al the Mighty scatters him, and puts Prince Sea to death".

Once Ba'al has perished and a substitute for him is needed, El, the father of the Gods, asks Atterat of the Sea to choose among her children a replacement for the dead God:

> "Aloud EL cries to Lady Atterat of the Sea,
> Hear, O Lady Atterat of the Sea,
> Give me one among your sons and I will make him king,
> And Lady Atterat of the Sea responded,
> Yes, let us make king one who knows how to shine"
> ....

The Kindly one, EL the Merciful, then asked:
Let us prepare unguents from the body of Ba'al
from the body of the son of Dagon"...
Then Lady Atterat of the Sea answered
Shall we make **'Attr** the Arrogant King?
Let 'Attr the Arrogant be King!"

It does seem that 'Attr the arrogant, turns out to be a poor substitute for Baal and voluntarily descends from the throne of Ba'al the Mighty, and reigns in the ground, god of it all...

Attar is a minor god, son of Atterat, with an astral significance. The Morning and Evening Stars, assimilated in the Ugaritic thought to be **Shr** and **Slm**, are the twin deities of Dawn and Dusk. A ceremonial human sacrifice appears to have been performed to the Venus star for Attar in Ugarit but other than on one occasion there is no mention of this god as worshipped in child- sacrifice in Ugarit.

Atterat does consent, at the request of Anat, to intercede before EL. Thus permission is given to build a palace for Baal, where he might live as a major god, and may live as an equal to the other gods, sons of Atterat.

"Lady Asherah of the Sea declares:

Saddle an ass,
hitch a donkey!
Put on harness of silver

Trappings of gold

....

Qds -and- Amrr

...sets Asherat on the back of the ass......

Qds begins to light the way,

....

Then she sets face towards 'IL

at the course of the two rivers

at the midst of the streams of the two Deeps.

She enters the abode of 'IL

and comes into the domicile of the King...

at the feet of 'IL she bows and falls

prostrates herself and honors him.

As soon as 'IL sees her

He breaks formality and laughs.

His feet he sets on the footstool......

He lifts his voice and shouts:

"Why has Lady Asherah of the Sea come,

Why came the Creatress of the Gods?

Are you hungry? Are you thirsty?

Then have a bite, have a drink

Eat bread from the tables!

Drink wine from the goblets!

From a cup of gold, the blood of the vines...

If the love of 'IL moves you............

And Lady Asherat of the Sea replied:

Your word, 'IL, is wise;

you are wise for eternity………

Our king is Ba'al, he is our judge,

and none is above him.

Let both of us drain his chalice

Both of us drain his cup!

Loudly…IL, her father, shouts,

King ëIL who brought her into being;

there shout Asherah and her sons,

The goddess and the band of her kin:

…Baal has no house like the gods

Nor a court like the sons of Asherah:

like the dwelling of 'IL, the shelter of his sons,

or the dwelling of Lady Asherah of the Sea,…

…The God of Mercy replied:

Am I both to act as the servant of Asherah

And am I to act like the holder of a trowel?

If the handmaids of Asherah will hold the bricks

a house shall be built for Baal like the gods,

Yes, a court like the sons of Asherah.

And Lady Asherah of the Sea replied:

"You are great O 'IL

You are really wise…

………………………………

Let it be told to Aliyn Ba'al:

A house of cedar let him complete,

> with much silver from the mountains
> with the choicest of gold from the hills
> from the mines bring lapis-lazuli
> And build a palace of cedar, silver,
> gold and lapis gems..."

BA'AL

The Ba'al of Lebanon is one of the four descendants of Time. Together with Ba'al Saphon (Jbeil of Akra), Ba'al Hermon (the Anti-Lebanon), and Ba'al Hamon (the Amanus mountain), they are described by Sanchuniathon of Berytus as «having being originally legendary giants that inhabited the mountains which later would take their names». Ba'al is the young god of thunder, the Hadad of Babylon, depicted as a warrior, not only the storm-god but also the king of heaven and earth, the lord of the fertility cult in Canaan. At Ugarit his initial name was Hadad, spelled in different ways and also abbreviated (**hd, addu, hada, hadad**). Ba'al came into use as the personal name of the god during the Hyksos period (18th to 16th century BC.), when he was still identified with the Egyptian storm-god Seth. He is primarily the Mighty (**al'eyn**) fighter against the powers of disorder. This is the Ba'al that has been identified in later times with the localities of his worship i.e. the Ba'al Shamem (**B'l ^smm** in phoenician, "Lord of the Heavens"). At Byblos he was known as the son of EL and Astarte.

Although EL is the head of the pantheon at Ebla, one of the four main gates of the city during the middle of the 3d millenium is named after Ba'al. At Ebla during the 25th century he is found as Hada, the storm-god, who along with Sipis, the sun-god and the star-god, besides other functions, they presided over international treaties.

At Ba'albeck there existed a temple dedicated to him when the city was an important center of religious worship. The city derived its name from the name of Ba'al. Explorations in the court of the temple of Jupiter, erected at Ba'albeck in Roman times have shown that Early and Middle Bronze Age artefacts were buried under its floor and consisting of painted pottery sherds, flint and obsidian flakes suggesting that occupation of the area dated back to 2900 to 2300 BC.

In Ugarit, during the 14th century BC., EL is the head of the pantheon, depicted with the horns of a bull, while Ba'al is the son of Dagon; both are symbols of fertility.

The title of Lord of Heavens is still applied to Ba'al in Hittite times (Anatolia), a fact confirmed in Summero-Akkadian writings. A bilingual inscription found at Karatepe (in modern Turkey) in Hittite hieroglyphic-Phoenician scripts describes Baal heading their pantheon. Futhermore, Ba'al will be identified with Tammuz in Mesopotamia, Osiris in Egypt and Adonis in Phoenicia. He is found still prominent much later, at the times of Yehimilk, on the 10th century BC, when he was worshipped at Byblos with Ba'alath-Gebel.

Jezebel, the Phoenician queen of the Hebrews, in the 9th century, introduced the worship of Ba'al among the Jews, a fact which eventually brought her downfall and death.

Hiram I build a temple to him in Tyre (Ba'al/Herakles), where a gold column was still standing in the times of Herodotus. Besides being a fighter againt the powers of Sea, he is also a great lover...In the Baal epic found at Ugarit his power of procreation is tested on numerous occasions and before his descent into the netherworld even with a heifer in order to leave a progeny in case of no return...as discussed below.

Allegedly, it is to Anat in the form of a heifer, that he makes love to; Anat, his sister and consort, 77 and even 88 times...The sexual vigor of Ba'al and Anat are legendary as shown in the texts at Ugarit where they take hold of each other's genital organs and copulate...a thousand times...(Ugaritic Literature, Vatican Press, 1949. Text 132: 1-4, Gordon translation).

According to certain portions of the correspondence of the Tell el-Amarna tablets, the city of Ugarit was voluntarily part of ancient Phoenicia, as shown by correspondence between the king of Beirut and his son, then governor of the Ugaritic country. Rib-Addi, king of Byblos, compares the attitude of the the royal family of Ugarit with that of Tyre in a letter to the pharaoh. Furthermore, Abi-Milki, king of Tyre indicates that the city of Ugarit was burned to a great extent during an invasion of the Hittites, around 1200 BC.

The initial arrival of the Phoenicians to Ugarit took place during the second half of the third millennium, as evidenced by ceramic finds dated from 2600 to 2100 BC. Furthermore it seems that it is at this time that the Phoenician (Canaanite) navigators were bringing to Ugarit their industrial products as well as their civilization and language: wine, wheat, gold from the Red Sea, perfumes, purple products and even exotic animals. In exchange they would take leather, wood and even objects in bronze and iron. Horses and chariots were also obtained in this manner and sold to the Egyptians.

Baal is prominent in Ugarit: his temple and the temple of his father Dagon were the most important there. He is the Hadad that mounts the clouds (**rkb 'rpt**) and who utters his voice in the heavens. The Phoenicians, according to Schaeffer and Dusssaud, were responsible for the construction of the temples to Baal and Dagon. Baal is commonly characterized as **bn dgn**. Ba'al appears to be his real name. The fact that no myths have been associated with Dagon is intriguing because he appears to occupy a prominent role in Ugaritic culture and religion. Besides, this god was worshipped by Sargon of Akkad and by the Amorite kings at the beginning of the second millennium BC after the fall of the 3d dynasty of Ur: the Amorite kings who took power were his worshippers as were Hammurabi of Babylon and his contemporaries the kings of Assyria. Alexander the Great had in mind to rebuild the temple erected in Babylon to Ba'al that had been previously razed to the ground by his contender Darius.

The center of worship for Dagon must have been near the middle to upper Euphrates, in Mari and Ebla. The name appears to be of Amorite origin and he and his son appear to be the gods of rain and fertility. The inscription of Eshmun'azzar of Sidon designates the region of Dor and Jaffa, once part of Phoenicia, as the abode of Dagon.

According to Dussaud the cults of Ba'al and Dagon came from the southern Phoenicia. It thus seems, following this view, that from the time of the dynasty of Akkad to the third dynasty of Ur, Dagon was the principal deity over the territory that extended from the shores of the Euphrates to the southern coast of Palestine. His role will soon be taken over in the land of Canaan by EL. In addition, Dagon is according to Philo of Byblos, the father of Demarus. Thus Ba'al is not the son of El but instead **bn dgn**.

The Myth of Ba'al at Ugarit: The Canaanite myths adopt the epic style towards the middle of the second millennium BC. The longest extant text deals with the cosmic theme of the mighty powers of Cosmos that maintain order in nature, over the powers of disorder or Chaos. The conflict between Baal and Mot or initially between Baal and the tyrannical waters of Sea and River is at the core of this epic. This segment seems to be the introduction to the main corpus of the Baal mythology. The characters of the epic include Ba'al, the son of Dagon; Anat and Mot, children of El; Asherat, consort of El; the Prince Sea and the Judge River. The texts seem to have been written in the times of king **Nqmd** of Ugarit in the early 14th century but may have originated much earlier perhaps, several hundred years before. The story begins with the messengers of Sea sent to the divine assembly demanding the surrender of Ba'al for not having paid his tribute to Sea. The emissaries of Sea deliver their message to El, the head of the pantheon, without any respect. El agrees to hand over Ba'al as a slave to Sea. Ba'al, infuriated, refuses, grabs a knife to slash down the messengers but is restrained from attacking them by the goddesses Anat and Asherat.

Eventually Ba'al proceeds against Sea, whom he defeats by using two clubs prepared for him by Chussor, the divine craftman. In the meantime Anat, after battling victoriouly the **ltn** and **tnn** monsters, is invited by Ba'al to his sacred mountain. Upon seeing the messengers of Sea, Anat at first fears that Ba'al has been attacked and is ready to seek the possible offenders but after being informed that Baal is good health she goes to comply with Ba'al's request and is received lavishly by Ba'al who asks her to help him build a palace according to his new rank as a god, after vanquishing Sea and River. Anat then proceeds to obtain authorization from EL to build the palace for Ba'al. Asherat's messengers are also sent to get confirmation from El. Finally the house of Ba'al is built by the divine craftman and a celebration takes place. The myth continues with the god of the underworld Mot threatening Baal, who refuses to pay his respects to Mot.

Ba'al is cautioned against destruction in the underworld by Mot who has laid rival claims to his kingship. But he goes down to the underworld where Mot reigns and Ba'al meets his death despite the great sorrow of Anat and her father EL.

Anat, in her grief, goes in search of Ba'al's corpse which is eventually found with the help of the Sun goddess and buried. Anat then proceeds to look for Mot who confesses to having killed Ba'al and is in turn slain by her. The final portion of the story contains a battle between Mot and Ba'al that is broken up by Sun, who frightens Mot off.

The reconstructed myth of Baal begins with the messengers of Sea sent to El and the Heavenly Assembly of the gods in the sacred mountains, demanding the surrender of Baal.

> Give up, O gods, the son of Dagon
> Whom you guard, yes, Ba'al himself
> ....
> The gods saw the messengers of Sea
> The witnesses of the Judge River
> and lowered their heads to their knees

and then responded:

> O Sea, Ba'al is your servant, your slave,
> the son of Dagon is your prisoner
> and will give you tribute.........

But Ba'al would not readily surrender and replies in anger to the insolent messengers as follows:

> He seizes a knife in his hand
> to smitte the servants
> ....

Among them Ba'al cries out:

> "Lift up, O gods, your heads
> from……your knees
> Return to your princely thrones
> and I will answer to the messengers of Sea
> and the witnesses of Judge River…"

Restrained by the goddesses Anat and Atterat……a battle betwen Ba'al and the powers of the Sea and River ensues with the outcome…that Ba'al strikes Prince Sea on the shoulders

> and smites the head of Prince Sea,
> expels Sea from his throne
> strikes Judge River between the eyes
> and drags River from the seat of his sovereignty…
> Baal…smites the head of Prince Sea…
> Sea collapses and falls to the ground…
> Baal drags him away and disperses him…

Atterat with joy shouted the name of Baal while saying:

> "Hail Ba'al the Conqueror!
> Hail, Rider of the Clouds!
> For Prince Sea is our Captive

> and Judge River is too……
> Baal the Mighty then goes out
> and scatters Sea and River…

Within the Ba'al mythology at Ugarit there is a fragment where both Ba'al and Anat are given credit for the slaying of the monsters **ltn** and **tnn**…**ltn** is actually mentioned only once, when killed by Ba'al…

> "You did smite **ltn**, the Primaeval Serpent,
> ……did annihilate the Crooked Serpent
> The Foul-fanged of Seven Heads
> ………………………………………
> …shall indeed go down into the throat of Mot, the son of El"

On the other hand, the list of monsters slain by Anat is much longer…when approached by the emissaries of Baal, Anat replies:

> What enemy rises up against Baal?
> What foes rise against him, who mounts the clouds?
> Have I not smitten Sea, beloved of El?
> …annihilated River, the great god?
> …put a muzzle on tnn?
> Have I not smitten the Crooked Serpent
> the Foul-fanged with Seven Heads?

I have smitten the Darling of the Earth-deities Mot,

……the Bitch of the gods, Fire

……annihilated Flame, the Daughter of El…

The discrepancy between the texts giving credit to either Ba'al or Anat in the slaying of the Serpent may be explained by either the fragmentary nature of the texts, the age of the different texts, (mixing both older and newer material) and the time of integration of the stories into the mythological tradition at Ugarit.

The main corpus of the Ba'al myth continues with a banquet in the house of EL:

…Serve Ba'al, the Mighty

Satisfy the Prince, lord of the Earth,

Let preparations be made

to feed him…let him have cool water

feast him and give him to drink

give him a cup in his hand, a jar of the folk of heaven…

a cup proper to the gods…El takes a jar with wine

He took a thousand jugs of wine,

mixed them up in a large bowl

Baal arose and sang a song,

the Hero sang with a sweet voice

………………………………………

and then looked upon his girls:

Watches Pdry, the girl of Mist,

Anthony Strong

>watches Dewy, the girl of Rain…

This feast is an initiation rite whereby the god is re-integrated into the living. Instances where a meal marks the end of a period of mourning are quite a common ocurrence in middle Eastern cultures even in modern times.

The beginning of the New Year in the autumnal season of Ugarit is marked by preparations in anticipation of Baal's rehabilitation and the upcoming demonstration of his virility

>……for the love of Ba'al the Mighty
>the love of Pdry, daughter of Fire,
>the affection of Dewy, daughter of the Showers,
>the love of the Arsy, daughter of the Wide World;

In a message of Ba'al to his sister Anat he announces through his messengers, **Vine** and **Field**, his new creation: lightning…

>I have to make a declaration to you
>a word of the tree, a wisper of the stone,
>the heavens murmur to the earth,
>and the voice of the deep to the stars
>I will create lightning, which the heavens do not know,
>a matter that men do not know
>or the multitudes of the Earth understand.

> Come now and I will show it to you
> in my sanctuary in the mountains
> in the pleasant place, in the Hill of Power…

Anat in a great misunderstanding is first under the impression that Ba'al is in some kind of danger and replies to the messengers of Ba'al, Vine and Field, as follows:

> What enemy rises up against Ba'al,
> What adversary against Ba'al, who mounts the clouds?
> Have I not slain Sea, beloved of EL?
> Have I not annihilated River, the great god?
> I have slain the Crooked Serpent
> the Foul-fanged with Seven Heads.
> I have slain Mot, the beloved of the underworld,
> I have slain the Bitch of the gods, Fire
> …the daugther of EL, Flame,
> smitten and dispossesed the Flood,…

and then Anat agrees to the suggestion of Ba'al

> to effect unions in the land,
> diffuse love in the earth
> pour out well-being into the midst of the earth,
> and increase love amidst the fields…

Anat also agrees to approach EL and Atterat, as seen earlier,..with a request to build a house or palace for Ba'al with the help of the divine craftman, **Ktr-w-Hss**, the Skilful and Percipient One, in anticipation of the upcoming demostration of his virility and as sort of reward for having vanquished the Prince of Sea. This requires obtaining permission from EL, a task that first Anat, Ba'al's sister, and later Atterat, EL's wife, have to get from EL through both threats and praise for EL who in his great wisdom undestands that Baal needs a palace in accordance with his new status because Asheratt says he is "our king and our judge...and none is above him". Finally EL gives his consent and the mansion for Ba'al is built in the mountain of Sapon with cedar from Lebanon, lapis lazuli, gold and silver from the hills and mountains, a palace in keeping with his rank, similar to the palace of the other gods.

The palace built, Ba'al then gives a banquet with slaughtering of animals for the meal including oxen, sheep, calves, goats and with the invitation of the gods, the seventy sons of Asheratt and all the fertility gods, the king and his men: everyone participated in the sacrificial meal, part of it cult and part myth.

The instalation of Ba'al in his house brings about the opposition of his enemy Mot, forcing Baal to send his messengers, Vine and Field, to the underworld, realm of Death, they

> descend to the House of Corruption of the Earth,
> towards the city Ruin,...of the most ruthless of the gods...

The death of Ba'al sometimes during the summer, when the fruits begin to mature, eventually takes place and he descends to the underworld with his clouds, his winds, his rain, his swine and his girls **Pdry** and **Dewy**;

> towards the mountain of Concealment
> he descends to the House of Ruin in the underworld,
> to be numbered with those that go down into the Earth
> thus to know the annihilation of the dead......

But before this happens Ba'al mates with a heifer. The heifer is considered by some scholars to be a personification of Anat, his virgin sister and consort, in order to leave progeny in case of no return. The often quoted passage, a show of his virility, goes as follows:

> Ba'al the Mighty loves a heifer in the pastures
> he lies with her seven times and seventy times,
> yes,...eight times and eighty times;
> and she conceives and bears a male...

The **number seven** or its multiples must have had a special significance among Canaanites, Phoenicians and Hebrews. Ba'al is sent to seven years of atonement for having vanquished the seventy children of Asherat; he copulates with Anat seventy-seven times before dissappearing into the underworld; Kadmus has to serve for seven years before he is allowed to wed Harmonia; king Krt after losing all his progeny of seven male children is promised to have seven new children with Hry, his new wife; for the funeral feast that Anat gives in honor of Ba'al the sacrificed animals include deer, oxen, sheep and wild goats (seventy of each); Ba'al copulates with the heifer, presumably Anat, 77 times; Mot returns from the realm of death seven years after Anat has destroyed and seeded his remains on account of what he did to Ba'al in the Netherworld; king Krt arrives at the sunset of the 7th day to 'Udum the great, in search of his new bride; the Athenians had to bring seven youths and seven virgins every year to be devoured by the Minotaur in the Labyrinth; Kronos had seven daughters with Atteratt and seven sons with Rhea, both of them being his sisters sent by Uranos, his father, to kill him. Many more examples of this nature are found in the Canaanite dialects and also in the Hebrew Bible.

The precise meaning or connection of Baal with the swine (**khnzr**) is unknown. The pig may have been taboo among the Canaanites and among other Middle Eastern people. In this connection the death of Adonis in Phoenicia, killed by a wild boar during a wild boar-hunt comes to mind.

After the death of Ba'al the extant material of the Ugarit tablets contains a vivid description of EL's mourning for Ba'al and the search by Anat of her brother in the Netherworld.

> Ba'al has fallen to the Earth
> Dead is Ba'al the Mighty
> the Prince, Lord of the Earth has perished.
> El, the Kindly One, the Merciful,
> then descends from his throne
> and leaps to the ground,
> removes the turban from his head,
> and makes the mountains echo his lamentations
> and his clamour the forest to resound.
> He raises his voice and cries
> Baal is dead. What has become of the son of Dagon?

Then Anat's search for Baal begins: this is a common theme in middle Eastern cultures from Egypt and Mesopotamia to Phoenicia; reminiscent of the search of Isis for Osiris, Ishtar for Tammuz, Baalath for Adonis.

> Anat goes in his search
> from every mountain to the heart of the Earth
> from the hills to the midst of the fields
> She comes to the pleasant land of pasture
> She comes upon Baal fallen to the ground
> Anat recovers his body and after
> weeping and drinking her tears like wine
> she shouts to **Sps**, the Light of the gods,
> lift upon me Ba'al the Mighty

> then…Sps lifts his body upon the shoulder of Anat,
> Anat weeps for Ba'al and buries him
> ……in the niches of the divinities of the earth.

Anat then gives a funeral feast for Baal which marks the end of the ritual of mourning. This practice is still current in Phoenicia until today following the death of certain figures, leaders or peasants.

The text continues:

> She slaughters seventy wild-oxen
> ………………seventy oxen,
> ………………seventy sheep
> ………………seventy deer
> ………………seventy wild-goats
> at a funeral due to Ba'al the Mighty…

While Ba'al is in the underworld a substitute should be found: the duty to find a replacement falls upon two goddesses, his sister Anat and the **sun-goddess Sps** but it is started by EL himself:

> El cries aloud to Lady Atterat of the Sea
> Hear, O Lady, Atterat of the Sea
> Give me One of your sons and I will make him king
> Lady Atterat replies:
> Yes let us make king one who knows how to shine

> ....
> Shall we make king **'Attr** the arrogant?
> Let **'Attr** the Arrogant be King....................
> **'Attr** then takes his seat on the throne of Baal the Mighty
> his feet do not reach the footstool
> nor his head reach the top

somehow **'Attr** does not feel that he can occupy Ba'al's seat and finally descends from his throne declaring:

> I may not be king in the throne of Ba'al the Mighty
> while he reigns in the ground, god of it all......

Anat in the meantime has decided to get Ba'al back and begins to intercede before her brother Mot

> The heart of Anat yearns after Ba'al
> as the heart of the cow after her calf
> as the heart of the ewe after her lamb
> ......Anat raises her voice and cries:
> O Mot...give me my brother back

and because Mot is unwilling or does not seem to respond promptly Anat resorts to brute force

> She seizes Mot, the son of EL,
> with a blade she cleaves him,
> with a shovel she winnows him
> with fire she parches him
> with a mill stone she grinds him;
> in the field she sows him;
> his remains are scattered
> for the birds to eat and consume.........

Again EL has a dream that anticipates the return of Ba'al and restoration of his procreative vigor:

> In a dream of EL, the Kindly One, the Merciful,
> In a vision of the Creator of all created things,
> the Heavens rain oil,
> the valleys run with honey
> and EL the Merciful, the Kindly One rejoices;
> ....
> for Ba'al the Mighty is alive,
> for the Prince of the Earth exists again

In the meantime Anat and Sps still searching through the skies and the underworld, learned all the secrets of life and death.

> The Virgin Anat departs and sets her face
> towards Sps the Light of the gods

> she raises her voice and cries
> the message of the Bull EL, her father,
> …………………………………………
> Where is Ba'al the Mighty, the Prince Lord of the Earth;
> then Sps, the Light of the gods, answers:
> Close your eyes at sunset, and during the night
> I will seek for Ba'al the Mighty…………

Ba'al in the meantime is alive and thinking about vengeance upon his adversaries, the sons of Atterat. Eventually

> He smites them with a sword
> he pounds them with a club
> and makes the desolation of death light upon the underworld……

The penalty of atonement for seven years imposed for fratricide upon Baal by El is difficult to understand unless we accept Baal and the seventy sons of Atterat as his half-brothers due to Baal's love for their sister, the virgin Anat. The sons of Atterat can not be the brothers of Baal because he is the son of Dagon. They are the sons of El, thus brothers of Anat, daughter of El and consort of Baal.

After seven years of disappearence in the Netherworld, Mot re-emerges to avenge his injuries at the hands of Anat and resume his unsettled conflict with Ba'al. He says:

> To Ba'al he raises his voice and cries:
> your fault, O Ba'al, was my humiliation;
> …being scattered with a blade
> …being burned with fire
> …ground with a millstone, was your fault……
> ………Ba'al will be made a fellow of Sea
> smitten by my mother's sons, yes, destroyed.

Then the battle between Mot and Ba'al takes place and appears to have been won by Ba'al. But the extant evidence is interrupted and the end is unknown.

BA'ALATH

The most important religious characteristic of Byblos is the cult to Ba'alath, «The lady of Byblos». Although dating back to the beginning of the third millennium BC, she remains the main goddess until the end of the first. During the first millennium her cult becomes so important that the cult of Ba'al Shameen is discontinued. The inscriptions of Yehimilk, and his descendants Abibaal, Elibaal and Shipitbaal are all dedicated to «the Lady of Byblos», seeking her protection to confer upon them a long life and protect their graves from the robbers of ancient times. They also describe, as shown elsewhere, the modifications they made to her temple in order to preserve it for eternity. During the 5th century BC Yehowmilk was king and dedicated a stele, now preserved in the Louvre Museum, in Paris, where the king of Byblos appears dressed as a Persian king presenting his offerings to Ba'alath, here represented as Hathor, the Egyptian goddess. The inscription enumerates the modifications performed on her temple: an altar in bronze was erected in the middle of the yard, a door made of gold was placed at the entrance with a disc also made of gold, decorating the front in stone and finally a portico.

During their navigation through the Mediterranean, the Phoenicians, especially those from Byblos and Tyre, had touched upon several islands, including Melos, and their route continued from there to Cythere, where they had a port named **Phoinikus.** Here the cult to Ba'alath-Aphrodite had been started by Phoenicians, according to Herodotus (HISTORIES: I:105).

The relationship of Ba'alath to Egypt dates back to the pharaohs of the 25th-24th century and it is most likely at this time that the assimilation of the two goddesses (Hathor and Ba'alath) took place. The relationship persists until the dynasty of the Ptolemies because inscriptions exists of "Hathor-Lady of Byblos" in Egyptian as **Nbt Kbn/Kpny** until that time. She is mentioned in the Tell-el-Amarna tablets from the 14th Century and it is a little later when she becomes invoked as protectress of navigation, as it is to be expected from the mistress of an important maritime site such as Byblos. The assimilation of Baalath-Gubal to Aphrodite by Lucien of Samosate and to Astarte take place sometime later, during the 4th century BC.

The godess Baltis Caelestis of Carthage is assimilated by some scholars to Ba'alath of Byblos, as follows:

"The people of Phoenicia did adore Ba'alath, queen of Cyprus. Because she fell in love with Tammuz, son of Chussor, king of the Phoenicians, she came to live in a castle at Byblos, that was under Cypriote control by Chousor as well. Ba'alath had first been in love with Ares and later with Tammuz. Her husband Hephaistos, full of jealousy, had followed her to the mountains of Lebanon with the intention of killing Tammuz, when he was in the chase of the wild boar. Since then Ba'alath stayed in Byblos and died at Afqa, where Tammuz was also buried."

Ba'alath also is the consort of Tammuz in Palmyra, where the latter is also represented dying. Evidently this story is identical to the legend of the love of Ba'alath for Adonis, discussed elsewhere. In the Greco-Roman period Ba'alath is assimilated to Aphrodite and to the planet Venus.

The Lady of Byblos, is the oldest deity worshipped in the city of Byblos. At the beginning of the 3d millenium BC she is variously known as Ba'alath-Gebal (**Bilt Gbl** in phoenician) and **Kbn** or **Kpny** in the Canaanite and Egyptian tongues respectively. She would be further identified with Hathor, Isis and Astarte. Offerings to Ba'alath such as inscriptions in plates and alabater jars were found in her temple that dated to the times of the great pharaohs. These are the ones who built the great Giza pyramids, Cheops, Khephren and Mycerinus. The Byblian kings considered themselves members of her priesthood. She was even better known in Egypt during the 25th and 24th century BC and was still venerated there at the time of Ptolemy the X (circa 107-88 BC). The symbiosis with Hathor must have taken place in Egypt at an early period (because she is known as **Bilt** in the 17th century BC inscriptions found in the mines of the Sinai peninsula). It also seems that the mythic voyage of Isis to Byblos in search of the body of her lover Osiris must have ocurred by this time. In the times of Ptolemy the X (1st century BC) the Isis-Hathor cult is well established and as such she was venerated in Byblos during Abibaal, Elibaal and Shapatbaal reigns (10th and 9th centuries BC) until the time of Yehawmilk (5th century BC). The assimilation of Ba'alath to Aphrodite takes place later (? circa IV century BC). Her cult became widespread in the Mediterranean area as evidenced by her veneration in most places colonized by phoenicians during the first millennium BC i.e. Sardinia, Baleares islands, Gades, Almuñecar or Cyprus.

Ba'alath-Gebal, queen of Cyprus, falls in love with Adonis. The love of Adonis leads Ba'alath to commit adultery. Her jaleous husband goes after the lover to the mountains of Phoenicia and kills him. Ba'alath remains at Byblos to stay near the burial site of her dead lover at Afqa. She is thought to die there sometime later.

The temple of Ba'alath-Gebal at Byblos contained numerous artifacts (found by Pierre Montet), contemporaneous with the pharaohs of the Old Kindom: inscriptions were found in alabaster jars and bronze plates from offerings to the goddess by Khasekhemui, Cheops, Kephren and Mycerinus. Ba'alath of Byblos appears at this early time already represented as Hathor-Isis.

The main reason for the interest displayed by the Egyptians rulers for the goddess was the existence near Byblos of large amounts of cedar wood used by them in shipbuilding and construction of their tombs, and as well as cedar oil used in mummification. These products were easily transported by sea from Byblos to Egypt and have been recorded since the times of Senefru (c. 2600 BC.). The Egyptian pharaohs for over two millennia often send gifts to Ba'alath that were found in the Byblos excavations by Renan, Montet and Dunand. Artifacts representing most of the Old and Middle kingdoms periods made of alabaster, bronze, scarabs, stone and ivory were found with hieroglyphic inscriptions in the lower levels of the temple. This revealed the respect the pharaohs had for the goddess in ancient times. Recently, Egyptian archeologists have found two ships at Giza next to the pyramids, one of them has already being restored and is kept today in a special preservation enclosure next to the pyramid of Kephren: it does seem that cedar wood was used by the pharaohs to build these ships that were the ones destined to take them through the secret passages in their last voyage to eternity.

It appears that Ba'alat-Gebal, the Lady of Byblos, later on became Astarte during the Greek period. Since Egytian times she adopted the image of the Egyptian goddess Hathor with her head-dress, her long scepter with a lotus flower and the lion as her animal attribute. Her god consort was at the time Ba'al considered by some authors similar to Ashtar or to **Mlk 'dr**, the all powerful god, the almighty. The designation **'dr** is a phoenician word that applies well to Ashtar. According to Dunand two temples existed for these gods in Byblos since the early Egyptian period and they occupied adjacent locations for about the first three millennia BC. It seems that at Byblos **Ba'al Gebal**, **Ba'al 'dr**, **Mlk 'dr** and Reshep represented from the beginning different names designating a single god, the consort of Ba'alath Gebal. The Ba'al of the city of Byblos was venerated as the consort of Ba'alath Gebal until the 4th century BC, when on the offerings of King Yehawmilk, the Lady of Byblos appears alone. In the bas-relief found by Montet the goddess is designated **nbt Kbn**, "the Mistress of Byblos".

In a sculpture found near Byblos, now preserved in the Istanbul Museum and dating from the 5th century BC while Ba'alath is represented with the Hathorian dress, Ashtar is shown as a lion with wings and a human head. This original lion god from Egypt appears at Ugarit in the 14th century BC as a winged lion and later on at Byblos still with a lion head but the body of a man. In this representation of Ba'al Gebal and Ba'alath, the gods were the protectors of Nature while the goddess was the source of fertility and life.

KADMUS (CADMUS)

The name of KADMUS derived from the Phoenician word **qadam**, meant **easterner, newcomer**. The Greeks believed that

Kadmus (Cadmus) came from Phoenicia. Herodotus gives a detailed account of his arrival, the settlement with his companions and the introduction of the Cadmean characters into Ionia.

"The Phoenicians who came with Kadmus at their settlements in Greece, among many other kinds of learning, brought into Hellas the alphabet, which had hitherto being unknown to the Greeks. Most of those that dwelt around the Cadmeians were Ionians who having been tught the letters, used them with some few changes of form and in so doing gave to these characters the name of Phoenician."

According to Diodorus Siculus (LIBRARY OF HISTORY: V: 58) the Phoenicians had received from Cadmus the mission to keep custody of the temple of Poseidon, that he had just founded. They took for wives the women of the locality and started a hereditary line of priests. Archeology supports this fact by demostrating that by the second half of the VIII century BC a wave of Phoenician immigrants dealing in olive oil and perfumes came and established themselves in Rhodes. They left there numerous artifacts used in this industry.

The phoenician trade with the neighboring islands involved the creation of colonies in small Mediterranean locations: Malta, Crete, and Cyprus.

Cyprus was an important location for commercial and cultural relations with Phoenicia since the 14th and 13th centuries as demonstrated by the presence of Phoenician inscriptions such as one found on a bronze cup bearing a dedication to the Baal of Lebanon by the governeur of **Kartadasht** (Carthage of Cyprus, or New Town) In addition, during the 9th and 8th centuries large populations in Cyprus spoke the Phoenician language. Although their exact number is unknown they are assumed to have come from the neighboring Phoenician coast or from Egypt or Anatolia, places where these people had spread with their commercial enterprises since early on. A temple to Eshmun-Melkhart and another to Astarte have been found in Kition, dating to the 9th century.

In Malta the cult of Astarte enjoyed great popularity and so did the use of the Phoenician script until the 2d century BC thus showing that Malta was quite independent of Carthage and Sardinia. Two large stelae in Phoenician were found in Malta dating from the end of the second millennium and considered among the oldest found in the Western Mediterranean area.

Crete also sustained relations dating to the time when Ugarit and Byblos were in constant contact with Egypt: Crete must have played an important role as intermediary. During the middle of the second millennium Cnossos became the most prominent Phoenician city. It is generally accepted that Crete must have been one of the earliest sites where the alphabet first was introduced to.

The Abduction of Europa by the Bull from the Beirut Museum

According to most genealogies reported by classic writers from the 5th century on, Kadmus is the grandson of Poseidon. Curiously enough, Kronos, the great-grandfather of Poseidon in Phoenician mythology, gives him in custody the city of Berytus. As mentioned elsewhere Poseidon becomes the protector-deity of Berytus. The Berytians would later found at Delos the "Poseidon Society" that was responsible for the erection of places of worship for their main gods. Apollodorus has it that Kadmus, son of Agenor, king of Tyre, and brother of Europa, was sent by his father to assure the return of his sister after her abduction by Zeus. To achieve this objective he took along his two brothers, Cilix and Phoenix, and his mother. Agenor's

The Phoenicians in History and Legend

orders to his children were not to return without Europa. After their diligent search and unable to find Europa, they gave up the idea of returning home and dispersed: Phoenix went to Phoenicia, Cilix to Cilicia and Kadmus stayed with his mother and allegedly founded the city of Thebes in Boeotia. An alternative legend argues that it was EL, the Canaanite-phoenician god known as the Bull who abducted Europa and took her from Phoenicia to Crete. The god EL through his identification with Aten, became established in Crete and took her there. This is understood in the Ugaritic text (AB, IV-V, lines 38-39)…

> **hm yd 'El mlk yhssk**
> **ahbt ^sr t'rrk**
> "the hand of EL, your king, will take you
> the love of the Bull would blind you"

After the death of his mother, Kadmus, under advice by the Oracle of Delphi not to trouble anymore attempting to find Europa, decided to pick an appropriate site and erect a new city: this he did and founded Thebes (Cadmeia).

Pausanias in "Boeotia" describes de foundation of Thebes as follows:

> "As Cadmus was leaving Delphi by the road of Phocis, a cow guided him on his way. This cow had on each of her sides a white mark like the orb of the moon. Now the oracle of the

god had told Cadmus and his host with him were to make their dwelling where the cow would sink down in weariness. So this is the place pointed out for the foundation of the city. Here there is in the open air an altar and an image of Athena, said to have been dedicated by Kadmus. Those who think that the Kadmus that came to Thebes was an Egyptian and not a Phoenician find themselves contradicted by the name of this Athena, because she is called by the Phoenician name of Onga, and not by the Egyptian name of Sais. The Thebans assert that on the part of their citadel, where today stands the market place, stood in ancient time the house of Kadmus. They point out the ruins of the bridal chamber of Harmonia and that of Semele; into the latter no man is allowed to step in, even now. There is also a story that along with the thunderbolt that hit the bridal chamber of Semele there fell a log from heaven. Polydorus adorned this log with bronze and called it Dionysus Kadmus. Nearby there is an image of Dionysus, of solid bronze, made by the sons of Praxiteles."

After the foundation of Thebes, Kadmus would have to kill the dragon guarding the spring of Ares (his future father-in-law) as a revenge against the dragon for having killed his friends who went there to get water. As a consequence, Kadmus had to atone the slaughter of the dragon with eight years of work [(seven plus one) (one eternal year)] for Ares.

Pausanias continues: "At Thebes there are three wooden images of Aphrodite, so ancient that they are said to be votive offerings of Harmonia and the story is that they were made out of the wooden figure-heads on the ships of Kadmus. One is called Heavenly because Harmonia wanted to signify pure love, free from body lust; another one was named Common, to denote sexual intercourse and the third, that of Rejecter, thus that mankind might reject unlawful passion and sinful acts. For Harmonia knew of many crimes perpetrated not only by foreigners but also by Greeks, similar to those attributed later by legend to the mother of Adonis, the daughther of Minos."

The service of eight years by Kadmus before his marriage is reminiscent of the biblical accounts where obligatory labor sometimes was required before a man would be allowed to marry the woman of his choice. After Kadmus servitude, Zeus in recompense gave him in marriage Harmonia, daughter of the god of war Ares with Aphrodite (Mars and Venus in Roman mythology). All the gods quitted Heavens and came to celebrate the wedding of Kadmus and Harmonia in Cadmeia.

The descendants of Kadmus included several daughters and one son. One of the daughters, Ino, became the foster-mother of (Dionysus) Bacchus by her husband Athamus. An alternate explanation exists: according to Ovid, Bacchus was the son of Semele and this makes Ino his foster-mother not his aunt. However Ino seems to have been his custodian and would watch over him during his infancy. Ino, under attack by Juno, queen of the gods, leaped into the sea with her son and both were changed into deities by Neptune. According to Apollodorus, Semele who bedded with Zeus would die tragically hit by a thunderbolt but not before Zeus would snatch their son Bacchus (Dionysus), and assure his birth three months later.

Dionysus then would be raised by Hermes. Diodorus Siculus describes the birth of Dionysus as premature because Semele would die upon her being impressed by Zeus when he appeared to her in all of his splendor: Zeus would rescue the infant and send him to the nymphs to be raised by them and later by Hermes.

Kadmus was also the father of Polydorus and grandfather of Laius. The latter would be involuntarily slain by his son Oedipus. Oedipus, after solving the riddle of the Sphinx, received as a prize the hand of Jocasta and unknowning will marry his own mother. Thus by this account, Cadmus appears as the direct father of the House of Oedipus. Controversy exists regarding this point: some scholars even deny the existence of Polydorus and declare that Cadmus had no sons.

The tribulations of Kadmus and his descendants have no equal in recorded mythology. Rape, murder, sodomy, parricide, suicide, madness and incest run through their lives. Thus, according to this tradition, Kadmus is arguably one of the most tragic characters of Western mythology.

Zeus abducted and raped Europa. This union resulted in three boys, the oldest being Minos. The boys quarreled with each other for the love of another boy, Miletos, later founder of the city of the same name. As stated earlier, Semele would get a son, Dionysus, by Zeus and would die herself hit by a thunderbolt. Dionysus would discover wine and, driven mad by Hera, would wonder through Egypt and the Near East before settling in Phoenicia. In Berytus he would compete with Poseidon for the love of the nymph Beroe, eponyme of the city.

On his Roman re-incarnation as Bacchus he would give to the Phrygian King Midas the wish and the source of his unhappiness: turning into gold everything he touched. Dionysus is said to have been the one who first discovered tree-fruits, especially apples and figs, and of course the vine and the pine tree and certain flowers. There was a flowery Dionysus in Attica and in some areas of Greece he was associated with the ivy. Dionysus died a violent death but was brought back to life by his father Zeus. The Titans had murdered him, cut him and ate his flesh raw, in pieces mixed with herbs. His sister Minerva saved his heart and gave it to her father upon his return: he put the Titans to death by torture. Pomegranates grew from the blood of Dionysus, as anemones grew from the blood of Adonis. According to some writers the severed limbs were pieced together and buried by Apollo in the Parnassus. He rose from the dead and ascended to heaven. Another version has Zeus raising him while he was mortally wounded, swallowing his heart and giving it to Semele who conceived him again. In those geographic locations where his resurrection was part of the myth it seems that a general doctrine of immortality was taught to his worshippers.

Still others believe that Dionysus descended into Hades to bring his mother Semeleback from the dead. He is commonly represented in the shape of a bull with horns but also as a child with clusters of grapes and the head of a calf with sprouting horns. At his festivals he was believed to appear in the form of a bull and the Bacchanals of Thrace wore horns in imitation of their god. It was in the shape of a bull that he was torn to pieces by the Titans. In Crete the act of devouring live bulls and calves appears to have been a regular feature of the Dionysiac rites. The worshippers of Dionysus believed themselves to be killing the god in the form of a bull, eating his flesh and drinking his blood. The custom of killing an animal and devouring its flesh raw has been a very ancient practice; the myths would tell of the animal inflicting some injury to the god: the killing of goat in this worship rites has come to be considered not as a slaying of the god but as a sacrifice in his honor. In some places such as Boeotia tradition indicates that a human being, sometimes a child, was torn to pieces during the Dionysiac rites. The replacement of human by animal sacrifices is most likely a merciful development in recent times.

The account that Dionysus was born of Semele is traced to its beginning by Diodorus Siculus, (Book III: 62) offering the explanation that Thoune was the name that the ancients gave to the earth, and this goddess received the appelation Semele because the worship and honor paid to her was dignified (**semne**). She was called Thoune, because of the sacrifices and offerings to her.

Furthermore the tradition that Dionysus was born twice from Zeus arises from the belief that the fruits perish with the plant each season and are reborn again…as if there had been a second epiphany of the god among men, and so the myth was created and told once more that the god had been born again from the thigh of Zeus. However this may be, those who believe the name Dionysus signifies the use and discovery of wine, recount the myth in this way. Several individuals were said to have the same name: the last one of them, according to Diodorus, was the one born of Zeus and Semele, the daughter of Cadmus, in Boeotian Thebes. Zeus had become enamoured of Semele because of her beauty and had consorted with her, but Hera, jealous and anxious to punish the girl, assumed the form of one of the women who was an intimate friend of Semele and suggested to her that it was fitting that Zeus should lie with her while having the same majesty and honor that Hera had when falling in the arms of Zeus. Zeus, at the request of Semele that he appeared to her accompanied by thunder and lightning, did so but Semele unable to endure the majesty of his grandeur, died and gave birth to the child before the expected time. This child quickly hidden in his father's thigh, completed his growth. Zeus, taking up the child, handed it over to the care of Hermes, and ordered him to take it to the cave in Nysa, which lay between Phoenicia and the Nile, where he should deliver it to the nymphs thus that they should rear him with great solicitude and give to him the name Dionysus, from **dios**, the genitive form of Zeus, and **nysus** from Nysa.

After Dionysus left Herakles, cityholder of Tyre, he went to the district of Berytus.

Nonnos describes then how Aphrodite bore a second child to the son of Myrrha, that is Adonis.

"Dionysus, already having planted the clustering vintage of his glorious fruit in the land of Lebanon, he intoxicated all the wine bearing plants of the land and presented the vine gift to Adonis. Come now, you Muses of Lebanon on the neighboring land of Berytus, that handmaiden of law! The city of Berytus, the keel of human life, harbor of the Loves, firm based on the sea, with fine islands and fine verdure, with an isthmus narrow and long, where the rising neck between two seas is beaten by the waves of both. On one side it spreads under Lebanon in the blazing East, and there comes for its people a lifesaving breeze, whistling loud and shaking the cypress trees with flagrant winds......

The other part by the sea that Berytus possesses, where she offers her breast to Poseidon and her watery husband embraces the girl's pregnant neck,...putting moist kisses on the bride's lips...accepts Poseidon's familiar gifts from his hand out of the deep......About the southern neck of this delightful country sandy roads lead to the southern hills and the Sidonian land, where are all manner of trees and vines with thick foliage in the gardens,......"

And Nonnos continues about Berytus

"O Beroe, root of life, nurse of cities, the boast of princes, the first city seen, twin sister of Time, coeval with the universe, seat of Hermes, land of justice, city of laws,...hall of the Loves, delectable ground of Bacchos,......star of the Lebanon country,...Beroe the one brought forth by her mother in her bed in the deep waters."

Diodorus describes (Book III, 67)
"Among the Greeks Linus was the first to discover the different rhythms and songs, and when Kadmus brought from Phoenicia the letters, Linus was again the first to transfer them into the Greeks language, to give a name to each character, and to fix its shape. Now the letters as a group are called "Phoenician"...but as single letters the Pelasgians were the first to make use of the transferred characters, and so they are called "Pelasgic".

As knowledge about the Greek alphabet has increased and more early inscriptions have become available, all the evidence has come to confirm the Greek tradition that their alphabet was derived from the Phoenician. The question that remains is how early were the letters brought to Greece. A palace, said to be erected by Kadmus, has been discovered in Thebes, roughly dated between 1400-1200 BC. However, the existence of Kadmus as a historical figure is still unproven. Additional evidence now suggests that the letters may have come to Greece much later than previously stated, about 800 BC. The stele of Moab, written in Phoenician, dates back to the 9th century

BC, thus suggesting that if the letters came to Greece late, it must have been earlier than indicated above.

Minos, father of Ariadne, would keep in the Labyrinth, constructed for him by Daedalus, the Minotaur, a monster half-man half-bull, product of his wife's love affair with a bull: the Athenians had to bring every year seven youths and seven virgins to be devoured by the monster. With the help of Ariadne, Theseus would enter the Labyrinth, kill the Minotaur and rescue the children.

Althaemenes, grandson of Minos, fearing an oracle which predicted that he would kill his father, left Crete and went to Rhodes where he erected a temple for a Phoenician Zeus. This Zeus will be worshipped there in the form of a bull until Diodorus Siculus times. Unable to avoid his fate, Althaemenes would eventually kill both his father and his sister.

The Oracle had warned Laius not to beget a son with his wife for that son would kill his father. However, while drunk, he had intercourse with Jocasta, who begat him a son. Fearful of the oracle's prediction, Jocasta made her son disappear. This son would eventually be adopted by the king of Corinth: the King found the infant and gave him to his own wife to raise. She named him Oedipus.

Oedipus, upon learning of the curse pending over him would leave the home of his adoptive parents, attempting to avoid his own fate as predicted by the Oracle and while riding in a chariot in unknown territory, he would encounter his natural father Laius in a narrow road. The road was known as the Cleft Way or Triple Way, where three roads united into one before reaching the valley that would lead to Delphi: a dispute ensued and Oedipus unwittingly killed his own father.

Following the death of Laius, Creon succeeded him as king of Thebes. During his reign a great calamity befell Thebes when Hera sent the Sphinx to plague the city: it would snatch away one of their men every day unless a riddle told to her by the Muses was solved. Creon, after losing his own son to the Sphinx, proclaimed that to whomever solved the riddle of the Sphinx he would give both the kingdom and the wife of Laius. Oedipus, after solving the riddle of the Sphinx, succeeded both to the throne of the kingdom of Thebes and unknowingly had to marry his own mother. Jocasta begat him sons and daughters. Two of the children of Oedipus, Polynices and Eteocles, fought each other for the succession to the throne of the kingdom of Thebes and in the process killed each other. Pausanias tells us in his book BOEOTIA that the tombs of the children of Oedipus are in Thebes and the Thebans still regard them as heroes and offer to them sacrifices: As the sacrifice is being offered the flame and the smoke from it, so they say, divide themselves into two. Nearby is a spring called the "Fountain of Oedipus", so named because Oedipus washed off the blood of his murdered father there. By the Fountain is also the grave of Hector, the son of Priam, whose bones were brought there from Troy because of an oracle that said:

> You Thebans who dwell in the city of Kadmus,
> If you wish blameless wealth for the country where you live,
> bring from Asia the bones of Hector
> and reverence him as a hero, according to the bidding of Zeus.

Jocasta later on hanged herself, upon learning of her incest with Oedipus. Although differences of opinion exist about the circumstances of her death, her suicide most likely appears to have occurred by hanging, according to common custom among the goddesses of the Greek mythology.

Finally, Kadmus and Harmonia by the end of their lives would be converted into serpents and send by Zeus to the Elysian Fields for eternity. In this regard, Euripides is the only other early source from the 5th century BC that reports the transformation of Kadmus and Harmonia into snakes and speaks of their exile. All other writers send them after their death to the Isles of the Blest.

ESHMUN

Scholars today are of the opinion that in many instances Kings of the very remote past became deified and later incorporated into mythological stories. It is unknown who was the historical character that gave origin to Eshmun. He appears as the main god of Sidon. Recent excavations at Jaffa have revealed that a Phoenician presence existed there going back to the concessions of Dor and Jaffa to the

Phoenicians of Sidon by the king Eshmun 'azzar II, from the Persian period. The Persian king preferred to transfer these cities, that had been previously under Egyptian domination, to the Phoenicians whom he considered more friendly. Little however is known about the origins of the cult of Eshmun (**'smn** in Phoenician means **"unction oil"**). Thus it has been proposed to interpret the name of the god as the word **"oil"** in order to reasonably explain his character of a healer god. As mentioned elsewhere, Eshmun (Asclepius) had been considered by Sanchuniathon and Philo of Byblos as the eight god of the **Kabirs (Kbr)**. His sanctuary was built in the vicinity of Sidon, at at the modern Bostan-el-Sheikh: this was a site of pilgrimage during ancient times, as revealed by the numerous offerings found during the excavations of the area. Some scholars disagree with the identification of Eshmun with the eight **Kbr** and prefer the designation relating the god to the unction oil, thus making him a healer, later identified by the Greeks with Aeskulapius.

At Tyre and specially at Sidon, Eshmun is the youngest of the eight phoenician **kabirim** that were principally worshipped at Beirut. He appears during the Greek and Roman periods as a god healer, thus its association with Aeskulapius. According to Philo of Byblos from the 1st century BC, Eshmun was one of the eight Cabires, a group of gods originally from Ugarit in the 14th century BC. They were protectors and themselves navigators and known as the **Dioscures**, children of Skydyk. On a coin from Beirut and another from Tripoli the Dioscures are represented standing, naked, in circle, with a characteristic star on their forehead and next to a ship.

Philo divides them into two groups: they are a group of seven and the eight, presumably from a different mother, is Eshmun, identified with Aeskulapius. He was of extreme importance in the region of Tyre and Sidon as a healing god.

Eshmun was documented as early as the second millennium BC in the cuneiform texts and its divinity persisted and was reaffirmed during the second century AD by Pausanias (DESCRIPTION OF GREECE; VII, 23,:7-8) who tells the story that a Sidonian who went to visit the temple of Aeskulapius in Greece told him that the Greek Aeskulapius was

"the air that all humans needed to breath to remain alive, and being the son of Apollo, who was the Sun god that created the air, by such means he had given Aeskulapius the divinity as God Healer."

Curious story about a divinity quite ancient that persisted in the minds of men for well over a millennium and was transferred to Cyprus first and later on to Greece itself.

Eshmun (Aeskulapius), was the son of an immortal woman and a sun-god, worshipped in Sidon; he became the god of Medicine in subsequent tradition.

He was identified in Greece with the son of the healing Apollo in the Hippocratic Oath i.e. with Aeskulapius. According to Philo of Byblos one of the Titanids, daughter of Astarte, was his mother. She would mate with Skydyk and bear Aeskulapius. The mother of

Eshmun then was one of the seven daughters of Astarte who was always represented in Tyre as a Dove. The dove was the attribute of Astarte in the rest of Phoenicia in places such as Afqa and in Cesarea of Lebanon. In Aleppo the dove appears over the head-dress of a goddess following her husband Ashtar-Reshep.

The unearthed evidence at Sidon indicates that Eshmun was the main deity worshipped there. His healing power was evident as attested by the fact that many statues of children bearing dedications to the god were found at his temple. The inscriptions on the sarcophagi of the Sidonian kings refer to them as members of the priesthood of Eshmun and Astarte. These burial sites are proof of the widespread acceptance of the cult of Eshmun at the time (c. 5th century BC) of kings Tabnit, Eshmun'azzar and Bodashtart. The latter king build a magnificent temple to the god.

In the enclave within the ruins of the temple build by the kings of Sidon, the waters were thought to have miraculous curative properties; it was a site of pilgrimage for the ancients seeking relief for their ailments. Marble statues of children have been found within the enclosures of the Temple of Eshmun with inscriptions asking for special indulgence from the god. The statues depict strong, robust children, not weak or ill-appearing individuals.

Philo states that after founding Byblos, the first city, EL gave Beirut to Poseidon and the **Cabires** i.e. the Dioscures. The worship of the **Kabirim** is known to us by their presence on the coins from

Tripoli, Beirut, Sidon, Acre and even Jerusalem. Their worship appears to have been initially typically Phoenician before it was adopted by the Greeks under the name of the Dioscures. In most of the northern Canaanite languages kabire (**kbr**) means "great", "noble". According to Pausanias (Book III: 19...24) the Dioscures brought the culte of Athena Asia (Anat) into Laconia from Phoenicia.

The phoenician **Kabrim**, the great, **'ilim na'amim**, the graceful gods, were eight gods born at the Temple of the Obeliscs: Resheph himself (Ashtar), Shahar and Shalim, their youngest brother Eshmun and perhaps Adonis. We do not know what the names of the other "graceful gods" was. A hymn of Ugarit supports this interpretation when Mot, makes the offer to Ashtar to marry Pdry, the oldest daughther of Ba'al and reffers to Ashtar as the "most gracious of the gods". It does seem that Adonis was also one of the Phoenician kabires: a mirror found in Etruria from the 3d Century BC, supports this interpretation: eight youngters are depicted in an attempt to kill a wild bear, five of them have luminous rays over their forehead, one is under the animal and another god with a dog and a lance is in the process of attacking the wild bear. Finally, another is already bitten by the bear. Gerhard and Dussaud believe that this scene represents the kabiri, the phoenician children of Skydyk, during the death of Adonis.

Eshmun, '**Smn** (capital S) in phoenician is the designation for this healing god. The most recent unearthed evidence of this very ancient divinity suggests that he was already known as **Si-mi-nu/na** in Eblaite language. In Ugarit he is mentionned as **Smn**. Thuthmose the III mentions him in a list from Akko as **Gb`Smn**, which is translated as "The hill of Smn". The name of Eshmun has the same root of **smn**, oil used for unctions, thus the inference as the god of Healing. The Greeks took Eshmun as the God of Medicine, Apollo, and later on converted him into Aeskulapius. The Romans transformed Eshmun into **Apollo Medice**. The fist confirmation of Eshmun in Phoenicia proper dates back to the treaty signed on 754 BC between Assurnirari of Assyria and King Matiel of Arpad, where he appears in association with Melkarth. During the 7th century BC the archives of Nimrud and Niniveh mention Eshmun three times. Subsequently he is mentioned in another treaty, that between king Baal I of Tyre and Azzar'haddon of Assyria, where he is invoked with Melkarth again. The treaty mentions the **"unction oil"**, most likely related to the Healing god Eshmun. An inscription from Amrit in Phoenicia found near fountains of water, believed to have healing powers, mentions Eshmun during the V century BC. It is from here that his cult most likely spread to other areas i.e. his identification in Greece with Aeskulapius. In Southern Phoenicia we find again at Sarepta, near Sidon, a sanctuary dedicated to Askulapius during the IV century. It is in Sidon where Eshmun has his most important religious center. His sanctuary is found about a couple of miles from there at Bostan-el-Sheikh, next to the river known today as Nahr el-Awali. This is the Eshmun celebrated in the inscriptions of Eshmun'azzar II, Tabnit and Bodashtart.

A large temple dedicated to Eshmun built around the year 606 BC existed here with a mountain in the back that lasted until sometime in the IV century BC when, according to the inscriptions in Greek, Eshmun was already assimilated to Aeskulapius. On the other hand, in some receptacles from Cyprus, likely destined to be used as recipients to store either olive oil or water, the names of Eshmun-Melkarth appear together.

To the East and West of the Eshmun temple in Sidon there were two chapels, erected to Astarte. One had a "swimming pool", where children were brought in search of healing. Some of these statues of children are still preserved in Beirut National Museum. The cult of Eshmun existed also near Beirut, where **Qabr Smun**, "the tomb of Eshmun", seems to have been located. The god's healing powers were known also in Palestine, Egypt and Cyprus. They also spread to Utica and of course, Carthage. The Carthaginean Senate held its sessions at the Eshmun temple until the second century. It is in this temple that the people of Carthage took refuge when the Romans legions arrived to destroy the city in 146 BC. The wife of Hasdrubal and her entire family perished in the fire instead of surrendering.

MELKART

In phoenician **mlk krt**, means "King of the city". Most scholars assign Melkart to the city of Tyre. In a phoenician inscription from Malta dedicated to him he is named **B'l Sr**, "The lord of Tyre". He is identified with HERAKLES in Tyre. Alexander of Macedonia made sacrificial offerings at his temple during his passage through the city. This deity was known in Malta as Melkart-Herakles by the 2d century BC. The origin of the cult to Melkart may be traced back to Ebla during the 3d millennium, it passed through Ugarit during the 2d millennium and finally to Tyre in the first. His temple at Tyre, according to certain scholars, was built by Hiram I during the 10th century BC. It was dedicated to Melkart-Herakles-Astarte, all three gods heading the Tyrian pantheon.

The deity of Herakles, according to Herodotus was known since antiquity and had its origin at Tyre. Herodotus in his Histories (Book II, 44) himself moved by curiosity about the origin of this deity, went to visit Tyre. What he saw there was

"a richly equipped temple dedicated to Herakles with many offerings, a temple of great sanctity, dedicated to Herakles (the Tyrian god Melkart); the offerings that adorned it were numerous and valuable, not the least remarkable being two pillars in the facade, one of pure gold, the other of emeralds, which gleamed in the dark".

His conversations with the priests disclosed that the temple had been erected when the city was first founded, about two thousand three hundred years earlier. Herakles is supposed to have been the founder of Tyre around 2750 BC according to tradition. At Tyre Herodotus also saw another temple dedicated to the Herakles called the Thasian. He also confirmed later the existence at Thasos of another temple build to this god by the Phoenicians, who founded a settlement there when they went in search of Europa. This, according to Herodotus, they did five generations before the birth in Hellas of

Herakles, the son of Amphitryon. Thus the Greeks were right when practicing two kinds of worship of Herakles: one to the immortal Olympian and the other to the dead hero. The temple erected to this deity in Tyre, described by Herodotus, has not been found yet.

Herodotus continues:

"I have indeed many proofs that the name of Herakles did not come from Hellas to Egypt, but from Egypt to Hellas". (And in Hellas the Greeks gave the name Herakles to the son of Amphitryon and Alcmene, who were both by descent Egyptian).

Herakles is a very ancient god in Egypt and the Egyptians claim that because of him the Greeks changed the number of eight gods to twelve including him among them. Wishing to get a clear knowledge of the matter,

Herodotus repeats

"I took then a ship to Tyre in Phoenicia, where I heard that there was a very holy temple of Heracles. There I saw it, richly equipped with many offerings; besides there were in it two pillars, one of refined gold, one of emerald, a great pillar that shone in the night-time…"

Legend asserts that the first tunic dyed with Tyrian purple was offered by the Phoenician god Herakles to Astarte. A painful process is necessary to extract a few drops of the red dye from the murex mollusc and in order to fix the color in primitive times lemon juice was employed while later on sodium bicarbonate was added by the people of Tyre for that purpose. The Roman Emperors wore a purple robe and Helen of Troy and Cleopatra were fond of the color. The tradition has come even to our days in the habit of the high members of the priesthood of modern religions who still wear a purple dress. The earliest occurrence of the word purple is recorded in Ugaritic stones where it is described as being used by weavers to color wool. In ancient times the mollusc that produces the juice that generates the purple color or some other species were also found by the Minoans and Greeks. The Phoenicians, in order to save their molluscs, which were of higher quality, at one time imported the dye from as far as Carthage, Utica and Sparta. Crushed shells have been discovered in Ugarit.

Pliny the Elder described its manufacture in Book IX, of his **Natural History**, pp 253-59.

"It is desirable to catch the mollusc after the rising of the dog star and before spring-time, since then they have their juices fluid. The fluid is extracted from a vein to which salt has to be added,......three days is the proper time for it to be steeped and it should be heated in a leaden pot at moderate temperature. About nine days later the cauldron is strained. A fleece that has been washed clean is dipped for a trial and heated up until a red blackish color is obtained".

"The fleece is allowed to soak for five hours...it is blended to a moderate degree with sea-purple until it acquires a deep dark hue and brilliant scarlet appearence, which is very much in demand. For Tyrian purple the wool is first soaked in sea-purple for a preliminary pale dressing and then completely transformed by a second soaking...Its highest glory consists in the color of frozen blood, blackish at first glance but gleaming when held up to the light."

The Tyrian purple was very much in use in Rome from the earliest times: Romulus first used it for a cloak and later Cornelius Nepos adopted it for his personal dressing. The double-dyed Tyrian purple at the time was impossible to buy for less than one thousand denarii per pound...and its use was regarded as a lavish extravagance...

The father of Melkart seems to have been Demarus, himself born from the union of Uranus and a concubine, according to a phoenician version. Other possibilities link Melkart with the god of the Amorites, **Hadad, hd,** the storm-god of the 3d millennium at Ebla; the **Haddu,** the Baal of Ugarit; and finally during the 1st millennium, **Hadad**, the god of the Arameans.

The Arameans near Aleppo depicted him c. 8th century BC standing with a full beard, conical head-hat, a long robe and a lotus flower in his right hand.
Certain sources such as Philo of Byblos considered him the son of Zeus and Astarte. He is also considered by certain scholars as the son

of EL and Asherat in Tyre. Asherat is sometimes, especially at Tyre, designated with the name of Elat, i.e. spouse of El. Their son is Melkart. In this city Asherath becomes later identified with Europa, EL with Baal Shameen and also with Zeus while Melkart became Herakles. Herodotus believed his sanctuary at Tyre dated from the time of the foundation of the city about 2750 BC. Melkart is the main protector of Tyre where he is present since the foundation of the city, he assures the fertility of nature and men, favors the navigation and trade in the purple dyes and fabrics. Although known historically in Tyre only about the 10th century BC, his socio-political and sacred influence extends back in time to Ugarit. The discovery of the purple is attributed in mythological times by some accounts to the work of Herakles/Melkart and the king of the Tyrians, Phoinix.

The temple of Tyre was occupied by Melkart/Herakles and Ashtarte, who were considered the protectors of the royal family while in Sidon their local Ashtoreth and Eshmun played the same role. Thus in times of Hiram of Tyre, it was he who apparently erected or rebuilt their temple. In the 9th century BC, the gods of Ittoba'al, father of Jezebel, the queen of the Jews, were Baal and Astarte. They were introduced in Israel by Jezebel through her marriage to Ahab. The gods Baal and Melkart also became here one and the same.

The god Melkart is represented in the 9th century with a conical hat, heavy beard, carrying a heavy mace with his left arm and an inverted lotus on his right. The inverted lotus was a symbol of death followed by resurrection. The same lotus is also observed on the ornaments of the sarcophagus of Ahiram, found at Byblos by Dunand and today preserved at the Beirut National Museum.

During the 8th century BC the Tyrian pantheon appears composed of Asherath, mother of the gods, and Baal Shameen; Anat and Baal Saphon (The Baal of Ugarit); and Melkarth and Asherath. To these we may add Baal Malage and Eshmun of Sidon.

The triad of Melkart, Astarte and Eshmun does not become established in Tyre until the end of the first quarter of the 7th century BC, the era of Persian domination. It is evident in the treaty between Ezzar'haddon of Assyria and Baal of Tyre. A sculpture made of porous stone preserved at the Louvre Museum and found near Tyre depicts the figures of Melkart on the right and Eshmun on the left, both dressed as Phoenician kings. The main seat of the sculpture is flanked by two winged sphinxes, representation of Ashtarth=Astarte. As the goddess of health and fertility, Astarte in on a throne ornamented by two lotus flowers standing upright as a symbol of the passage from death to life. The monument is consecrated in an inscription in Phoenician indicating that this was the seat of Ashtarth and her guests Melkart and Eshmun. They represent the familial triad so popular in the Mediterranean environment: the Astarte of Tyre is represented next to her consort Melkarth and their son Eshmun, the healing god who will later be identified with Aeskulapius. The image of Eshmun is interesting to examine: his long robe to the ankles suggests a Phoenician priest of the Persian period but the long hair does not support the view that he is a priest. He is supporting himself with a sceptre ornated with a lotus, a sign of royal authority. In Ugarit and other parts of Asia Minor these are characteristics of "divinities" that give life: they are dressed in long attires that in Phoenicia are typically used by priests and kings. On the sarcophagus of Ahiram, the king and his son are dressed in a similar fashion and carry an inverted lotus, the deceased father, and an erected one, his son and successor. The similarities between the monument of Astarte found near Tyre and the images of Ittoba'al and his father Ahiram of Byblos are striking.

Melkart may have been originally a god of fertility along the phoenician Mediterranean coast such as Baal was in Byblos or Ugarit. He will sleep during winter time and awaken in early spring. He was the master of the thunder and the rains and had special powers over the fire of the heavens. He appears to have participated in the creation of Tyre. He was also the first to send a ship into the sea: A fire enhanced by a storm in the nearby forest allowed the first ship to be send into the sea. The image that we have of Melkart is derived from the stele of Aleppo dating to the 9th century BC. He is shown standing with a beard, a long robe and long hair. His head is covered by a rounded hat. In his left hand he carries a **hatchet** on his shoulder and in the right arm and hand what appears to be an inverted lotus flower, symbolic perhaps of his winter death. Melkart has been identified with the Baal of Tyre who was originally protector of the fertility rites and possesed power over the thunder and the rain. Under this aspect Melkart becomes the master of the heavens.

Nonnos, on the 6th century AD, designates Melkart as that "whose dress is decorated with stars". Some writers have attempted to make Melkart the "King of the Underworld" based on findings from Ugarit but no reliable evidence exists from the ancient sources to confirm this assertion.

Another god with whom Melkart is identified is Herakles but it seems that the Greek hero, as stated earlier, is derived from the Tyrian god and not the opposite, as evidenced by the presence of him in Phoenician coins since the 5th century BC. Melkart at this time was worshipped across the Meditarranean sea from Anatolia to Spain and from Cyprus and Carthage to Ibiza and Gades (Cadiz today).

From Ibiza (Spain) on the 5th century an inscription shows Melkart associated with Reshep. **Rsp mlqrt: l'dn l'rsp mlqrt**...There is another inscription found at Tyre on a seal with similar association **lb' lytn 's 'lm lmlqrt rsp** that translates "To Ba'al yaton, a man of the gods, who belongs to Melkart-Reshep". Dussaud translates **mlqrt-rsp** as "Melkart, the son of Reshep". The evidence from Spain and Tyre does support the interpretation that at this time Melkart and Reshep are identified as the same god. He retained a strongest link between Carthage and Tyre through the entire first millennium. In the 7th century BC he is the god guarantying the treaty between Baal, king of Tyre and Ezzar'Haddon of Assyria and much later, according to Polybius, Hannibal invoked his protective power against Rome. He is commonly identified by some historians with Eshmun, the healing god of Sidon and with Herakles in Cyprus, at least since the 6th century BC. During the Greek period several changes will take place:

Melkart will be identified with Herakles, Eshmun will become Aeskulapius and Ashtarth will be Astarte.

TANNIT OF SAREPTA

In phoenician **tnt** and in punic **Tnt pn B'l**. The name designates the goddess who acquired great importance in Carthage but whose origin can be traced back to Sarepta in Phoenicia proper. Sarepta was a town located between Sidon and Tyre, mentioned in the Ebla texts of the 25th century BC and later on by many other ancient sources. The excavations of Sarepta in the sixties (AD) revealed several artifacts dealing with the goddess such as an ivory head of "The Lady at the Window" and a plate dedicated in phoenician to the goddess as Tannit-Astarte. These artifacts date back to the X-IX century BC.

The designation **Tnt pn Baal** has been a name subject to controversy sometimes translated as "lamentation before Baal". Other inscriptions such as **hnt tmt** meant "crypt of Tannit". Although started at Sarepta the cult of the goddess extended to Kition, Hadrumentum and Carthage in Africa, and to Palermo, Nora, and Ibiza in the Mediterranean islands. In Carthage the name of Tannit appears on steles preceding the name of Baal Hamon. She is the goddess in the inscriptions of the tophet of "Salammbo" that Gustave Flaubert made famous but she existed in other forms such as the **Tnt b-lbnn,** that is, the "Tannit of Lebanon".

Tannit is eventually associated to Astarte, not only in Sarepta but also in Malta and Carthage. In some coins of Malta she is represented dressed in mourning and in a sanctuary near Byblos in the Roman period she is the **Venus Lugens** next to Osiris and Isis. The Tannit of Hadrumentum and Ibiza was assimilated to the Winged Isis who protected with her wings the body of Osiris.

Sarepta was a town located about 7 miles south of Sidon, extending along the seashore (in phoenician **Srpt**) for about one mile and a half. A satellite of Sidon, it was already mentioned in documents from Ebla and Egypt since the 3d millennium BC. After 701 BC the town was put under Tyrian domination by Ezzar'Haddon. A head in ivory of the "Lady at the Window" and a phoenician inscription dedicated to Tannit-Astarte were unearthed there during the last third of the present millennium. Here in Sarepta is found one of the most ancient proofs of the cult of the goddess Tannit.

In phoenician **Tnt** or **Tmt** must likely is translated as the "Lament Lady" and she is designated as such many centuries later at Carthage as revealed by the designation **Tnt pn B'l** meaning "lamentation before Baal". The goddess name appears subsequently in multiple artifacts from either Phoenicia proper (**Tnt b-Lbnn**), Carthage, Hadrumentum, Nora, Malta, and Ibiza. Tannit is usually associated with Astarte especially in Sarepta, Carthage and Malta, as a warrior goddess, in contrast to those who share the belief that she was always in the service of Baal. The Tannit of Hadrumentum and Ibiza is associated to Osiris in the role of Isis. In the coins and later in a stele from Hadrumentum she is assimilated to Artemis and becomes later in the Roman period the "Nurse of Saturn" when she is depicted as mother (**Nutrix**). The symbol known as the "sign of Tannit" is represented either as a triangle or a trapezoid, above which reposes a bar, with or withouth elevated extremities: in reality it seem to be the stylized figure of a woman with the arms extended. The best preserved image was discovered at Kerkuane, north Africa, in a mosaic pavement. The sign is found on coins of the time of King Ainel, who was in power in Byblos at the time of the conquest of Phoenicia by Alexander the Great in about 332 BC. Symbols probably having the same significance to the sign of Tannit appear in Egypt, such as the **ankh** or symbol of life, found to the south of Thebes but also at Dura-Europos on the Euphrates.

Tannit is the goddess of fertility, sexuality and vegetation. As such her signs have been assimilated to genital organs in several locations, including in America, where these signs have been found in parts of New England. In Phoenicia proper, in the cave of Wasta, between Tyre and Sidon, a Phoenician inscription has been found representing feminine genital organs. The phoenician inscription reads **'bd'n bn 'bdspn nsh 't 'mt hdst l-Pm** and translates "Abed'enna, son of Abedsaphon, brought a new servant to Phallus". It appears to refer to the phoenician word **p'm** which means "phallus". The same was found at Ugarit with the equivalent term **p'n** followed by the word **Hrz**, meaning "penis" or Phallus. In the phoenician site of Motya in Sicily "phallic stones" have been found dating from the 7th to the 5th century BC, suggestive that a cult existed here. This is the earliest evidence of the divinization of the Phallus as proved by the inscription found that reads **'bdp'm**, "Servant of the Phallus", engraved in phoenician characters in Abu Simbel, Egypt. The cult of the Phallus remained closely associated to Dionysus until the greco-roman period.

In the Cueva d'Es Cuieram in Ibiza, on the flank of a mountain, numerous objects dedicated to the goddess Tannit were found dating back to the 2d century BC, together with a neopunic inscription where a priest makes a dedication to "our Lady the powerful Tannit of Good Fortune". The most characteristic objects found are religious symbols such as the lotus flower, symbol of the eternal return to life; a disc and a crescent surmounted by a star, astral representations that reveal the Egyptian influence of Isis, very common in the punic steles dedicated to Tannit and Baal Hammon.

The Tannit of Carthage was also venerated in a cave, a choice dictated by the belief that a subterranean place was the ideal site for a close relation between the faithful and the divinity. Finally, sacrifices made to the goddess were most commonly located in tophets, the human sacrificial places, of which the best known were those of Carthage and Constantine, in Algeria. They contained numerous incinerated rests of animals and infants and also inscriptions indicating mostly the dedications to Baal Hammon and less often Tannit.

Evidence from temples found in eastern North America suggest that veneration of Tannit had come from Carthage through Iberia brought by travelers from either Tartessus in Spain or from Phoenicia proper to the new world. Several signs depicting Tannit have been found in what are believed by American scholars to represent primitive temples built to the goddess in North America.

RESHEP

Over 50 inscriptions come from Egypt referring to Reshep. Recently two stelae regarding the god have been found and are now available: one is Cairo 2792 and the other the University of Pennsylvania E-13620.

Although the God is probably originally mentioned for the first time at Ebla, most iconographic documents available come from Egypt. The Sphinx stele of Amenophis II describes the assignment of this Pharaoh in his youth "to take care of the horses of the king's stable (his father) with the joy of Reshep and Astarte". This has been taken as evidence that Reshep was first adopted in Egypt at the times of Amenophis II. A contemporary stele found at Memphis states that "his majesty crossed the Orontes over the waters like Reshep". Other inscriptions referring to Reshep such as the Graphito of Nubia, the Berlin Stele and the Cairo stele number 70222, are all from the Eighteenth Dynasty.

The stele at the Oriental Institute of the University of Chicago, comes from Deihr el-Medinah (Thebes) in the times of Ramessses the II. Reshep strides to the right. He wears the crown of Upper Egypt with a gazelle-head in front and from the top two ribbons flow down his back. His skirt, affixed from the shoulder with crossed chest-bands, is ornamented at the bottom. An object hangs from his right arm which brandishes a fenestrated axe. To the left, on the stele, is the name of his dedicator, a priest of Horus.

In the stele at the Louvre, from Deir el-Medineh, there are from left to right, three ithyphallic divinities: Min, Qudshu and Reshep. Min and Reshep face Qudshu (Astarte) who stands on a lion's back. Reshep wears the Upper Egyptian crown with two ribbons and a gazelle head. He carries a lance in his right hand and an 'ankh in his left hand. He is bearded and the stele has a legend "Reshep, the great god, lord of eternity, sovereign everlasting, mighty master, amidst the divine ten gods". The Sphinx Stele, the Memphis Stele and the inscription in the Mortuary Temple of Ramesses III all depict characteristics of Reshep as a benevolent god more than a warrior. Reshep occurs as the divine element in several names on Phoenician inscriptions where he is the patron of individuals, several towns or their rulers.

Reshep is in phoenician **rsp**, pronounced **ras^op**. Although he was worshipped at the temple of the Obelisks in Byblos during the Amorite period (20th to 19th century BC) as the deity of war, his origin is still a subject of controversy. The image of the deity that has reached us comes from what is depicted in numerous stelae, papyri, scarabs and amulets found all over the Middle East and the neighbouring Mediterranean islands where he was worshipped for well over two millennia. Reshep is a prominent god at the city of Ebla, where one of the four main gates of the city was named after

Rasap, making him as prominent as Sipis, Ba'al and Dagon, during the middle of the third millennium BC. Resheph is not the major figure at Ugarit, where El and specially Baal are the main presiding gods of the Canaanite pantheon. However, at Ugarit he is still a feared deity in control of plagues and war and paradoxically he is also described as the "Lord of Good Fortune". This designation remains unchanged, for a thousand years later it is still found in Cyprus. He appears in Phoenicia proper contemporaneusly with Baalath much earlier towards the 28th century BC. He is worshipped as a powerful military protector during the 18th and 19th dynasties in times of Amenophis II of Egypt. Some scholars believe that Resheph was formaly introduced into Egypt during the reign of Amenophis II: a stele from Giza describes the youthful equestrian and martial power of Amenophis II in the following terms and partially reads: "Now after the care of the horses in the stable has been entrusted to the king's son...Reshep and Astarte were rejoicing in him for all that his heart desired". Another stele from Memphis reads: "His majesty crossed the Orontes over the waters like Reshep" and the pharaoh is likened to Reshep as "an awsome warrior out to battle". Two stelae published relatively recently from the early period in Egypt are of importance, especially the so-called "stele of Cairo" which bears an inscription reading **rsp ntr nb pt** that translates "Reshep, the great god, master of the heavens". During the 18th Dynasty several stelae from Nubia, Thebes and Cairo depict him with a high conical hat, holding a mace over his head, a shield with his right hand and a spear in his left. He wears a short kilt, upper garment, collar, Upper

Egyptian crown and a gazelle-head in front. On a graffito from Nubia, Reshep is represented with five offerers, all walking to the right and bearing gifts. From left to right there is a male offerer carrying two boomerangs; a male carrying a pair of sandals and a bird; a male carrying a bow, arrows and a dead gazelle; a female with a conical bread loaf; and a male offering incense and pouring a libation on an altar. Seated facing the offerers are the god Horus, the pharaoh Sesostris the III with a lotus and Reshep.

The stele preserved at the Oriental Institute of Chicago most likely came from Deir-el-Medinah (Thebes). Here he wears the crown of Upper Egypt with a gazelle-head in front and from the top two ribbons flow down his back. His kilt is affixed from the shoulder with crossed chest-bands and what is possibly a "lute" hangs from his right arm which brandishes a fenestrated axe. In his left hand there is a spear and a shield. To the left on the stele there is the name of the dedicator, likely to be "a priest of Horus".

The stele preserved in the Museum of the University of Pennsylvania appears to be from the same period: here a man, a woman and a small boy approach Resheph who is standing and facing to the right: there is a spear, a mace-axe and a lute as well. Both stelae and the one immediately described below, from the British Museum, appear to be from the Ramesside period.

The stele from the British Museum shows the god with Anat and three figures making offerings to Anat who is seated on a throne, holding a spear and shield in her right hand, a mace-axe in the left and wearing a long gown and plumes on her crown. We must remember that in Ugarit frequently Reshep and Anat are listed together. On several stelae, mainly from Deir-el-Medinah, Thebes, Reshep is depicted with other gods: Horus or Anat.

A stele from the Aswan Museum in lower Nubia, found in the temple of Amenophis the III, shows Reshep with Amon-Ra, "lord of the road" and Seth, "great in might, lord of the sky" seating on a throne and below them the usual image of Reshep.

The stelae from Deir-el-Medinah depict Reshep in a benevolent attitude rather than a warlike stance. His weapon is resting at his side and he holds in his hand an **ankh**, the symbol of life. According to certain scholars this suggests that although Reshep is usually the god of disease, pestilence and death, he sometimes represents, as in other areas of the Near East, a dual role thus he is also the god of healing, fruitfulness and fertility. This is in keeping with the fact that Reseph is at times represented with Eshmun, the Phoenician god of healing.

It is most likely that the initial introduction of Reshep into Egypt took place during the period of Amenophis II who followed Thutmose the III, the greatest conqueror of all pharaohs, who was the first to invade the neighboring Asiatic lands. Amenophis II' motivation in introducing his cult is unknown but speculation suggests that he simply experienced a personal fascination with Reshep and a natural wonder at the might of the Canaanite god thus he decided to adopt him as his patron because he was the prototype of his own military spirit. Reshep was initially a royal patron and his popularity did not extend to the people until the times of Ramessess the II. During this period he enjoys immense popularity, being represented with the head of a gazelle projecting from his helmet, above his forehead. Thus it is during the Ramessess II period, at the beginning of the 13th century, that the cult of Reshep becomes official and extremely popular in Egypt.

At Ebla (and perhaps Babylon) he is considered the guardian or god of Hell and Epidemics. This is the interpretation that remains prevalent until the period of the Tell-El-Amarna letters. Despite his characterization as a feared deity, Reshep is also capable of good deeds and is known to afford protection to his followers: this was evident until Carthaginian times: a temple in gold erected to him existed at the center of the city until the? 3d century AD. Several Phoenician (?Canaaanite) gods were venerated in Carthage when the city passed under Roman domination: Merkart, Eshmun, Astarte, Dagon and Reshep. Apollo had a prominent cult at Carthage but there is considerable discussion about the fact that Apollo here may have been a hellenization of Reshep. In Karatepe (Turkey) during the 8th century BC, Reshep was considered together with Ba'al among the dynastic gods.

In the 5th century at Sidon, during Bodastart's reign, several inscrptions show that a part of the city was known as "land of Reshep" despite the fact that Eshmun was the principal god of Sidon. The worship of Reshep persisted more prominently in Palestine as Apollo during the 5th century and in Cyprus where he was identified with Apollo in the 4th century BC. In a bilingual text from Cyprus dated at 363 BC from Tamassos Reshep is identified with Apollo, the archer. This is seen in other inscriptions from the same period at Cyprus and Egypt where he is depicted wearing "a quiver full of arrows". The Apollo of the Iliad is described with the characteristics of Reshep.

It is also assumed that Reshep was the main deity worshipped in the "Temple of the Obelisks" at Byblos. According to Dunand his worship at the temple was prevalent during the Amorite period but Montet believes the identity of the deity to whom the Temple of the Obelisks was dedicated is still unresolved. In Byblos certain buildings apparently used for sacrifice still may be seen today but it remains unclear whether they were used for human or animal sacrifice.

Anthony Strong

Reshep "Au Foudre" As Depicted in the Stone of the LOUVRE MUSEUM, serial # AO 22 247

At the beginning of the 3d millennium or perhaps earlier, the Egyptians decided to start commercial relations with Byblos in order to obtain wood, cedar and pine, mainly bought or exchanged from them for their funerary and architectural purposes. Thus in order to strenghten their ties and their treaties they decided to establish relations between their gods and the local divinities. But the Egyptians, even in a foreign country, could not conceive a creator god other than Ra. Thus they decided to assimilate EL to Ra who was named the "Ra-of Foreign countries". But as the spouse of EL they had the appropriate goddess: Hathor. She was the great creatrice, mother of the gods and even as companion of EL, the Bull, she was the "Holy Cow". Another couple at Byblos was that of Ashtar and Ashtarth, originally the Evening and Morning Stars. Ashtarth became in the Greek period Astarte, the Ba'alath Gebal, the Dame of Byblos, but since the Egyptian beginnings until the Persian times she adopted the characteristics of Hathor, especially in her head-dress and her animal became the lion. The consort of Ba'laath Gebal, Ashtar, has adopted a human form but with a lion as companion. In some phoenician inscriptions Ashtar became **B'l 'dr**, Ba'al the powerful or **Mlk 'dr**, Ba'al the King.

Next to the temple of Ba'alath Gebal there existed for about three millennia BCE another temple excavated by Maurice Dunand that contained about twenty obelisks measuring between one and three and a half metres in lenght, thus the site was named "the Temple of the Obelisks". On one of the obelisks there is an inscription to Herishef-Ra, which has been interpreted by Dunand and other scholars as belonging not to an Egyptian deity but to a Cannaanite one: Reshep. At Byblos while EL was the god "Ra-of the mountinous country", Reshep is just one more of his children but he is the principal god of this temple. According to some European scholars the head of antelope that he wears before his head-dress should be interpreted as a trophy and while Astarte is represented as a naked goddess, named **Qds**, "mistress of the Heavens"; Reseph is named **Rspw**, "the great god", "master of the Heavens and the all powerful". Thus it seems that at Byblos, Ba'al Gebal, Ba'al 'dr, Mlk 'dr and Reshep, all represent Ashtar. This is also the case in Cyprus in a Phoenician inscription of the 4th century BC found at Larnaca where Reshep is accompanied by two lions and in Ugarit where he is **Rsp-gn** "Reshep of the gardens". In Palmyra he remains as the main god until 300 BC.

In one Egyptian stele of the Ancient Empire the consort of Astarte, considered here as goddess of war, is always Reshep (**Rspw**) and the same appears to have been the case in Byblos. It shoud be remembered that commercial relations with Egypt existed here since the early 3d millennium. The god has his head-dress surrrounded by an Egyptian "white crown" ornamented in front by an antelope head, symbol of the night, freshness and prosperity. This image of Reshep is quite similar to the bronze images found at Ugarit. The "white crown" in Egypt was worn by both Osiris and Reshep.

In Ugarit at the temple of Reshep the local Astarte was his companion. Ashtar, the male counterpart of Astarte, was considered here the Morning Star and as such his name was translated into Latin as "Lucifer=the Brilliant, the one who carries the light" while Reshep was designated Diabolus=Satan. Lucifer, also known as the "Brilliant", because he dared to compare himself with the Allmighty, was sent by EL to Hell where he became the ruler. This latter designation of Lucifer was later adopted by Christianity.

Reshep appears in a many proper names throughout the area. It is found at Mari in Akkadian, in Babylonia during the realm of Sargon and in Amorite times. Under various names the translation of his name in inscriptions is "Reshep is eternal" or "Reshep is unique". In Ugarit, although not quite common, it must be remembered that Keret lost his first generation of children because of pestilence, a characteristic usually assigned to the power of Reshep. In the Hammurabi Code of Law, Reshep is identified with Nergal as god of pestilence and warfare. In an Egyptian stele he is designated as the **ntr nfr** "the good god". In other locations he is identified with Herakles and Apollo.

In a somewhat different respect Reshep has been, according to Dahood, identified as a solar deity probably since very ancient times, a satellite of the Sun or as the Sun itself: Given "the conservative nature of the Canaanite religion it is not surprising to find some of his features delineated in the texts of the 14th century BC" (Keret, text 127: 56). It is identified with the planet Venus according to Gray. Perhaps this assumption is related to the occurrence of a total solar eclipse observed at Ugarit on May 3, 1375, BC. The text has been translated as "The day of the new moon in the month of Hiyar was put to shame. The Sun went down in daytime with the planet Mars (=

Reshep) in attendance". The mention of a solar eclipse in this context fits well with the mythology of Reshep. In the Mesopotamian mythology the Sungod descends at night into the Sea where he passes the night in the underworld while in the Ugaritic mythology the goddess SAPS, mistress of the dead, does the same in the netherworld. Such is the interpretation of Dahood, Caquot, Dussaud and Gray.

Other Ugaritic texts mention Reshep with Astarte, Baal and Anat. The evidence from the texts of Ugarit indicates that Resheph was a god who had a shrine or temple there as "Reshep of the garden" or "Reshep of the Field".

More inscriptions in Phoenician and Aramaic exist mentioning Reshep from the 8th to the 3d century BC. In the Zinjirli inscription it reads: "the gods Hadad, El, Reshep and Shamas stood by me and…Reshep put into my hand the scepter **hlbbh** while Hadad, El,…provided abundantly and gave me greatness". Indeed Reshep enjoyed here a high place in the pantheon.

The Karatepe Phoenician-Hittite bilingual inscription which dates from the end of the 8th century (? 720 BC) in Anatolia mentions **rsp sprm** which has met with a difficult translation and most likely relates Reshep with either "birds" or "goats" but the inscription suggests that Reshep occupied a high position in their pantheon also. Other inscriptions in Phoenician mentioning Reshep date from the 7th century and come from Cyprus, Spain and Carthage. The inscription from the time of Bodastart of Sidon is dedicated to Reshep by a priest of Eshmun most likely and refers to "Sidon of the Sea…the high

Heaven...the land of the Resheps". The last expression probably means "Sidon, land of the warriors".

An inscription from Ibiza and another from Tyre from the 5th-4th century is translated as "...To Baal-yaton, the man of god, attached to Melkart-Reshep". Of course Melkart and Reshep represent opposites as gods of "healing and disease", attributes of both gods. The problem has been to translate the expression **rrsp hs** for which practically every scholar has proposed a different interpretation. A discussion of this problem is beyond the scope of this writing.

Finally, several inscriptions from Cyprus, some bilingual, 4th century BC, link Reshep, Herakles, and Apollo with another as yet unknown god named **mkl**. Some have postulated that the name would be **Mika=el,** "who is like EL." "If he represents a local type of the god EL, it is understandable that he be depicted in a manner similar to that of the god of Ugarit, whose image appears on a stele found at Ugarit in 1936 AD."

The question is that no acceptable meaning has been agreed upon on the sense of the word **mkl**. A popular interpretation has been that this represents a peculiar syncretism in Cyprus and Cyprus only, where Reshep, Apollo and **mkl**, would be homonymous gods. Lipinski has argued recently that there is no historical reason to jump over ten centuries of history to identify Reshep, a god from the Jordan valley, with Apollo, a Cypriot god. The word **mkl** appears twice in a list of items bought for the temple of Astarte in Kition. Thus he has translated the word **mkl** simply as meaning "a part of the large building that closes the southern domain of the sanctuary of Astarte".

In Egypt Reshep is viewed as a warrior god as evidenced from the images and inscriptions of the stelae, most of them thought to have been of Canaanite origin. The texts of the inscriptions also support the idea that he represents primarily a god of battle. Reshep is most likely of Amorite origin and may have been originally conceived as a god of the underworld, involved in the darker sides of human life such as plagues and calamities and death. The texts of Ugarit and Cyprus support this interpretation. In Cyprus, Carthage, Sidon, Kition and Phoenicia proper he is often identified with Apollo. He is more rarely considered as a divine protective element especially in Phoenician inscriptions where he appears as patron of towns or their rulers. This is the way he was introduced in Egypt under Amenophis the II and much later the way he was worshipped in Ramesside times and finally in the temples of Carthage and Ibiza in Spain.

Reshep was indirectly related as god of pestilences to the practice of **human sacrifice**, most specially of children. In the Phoenician and Punic religion this seems to have been rare, and practiced only under exceptional circumstances. The descriptions with crude details that have come to us often reflect anti-Carthaginian propaganda. The most important historians are silent on this matter: Herodotus, Thucydides, Polybius, Livy, do not even mention these sacrifice rituals. With the exception of biblical accounts, the Phoenician East is mostly silent on the subject. Human sacrifice was practiced in precints known as tophets. No evidence of its use in Phoenicia proper exists but the tophet was somewhat frequently used in Carthage, Sardinia, Malta, Cagliari and Nora.

The tophets were always located outside of the cities and towns because it seems the Phoenicians customarily kept the dead apart from the living. They would carefully prepare the body of the dead and dress them well. But never used mummification They practiced burials in Phoenicia itself. Cremation was practiced mainly in Carthage and several Mediterranean islands, in later periods. Usually a virgin site was chosen to locate the tophets, one for every community, usually away from the populated areas of the site. They were always respected places. Furthermore, today it is generally accepted by scholars that tophets were most likely used as cemeteries for children (stillbirths, premature and deformed infants.)

Human Sacrifice in antiquity appears to have been quite widespread during the Dynastic period in Sumeria (early dynastic Ur) and the Shang period in China but in predynastic or Dynastic periods in Egypt human sacrifice appears to have been a rare practice. In lower Nubia it did however exist; but sacrifices were not practiced **en masse** but as individual acts of self-sacrifice. During the first Dynasty it may have occurred but by the end of the second Dynasty these forms of experiments introduced by kings in the form of demonstrations of their power were soon a failure and thus abandoned quickly. In Byblos the practice may have started as an imitation of the early Egyptians or Sumerians but was never done after 2700 BC.

The most recent view suggests that the great majority of the alleged instances of human sacrifice in Phoenicia may have been just a ritual of purification with no sacrifice of life. The **tophet** of Carthage served the function of a child necropolis to receive the infants that had died prematurely of natural causes or illnesses.

In Phoenician culture sacrifices were performed to ensure the benevolent protection of certain deities for the children that survived (Tannit and Baal Hammon in Carthage were not by any accounts blood-thirsty gods). Human and particularly child sacrifice was not included in their ordinary forms of worship but seems to have taken place in situations of extreme danger to the communities, i. e. the priesthood class practiced it in times of disaster in the hope to placate the ire or obtain the favors of the gods. However, it must be pointed out that human sacrifice appears to have been, otherwise, a widespread practice throughout the ancient world. Evidence exists that the Phoenicians had completely abandoned this practice by the 6th century BC. The topheths were altars erected in the open air mostly on high mountains. They have been found in Carthage, in Sardinia but not in Eastern Phoenicia itself. The Phoenicians, however, abstained from burning humans alive and for sacrifice would instead burn a lamb. The Hebrews seem to have practiced human sacrifice if one is to believe the biblical prophets who commanded their people not to burn their sons or daughters. This custom may have been abandoned by the time the biblical Moses came to power.

Recent documents from Ugarit indicate that Reshep had a close association with Anat, especially in ceremonies dealing with human sacrifice and with the Babylonian Nergal, who is related with plagues and epidemics. Nergal, it is confirmed by documents from Ugarit, participates in the extermination of families or individuals. However Reshep is conspicuous for his absence in the mythological texts and his role seems to be more prominent in rites involving both public and private ceremonies. The rituals directed towards Reshep involve sacrifices intended to prevent his intervention as the cause of disasters. Indications also exist that the god lacks powers as a healer and that he is commonly associated with the goddess Shapash, an astral deity related to hell and the netherworld.

The evidence from Ugarit associates Reshep mainly with fearsome deities, mediators of suffering and diseases. He appears to be the guardian of hell and his followers render him respect and honors more out of fear than of gratitude. It is easy to conceive his followers in their prayers asking from the god to help them exterminate their enemies using the same weapons they know he has used against themselves.

While at Ugarit Reshep does not appear as a benevolent god, it is not unlikely that in other times and at different periods he may have been perceived as protector especially among his phoenician worshippers in Egypt where he was invoked as "master of the heavens" to his followers in Phoenicia proper (Karatepe, Zincirli) and even in Carthage. Some scholars argue that at Ugarit Reshep has become during the late 14th century BC an astral deity as cited earlier in the solar eclipse that occurred on May 3, 1375. On the other hand the god seems to have remained on earth grounds and had a shrine at Ugarit under the designation of "Reshep of the Garden".

CHAPTER FOUR

JEZEBEL AND MONOTHEISM

It is rather difficult to assess impartially the facts about the life and death of the tragic character of Jezebel. The fate of her descendants is also obscure because most of the historical information that has come to us departs from the story told by the biblical writers. Daughter of Ittobaal, king of Sidon and Tyre, she married Ahab of Israel (son of Omri, a contemporary of her father). Omri, who may have been of Arabian stock, had stabilized the country and was an astute ruler and gifted commander. After his ascension to power he reconciled the kingdoms of Judah and Israel. Furthermore, he conceived the idea of strenghtening his relations with his neighbor to the North: Phoenicia, by using the old custom of negociating a marriage between his eldest son and a daugthter of the king of Tyre and Sidon, Ittobaal: Jezebel's father. Although no historic evidence exists, Jezebel may have been a quite attractive woman and Ahab, her would-be husband, accepted the alliance. He was probably not a brave soldier and leader like his father. He accepted this marriage of convinience and fell under the spell of Jezebel. She became his wife but retained her own religious faith. This was not an unheard of event; it was rather the custom that the bride and groom retained their own religious beliefs. She introduced into Samaria during her husband's life, and with his consent, the worship of the Tyrian gods. The adoption of similar religious practices were customary in mixed marriages between royal families. After the death of her husband in battle against the king of Damascus, she continued the practice of the cults of Baal (Melkart, according to Albright) and Astarte within her former husband's kingdom.

But as new Queen she soon met with oposition to her policies and this opposition mounted under the leadership of the Hebrew prophets. She appears to have ordered the assassination of many priests of the Hebrew god in retaliation for a similar crime against her own Phoenician priesthood. The angry Elijah had put to the sword 450 priests of Baal. Thus she retaliated. The measure would, however, bring upon herself not only the animosity of her new subjects but eventually her own downfall at the hand of the Israelites.

JEZEBEL, queen of the Hebrews: Jezebel was the daughter of Ittobaal, king of Sidon, priest of Astarte, who later became also king of Tyre. Jezebel was to marry Ahab, the first Hebrew character of whom we have information in recorded history ouside biblical sources. Omri, an army commander probably of Arab origin, brought stability to Israel at about 875 BC and was the first to conceive a union with neighbouring Phoenicia. Thus he proposed to Ittobaal, king of Tyre, to have a familial union between his oldest son Ahab and Jezebel. Ittobaal aggreed and so did Jezebel and Ahab. Once marriage took place, Jezebel changed her nationality but retained her religion. This was customary, not illegal, and was a normal political manoeuvre. The union between princes of two kingdoms was supposed to take place not only in the royal bed but also was a cultural, spiritual and religious union. Wives and concubines of foreign origin throughout the Near East in ancient times were allowed to worship the gods of their native homeland. In Israel apparently many religions co-existed at a time but usually the Jewish priesthood was never tolerant. However, the powerful kings did not pay much attention to the priests of their times. In the case of Jezebel, the implementation of the cults of Ba'al and other Phoenician deities was not regarded with sympathy despite the fact that a temple to Ba'al existed in the Be-Hinnon valley, just beneath the walls of Jerusalem.

The phoenician pantheon essentially consisted of the God father EL, his wife Astarte and a son Ba'al. Ba'al was peculiar because as the god of the Canaanite fertility cult he had to die and resurrect with the seasons every year, and eventually came to represent a god who suffered death as a sacrifice for mankind. This is an idea that would be centuries later adopted by Christianity in the person of Christ. As indicated elsewhere Ba'al soon superseded his father El and became not only the warrior god but also a superb lover: his strenght in copulation became legendary.

Following the death of Ahab in the battlefield as one of the many warriors fighting against the king of Damascus, Jezebel then attempted to impose her religion on her new kingdom. While her husband was alive he had allowed her to build temples for Ba'al and

Astarte, a prevailing custom when marriages of convenience such as this were made in order to strenghthen relations between the new couple and their original families or country of origin. But following her husband's death the Israelites under the leadership of the prophet Elijah rebelled against the foreign queen, supported by the farmers, peasants and nobility. In time they eventually killed her son (Ahab's son), the succesor to the throne Ahaziah and later managed to kill Jezebel herself and the rest of her children. However a daughter, Athalia, survived as queen of Judah, attempted to kill the descendants of prior kings and eventually was attacked for maintaining relations with the Phoenicians and assassinated. Forty years later the union between the kingdoms of Israel and Judah as well as Phoenicia were conquered and dissolved by the Assyrians and Babylonians.

The father of Jezebel, Ittobaal, high priest of Astarte, was the alleged founder of small colonies in Lybia and of the city of Botrys (Beruna, Batrun) in northern Phoenicia. There is no certainty concerning the time of the foundation of Batrun by Ittobaal. The evidence from the Tell-El-Amarna letters makes the foundation of Batrun by Ittobaal highly unlikely. The date of the foundation of Batrun is unknown but it is improbable that Ittobaal had anything to do with it since Batrun is mentioned in the Tell-el-Amarna Tablets (14th Century BC). Batrun was then one of the Byblos-dependent cities that passed over to Abdi-Ashirta during the time of intrigues in the reigns of Amenhotep III (Amenophis III) and his son Amenhotep

IV (Amenophis IV), intrigues that involved, among others, the Canaanite cities of Tyre, Sidon, and Byblos.

The phoenician priests and scribes appear to have accepted the reforms imposed by Amenophis IV concerning the god Aten not only as supreme god but as a unique and universal god. Thus they identified Aten with their god EL. Both appear as creators of the universe and related to the Sun worship.

This period of unrest and rebellion was especially intense during the reign of Amenhotep IV, the pharaoh most commonly given credit for the creation and implementation of the idea of monotheism. Amenhotep IV changed his name to Akh-en-Aten, meaning "Aten is satisfied" and moved the site of his kingdom from Thebes in Upper Egypt to a new place named Akh-et-Aten, "horizon of Aten", in Middle Egypt. This became the new capital of monotheism personified in the image of the sun-god. When the affairs of state in Egypt became troublesome, to carry on his religious ideas after his father's death he moved the capital away from Memphis and did not appear to care that much for the business of governing his vassals, focusing on his religious beliefs. To assure control of the kings of the many city-states who were avoiding payment to support the lavish lifestyle of the pharaohs, he continued the correspondence his father had initiated and sustained with his vassals for a few more years until he died.

Akhenaten died prematurely, unable to achieve the perpetuation of his monotheistic ideas. It will take many generations and transmutations until the monotheistic idea would gain support in a somewhat different form and spread to the Western world.

Following his death the old priesthood would regain control and resettle back in Thebes. Thus for over three millennia the location of the original capital of monotheism will be forgotten. The correspondence of the pharaohs and their vassals remained buried under the desert sands until discovered incidentally by a peasant woman during the 19th century of our era. Preserved in baked clay in the modern village occupying the ancient locality, the correspondence has become known as the Tell-El-Amarna tablets.

The evolution of the idea of monotheism took well over two millennia until taking shape as the final doctrine of a unique deity with universal dominion. The Egyptian intellectual aristocracy of the Pyramid age (~ 30th century BC on) was the first in recorded history to appreciate the moral value of the family and to initiate the most elementary veneration of their departed. From the material welfare in the hereafter, the next stage in the moral development of man showed the importance of the family as shaper of the ethical ideas that were to characterize evolving human behaviour.

The inscriptions in the tombs from this ideal age of innocence are the earliest surviving evidence that the moral ideas of man were the product of the social conditions prevailing then, towards the end of the fourth millenium before the beginning of our era. The belief that good behaviour was to be rewarded in the afterlife seems to have been evident since then: if wrong and injustice were perpetrated by man during the earthly life he would have to respond before the Sun-god Ra as a supreme judge in the afterlife. The demands for justice and righteousness applied not only to the lower subjects but also to the king who eventually had to respond to the god Ra. It was the intelectuals of the Pyramid Age that put together society; government and social behaviour in terms of moral convictions and conceived of a divine ruler in control of that order, thus moving for the first time in human history towards the concept of monotheism. This step could not have taken place at once: over a span of two centuries the Sun-god became the divine ruler, supreme judge of the afterlife.

The moral and intellectual elite of the times included Imhotep, the physician, Ptahhotep, the philosopher and Khafre, the pharaoh. All three conceivable made contributions to the concept of the unique divine ruler, Sun-god. This idea either spread rapidly or appeared independently soon afterwards because it is already formulated in clay tablets found at Ebla.

The literary texts found at Ebla (25th century BC) already speak of a unique god

> "Lord of Heaven and Earth:
> the earth was not, you created it,
> the light of the day was not, you created it,
> the morning light you had not yet made…"

The document where these words are contained was found at Ebla in triplicate but written in Sumerian, not in Canaanite. The Eblaite culture, although certainly polytheistic, as proven by many documents in clay, in this hymn suggests evolution towards a new religious conception based on monotheism. The use of the Summerian script permits us to postulate that the origin of the text was likely to be foreign to Ebla.

The well-known Egyptian Amon hymn of the 15th Century (conceptually older) preserved in a papyrus at the Cairo Museum, expresses the same ideas:

> Far-traveller,...prince of Upper Egypt, lord of the land of Nubia,
> ...greatest of Heaven, oldest of the earth, lord of what exists......
> father of the fathers of all the gods, who created man and made the animals...
> ....
> the unique one who created what exists...from whose eyes came men,
> from whose mouth sprang the gods.........

From the Byblos of King Zakarbaal came the Wen-Amon papyrus (11th century), now preserved in Moscow, in which the Egyptian envoy, although humiliated and offended, dares to say to the Byblian

King: "There is no ship on the waters that does not belong to Amon, for his is the sea and his is Lebanon......" The Canaanite prince then admits the supremacy of the Egyptian god.

The recognition that many different deities are just the manifestations of a single god, and that the domain of a high god is universal, preceded the sophisticated idea that would evolve into a practical monotheism. From humble beginnings the idea would acquire strenght during the reigns of Amenophis III and especially his son Amenophis IV, who upon adopting the new ideas under the new pressures, would change his name to Akhenaten, "Aten is satisfied".

Most authorities now believe that the concept of monotheism was then probably quite prevalent and counted with many adepts among the Egyptians during the 14th century BC before the ascent of Akhenaten to the throne of Upper Egypt, circa 1377 BC. Because he was not older than 11 at the time of his father's death, scholars believe that perhaps other individuals were really responsible for the imposition of monotheism.

His father Amenophis III, his mother or even his wife, Nephertiti, a beautiful woman of Mitannian origin, who was older than he, have all been considered among the most likely candidates to being creators or the developers of the original idea. Adoring Aten, the solar disk, as the only god, as a universal sun-god, was to become the first step towards the conception of true monotheism.

Aten will replace Amun in the following hymn:

> O Creator of what the earth brings forth......
> Mother of gods and man...
> creator who takes the pains of his innumerable creatures...
> who reaches the end of the lands every day......

Aten then becomes the father and mother of creation, the lord of all lands and men. When he became pharaoh, Amenophis IV, was about 11 years of age. He would die at approximately the age of 28. The mummy of Amenophis IV was found in the tomb of his mother and has been examined forensically. The physical characteristics are worth mentioning: large (brachycephalic) head, protuberant abdomen and abnormally-shaped pelvis and extremities. His nephew, Tut-ankh-Amun, shared a similar appearance. Both died quite young. Hereditary diseases based on consanguinity have been postulated as the cause of their shortened life-span.

The presence of gynecomastia (enlarged breasts) in the mummies and artistic representations of Thutmose IV, the father of Amenophis III, and grand-father of Amenophis IV (otherwise known as Akhenaten), and Tutankhamun has led to considerable controversy among scholars, historians, archeologists and pathologists. Their real genetic sex has motivated considerable speculation but Harrison, who did the autopsy of Tutankhamun, concluded that he found "no anatomic or pathological evidence (apart from minimal skeletal trends towards femininity) in the remains of the young king". The number of possible pathologic conditions described by the different medical students of these individuals is numerous and until today the issue remains unresolved. What seems certain is that Tutankhamun did not father any children. Upon his death, a letter exist sent by the wife of Tutankhamun to Suppiluliumas, king of the Hittites. In this letter she begs from him to send her one of his children for husband because she could not marry any of her subjects or close family members and she explains that she did not wish to remain without children. The text of this letter that was sent by private courier to the Hittite king took two whole weeks across deserts and mountains and has come to us. Here it is:

"My husband is dead. I have no son. But you, they tell me, have many sons. Were you to send me one of your sons, he would become my husband. I shall never take one of my subjects and make him my husband. That I should find too abhorrent".

The letter had been sent by the widow of Tutankhamun and daughther of Nefertiti named Ankesennamun, a woman less than twenty years old. The young widow was declining to marry her own grandfather. Following consultation with his advisors and confirmation that this was a legitimate request Suppiluliumas decided to send his son Zannanza to Egypt. A Hiitite cuneiform text provides information indicating that he never made it to his destination, having been killed en route to Egypt. Apparently, Nefertiti's father, known as Ay, who was high priest and court chamberlain, married the young widow and became pharaoh.

The femininity of Akhenaten (the roundness of his body and the exaggeration of his breasts), and his inability to father any children, caused him to be taken for a woman. There are however, many relics of him depicted with six daughthers either alone or with his wife Nefertiti thus supporting the idea that despite his odd physique Akhenaten was fertile. Other scholars have suggested that the depiction of Akhenaten with a family of daughthers was a deliberate cover-up. Amenophis III, Akhenaten's father, they claim, was the actual father of the daughthers of the beautiful Nefertiti. Thus in such a short life-span scholars speculate that, most likely, the idea of monotheism, that Akhenaten will be remembered for, was quite prevalent in his entourage, had probably existed during his father's reign, may have been supported by his mother and was familiar and popular with the priesthood of his inner circle. His wife, Nefertiti, who was older than he, may have played a role in the implementation and diffusion of monotheism, as well. Akhenaten only had to attempt to implement the idea and it would find favorable reception. In the Hymn to Aten, he is explicitely addressed as

"the only god,...besides him there is no other, the creator of everything, lord of the universe..."

The new monotheism was based on a triad consisting of the worship of Aten, "the solar disk", Aten in the new temple of Akhetaten, and a third element, the pharaoh himself. The pharaoh is then said to be "born anew every morning, like the Sun-god his father".

The middle portion of the triad linked the sun-god in Heaven with his Earthly incarnation in the new temple. In the new cult the followers of Aten, the sun-god, were ordered to erase the name of Amon from all places where it occurred and the names of all previous deities were to be eliminated from inscriptions. The king ordered to replace and substitute the language spoken by his new followers for a dead tongue with rules consistent with the new ideas.This led to a change not only of the inscriptions erased but total elimination of the language in use before Akhenaten death and replacement. The courtiers were led to imitate the new royal family and even are depicted from then on with the abnormal head and limbs of the pharaoh.

The opinions of certain scholars about the character and behaviour of Amenophis IV vary and may appear as being almost diametrically opposed: to Breasted,

"Akhenaten was a "God-intoxicated man" with marvelous sensitiveness and in ecstasy before the beauty of the eternal and universal light";

while to Albright "the monotheism of the new religion was characterized by little sexual ethics and predominantly materialistic tendencies, without regard for the poor lot of their subjects".

The new cult did not survive, at least in an open fashion, after the death of Akhenaten. The priesthood used his demise to enhance their own power and return to the cult of Amon. Now Seth, the god of the Ramesside family, was imposed. The resentment generated in lower

Egypt was responsible for the return of the Hyksos ideas and traditions which had dissappeared.

It may be recalled that the Hyksos had invaded Egypt late in the 18th century BC, as explained elsewhere, and were expelled after 1560 BC. Hyksos was the name given by the Egyptians to invaders from Asia Minor. The best translation of the word Hyksos is "rulers of foreign lands". The worship of Seth gained again unusual power during the reign of Ramesses II, who himself claimed to be of Hyksos origin.

During the 13th century Ramesses II mainly for political reasons will amalgamate the gods of Canaan and Egypt: Seth and Baal became the same divinity. Anat, the sister of Baal, became identified with Nephthys, the consort of Seth; Astarte with Hathor and so on. Although this was clearly a great step in support of polytheism, on the other hand the internationalization of the gods, would result in the eventual return to monotheism.

When Ramesses II, signing the peace treaty with the Hittites, after the battle of Quadesh, invokes a common god for both people, he is in reality supporting inadvertently the long-existing process of internationalizing the high gods. The main deity of the pharaoh becomes then the chief god of Canaanites, Hittites and Mesopotamians. Along this line, the development or adoption of monotheism, according to some scholars (Breasted, Albright), by Moses who probably was born in Egypt towards the middle of the

14th century BC, may have derived from the prevalent idea among the elite of Egyptians then in control i.e. soon after the fall of the Aten worship. It is difficult to know if there was any connection between the failure in the worship of the sun-god and the origin of the idea of an all powerful god, unique immaterial being. It is well-known that some modern religious historians attributed the creation of monotheism to Moses. However, both movements share the idea of monotheism; their "god is the sole creator and besides him there is no other". The Tell-El-Amarna monotheism rested on a triad which included the pharaoh himself. In contrast, the God of Moses was one, created all and reigned over all.

The name Moses is Egyptian but originally appears to have been connected with the Canaanite word **mt**, meaning "lord, master". The original word **Mose** means "child" in Egyptian and was a form commonly used as a second element in personal names that started with the name of a divinity i.e. **Thuth-mose, Ra'-mose, Akh-mose, Amon-mose**. The extra letter **s** to make **Moses** was added in the Greek translation of the hebrew Bible and did not exist in the original biblical writing. Yahveh, the hebrew god, was found by Moses in the wilderness, south of Palestine, among the tribe of the Midianites. The escape of the Hebrews from Egypt must have been accompanied by some natural catastrophe, most likely volcanic in nature, with an earthquake and a tidal wave which destroyed their enemies. This might have led to the belief that a national God delivered them by extraordinary demonstration of his favors and power.

Discrepancies exist between this view and the opinions of other scholars about the historicity of Moses and the events taking the Israelis from Egypt to the land of the Canaanites. The Canaanite mythology established a liaeson betwen EL and Yahweh. In the Ugaritic texts it appears as **Yw'elt** translated as **Yw** son of **EL**. By the same token the word Israel is translated as "EL fights".

According to Maurice Dhorme the primitive Canaanite form was **yhwh** which translates "makes being", in agreement with the role of creator attributed to Yahweh. Following Kuhn, another biblical scholar, the primitive form **yw** became **yhw** before being converted to **yhwh** in Canaanite and **Yeuo** in Byblos. It appears that Moses adopted the cult of Yaw-Yahwe confirming the biblical saying in Jeremiah II, 2-3.

In the Canaanite tablets VI AB, IV, 13-14, found at Ugarit, in the Gordon translation, it is written **<sm bny Yw'elt**. Thus "the name of my son is **Yw**, son of EL".

It is sort of inconceivable that biblical scholars could in the middle of the 20th Century AD make statements such as the one that follows, quoted from Albright, motivated more by political-religious beliefs rather than historical extant documentation:

> "It was fortunate for the future of monotheism that the Israelites of the Conquest were a wild folk, endowed with primitive energy and ruthless will, since the resulting decimation of the Canaanites prevented a racial mixture which

would inevitably have depressed the standards of Yahveh to a point beyond recovery. Thus the Canaanites, with their orgiastic nature worship, their fertility cult in the form of serpent symbols and sensuous nudity, and their gross mythology were replaced by Israel, with its pastoral simplicity and purity of life, its lofty monotheism and its severe code of ethics. In a not altogether dissimilar way, a millennium later, the African Canaanites (or Carthaginians) with their gross phoenician mythology from Ugarit and described by Philo of Byblos, with human sacrifice and the cult of sex, were crushed by the immensely superior Romans, whose stern code of morals and singularly elevated paganism remind us in many ways of early Israel."

This statement is obviously biased and full of puritanism, fear and even obscure, suppressed desires, from the part of an otherwise important biblical scholar, disregarding history and archeology and replacing it with distorted views no longer acceptable by today's historians: human sacrifice was practiced by most people of antiquity, and in Carthage it was done only in the form of cremation of children dying of certain epidemic illnesses. On the other hand, their primitive art depicting nudity was just that, very primitive. Human sacrifice of any kind was never practiced in Phoenicia proper, at least no evidence for it has yet been found. The Romans could not be considered as the best example of stern morality and any scholar with knowledge of how the events evolved during the Punic wars can hardly justify considering the Romans immensely superior to the Carthaginians.

The entire set of opinions reflects an undue fanaticism derived from an ill-understood interpretation of historical reality. The Canaanites were not decimated and have survived until today: This is fortunate, because under the name of Phoenicians, they made to humanity one of the greatest contributions in history: the creation and dissemination of the alphabet, which made possible worldwide communication and continues to survive today in the modern languages, that we all speak and write, in the Western Hemisphere.

CHAPTER FIVE

GODS OF EBLA AND UGARIT

Until 1975 AD, when the Royal Library of Ebla (about 20,000 tablets in clay) was unearthed the exact location of the ancient city and its identification with Tell Mardikh in Northern Syria were not generally accepted. The Library, with more tablets being discovered and deciphered in the subsequent years, is the largest source of information on this area in the third millennium. It now appears that a quite advanced civilization had developed in that region now buried in the sands 40 miles south of modern Aleppo. The data obtained from the deciphered tablets has helped to clarify not only historical facts thought before to be legendary but also revealed the entire network of events that occurred in Ebla vis-a-vis Mesopotamia (Sumeria) and Egypt in the times of the 4th Dynasty.

The Eblaites had developed a language that was a mixture of Sumerian and Akkadian but spoken in their own way and written by their scribes in a fashion that made it a distinct Canaanite tongue. The marked bilingualism of the scribes allowed them to pass from one language to another with great ease: the syllabic nature of some words but not others, lead to the inference that a new tongue had been developed: Eblaite. This language used a cuneiform set of signs: a remarkable achievement, because it was developed a millennium before Ugaritic. The Eblaites used the Sumerian in a purely phonetic manner but the extent of this use is still unknown and most likely incomplete, because more material needs to be studied. The Library with over 20000 tablets dveloped during the third millennium; was arranged then at Ebla like today as an alphabetic syllabary. The royal archives of Ebla compare in intrinsic value historically with the great cuneiform libraries of the second and first millennia found at Niniveh, Boghazkoy, Ugarit and Mari. The bilingual vocabularies at Ebla were remarkably modern for their times: modern vocabularies use the alphabetical organization of their libraries and the same method was already used in the texts at Ebla.

The singular nature of the Eblaite language and script is to be emphasized: roots of certain words that already existed then have persisted through five millennia until today in languages such as Arabic. The Eblaite root **KTB** = iktub is read as "to write". From the Arabic root **ktb** derive kitab= book, kutub= books; katib= scribe; maktub= a letter; maktab= an office.

At Ebla the system of government was also quite modern: the royal mandate appears to have consisted of periods of seven years after which there was no ban on re-election i.e. king Ebrium was elected four times and one of his sons Ibbi-Sipis was king for ten to fifteen years. The king of Ebla was known as "lord", a word rendered in the bilingual vocabularies of the tablets as "**malikum**"= king; the queen is known as "**malitkum**" the femenine form of king. The

Sumerian equivalent of malikum is **nam-en**, which means kingship. That is why one of the words for King in Phoenician is **mmlkt**. The king did not rule alone: the queen had several well-defined functions and so did the queen-mother. The advice and consent of the Elders was also necessary in matters of election and regulation of the desirable behavior of successors to the main seat of government: that of king or governor. This was quite a remarkable democratic society for the times, compared to the contemporary Mesopotamia, where the king was an absolute despot, who exercised the right of life and death over his subjects.

This also contrasts with the behavior in other cultures. In the Poem of Gilgamesh, in the segment regarding the struggle between Uruk and Kish, before engaging in the epic duel Gilgamesh seeks first the opinion of the Elders and after that the consent of the chamber of Youths. Gilgamesh then describes the king of Uruk's trip into Syria and his intention to take possession of the Cedars of Lebanon. If Gilgamesh was a historical character, this is the first recorded attempt to come in search of wood and in effect begin the deforestation of the legendary trees of Lebanon. In is interesting to recall that at this point in time the Egyptian pharaohs of the fourth dynasty had started to use the cedar wood from Byblos (a trade that appear to have started with Byblos and the pharaohs of the second dynasty) in their constructions either of a funerary nature or for the living for building their temples and palaces.

The queen at Ebla was in charge of the supervision of the "receipt and delivery" of goods as well as the function of the mills that produced textiles, Ebla's main industry. In addition, the queen mother had others function as seen from the message sent by king Ebrium to his son and successor Ibbi-Sipis where he clearly notifies him of assigning some of his properties to three other sons and explicitly mentions that this allotment was decided by the queen mother.

The construction of the royal archives appears to precede the rise of Akkad and is contemporary with the first dynasty of Kish. In the future, when deciphering will advance, the archives of Ebla will help determine the historical setting of kings from neighboring areas such as Byblos. Some rulers such as Tudia of Ashur, until recently considered legendary, are now recognized as historical figures.

It is well accepted that the so-called Dynasty of Ebla known today consisted of Ebrium and his sons, including Ibbi-Sipis. Before him the tablets record only three kings. Concerning king Ebrium the tablets reveal that he had 44 children: 24 princes and 20 princesses, clearly designated as sons or daughters of the king. Polygamy must have been the prevailing state of life. One should remember that twelve centuries later Ramesses the II in Egypt fathered closely to 100 children. In a single burial site in Egypt more than fifty of them have been found because their father having survived them and, being in power, had everything to build such a mausoleum for his children's stay during their afterlife. That was not the case with Ebrium, who stayed in power a longtime but was eventually succeeded by his son. He also married some daughters to neighboring kings, rulers, and even to mercenaries for political reasons because Ebla did not have an army of its own. The tradition of hiring mercenaries was to persist for several millennia from Canaanite times through Phoenicia until Carthage, where the practice of using mercenary armies was not only costly but at times dangerous.

In the ordinary life Ebla consisted of a peaceful society which only engaged in war when absolutely necessary due to foreign attacks: thus their use of mercenaries. This practice was not always desirable as shown by what happened much later in certain phoenician city-states and even in Carthage some centuries after. Ebrium appears to be the first king to use the practice of family marriages as a political weapon: he gave in marriage some of his daughters to neighbors, powerful rulers, friends or enemies in order to maintain peace and avoid war. Ebrium also made another one of his sons, Sura-Damu, king of the age-old rival city of Mari, at this time under Ebla's dominion.

His son Ibbi-Sipis was the first to stop the practice of using an elected ruler form of government and initiated a hereditary monarchy. He reformed the calendar and entrusted to two of his sons the highest positions in his government. It seems likely that it was his excessive abuse of power that brought about the collapse of the dynasty in the Eblaite state. Another possibility is that the downfall of the dynasty was due to internal power struggles although the destruction of Ebla may have been inflicted from outside by Kish, according to

Mesopotamian sources. Decipherment of more material may provide a definitive answer about the collapse of Ebla.

Ebla maintained commercial relations with an extensive area in the Near East: in the tablets prominent cities mentioned are Byblos, Sidon, Sarepta and Beirut in Phoenicia; Damascus and Jaffa in Syria-Palestine; Karkemis and Mari in the Euphrates region; the island of Cyprus and also Kanis in central Turkey.

At Ebla the language of the syllabaries, in cuneiform signs, was arranged according to the initial formative elements, just as it will be done centuries later in Mesopotamia. The bilingual vocabularies represent their most advanced cultural achievement and they list the Sumerian words with their translation into Older Canaanite, the language currently spoken at the time in Ebla. Literary compositions included more than 20 myths, some preserved in more than one copy. The text of the Epic of Gilgamesh has been found in two copies and a list of professions has been found in identical copies in southern and northern Mesopotamia and at Ebla.

The religion at Ebla had attained quite a high degree of sophistication and despite their advanced economic and political status denied power to the clergy. Among the male gods Dagan occupies the first and central position: he is the "lord" and also a quarter of the city and one of the main gates is named after him. He is the "lord of Canaan" and "lord of the lords". In subsequent times only EL seems to compare to him. The female counterpart is **belatu,** lady, a designation that perhaps identifies a goddess similar to the contemporary lady of Byblos, Ba'alath. Other male gods include

Dabir, the male god of the city of Ebla who controls the "plagues"; Hada, the storm god; Baal and Reshep in the phoenician group; Sipis, sumerian; Kamis, the main god of Moab; Lim, the amorite god of the Mari tablets and Ashtar, the god of love and war. Among the female goddesses are Astarte, Isatu, the fire goddess, and Tiamat, the goddess of the primordial ocean waters.

IL and **Ya** are two other divinities of uncertain significance. IL appears to correspond to the EL in the Ugarit-Phoenician tradition but Ya is more difficult to classify. The overall picture of the religion at Ebla does suggest the existence of an advanced concept of the divine. The names of the months are often associated to a divinity: Dagan, Ashtabi, Hada, Adamma, Ishtar, Kamis, Rasap are all assigned a month in their calendar. From the study of the personal names of Eblaites it appears that gods such as Malik, Damu, IL and Ya were the most popular divinities. Thus from the religious viewpoint the Eblaites are Canaanites and predecessors of the Phoenicians. Priests and priestesses, temples and chapels did exist at Ebla; and it is also remarkable that prophets already went around spreading their teachings: the **nabiutum** of Ebla were known from the root **nb'/nby**, "to call, to announce" that came from Mari.

In summary, some of the gods of Ebla persisted until much later: Dagan seems to have been the head of the pantheon during the 3d millennium in Ebla. He is designated not only the "lord of Canaan" but also the "lord of the gods". The female consort of Dagan is named **Belatu**, "lady", with no other designation. Among the male divinities

Sipis, the sun-god and Hada, the storm-god, presided as witnesses over international treaties. Baal, the young god of Canaan, with Sipis, Dagan, and Rasap, have the gates of the city named in their honor. Ashtar is the male god of love and war while Ashtarte is his female companion. Rasap is the god of plagues and pestilences. Dabir is the protector of the city but also companion of Rasap. Finally **Isatu** is the fire goddess and Tiamat the goddess of the primordial ocean.

A separate problem is posed by the identification of **Il** and **Ya** in the pantheon of Ebla. According to Pettinato these terms should be considered equivalent to the **El** of the Ugarit script and the **Yahveh** of the Hebrews, repectively.

DAGON was during the 3rd and 2d millennium BCE one of the most important figures of the pantheon in the Euphrates region. From here his cult spread to Ebla and the land of Canaan. Since the 3d millenium his power extended to the Amanus mountain, the mountain of the Cedars. In Assyria he was the god of vegetation and the father of the young god of the storms, Baal-Haddu. Under this personification he appears in the mythological texts of Ugarit. During the second millennium he was among the gods of the Amorites of Mari, who sought him as a guide in the important afffairs of the state through the help of his oracles. This idea persists during the 13th and 12th centuries BC at Emar as a **Dingir-Kur**, suggesting that he represented a "divine mountain". Some time earlier, 14th century BC, the most imposing of the temples of Ugarit was dedicated to Dagon under the name of **Bet Dagon** and his cult had spread to Phoenicia in places such as Tyre and Beirut. A town near Jaffa bearing the name of

Dagon is mentioned in the Annals of Sennacherib. In the areas where Phoenician was spoken he was venerated as Dagon, such as Palestine and in the inscription of of Eshmunazzar II. Some sources have suggested that Dagon was given the name of Kronos by the Phoenicians. This name was greatly popular in the region before the Palestinians came, as attested by Ramesses the III who mentions a city of **Bet Dqn** in the 12th century BC. In the political treaties between Assyrians and Arameans in the middle of the 8th century BC he is invoked as "Dagon of the Egyptians". The Palestinians seem to have borrowed the elements of the cult of Dagon from the Phoenicians. During the first millennium Dagon, the god of agriculture, gave his name to the grain of wheat. Under the name of **B'l Hmn**, Baal Hamon, the Carthagineans will represent him later as a god with a heavy beard, sitting on a throne, with a vegetal crown, supporting a branch of wheat in his left hand and imparting a benediction with his right hand.

The head of the Ugaritic pantheon is **El**. He is known under the epithets of "the King" and "the father of the gods". The word **El** originally meant "god", and also "the first" as well as "the strong". From his home in Mount Kassios originated the two great rivers that supplied fresh water to the entire world. He presided as a patriarchal figure over the other gods, his children, and he was the "creator of all". Furthermore, he is the "Father of Time", the "Bull" and the "Eternal One". Several of his attributes were later adopted by the Hebrews, together with those of Baal, and applied to Yahveh.

In the Ugaritic pantheon **El** is the proper name of a deity and not just a name to designate the divine. The texts of Krt and Aqht show that El was the main authority in social affairs while the fertility cult was under the power of Baal.

El is the **'ab s^nm,** that is, "the father of the years". This refers to his function of regulating the seasons, either with the solar or lunar deities. Differences exist among scholars in the Ugaritic tongue in the interpretation of the words **'ab s^nm**: some believe the correct translation is "father of mortals" while for others is "father of the divine family".

El is also given the title of **mlk**, "king", meant to reflect the relation between worshippers and their god, between masters and slaves. Moreover, the human king is considered the "son of El".

El is also known as "the bull", **tr'el**, title referring either to his strenght or to his power of procreating. The extant literature from Ugarit shows him as the father of the divine family, and in this active role he begets offspring of whom the first are the divine twins **s^hr** and **s^hl**, the deities manifested in the morning and evening stars.

Another title that El appears to have because of his relationship with the community of men is **'ab 'adm**, that is "the father of men".

The term **'EL** or **ilu** seems to refer to the supreme god of the early Amorite pantheon, to a proper name, such as it is found in the names of places or personal names, as in Yibne'el, Yishma'el, Isra'el. El is the most primitive form of the god while Baal is a more recent arrival to the Ugaritic pantheon.

King Krt addresses El as "father" and El later directs him to do no harm to the people of the town of **'Udm**, the town where he went in search of a new bride, thus revealing the moral aspect of the character of El. He is the senior god of the Ugarit pantheon. However, El is willing to give up his power to Baal; upon learning of the news of Baal's revival, he is ready to gladly resign his functions and dedicate himself to "retirement with dignity".

The gods Reshep and Astarte were the first divinities adopted by the pharaohs and they remained popular in Egypt. However they do not seem to play a prominent role in the texts from Ugarit. Only Anat is prominent both in Ugarit and in Egypt. The religion at Ugarit is polyteist but because many documents are most likely missing from the library found there, it is likely that the place and importance of some gods are not fully clarified. The chief of the pantheon is EL, meaning "god" in all local languages of the area. He is the father of the gods and father of men, "the creator of everything" and "the father of the years". He resides in a mysterieous place at "the origen of the two Rivers". He is the supreme arbiter and the guardian of the cosmic order and it is him who decides in the interests of gods and men. It is possible that he had played a more important and active role in earlier times but that information has not been documented at Ugarit and has not reached us. The gods Reshep and Astarte were the first divinities adopted by the pharaohs and they remained popular in Egypt. However they do not seem to play a prominent role in the texts from Ugarit. Only Anat is prominent both in Ugarit and in Egypt. It is possible that he has played a more important and active role in earlier times but that information has not been documented and has not reached us. His power of fecundation is not very prominent in the Ugaritic literature but is mentioned in relation to two women that he impregnates and who give birth to Dawn and Dusk. His official spouse is the goddess Asherat who gave birth to his seventy divine children; thus she is the "mother of the Gods". She exerts power over the heart of EL and the other Gods usually seek her help to mediate before the father of all gods.

This couple is later replaced by two younger gods: Baal and his sister and lover Anat. Baal is the son of EL although frequently the texts mentioned him as the "son of Dagon". Baal is the "Master" and later on Haddu or Haddad, the god of the storms, who brings the rains and the fertility to the land. He is the "Master of the Earth" and the "Rider of the Clouds". His abode is in the mountains located to the North of Ugarit, where the "assembly of the Gods" takes place.

Anat is a goddess of war and love, occasionally cruel but also the type of the young woman, beautiful, desirable and giver of life. The other gods all appear in the extant tablets of Ugarit playing lesser roles.

ANAT

The virgin sister of Baal and also his consort, Anat, (in phoenician **'nt**) is chiefly a Canaanite goddess, adopted fully later on by the

Egyptians. She is a warrior goddess who delighted occasionally in slaughtering her enemies; "she plunged her knees into the blood of warriors, her thighs into the blood of youths". Other designations commonly found applied to her were btlt 'nt "virgin Anat" and ^st 'gr "lady of the mountain". In ancient times when Baal was not yet the head of the Ugaritic pantheon, Astarte was the wife of El and mother of all gods. When Baal seems to have driven EL from his leading position he also took over his wife. Anat is commonly designated as both "sister" and "consort" of Baal: this has lead some scholars to confusion in the interpretation of the texts: perhaps the ancient use of the terms "brother" and "sister" should not be taken too literally because in the majority of the myths Anat is Baal's principal wife. Besides, other wives are often referred as "sisters of Baal".

The goddess Anat is depicted as both protective and destructive, both characteristics undoubtedly reflecting the early beliefs of primitive men. When Anat found the dead body of Baal, in reaction to the beauty and charm of his dead body, she devoured his flesh without a knife and drank his blood without a cup. She is also considered the goddess of passion, love and fertility. In Egypt, especially in the times of Ramesses II, she was regarded as the goddess of war, "queen of heaven and mistress of all the gods". The figure of Anat will grow less and less important, especially in Phoenicia, from the 3d millenium on into the 2d, where she will be slowly replaced by Astarte. Other scholars paint a different picture of Anat and point out that her tenderness or cruelty were unequaled: when she attacked Mot (Death) in order to rescue Baal from the underworld, "she seized Mot, son of El, and with her sword she split him open". Following Baal's death his vengeance is achieved by Anat who finds Mot and kills him in battle:

> "She seized Mot, son of El and Astarte,
> with the sword she cut him up,
> with the sieve she winnowed him,
> in the fire she burned him,
> in the mill she ground him,
> in the field she sowed him,
> she scatered his body for the birds to eat,
> for them to destroy the seed…"

This is the basis for the identification of the body of the god with the grain, a central theme in the fertility-cult of Canaan. It should be indicated here that the original meaning of the word Dagon, Baal's father, is "grain of wheat". Dagon is thus considered the main god associated with germination.

Anat is an active participant in most of the legends of Ugarit side-by-side with Baal and next to her father El. Some scholars believe these legends had been used in the shrines of the goddess with the attributes that were customarily characteristic of Baal. The variable nature of her character, at times generous at times capricious, is evident on several occasions. She is always on the side of Baal and exercises her power as a warrior at any occasion: When a company of raiders, presumably enemies of Baal, attack the palace of Anat she responds in a ferocious battle:

> …marauders came to the gates of Anat's house
> mightly she cuts to pieces the sons of the two cities
> she exterminates the people of the Seashore and Sunrise
> she plunges her knees into the blood of the swift ones,
> her thighs into the gore of the fast ones,
> she drives raiders with her staff………
> ……………………………………………
> Anat hews in pieces and rejoices,
> her liver expands with laughter,
> her heart is filled with joy,
> she washes her hands from the blood of her enemies
> ……………………………………………
> and bathes with dew of the heavens……

Then Anat receives a message from Baal, a word from the Mightiest Hero,

> Withdraw war from the Earth,
> set love upon the land,
> put forth peace in the midst of the earth
> increase love in the midst of the fields
> spare your rod, put back your sword,
> ……………and come to me

> I have a word to speak to you
> a message to tell you
> a word of the trees, a whisper of the stones,
> stones of lightning…………
> unknown to heavens and to man,
> ………in my sanctuary of the mountains,
> in the hills of might…………

Upon her arrival to Ba'al's dwelling he reveals to her that the building of a palace beffiting a King would be of greater help to him in his conflict with Mot and his belligerent acts. Thus he asks her to obtain her father EL's permission to build a palace in agreement with his status.

This she does by going to her father and requesting, in a well-known passage, combining charm with threats, that El grant Baal his desire to have a house built for him. Apparently a large portion is missing from the extant tablets but it appears likely that Anat also took her request to Asherat and that she also agreed to present the case before El who agrees finally to Asherat's request. In the preserved segment Asherat then orders her messengers to go to the god of craftsmanship, Ktr-w-Hss, and ask him, in Baal's name, to build a palace.

In another episode of the texts a different aspect of her character is revealed: when Anat desires the bow and arrows of Ahkat, the son of Daniel, she can use all her charm or instead resort to crime.

When the god of craftmanship, the Skillful and Percipient One, (Ktr-w-Hss), passing by with a stock of bows and arrows decides to give one to King Daniel, who in turn gives it to his son Akhat, the Virgin Anat in her whim decides to have the bow and uses all of her charms in order to secure it. Since she was attending a feast

> Anat poured her cup to the ground
> raised her voice and shouted:
> O young Akhat! ask for silver and I will give it to you
> ask for gold and I will give it to you
> But let me have your bow
> Let the sister of the Prince Baal have your arrows

Akhat responds:

> I would donate wood from the cedars of Lebanon
> I would give you tendons from wild oxen,
> sinews from the hocks of the bull,
> reeds from the vast marshes
> to make bows for you, O Virgin Anat,

Anat persisted

> If you want eternal life I will give it to you,
> Immortality! I will make it yours
> I will make you number years with Baal

Akhat rejects the offers of the goddess with scorn:

> Do not lie to me Virgin Anat,
> to a hero your lies are wasted,
> what do mortal men get in the end?
> what does a mortal finally get?
> Plaster is poured on his head
> the death of all men I will die
> the bow is the bow of warriors
> and women are not hunters…

Deeply offended she marks the young hero for death:

> Then she left the earth and went to El, her father,
> At the confluence of the two rivers
> in the midst of the source of the two deeps,
> she arrived to the tent of El
> and entered the shrine of the King, the Father of Time.
> She prostrated herself at the feet of El
> honouring him and pleading obeisance
> She slandered the son of Daniel…
> ……………………………………
> Then El, the Kind, the Merciful, replied:
> "I know, daughter, how gentle you can be,
> store your feelings in your breast,

whatever you desire you can do…

whoever slanders you should be crushed…"

………………………………………

The Virgin Anat left, headed towards Akhat the Hero,

to hire **Ytpn**, the assassin………

When approached **Ytpn** replied:

"Will you O Virgin Anat

will you really kill Akhat for his bow?

kill him for his arrows? not let him live?"

And the Virgin replied:

"Pay attention, Ytpn, I will give the orders,

I will carry you as a vulture in my mantle

When Akhat sits down to eat

vultures will swoop over his head

I will be swooping among the vultures

and drop you over Akhat, the Hero,

strike him twice on the skull

and three times over the ear

like a slayer you will make his blood run…

his breath will leave him like the wind

and his spirit like the breeze……

After completion of the deed, the bow is obtained but, on his return from the scene of the crime, Ytpn, unwillingly drops it into the sea where it is lost.

Upon knowing of the mischance, Anat then wept:

"I killed him for his bow, I killed him for his arrows,
I did not let him live and his bow is not mine...
his bow has been broken and fell into the water......"

The story ends with the father Daniel searching for the body and the youngest sister of the hero punishing the assassin. This is a common theme in the writings of the land of Ugarit in Canaan, reminiscent of the story of Anat searching for Baal's body while El was lamenting his death.

Anat's disrespectful attitute towards her father El is, according to some scholars, contrary to the idea that monotheism had already developed by then in Canaan. However, others believe that monotheism was probably a doctrine shared by a certain elite of learned men in Ugarit. In favor of this view it is argued that common titles given to El denoting special characteristics such as his Mercy, his Eternity, his Perfection, his Nobility, etc. are certainly consistent with the idea that places him as the unique highest God at Ugarit. In this respect it is worth mentioning that Dussaud is of the opinion that Moses did not introduce the Hebrews to a new God but simply made them adopt the Canaanite god **Yw**, who was the son of El.

Some scholars have claimed that the presence of Anat in the pantheon of Tyre by the 7th century BC is due to the fact that by this time she has already been identified with Athena. Both share several characteritics: Anat is the daughter of EL at Ugarit and according to Philo of Byblos the daughther of EL at Byblos while Athena is the daughther of Zeus. Both are the the prototype of warrior goddesses, both possess the capacity to fly, both are designated "virgins" quite often, both have contacts with Kushor, both fight either the Sea God or Poseidon, Anat at Ugarit and Athena at the Acropolis respectively. Some writers believe that Athena fights Poseidon as an extension of the Phoenician myth of Anat fighting against the Sea God in Ugaritic times. Their complete identification is already established by the 4th century BC as proven by a Greek-Phoenician bilingual inscription found at Larnaca in Cyprus: Athena was the Greek form of Anat imported from Phoenicia. Philo of Byblos considers Athena as the goddess daughter of EL-Kronos in Tyre who was given the royalty of Athens.

KING KRT

King **Krt** (? of Sidon) had a numerous progeny and lost his entire family to pestilence, being left without legitimate heirs. In his sadness, he sobs himself into sleep during which EL appears to him in a dream. The god instructs Krt to perform certain rituals, organize an expedition and besiege the city of **'Udm**, whose king **Pbl** has a granddaughter **Hry**, who is to wed Krt and bear him offspring. Krt follows the instructions of El not to accept gifts from Pbl, to insist on obtaining Hry's hand in marriage, and to stop in southern Phoenicia to make a vow to Asherat of Tyre and Sidon asking that if she blesses his mission with success, he will give Asherat much gold and silver. Krt then proceeds to **'Udm**, lays siege of the town, rejects the offers of **Pbl** and insists on wedding Hry. Finally the grandfather accepts, the wedding takes place with the attendance of all the gods and the prediction that they will have seven sons and eight daughters. The prophesy is fullfilled but Krt conveniently forgets to keep his promise to Asherat. After a banquet given in celebration of the restoration of his family, Krt becomes gravely ill presumably because of Asherat's doing after having been forgotten by Krt. Following this, the kingdom suffers a famine because of the king's illness. **Ilhu**, a son of Krt, begins to have doubts about the immortality of his father and **Ysb**, the crown prince, is impelled to request his father to abdicate. Finally the father's disease is exorcised and he returns to his throne, not before giving a malediction to his eldest son. The extant text reads as follows:

>The house of the king had seven brothers,
>………eight sons of one mother
>his rightful wife, that gave him offspring
>perfect in health, in princely dignity,
>the woman he married had left him
>Reseph gathered them into himself;

Krt saw his offspring destroyed

his royal house completely finished

his line was utterly ruined

and he had no heir in his household

king Krt's dynasty was finished

his dwelling entirely ruined……

repeating his own words he sheds tears.

Krt goes into seclusion, he enters his chambers and weeps, he sheds more and more tears and then falls sleep: a consolation comes soon in the form of a dream-vision:

In his dream, El comes down

in his vision, the Father of Men,

approaches him asking:

why is Krt weeping, the Gracious One,

the Lad of El? Why is Krt shedding tears?

Is it the kinship of the Bull his father that he demands?

or governement, like the Father of Men?

……Go and wash your hands, fingers and forearms

Take with your right hand a lamb for sacrifice,

a bird of sacrifice, a cup of silver, a cup of gold

pour wine into the golden cup…

go up to the top of the tower

and raise your hands to the heavens.

Sacrifice to your father the Bull El;

Offer the lamb in sacrifice to Baal
the son of Dagon;
then Krt comes down from the roof
and prepares food for the city:
Let the crowd gather and come forth
let the elite of the fighting men come together
three hundred times ten thousand freemen,
march in thousands like a dust-storm,
in tens of thousands like winter rain

gathering in excitement all sorts of people, from the lonely widow to the blind man, they march for several days, in a bizarre expedition to find a bride for Krt, thus he can have a new progeny.

They reached the shrine of Asherat of Tyre,
………the Goddess of Sidon;
Then Krt, the Generous, made a vow:
In the presence of Asherat of Tyre and Sidon
"If I take Hry into my house
if I bring the damsel into my court
I will double her price in silver
and triple her price in gold………"
Then at sunset on the seventh day
they arrive to 'Udum the great,
the city of the Abundant Waters,
…………………………………

> do not lay siege to 'Udum the great
>
> do not aim your arrows at their fortress

is the request of Pbl to Krt. Pbl does not want 'Udum attacked or destroyed. A passage of similar significance is found in the Bible when Yahveh requests the Israelies not to attack Edom and Moab.

Will Pbl, the king, pay attention to the demands of Krt? The grandfather of Hry responds:

> "Take silver and gold in token of her value instead,
>
> …take a chariot that stands in the stable of your servant
>
> take, O Krt, these peace offerings and depart
>
> and depart, O King, from my House,
>
> far away, O Krt, from my court."
>
> Do no harm to 'Udum the Great
>
> 'Udum is the gift of El
>
> a present from the Father of Men"

King Krt then sends in return this message to king Pbl

> "What is the purpose of silver and gold,
>
> slaves, horses and chariots………
>
> give me rather what is not in my house,
>
> Give me the damsel Hry,
>
> the fairest of the offspring of your first-born,

> whose grace is like the grace of Anat,
> whose beauty is like the beauty of Atterat,
> whose eyes have the shine of lapis-lazuli,
> whose eyelids are bowls of carnelian
> ....
> I shall repose in the clear glance of her eyes"

This is indeed great poetry in 14th century Canaan.

The text describes in epic style how Krt carried on the instructions given to him by El in his dream. Krt, in his journey to the home of the bride, stops to visit the shrine of Asherat of Tyre and Sidon (in phoenician **srm** and **sdynm**) where he makes a vow which we learn later he will neglect to comply with.

> "In the presence of Astarte of Tyre and Sidon
> If I take Hry into my house,
> If I bring the damsel into my court,
> Twice her worth will I give in silver
> Yes, and triple her weight in gold…"

The king of 'Udum eventually gives **Hry** in marriage to **Krt** and thus she becomes his queen. In Krt's palace the wedding takes place with the attendance of all the gods and the blessing of El:

> With a cup in his hand, El blessed Krt,
> the gracious One, the son of El,
> "The wife you have taken, O Krt,
> the wife you have taken into your house,
> the damsel you brought into your court,
> will bear you seven sons,
> and eight daughthers…
> she will bear the lad Ysb
> who sucks the milk of Atterat,
> and the breasts of the Virgin Anat……

The attendance of all the gods is an event of special significance. One must recall that at the wedding of Cadmus and Harmonia all the gods came from Heaven to feast with the mortals.

King Krt then falls sick, having forgotten his vow to Atterat, the goddess seeks vengeance and proceeds with punishment.

> "Krt will reach the sunset,
> Yes, the lord will go with the sundown…"

Because a great famine has taken over the kingdom during the king's illness and his crown prince is asking him to abdicate while Ilhu doubts more and more about the immortality of his father, El eventually decides to heal the sick king.

Some scholars have seen this turn of events as a suggestion that belief in personal immortality was an idea already prevalent in Canaan. The later couplet recalls the Egyptian belief that immortality awaited the King in the West, in the dwelling of the gods. In the Golenischeff papyrus, preserved in Moscow, Zakarbaal, the King of Byblos is reminded by the Egyptian envoy Wen-Amon of the immortality of the pharaoh.

THE GOD EL

He is frequently mentioned in the Bible and later on by writers such as Philo of Byblos. Scholars have argued for a longtime about his importance and his place in the mythology and religion of the Near East. Sources of the 19th century AD regarded as reliable the tradition that designated EL, **Il**, as a legitimate ancient Phoenician deity. However, later on some scholars questioned the vality of such opinions until the documentation unearthed at Ugarit came to corroborate the writings attributed to Philo of Byblos (from about the 1st century) and left no doubt that EL was a true Phoenician deity. His name was commonly used as a proper name. The worship of EL in Ugarit is now accepted without any question. In most instances EL is mentioned in the mythological texts as the proper name of the head of the Ugaritic pantheon and as the Canaanite-Phoenician god.

The designations ^**il** and ^**ilah** appear to be connected in most languages of the area and are referring to a deity: ^**ilah** is either an expansion of ^il or ^il is a contraction of ^ilah. The use of the plural of majesty by the Canaanites and Egyptians as a form of flattery for pharaohs and gods to indicate that a given individual god was the equivalent of the entire pantheon suggests this as the mechanism whereby the plural developed a singular meaning. That is the reason why the plural **ilm** in Ugaritic refers to a single god and was the equivalent of the Phoenician ^lm.

A study of the proper names compounded with El through the Aramaic, Canaanite, Hebrew, Phoenician, Amorite and Arabic cultures discloses a widespread use of it from BC 2700 into AD 500. Its meaning is very broad: El is father, uncle, king, master, ruler, lord; he is a bull, a lion, a bear, a rock; he is light and peace, first, great, exalted, perfect, strong, merciful, honored; he produces, builds, commands, speaks, judges, thinks, hears, chooses, lives, knows, remembers, provides, forgives, gives, heals, helps, inspires, saves, rescues and loves. The attributes and actions predicated of EL show how ancient and important deity he was.

Some of the attributes in the Ugaritic documents are worthy of further analysis since they disclose important characteristics. It has been suggested that in Phoenicia the name **mlk**, used to designate a cosmic deity in Tyre, probably refers to Melkart but there is nothing to oppose the view that the Melkart of Tyre may be identical with the El of Ugarit. Thus mlk also is likely to refer to El.

El is featured in the Ugaritic Texts as King of the gods, Father of the gods and men, as the Bull, the Creator, the Senior figure of the pantheon and as the personification of Wisdom.

Wisdom is a characteristic applied only to El. This is the natural result of his age: Asherat and Anat both flatter and praise him for his wisdom before requesting any favors. However, he does not often demonstrate this wisdom in any of his actions. His wisdom is accompanied by benevolence, benignity, and affability. He expresses joy and sorrow but never anger: this is seen for instance when Baal dies or comes back to life and when Asherat comes to visit him to request permission for the building of the palace for Baal.

EL's forebearance and calm is evident when facing Anat's insults and threats in the incident of Ahkat's bow: he responds with composure and courtesy.

The amorous adventures of El were frequent especially in his prime: he fathered the seventy children of Asherat and keeps for her a special feeling even when they appear to have been estranged: when she returns to see him for the business of building the house of Baal, he seems happy to see her and does not hesitate to make it known: "The love of King El will excite you, the affection of the Bull arouse you".

The physical appearance of El is depicted in a stela from Ugarit: majestic figure seated on an ornate throne, with full and prominent beard, long robe and high tiara crowned with horns. Over his head is shown a winged solar disc. This evidence of Egyptian influence that goes back to the beginning of the 3d millennium at Byblos is still seen in the middle of the 2d millennium in Ugarit.

The coins of Byblos represent El as a man with six wings, perhaps influenced by similar images depicted in Mesopotamian deities. The

Ugaritic evidence indicates that El as creator is not only concerned with paternity. The Ugarit Texts do not show any deity preceding El. His sexual capacity seems to have declined by the time the extant texts describe him and in this respect Baal seems to have replaced him.

But Baal describes him as "the Creator of all of us". Kings Krt and Danel both refer to El as "Father". His procreative capacity seems to have come to an end because by now he has to use the rejuvenation ritual of consuming a roasting bird before being able to impregnate two females and thus father several minor gods.

According to some hebrew scholars such as Cassuto "the Lord, most High God, Maker of Heaven and Earth, of the Canaanites" was identified by the people of Israel with their own One God, althought in the eyes of the Canaanites El exhibited some of the characteristics of mere mortals. The Canaanite prince of Tyre says of himself

"I am El, I sit in the seat of the gods, in the heart of the sea", to which Ezekiel responds "and yet you are but a man and not a god".

Taking similarities further El is considered to have had many children, among them the seventy children of Asherat. Three of these children rebelled against him; Baal, ruler of the Heavens; Mot, reigning over the underworld and another son designated "Prince of the Sea". The Greek legends concerning Kronos follow the same pattern and if El is succesfully dethroned by his sons; Kronos is also deposed by his sons with Zeus controlling the heavens, Pluto the netherworld and Poseidon crontrolling the sea. In addition, both Kronos and El are designated as "fathers of time", **'ab ^snm**.

The abode of EL: There is nothing in the Ugaritic texts to suggest that the residence of El was located in a geographic area far away. If Baal's abode is in nearby Mount Kassius, it is reasonable to assume that El's residing place would be in a neighboring locality as well. In the descriptions of the visits of various gods to El there is no suggestion of remoteness. When Danel searches in the distance the approach of Ktr and Hss "On lifting his eyes he perceives by the thousand acres and myriad of hectares the going of Ktr and the course of Hss": this is naturally somewhat quite a short distance.

By the same token, the interval between the abode of Baal and that of Mot is described with the same expression. The distance between the abodes of Anat and Baal is also described in a similar manner

> The Virgin Anat rejoices
> she jumps with her feet and leaves the earth
> she sets face towards the lord of Sapan's place
> By the thousand acres and myriad hectares
> she lifts her voice and shouts:
> a house will be built for you
> ....
> a house of silver and gold...
> Eliyin Baal rejoices...

The distance between the residences of El and Baal, Baal and Mot, between Anat and Mot, Anat and Aqhat, between Asherat and El, are all described using the same expression.

When Asherat goes to visit El to ask permission to build a house for Baal, El's place is said to be

> At the course of the Two Rivers
> At the midst of the streams of the Two Deeps
> She enters the abode of Il
> comes into the domicile of the King
> at the feet of Il she bows and falls
> at his feet she postrates herself
> ....
> El breaks the formality and laughs
> He lifts his voice and shouts:
> "Why has Lady Asherat of the Sea come?
> Are you hungry? Are you thirsty?

The location of the abode of El has been accepted by most scholars to be related to the use in the Ugaritic and Canaanite languages as well as in more recent sources of the words **nbk** and **'pq** both meaning "fountain". The location of the ancient Afqa in Phoenicia is today known to be about 40 km northeast of Beirut and midway between Baalbek and Byblos. Afqa possesses the features that characterize El's mythological residence as described in the

Ugaritic Texts: the river emerges from a cavern, near the bottom of towering cliffs and plunges in a series of cascades into a deep and greenish gorge. Over the cavern the cliffs rise more than a thousand feet. On the other side of the mountain there is an intermittent lake ("the little Sea") fed by a spring that erupts every year at approximately the 10th of March (Adar) and continues to flow until the last day of July (Tammuz). In the Autumn the spring drys up and the lake tends to disappear: a remarkable natural phenomenon which must have greatly impressed the ancients.

A tradition exists in support of the belief that the waters of the Lake and those of Afqa on both sides of the mountain are connected by a tunnel: the river Adonis would flow for a long distance below the surface from the eastern slope and after winding for about 12 km. under the surface it would re-appear on the western slope at 4000 feet above sea level. Local tradition would expand on this phenomenon of nature and create future legends making figures such as Gilgamesh, Moses and Alexander the Great, traverse the same subterranean tunnel, in their trip to eternity.

A subject of considerable controversy has been the **monotheism of El**: early on the 20th century AD eminent European scholars postulated the existence of an elite of monotheist priests at Ugarit who held such a belief. The basis for this is to be found in the documents listing EL as the father of the other gods in the Ugaritic pantheon. None of the Ugaritic gods has been shown to stand alone and exist out of the family of EL: at least a segment of the population worshipped EL not only as the highest god but as the absolute God. The point has been made that there was a movement that gave El monarchical powers and regarded the other gods as emanations of his divine power.

Similar monotheistic movements in the Middle East started in the middle of the 3d millennium and included the one where the priests of Ptah in Memphis ascribed to their god all the powers of creation and the embodiment of all deities. The Ihkenaton movement of Tell-el-Amarna was to happen a millennium later.

CHAPTER SIX

THE ALPHABET

Aleph, Beth, Gimel, Daleth,…Teth…Herodotus in his **Histories** (Book V, 57-59) describes the often quoted arrival of the Phoenicians in Greece.

"My own inquiry shows that there were some Phoenicians who came with Cadmus to the country now called Boeotia, and in that country the lands of Tanagra were allotted to them, where they settled. The Cadmeans having been first expelled by the Argives". This happened sixty years after the fall of Troy, according to Thucydides. But Herodotus continues:

"These Phoenicians who came with Cadmus at their settlements in this country, **among many other kinds of learning, brought into Hellas the alphabet,** which had hitherto been unknown, as I think, to the Greeks; and presently as time went on, the sound and the form of the letters were changed. At this time the Greeks that dwelt around them for the most part were Ionians; who having been taught the letters by the Phoenicians, used them with some few changes of form, and in so doing gave to these characters (as indeed was but just, seeing that the Phoenician had brought them to Hellas) the name of Phoenician. Thus also the Ionians have from ancient times called the papyrus-sheets **skins**, because formerly for lack of papyrus they used the skins of sheep and goats; and even to this day there are many foreigners who write on such skins." There is certainly a great similarity in the form and order of the early Greek and Phoenician letters.

And Herodotus continues: "I have myself seen Cadmean characters in the temple of Apollo at Thebes of Boeotia, engraved on certain tripods and for the most part like Ionian letters. On one of the tripods there is this inscription:

I am Amphitryon's gift, from spoils Teleboan fashioned.
This would be of the time of Laius, the son of Labdacus, who was the son of Polydorus, who was the son of Cadmus.

A second tripod says in hexameter verse:

I am a gift that is given by Scaeus, the conquering boxer,
Archer Apollo, for you in your temple is this beautiful adornment.

"Scaeus the son of Hippocoon, if indeed the dedicator is him and not another person by the same name, as Hippocoon's son, would be of the time of Oedipus, son of Laius"

The entire genealogy from Kadmus to Oedipus is described here, coinciding with a similar account by Philo of Byblos. Concerning this point, Pliny the Elder, who lived in the first century AD, states in his NATURAL HISTORY (Book V, chapter XIII) that "Phoenicia is surrounded by Syria......The whole of the sea lying off the coast is called the Phoenician sea. The Phoenician race itself has the great distinction of having invented the alphabet and the sciences of astronomy, navigation and strategy".

Diodorus Siculus in his "LIBRARY OF HISTORY" (Book III, 67) also described the origin of the alphabet in the following terms:

"Among the Greeks Linus was the first to discover the different rhythms and songs, and when Cadmus brought from Phoenicia the letters as they are called, Linus was again the first to transfer them into the Greek language, to give a name to each character and to fix its shape. Now the letters, as a group, are called "Phoenician" because they were brought to the Greeks from the Phoenicians, but as single letters the Pelasgians were the first to make use of the transferred characters and so they were called" Pelasgic". As the knowledge of the history of development of the letters has increased recently and early Phoenicians inscriptions have come to light, all the evidence confirms the Greek tradition that their alphabet was derived from the Phoenician. What remains controversial is the time at which the Phoenician letters appeared in the Greek mainland. If Cadmus was a historical figure, as some evidence discovered in Thebes seems to indicate, he must have come to Greece between the 14th and 12th century BC but the Phoenician letters were adopted sometime in between.

Kadmos, the Phoenician, is accepted by most scholars, as the evidence just quoted shows, to have introduced **"the letters"** into Greece sometime between the early and middle part of the 14th century BC. This appears to be the date that fits best because Cadmus is credited with founding a dynasty at Thebes roughly nine generations before the Trojan war. This is assuming a generation being 30 years and the fall of Troy occurring at about 1190-84 BC. The foundation of Thebes by Cadmus must have been a re-foundation since the city existed in Neolithic times and probably underwent trade penetrations from the East at various times notably during the 12th and 11th centuries. Trading and seafaring by the Phoenicians (Canaanites) is known to have been well-developed by then. This places the coming of the Cadmeans and the sack of Troy within 50 years of each other.

In the **Annals** (Book XI, Chapter XIV) Tacitus describes how Claudius during his reign, after making the discovery that not even the Greek alphabet was begun and completed at the same time, invented and gave to the world some additional Latin characters. These included an inverted digamma for the consonantal U, an antisigma, and a Greek sign to express the sound Y, heard between U and I.

"The Egyptians, in their animal-pictures, were the first people to represent thought by symbols: these, the earliest documents of human history, are visible today, impressed upon stone. They describe themselves also as the inventors of writing: from Egypt, the Phoenicians, who were predominant at sea, imported the knowledge into Greece and gained the credit of their discovery. For the tradition runs that it was Kadmus, arriving with a Phoenician fleet, who taught the art to the still uncivilized Greek peoples."

It is said also that the Egyptian writings, although hieroglyphic, contained implicit the consonant letters that they taught to the Phoenicians, who transferred them to Greece. The letters were most likely developed at the beginning of the second millennium and transferred to Europe around the 15th century BC. They were further transferred by the Europeans to America about three thousand years later. Thus in a span of three millennia the alphabet spread to the entire world including the modifications made by Greeks and Romans.

In 1923 AD the French scholar Pierre Montet discovered in Byblos the "Sarcophagus of Ahiram" which has inscribed in stone the most advanced form of the Phoenician alphabet. It now rests in the Beirut National Museum. Its dating may be between the 13th and 11th century BC. The sarcophagus may have been made earlier than the time of Ahiram and according to some scholars may have been re-used for the burial of Ahiram by his son.

Other inscriptions in stone or bronze have been found in Byblos, Sidon and Tyre, of more recent vintage, depicting the same alphabetical system which consists of 22 consonants and no vowel signs. The Yehimilk inscription, and the Roueisseh spearhead inscription, date from the 11th while the Abiba'al and Eliba'al inscriptions are from the early tenth century. Among the inscriptions in stone, the one found by Dunand and termed linear pseudohierogliphic contains a mixture of the pseudohierogliphic writing and the archaic alphabetic writing signs. It has been dated to the early 19th century BC. A reproduction is seen here on page 248.

The alphabet of Ugarit discovered in 1929 by Schaeffer was inscribed in **cuneiform** with thirty letters in clay but with no connection with the cuneiform writings of Mesopotamia. Interestingly enough is the fact that Ugaritic contained three signs expressing the 'a, 'i and 'u. The Ugaritic dated to the fourteenth century and was likely, according to most scholars, derived from an earlier extant alphabet, perhaps the pseudo-hieroglyphic script of Byblos, that may have existed already in the sixteenth or fifteenth century BC but which most likely began to develop two to three centuries earlier. This early Canaanite script was written vertically while Phoenician was written from right to left. This is also true of early Greek.

The creators of the Phoenician writing must have been aware and familiar with all previous scripts in existence before them and during their own time in order to achieve the conceptual leap that led to the creation of their mature Phoenician language and script.

The Aramaic may have appeared in the tenth or early ninth century BC and spread early throughout the Near East. "Syria" and "Syrians" were terms used by the Greeks for "Aram" and "Arameans". Herodotus much later regarded the term "Assyrians" as the barbarian form for the Greek spelling "Syrians". Others considered "Syria" as a derivation from the term **Suri** of the cuneiform inscriptions, the Babylonian designation for "the west". This word has persisted in the modern Arabic language. The Nabateans of Petra, in present day Jordan, were Arabs that used Arabic as their language in daily life but adopted Aramaic as their written language. Arabic, of course, was also derived from Phoenician and is today one of the most widely spoken languages in existence.

Like other alphabetic scripts the early Greek was also written from right to left: the Greeks took directly the letters **beth, gimel, daleth, zayin, kaph, lamed, mem, nun, pe, resh and taw** without change in their phonetic values but their revolutionary change was the transformation of the letters **aleph, he, waw, 'yod and 'ayin** into the vowels **alpha, epsilon, upsilon, iota and omikron.**

The Coptic alphabet was the only non-European offshoot of the Greek used in Africa to which they added seven letters taken from the Egyptian demotic writing, to express sounds that did not exist in Greek.

The Etruscan was probably a non-Indo-European alphabet that adapted the Greek symbols most likely during the eight or early seventh century BC as observed on the Marsiliana Tablet

(Archeological Museum of Florence). It depicts the archetype of the Etruscan with 26 letters carefully engraved from right to left vis-a-vis the 22 consonants taken from Phoenician with the additional four Greek letters.

THE ARROWS OF ZAKKUR AND AZORBA'AL

Another bilingual inscription in Phoenician and Etruscan, datable perhaps later towards the year 500 BC, made in a **lamine di Pyrgi** in gold, is preserved in the Museo di Villa Giulia in Rome. From the same time and the same sanctuary of Pyrgi is another inscription **in etrusco e in fenicio**, relative to the consecration of the temple of the godess Uni/Astarte by Thefarie Velianas. At the end of the 5th century Etruscan took its final form with a total of twenty six letters: four vowels and twenty two consonants.

The paramount offshot from the Etruscan, of course, was the Latin alphabet that took place around the seventh century BC. The Romans adopted only twenty one letters and the others were made into numbers while from the Greek, after their conquest, they took the **y** and **z** and placed them at the end of the alphabet. During the medieval period the letters **V** and **I** served as the basis for the **U, W** and **J**. The Latin transformed after the first century BC by adapting to the other languages and adopting the cursive style as well. The rest is recent history.

The Byblians who dealt commercially with papyrus obtained through trade from the Egyptians used it for a variety of purposes: one seems to have been their use in writing and as a consequence most of the literature of the Phoenicians such as Sanchuniaton of Berytus got lost because this perishable material did not have the resistance of clay used in Ebla, Tell-el-Amarina and Ugarit. Furthermore, the word used later by the Hebrews to record their religious beliefs, the Bible, (βψβλοσ) is derived from the word for paper, papyrus, used at Byblos.

The pseudo-hieroglyphic script of Byblos was discovered in 1929 AD by Maurice Dunand and published in 1945. The superficial similarity of this script with the phoenician alphabet on the one hand and with hieroglyphic symbols on the other, lead Dunand to call it pseudo-hieroglyphic. More recent studies confirm some of his original postulates but tend to provide a somewhat different interpretation for this form of writing.

The extant material containing this script includes two bronze tablets (2); four bronze spatulae (4); one (1) stone stele and three (3) stone fragments containing a total of 114 symbols or signs; representing, it was believed earlier, either a transitional form of writing or a syllabic system. A total of 13 inscriptions are now known. A more advanced form of this script named linear pseudo-hieroglyphic by Dunand has been found. (Figure on page 228). It is intermediate between the pseudo-hieroglyphic and the archaic alphabetic phoenician system, as mentioned earlier. It shows signs of both systems of writing. This fact appears to resolve the long discussion about the origin and evolution of the phoenician alphabet. It suggests not only a transition but shows that both scripts were in use simultaneouly at a certain time in Byblos. These signs according to Dunand originated around the 22d Century BC from the? Egyptian consonantal system. More recent opinions trace the origin of the pseudohieroglyphic system to the 19-18th centuries BC. This is the main corpus that scholars have had to examine in their attempts to decipher it. When compared to the material unearthed at Ebla, Ugarit or Tell-El-Amarna, the Byblian corpus represents quite a small amount of material.

This pseudo-hieroglyphic script according to **Edouard Dhormé** definitely represents a syllabic script of the Phoenician language originating during the times of the Pharaoh Amenophis IV (early 14th century). It consists of over 100 symbols that were **borrowed** by the Byblians from foreign scripts, particularly **from the Egyptian hieroglyphic writing**.

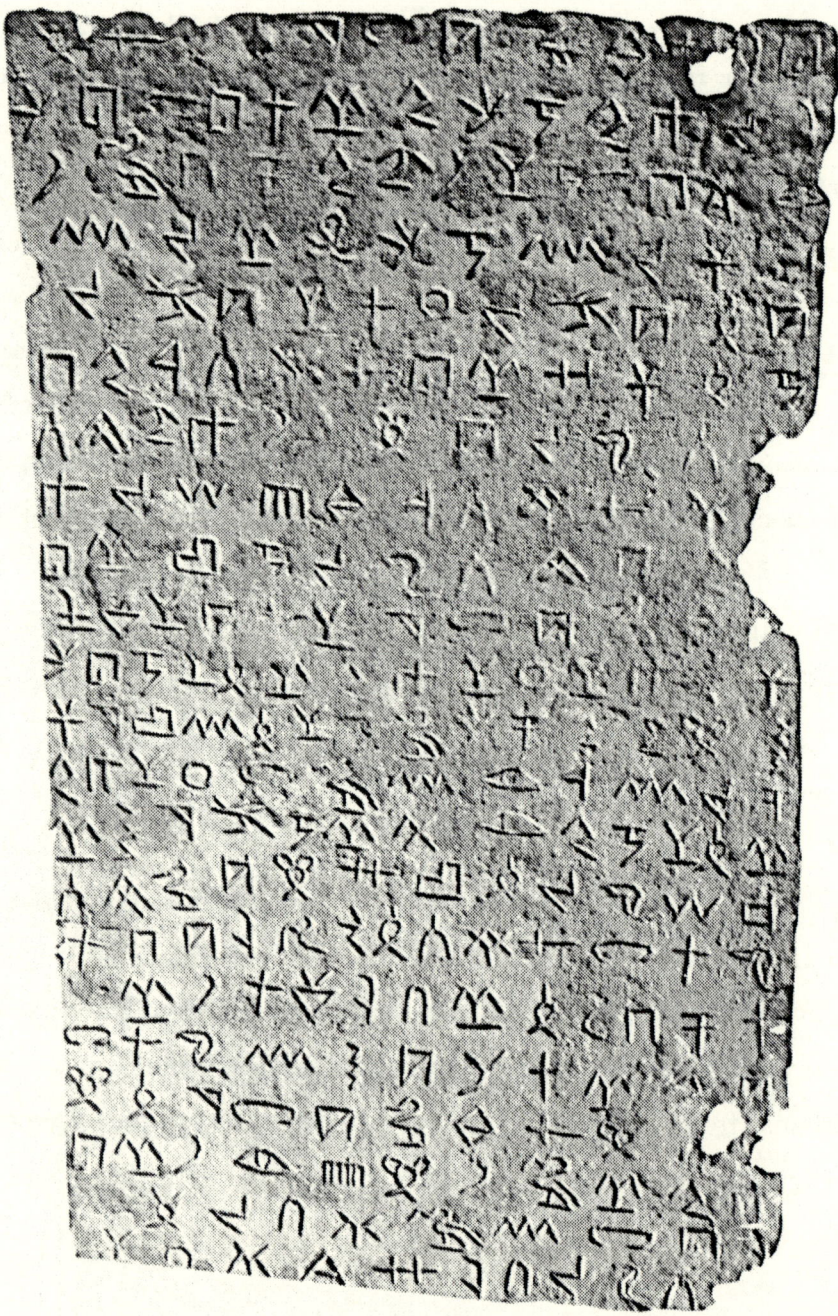

The Inscription in the Pseudo-Hieroglyphic Script from Byblos, showing a combination with Archaic Phoenician Signs.

A more recent attempt to decipher this script has been undertaken by **G E Mendenhall**. His work has taken almost four decades to complete; it represents a definitive fresh approach with a meaningful interpretation based on the historico-socio-political circumstances of the time: this has been one of the epigraphic problems most difficult to solve during the last seven decades since its discovery.

The syllabic nature of the pseudo-hieroglyphic script of Byblos is no longer in doubt but its dating appears now to go back to the middle of the third millenium BC according to Mendenhall; based on a careful study of its similarities and differences in relation to/and with other syllabic sytems. Thus some writers now believe that the Phoenician alphabet may have been well developed by 1750 BC during the reign of the pharaohs of the fourth dynasty.

The study by Mendenhall proposes challenging conclusions that should be given serious consideration in the future. At least this study will certainly remain as the basis for a more comprehensive and, hopefully, definitive approach to the complete decipherment of the Byblian pseudo-hieroglyphic script. His most recent analysis indicates the existence in the script of about 63 different syllables. A syllabary of approximately 90 consonant-vowel (CV) characters was initially conceived under the assumption that the Byblian script was analogous to Ugaritic with a somewhat similar number of consonants (about 28 to 30) and a system of three vowels..**a, i** and **u**...Because there is considerably larger number of graphic variants depicting somewhat similar characters, the most recent working hypothesis has reduced that number to approximately 60 signs. Only 24 consonants have been identified in the **signary of the Byblian syllabic script at present.** Three (3) **"proto-semitic" vowels a,i,u** and 3 half-vowels **y, ω** and **h.** The **u** vowel sound is preferred to the letter **i.**

The **primitive, archaic, nature of the Byblian syllabic system** is obvious when compared to other systems, especially **Ugaritic.** The evolution of Ugaritic ended by the 12th century BC following the destruction of the city by fire during an earthquake. **Ugaritic cuneiform alphabet** tablets date from the 14th century BC, written from right to left or left to right, discovered in 1929 AD by **Claude F.A. Schaeffer.** It consists of 30 letters (?29)…Six (6) letters of Ugaritic cuneiform resemble Phoenician alphabetic letters but Ugaritic cuneiform contains also three signs for **a, i** and **u.** Thus the creation of the vowel symbols took place most likely around the 14th century BC, most likely starting at Ugarit. This supports the view that an alphabetic script already existed by the 16th or 15th century BC; thus the creators of Ugaritic may have been influenced by an **already extant alphabet** or perhaps by the **pseudo-hieroglyphic script** of Byblos just briefly discussed. Furthermore, the Greeks took from the Arameans the vowels in the middle of the 9th century and began to use the **a, e, u, i** and later on introduced the **omega.**

The **Asdruba'al (Azarba'al) Spatula** dates from the 14th century, contains **a form** of **pseudo-hieroglyphic** writing on one side and a **Phoenician alphabetic** inscription on the other. This supports the view that Phoenician writing most likely developed when the Byblian pseudo-hieroglyphic script was still in use.

Zakar-Ba'al, a Byblian ruler whose palace has not been unearthed or may have disappeared altogether under the modern Crusader's castle at Byblos, was contemporary with the beginning of the 21th Egyptian Dynasty, circa 1080 BC. The Wen-Amon papyrus; now conserved in the Moscow Museum describes a mission sent by the Egyptians during their period of decline to Byblos to obtain cedar wood. The details of this mission are described elsewhere in this book. Because they were lacking in funds sufficient to pay for their load, Zakar-ba'al, the king, boasted about his power and political independence:

"If I cry out to Lebanon, the heavens open up and the logs are here lying on the sea shore..."

As payment for the timber the pharaoh had sent five hundred rolls of papyrus and five hundred coils of rope. Is this evidence that the pseudo-hieroglyphic script of Byblos, previously used to write in metal or stone, had now been replaced by another system of writing in papyrus?. Archeological (and/or epigraphic) evidence is needed in support of this speculation. Papyrus ropes exported from Egypt were used for hauling and binding cedar logs and for manufacture of the cables of ships from papyrus.

The palace of **Zakar-Ba'al** has never been found but most of the ancient city dwellings have not been excavated because they are occupied by the modern town of Jbeil. It is also possible that the palace may have existed beneath what is now the Crusaders' Castle. The obvious proximity to the sea of the ancient royal palace is observed in the description of the Wen-Amon papyrus, discussed earlier in a previous chapter. The constant erosion during the torrential rains that occur commonly in this region may have changed considerably the topography of the ancient constructions and modified considerably the sealine over the last thirty centuries. One must remember that the location of Byblos remained practically unknown until the expedition that Ernest Renan conducted in 1860 AD under the auspices of Napoleon the III. And only at the beginning of the 19th century, torrential rains produced in Byblos the mud slides that uncovered the Sarcophagus of Ahiram and several other tombs, thus allowing Pierre Montet the serendipitous discovery of the most advanced form of the ancient Phoenician alphabet.

The Yehimilk stele with inscription was found at Byblos and preserved at the Beirut National Museum, is dated by some scholars at the 11th century BC and by M. Dunand at the first half of the 12th century BC.

The inscription, translated by M. Dunand, reads:

"This is the temple built by Yehimilk, king of Byblos. It was he, who restored the ruins of these temples. May Baal-

Shamen and Ba'alath-Gebal and the entire assembly of the holy gods of Byblos prolong the days of Yehimilk and his years over Byblos as a rightful King and a true king before the holy gods of Byblos. May the Lady of Byblos prolong his years as king. Whoever you are, who come to restore this temple in the future, you may place your name next to mine. Otherwise, the Lady of Byblos will destroy your name and your posterity before all the gods of Byblos."

Sarcophagus of Ahiram

The Epitaph of the Ahiram Sarcophagus (11-10th century BC) of Byblos was discovered by **Pierre Montet in 1923 AD.** King Ahiram, in phoenician **'hrn** (my brother, the exalted), was the father of **Ithoba'al.** The three-line inscription on the lid of his sarcophagus represents the **most developed extant ancient form of the**

Phoenician alphabet found thus far. Its dating is still a topic of controversy: The features and dress of the figures on the sarcophagus are similar to those observed in Egypt during the 18th Dynasty. The "lotus and bud" decoration is of Egyptian origin. The appearance of the lions is characteristic of the Hittite sculptures. The Egyptian and Hittite influences were at its height in Phoenicia during the 13th century BC. The presence in the tomb of vase fragments with an inscription of Ramessess the II, all suggest that the sarcophagus dates from the 13th century. However the letters themselves are suggestive of a later period due to their similarity with more recent inscriptions in the Phoenician language.

Here is the translation of the proud imprecation written on the lid of the sarcophagus:

"This is the coffin which Ithoba'al, son of Ahiram, king of Byblos, made for his father as his dwelling in eternity. If any king or governor or army commander attacks Byblos and exposes this coffin, let his judicial scepter be broken, let his royal throne be overthrown, and let peace flee from Byblos; as for him let a vagabond efface his inscription".

The 22 consonants and the absence of symbols for the vowel sounds is the mature **most evolved** form of the script that was transferred to the Greeks and eventually to the entire West. Although the creation and addition of the vowel signs to the phoenician alphabet of 22 consonants has long been attributed to the Greeks, it is known that some vowel sounds were represented already in Ugaritic and Aramean. Some scholars now believe that the invention of the vowel sounds was likely to be the product of the Aramean culture. Their transfer to Greece may have occurred later. This is, however, not a settled question.

The Roueisseh (Ruweiseh) bronze (arrowhead) **spearhead** inscription (11th - 10th century BC.) is written with Phoenician signs.

The inscription on the **Azorba'al** bronze **spatula** apparently describes a commercial transaction with a certain individual named Azorba'al as the beneficiary.

Abiba'al and Eliba'al inscriptions (10th century BC) are in a script similar to that of the Ahiram sarcophagus: a consonantal writing of 22 symbols.

The **Abiba'al** inscription is dated to the time of the Egyptian Pharaoh Sheshonq I (945-924 BC). The translation given by Albright is as follows:

> "This is the statue which Abibaal, king of Byblos, son of Yehimilk, king of Byblos, brought from Egypt for Baalath Gebal, his lady. May Baalath Gebal prolong the days of Abibaal and his years over Byblos."

The **Eliba'al** inscription is dated to the time of Osorkon I (924-895 BC.), son of Sheshonq I. Is Eliba'al another son of Yehimilk? Some scholars believe he was a brother of Abiba'al. The statue of Osorkon I is now in the Louvre Museum and the letters of the phoenician inscription are almost identical to those of Abibaal. It reads:

"This (is the) statue which Eliba'al, king of Byblos, son of Yehimilk, king of Byblos, made for Balaath Gebal, his lady. May Balaath Gebal prolong the days of Eliba'al and his years over Byblos."

During the "Fouilles de Byblos" Maurice Dunand found in the space located between the set of Columns of the Roman period and the Crusader's castle, a number of objects and inscriptions among which the most important were the Stele of Yehimilk mentioned earlier, a plaque of white marble with a phoenician inscription pertaining to Batno'am, mother of Ozba'al, king of Byblos, who (based on numismatic material preserved at the British Museum may have been in power towards 350 BC) and several partially incomplete inscriptions on flagstones of the time of Shaphatba'al.

These inscriptions are very well preserved and written in the phoenician language. That of the mother of the king reads in translation made by Dunand (in agreement with Dussaud):

"In this sarcophagus I, Batno'am, rest, mother of 'Ozba'al, king of Byblos, son of Pillet-Ba'al, priest of Ba'alath. I rest duly dressed and ornated with a gold mask covering my mouth, as it was customary for people of royal rank that preceded me".

It has been said that the latter part of this inscription was rather innaccurate because she was not a Queen but by the power of her son, the King of Byblos, she was given burial with royal honors.

The **Shaphat-ba'al** inscription was engraved on a wall likely to date after the inscriptions of the Abiba'al and Eliba'al brothers, from about 850 BC. Shipit-Baal I, in the Assyrian records, is the son of Eliba'al and grandson of Yehimilk. The text of this inscription is quite similar to those just described. It says:

"This is the wall which Shipit-Ba'al, king of Byblos, son of Eliba'al, king of Byblos, son of Yehimilk, king of Byblos, built for Ba'alath Gebal, lady of Byblos. May Ba'alath Gebal prolong the days of Shipit-Ba'al and his years over Byblos."

An inscription which was long considered the most ancient one, written in the Phoenician script, is preserved at the Louvre Museum in Paris and dated to about the year 800 BC. It is known as the **Stele of Mesha, King of Moab**. It reads in abbreviated fashion as follows:

"I am Mesha, son of Komash, king of Moab, the Dibonite. My father was king of Moab for thirty years and I became king after my father. I built this sanctuary for Kamosh of Kerihoh; with all my salutations because he saved me from my aggressors and he made me enjoy victory over all my enemies.

Omri, (the King of Israel) having taken the country of Modaba, kept the country of Moab under oppression for many years and was followed by his son that succeeded him for 40 years. During my days Kamosh was restored as the king and I was full of joy following my victory against the people of Israel, against their king and against their house. Israel has been ruined forever.

The men of Gad stayed in the country of Attarot: I attacked their city and took it. I killed all their people. I entered during the night, attacked all night and the day after until the afternoon. I took seven thousand men and women, young men, young women and all their concubines. I took the vases of Yahwe and offered them before Kamosh."

It is remarkable that over three thousand years later the differences among the people of the area continue still unresolved.

"THE STELE OF MOAB" picture from the Louvre Museum. Serial # AO 5066

Ignace Gelb, in his classic book on the history of writing, has suggested a modification to the opinion of Maurice Dunand in the dating of the inscriptions found under his direction at Byblos by his archeological team. Thus he states "in connection with the dating of the earliest Phoenician inscriptions, the epigraphic differences between the oldest inscriptions -like those of Ahiram- and the younger ones -like those of Abiba'al and Eliba'al- are so negligible that one may justifiably wonder how correct it is to assume the wide gap of three hundred years between them. As the dating of the Abiba'al and Eliba'al inscriptions to about the 10th century is beyond question, the lowering of the date of the Ahiram and related inscriptions by about two hundred years would seem to be much more satisfactory from the epigraphical point of view". However, the differences observed in modern European languages show that they have changed to the point of becoming different in a shorter time, about 400 years.

The Yehawmilk stele, 4th - 5th Century BC, records improvements to the temple of Ba'alath in a lengthy inscription conserved at the Louvre Museum. A picture of it is represented in the Figure shown here which depicts in the upper part Lady Ba'alath and the King of Byblos. The goddess is represented with the solar disc over her head, between the cow's horns, characteristic of the Egyptian Hathor-Isis, holding a staff with a lotus flower in her left hand while the King is bent in front of her. This is the same Ba'alath, **B'lt**, whose inscriptions on stone were found in the Sinai Peninsula by WM

Flinders Petrie, presumably carved by Phoenician miners who dug for cooper and turquoise in this area during the 16th century BC.

Stele of Yehawmilk. Serial # AO 22368 from the LOUVRE MUSEUM

The language spoken by the Phoenicians during the 1st millennium had, no doubt, its roots in the second and even perhaps the latter part of the 3d millenium BC. Their writing most likely was developed through multiple modifications during the second. The Phoenician tongue was spoken for at least two millennia. The finds at Tel-El-Amarna, Boghazkoy, Ugarit and Byblos during the Late Bronze Age have shown that Akkadian was the **lingua franca** in the Near East for an extended period. The standard Akkadian language was used in Mesopotamia in the 18th century BC. and was thereafter taught in scribal schools. The scribes translated it (or rather transcribed it) phonetically, adapting it to the various forms of the local dialects. During the 15th to the 13th centuries the Egyptians corresponded with Babylonians, Assyrians, Hittites and Phoenicians in Akkadian. While expecting to receive responses in Akkadian, in many occasions they received responses in several other languages. During the 14th century, Egyptian scribes attached to the city-states of Tyre, Sidon, Berytus or Byblos, answered to the correspondence of the pharaohs in Akkadian sprinkled with many Egyptian words, ideas and idioms. By so doing the scribes were indicating their origin and demonstrating unfamiliarity with the local dialects that they had learned at schools. They devised bilingual and multilingual vocabularies that were used for education by the scribal schools. Their tongue was not contemporary Babylonian but a corrupt form of it, similar to the language used in the inscriptions from Mari dating back to the 18th century BC. Canaanite scribes also wrote part of this correspondence in vulgar Akkadian with frequent inclusion of

Canaanite words. Thus it seems that from the 16th to the 14th century BC., the evolution of a completely unrelated type of language and script (the Phoenician proper) was taking place or was being developed at places such as Byblos. This is evident by the epigraphic finds in both stone and bronze, such as the inscription on the sarcophagus of Ahiram and the pseudo-hieroglyphic inscriptions translated by Dunand, Dussaud and Mendenhall. This new Phoenician script would spread to the Western world and become the only means of transferring written information for the next three millennia.

Phoenician Alphabet

Sign	Name	Meaning	Phone	Latin
⌧	Aleph	Ox	A consonant laryngeal	A
◿	Beth	House	B consonant	B
⌐	Gimel	Camel	G consonant	C, G
◁	Daleth	Door	D consonant	D
∃	He	?	H consonant	E
Y	Waw	?	W semi-consonant	F
目	Heth	Wall	H laryngeal consonant	H
⌐	Yodh	Hand	Y semi-consonant	I, J
⌐	Kaph	Hand	K consonant	K
⌐	Lamedh	?	L consonant	L
w	Mem	Water	M consonant	M
∫	Nun	Fish	N consonant	N
O	Ayin	Eye	3 laryngeal consonant	O
⌐	Pe	Mouth	P consonant	P
φ	Qoph	Monkey	Q voiceless velar	Q
⌐	Resh	Head	R consonant	R
W	Sin	Tooth	Sh consonant	S
†	Taw	Mark	T consonant	T
Y	Waw	?	W semi-consonant	U, V, W
⌐	Samekh	Fish	S consonant	X
Z	Zayin	Sword	Z consonant	Z

Two major forms of the Phoenician language and script existed:

i) The **Phoenician proper,** in use in mainland Phoenicia until the 2d or first century BC and

ii) The **colonial branches** that existed in 3 different varieties:
   1) The Cypro-Phoenician script, which already contained the vowels **a, e, i, o,** and **u,** consisted of approximately 45 symbols; it was in use from the 10th to the 2d century BC.
   2) The Sardinian branch: the Nora stone is the prototype of this script which started in the early 9th century BC.
   3) The Carthaginian writing (named Punic by the Romans) remained in use until the 3d century AD. This appears to have been the language that most strongly influenced the Lybian-Berber script and the Iberian scripts.

The Lybians borrowed the idea of writing from the Carthaginians but they did not take the entire Punic alphabet: they took some signs, the direction of writing from right to left and the consonantal system but in their own languagethey used some local signs and modified the Punic letters, thus ending with a different system of writing.

The Iberians developed two distinct systems of writing: the Iberian script in the narrow sense of the word, Iberian proper, and the Tartessian system, also known as Andalusian, supposedly the script of the ancient city of Tartessus. Their inscriptions are engraved in stone, lead, silver, bronze and pottery. Most of them are stored in Valencia (Spain). Their decipherment indicates that the Iberian Script consisted of thirty letters: twenty five consonants and five vowels, written from right to left. The Iberian script proper was derived from the Phoenician or Punic while the Tartessian script appears to have been derived from the Lybian. The Celtiberians appear to have been the people who developed the latter script. The baron von Humboldt considered the present Basques, who now inhabit the region of the Pyrenees, as the descendants of the ancient Iberians who are supposed to have been in the peninsula since the Stone Age.

Finally it should be pointed out that Phoenician being the predominant language in Iberia for over a millennium, numerous bilingual inscriptions have been found in the Mediterranean area. Worth mentioning are the Phoenician-Hittite bilingual inscription of the 15th century BC, the longest, found in Karatepe, Eastern Cilicia, in modern-day Turkey. It consists of approximately 80 lines in four columns. Another one is the Phoenician-Etruscan bilingual inscription from the 6th-5th century BC, found at Pyrgi and now preserved in the Villa Giulia in Rome, engraved in gold laminae.

Punic Alphabet

Sound	Style of Carthage 800-600 B.C.	Style of Phoenicia (Iowa) 800-600 B.C.	Style of Phoenicia (Spain) 800-600 B.C.
b	◁	ꓶ,9	ꓶ,9
g	ꓶ	>	>
d	◁	△	△
h	≋	⊓	⊓
w	Ч	↑,	↑, Y
z	I	N, н	N
ḥ	目	///	///, 目
ṭ	⊕	ᗱ	ᗰ
k	⊁,ꓘ,ꓤ	ꓘ⊤	ꓤ,K
l	⌐	∧	∧
m	ꟽ	⋌ⱳ	W,ꟽ
š	W	⋎	⋎
', i	O	O,⸫	O,⸫
s	⟊	⸝	⸝
t	✝	ⴘ	ⴘ

THE VISITORS TO THE MOUTH OF THE "DOG" RIVER

The site known by the Greeks and Romans as Lycus (Λψχυσ) and later on until modern times as the Dog River is located about 9 miles north of Beirut. According to legend at the highest part of the route there existed in antiquity a large promontory on the top of which was placed the statue of a wolf or a large dog which gave its name to the river. In its "Memoires" the Chevalier d'Arvieux in 1735 AD described it as "a site where the Pagans have erected the statue of a big dog on the rock of the Cape which entered into the sea and allowed the local defenders to discover the armies approaching the site. They would then communicate by using their strong voices that, it is claimed, were heard as far as the neighbouring inland of Cyprus".

What unique attraction did this site have upon the minds of people and conquerors of antiquity from Ramesses II to Alexander the Great? Large armies passed through here and their commanders always felt a compulsion to perpetuate their names on stone. Nineteen inscriptions have been found here in many languages from Egyptian, Greek and Latin to French, Arabic and English. From Ramessess II, Ezzar'Haddon of Niniveh, Nebuchadnezzar of Babylon to the emperor Caracalla, all left inscriptions to indicate having been there at a certain point in history. The area was used by the natives, in most instances unsuccessfully, to defend themselves from foreign invaders. This was a site of great natural beauty but also of strategic importance.

Amin Maalouf, a prominent present-day writer put it this way:

"Near the mouth of the Dog River the route narrows skirting cliffs and steep hills...Nahar-el-Kalb has been the bane of conquerors since remote antiquity. Whenever one of them managed to get through to the pass unscathed, his pride would be such that he would chisel an account of his exploits into the walls of the cliff......From the hieroglyphs of Ramessess II and the cuneiform characters of Nebuchadnezzar to the Latin speeches of Marcus Aurelius Antoninus Caracalla, grand-uncle of Septimius Severus, whose father was born in Lebanon".

All sorts of ancient scripts with various characters are found here because the conquerors felt compelled to satisfy their pride and leave a message of their visit. Ramessess II left three inscriptions on three stelae, one of which was erased by the French in 1860 during the expedition sent by Napoleon III and the other two are nearly illegible today. They commemorated the triumphs during his campaigns, one of which marked "Year 4" testifies of the consolidation of the territories conquered by his armies to that date. The others are marked "year 2" or year 10 (this is unclear). Further down a third inscription left by Ramesses is probably from an even earlier date. The best preserved extant stele of Ramesses is located next to one of Ezzar'Haddon. It represents Ramesses II holding a captive by the hair and ready to decapitate him in the presence of a deity, most likely

Ptah. In another stele the god has a bird's head over which is shown the figure of the sun disk (Ra-Harakhte) and in front of him is the King, showing a captive.

The Assyrian conquerors engraved on stone six inscriptions here (Shalmanaser III, Sennacherib, Ezzar'Haddon and Nebuchadnezzar), most of them erased by the passage of time. Only that of Ezzar'Haddon remains and although the inscription is poorly legible today and badly damaged it had been translated earlier by Weissbach in 1922 and published by Luckenbill. Ezzar'Haddon passed by Tyre in the course of his tenth campaign, put a siege to Ba'lu, King of Tyre, who had rejected the Assyrian yoke and was allied to Tirhakah, king of Nubia. Ba'lu responded to the Assyrian demands with insolence and thus they withheld from Tyre food and water until they surrendered. He then marched over to Egypt, defeated Tirhakah, king of Egypt and Ethiopia and after taking Memphis, on his retun left the inscription on the mouth of the Lycus River to commemorate his exploits. It reads something like this, in free translation:

"To Asshur, Anu, Enlil, Ea, Sin, Shamash, Hadad, Marduk, Ishtar, the Seven great gods who decree the destiny of kings, granting power and might: Eza'arhaddon the great king of Asyria and Babylon, king of kings of the four regions of the world, son of Sennacherib, the king of the Universe......"

"I entered Memphis and the royal city of Tirhakah amidst gladness and rejoicing, I took their gold weapons and gifts of gold and silver…Its palace, its gods, its goddesses, I declared as booty. His "queen", his harem, his heir, his courtiers…properties, ivory…vessels of gold, silver, precious stones of all kinds, 30 tiaras of the harem women, the heir to his throne, his court officials……his possessions……I took the treasures of gold, silver, antimony, bronze, lead, magnesium, ivory, cooper, tin,…his son-in-law, his family, princes…physicians, divinitation-experts…"

Instead of the former officials he left new people in charge of the conquered towns and countries. It is hard to believe that the ransacking and plundering of the people's property were received by the inhabitants with "gladness and rejoicing".

However, within a year of this campaign, it is not surprising, Tirhakah was re-instated and Ezzaar'Haddon died leaving in his throne his son Ashurbanipal. The latter then undertook new campaigns to reconquer Egypt and southern Canaan. He reconquered Tyre on his third campaign. Ba'lu of Tyre after his defeat offered Ashurbanipal his own daughter and the daughters of his brothers as part of the booty. The latter accepted them with their great dowries. He then proceeded to tranfer all these people as slaves to Assyria. The Assyrian kings then followed tyrannical and cruel practices against the Phoenician cities. Finally towards the end of Ashurbanipal's rule his kingdom weakened and deteriorated, Niniveh fell in 612 BC. The Phoenicians regained their independence without struggle.

The Phoenicians in History and Legend

Nebuchadnezzar the II left an inscription recorded for posterity, translated in the past and now almost erased. A similar copy, it is agreed, remained over the rocks of Wadi Brisa, between Homs and Tripoli, in present day Northern Lebanon. The text has been saved and although partially mutilated it reads:

"......Lebanon, the cedar mountain, the luxurious forest of Marduk, the high cedars no other god has desired, my **nabu** Marduk wanted as a fitting adornment for the palace of the ruler of heaven and earth, this Lebanon over which a foreign enemy was ruling and robbing its riches...

Trusting the power of my rulers, Nebo and Marduk, I made an expedition there and made the country happy by eradicating its enemy. All its scattered inhabitants I led back to their settlements.

What no former king had done I achieved: I cut through steep mountains and split rocks, opened passages and constructed a straight road for transport of the cedars...mighty cedars for Marduk, high and strong, of precious beauty and excellent dark quality...I made the inhabitants of Lebanon live together in safety and let nobody disturb them...I erected a stele showing me as everlasting king...and beside my statue I wrote an inscription with my name for posterity..."

Throughout history during the invasions by Egyptians, Hittites and Mesopotamians, the Phoenicians followed the same policy: by paying tribute they purchased immunity and sought compensation during their freedom by expanding the markets for their trade. History has never been merciful to the defeated: the recognition of the Phoenician contributions to history has been lessened by the fact, that as a traditionally peaceful people, they rarely engaged in war. When they did, it brought them often disastrous consequences: One case in point is that in which they sided with the Persians against Greece and were defeated. Much better known, their descendants, the Carthaginians, were to be defeated by Rome in the ferocious Third Punic War.

The Roman emperor Caracalla (211-216 AD) also left here at the mouth of the Dog River an inscription in Latin that reads as follows:

> "Imperator Caesar Marcus Aurelius
> Antoninus Pius Felix Augustus
> Part (hycus) maximus, Britannicus maximus, Germanicus
>   maximus,
>   Pontifex maximus, montibus inminentibus
>   Lyco fluminis caesis, viam delatavit,
>   per legionem III Gallicam
>   Antoninianam suam".

"The Emperor Ceasar Marcus Aurelius Pius Felix Augustus, supreme vanquishing of the Parths, the Britons and the Germans, suzerain pontif, having opened the way through the mountains that lay

The Phoenicians in History and Legend

above the Lycus River, expanded the passage with the efforts of his Antonine legion".

Beneath the above legend there was an altar in the past and in relief the exclamation in a brief inscription:

"Invicte Imperator, Antonine Pius Felix Auguste, multis annis imperes".
"Invincible Emperor Antonin Augustus, may your reign last many years."

More inscriptions of the early 20th century AD were left by the French and one by the British at their passage through Beirut and Tripoli. The most recent inscription is in Arabic and celebrates the end of the French mandate that followed WW 2 in the 20th century AD and the creation of the modern country of Lebanon.

CHAPTER SEVEN

MERCHANTS AND NAVIGATORS

The many inscriptions in Phoenician as well as in bilingual vocabularies found around the entire Mediterranean area testify to the tenacity of this singularly industrious and adventurous people. For over a millennium they controlled vast areas of the southern European Mediterranean towns and cities and founded new ones through northern Africa. The geographical locations of various Phoenician ports reveals that very little stopped them in their advance through the seas: in the absence of navigational instruments, distance and winds were not obstacles, even during the night their ships navigated. It seems that they were the first to use the constellation of the Ursa Minor to guide themselves in the uncharted seas. They navigated at night guided by the stars: they would advance towards the unknown, and the high seas would not frighten them.

The most superficial knowledge that has reached us tells of the enormous capacity and perspicacious attitude of the Phoenicians in comparison with other Meditterranean people in terms of their thirst for richness and their love for the sophisticated pleasures of life. Severely criticized by some ancient writers and praised by others, the truth about them has begun to emerge in the first quarter of the 20th century AD when their significant contributions to the development of Western civilization have been slowly accepted. Besides their intelectual contributions, they were essential participants in many of the events of their time that today are taken for granted. Here we will attempt to describe briefly some of their "minor" contributions:

Glass: The forests where cedar and pine wood came from were eventually exhausted and did not grow back although demand continued. What could then be made of the mountains facing the sea?. They noticed that their sand contained quartz. Quartz is crystalline silicic acid, the main component of glass. Quartz mixed with sodium bicarbonate and alkaline substances, heated at 700-800 degrees centigrade, leads to a quickly solidifying substance that the Egyptians in the 4th century BC converted into an opaline, opaque glass they used to make liquid containers and sold them as luxury articles. The Phoenicians learned this technique from the Egyptians and began to produce their own glass. The phoenicians developed their own glass industry and succeeded in making the milky substance into transparent moulded glass, a secret kept by them until the advent of the Christian era; from the furnaces of Sidon came the first transparent glass in history. They also discovered the technique of glass-blowing. Mass production allowed economical prices and their elegant and attractive containers soon replaced clay and metal vessels, flooding the

Mediterranean areas. Besides perfecting glass they learned to color it for trade.

Pliny has described how was it done by them (Nat. Hist. Book XXXVI, Chapter LXV, pp 149-155, Loeb Classics) in Phoenicia. Between Syria and Judea, on the lower slopes of Mount Carmel, originates the "River Belus, which after traversing a distance of 5 miles flows into the sea near the colony of Ptolemais. The river is muddy and flows in a deep channel, revealing its sands only when the tide ebbs. For it is not until they have been tossed by the waves and cleansed of impurities that they glisten......The beach stretches for about half a mile, and yet for many centuries the production of glass depended on this area alone."

The fact that this beach was an important source of sand for glass-making at Sidon and elsewhere gives support to the story of Pliny that continues:

"There is a story that once a ship belonging to some traders in natural soda (sodium carbonate and bicarbonate) stopped here and scattered along the shore to prepare a meal. Since no stones to support their cauldrons were available, they rested them on lumps of soda from their cargo. When these became heated and were completely mixed with the sand on the beach, a strange translucent liquid flowed in streams; and this, it is said, was the origin of glass".

Glass is usually made by the fusion of silica, soda and alkaline earth (lime). Without lime only water-glass would have been produced but at extremely high temperatures the liquid glass solidifies.

"Next, it was expected that man's inventive skill would no longer be satisfied and would add **magnes lapis** and crushed quartz which attract molten glass. Similarly crushed shells and quarry sand is added to the mixture......" Glass like copper is smelted in a series of furnaces and dull black lumps are formed. Molten glass is everywhere so sharp that, before there is the least sensation, it can cut any part of the body to the bone......Sidon was once famous for its glassworks, since apart from other achievements, glass mirrors were invented there".

This was the old method of producing glass but using modifications of the same method glass was from then on produced in Greece, Italy and the Gallic and Spanish countries. Some historians trace the invention of transparent glass to Babylon from where it passed to Egypt, India and Phoenicia. Glass-blowing was introduced later, perhaps towards the middle of the first century BC.

Ship-building was for several centuries their main industry: with the forests of fine timber behind them they proceeded to build ships for themselves and for their Egyptian friends and customers. Ivory carving was also prevalent among them and originated in Ugarit, Byblos and Sidon. It is speculated that their ivory was brought by them from India: recent scientific studies favor this interpretation.

Music: Among all of the Near Eastern people the most gifted musicians were the Canaanites: the lute and the harp were of their invention. Cyniras, the father of Adonis, himself was praised for his musical ability and his name appears to be related to the word for "harpist".

The Phoenicians also were the most skillfull technicians of antiquity: they discovered fire by rubbing two pieces of wood. In addition, they brought to Europe the vine, wheat, fig and olive.

Wine: Wine appears to be have been a product of high quality exported from Byblos to Egypt from the 8th Century BC until the 5th AD. Hesiod (8th century) and Theocritus mentioned the Byblian wine in terms of quality next to the one produced in Lesbos and highly appreciated. Herodotus described the earthen jars he saw in Egypt with the wine imported from Byblos which was held in high esteem by the governors of the various Egyptian provinces.

Diodorus Siculus (THE LIBRARY OF HISTORY, book III, 64: 2-6) tells us of the invention of wine by Dionysus.

"He was a Boeotian born in Thebes, from Zeus and Semele, the daughther of Cadmus. The myth says that Zeus had become enamoured of Semele and often, lured by her beauty, had consorted with her, but Hera, jeakous and anxious to punish the girl, asumed the form of one of the intimate friends of Semele and suggested to her that it was fitting that Zeus should lie with her while exhibiting the same majesty and honor in appearance as when he made love to Hera. As a consequence, Zeus at the request of Semele that she be shown the same honours as Hera, appeared to her accompanied by thunder and lighting, but Semele unable to endure the majesty of his grandeur, died and brought forth the babe before his term. Zeus quickly took the baby and hid it in his thigh until the appropiate time that nature prescribed for the baby to complete his growth. Zeus took him to Nysa in Arabia. The boy was reared by nymphs and given the name Dionysus after his father (**Dios**) and after the place **Nysa**. He grew to be of unusual beauty and at first spent his time at dances with bands of women and in every kind of luxury. He also made an army of women and travelled over all the inhabited world. He also instructed all men who cultivated a life of justice in his rites and initiated them into his mysteries. He imposed peace between the nations and created concord where there had been civil strife and wars."

The presence of the god and his mythical exploits became known throughout the ancient world. Many places claimed to be his birth place although it seem that the most accepted is that described here. Of the seven explanations offered in antiquity for the origin of the name Dionysus the most likely sems to be thet Zeus changed the infant Dionysus into a kid which Hermes took to Nysa and turned over to the Nymphs.

The tombs at Byblos, located next to the sea today, were uncovered during torrential rains in the first quarter of the 20th century by French excavators. They revealed a large number of sarcophagi located on rock burial sites: they contained numerous artifacts such as a gold pectoral encrusted with precious stones, a gold pendant with stones resembling the façade of an Egyptian temple and many more objects of art such as human figures, gold pendants decorated with lotus flowers, gold bracelets and alabaster vessels decorated with gold bands. Scimitars were also found bearing the name of Ipshemuabi, king of Byblos, a contemporary of Amenhotep the IV. Without doubt the sarcophagus of Ahiram was their greatest find. More recently a large number of ancient sarcophagi have been found near the houses of the old city: they are made of pure rock in single blocks which appear to have been commonly used by them, as evidenced by the fact that today several of them have been placed by the inhabitants of Jbeil in the backyard of the Crusader's castle.

The art found in Byblos reflects the strong influence of Egypt but the craftmanship was typically phoenician, i.e. Giblite. The Hebrews borrowed from all their neighbours: the cosmogony from Babylonia, from the Assyrians the winged bulls, from the Persians the idea of angels and archangels and from the Phoenicians the feast of the Tabernacle, their temple architecture and the hymns that became the psalms.

The Phoenicians and their descendants the Carthaginians never had an aristocrasy **per se** or based on nobility but a strong, very rich middle class, and especially in Carthage they never had a king but a ruler or a Council of Elders that ruled democratically. This also existed in Byblos of Phoenicia almost two millennia earlier and it seems that at Ebla there also was a Council of Elders.

The Phoenicians mined copper from Cyprus and the Sinai, silver from the Sierra Morena in Spain, tin from England and Ireland, and?

gold from the Sinai. They introduced the precious gold metal to the Greeks and taught them how to like and appreciate it.

During their Mediterranean trips the Phoenicians had established good relations with the indigenous people of the territories they approached for their commercial enterprises. Agriculture was not practiced by them for export but only in a minimum necessary for their own use. Especially at Malta there appears to have been a close integration between the Phoenicians and the indigenous population. Mixtures of populations were quite successful in some other locations such as Ibiza, as testified by Diodorus and Thucydides (VI: 17,2) «The cities are very populated by heterogenous ethnic groups and changes such as admissions of new citizens occur quite frequently».

Only Carthage seems to have achieved a considerable agronomic development and both Greeks and Romans, praised the luxuriant fields of the Carthagineans. An individual named Mago seems to have achieved considerable knowledge and wisdom in the science of Agronomy, to the extent that he wrote a Treatise on Agronomy in twenty eight volumes, widely used in antiquity. It was so famous that the Roman Senate, after Carthage was finally defeated in 146 BC, the Roman body proposed that Mago's treatrise should be translated into Latin for its use by the Romans. There is evidence that other translations followed, one of them in Greek.

The beautiful residences of the Carthaginean higher classes were surrounded by vines, olive trees, cereal plantations especially of wheat, and troopes of cattle, and horses became so well known that they were highly praised by Diodorus (Library of History; XX: 8, 3-4.) During the campaign of Hamilcar against Sicily, large amount of wheat, either bought or cultivated by themselves was sent by Carthage to support an army of about 300 000 men. Diodorus (XI, 20,4).

The **olive tree**, indigenous to the Middle East, was introduced by the Phoenicians into Greece, Etruria, Italy, North Africa and Spain. One of the earliest references to this tree is found in Ugarit. In their temples the phoenicians had it usually as their **sacred tree**, especially in Tyre, the olive tree but other trees were also occasionally in use: the cedar, the poplar or the oak. The sacred tree was placed either next to or between two large stones thus giving its shade as well as its aroma according to the type. In Tyre it appears that the olive tree played a role since the foundation of the city around 2700 BC. Aromatic trees were used by the Greeks later on in places such as near the Acropolis in Athens. In some instances a palm tree or cypresses were used in places such as Sidon. The olive tree was considered eternal and it appears that at Tyre it was considered resistant even to fire. On its branches it could sustain an eagle and a snake: when Oossos arrived to the island part of Tyre to found the city he sacrificed the eagle. The snake appears to have been a symbol of immortality and here it was probably associated to the god Eshmun, later identified by the Greeks with Aeskulapius. The two rocks near the temple probably existed since time immemorial before Oossos arrived and according to Nonnos (Dionysiacs, XL, page 50) they were known as Ambrosia, i.e. "The Divines". They were located next to an olive tree on the island where the city was founded. Nonnos describes the foundation of Tyre by putting it in the words of Bacchus (Dionysus), who

"Leaving the long stretch of Arabia with his deep shadowy forests, measured the Assyrian roads on foot...had in mind to see the Tyrian land, Kadmos' country,......he examined cloth dyed with the Tyrian shell, shooting out sea-sparkling of purple: on that shore once a dog busy by the sea, gobbling the wonderful lurking fish with joyous jaws, stained his white jowl with the blood of the shell and reddened his lips with running fire, which once alone made scarlet the sea-dyed robes of kings. He was delighted to see the city,...with a liquid girdle of sea,...and when he saw the mainland joined to the brine, he felt a double wonder, since Tyre lies in the brine, having her own share in the land but joined with the sea which has joined one girdle with the three sides together......Still more, Bacchus admired the city of Tyre;......How is this? How do I see an island on the mainland? If I may say so, never have I beheld such beauty. Lusty trees rustle besides the waves...A delicate breeze of the south breathes from Lebanon upon Tyrian seas and seaside plowland, pouring a breath of wind which fosters the corn and speeds the ships at once, cools the husbandman and draws the seaman to his voyage......O world-famous city, image of the earth, picture of the sky! You have a belt of sea grown into one with your three sides!".

If we are to believe that the long stretches of Arabia were covered by "deep shadowy forests", their extinction during mythological times left the vast desert lands that eventually resulted several millennia later in the largest deposits of petroleum products which during the 20th century AD served as abundant sources of energy for the entire world.

Nonnos continues:

"So he spoke, and wandered through the city casting his eyes about. He gazed at the streets paved with mosaic of stones and shining metals, he saw the house of Agenor, his ancestor, he saw the courtyards and women's apartments of Kadmos; he entered the ill-guarded maiden chamber of Europa, the bride stolen long ago, and thought of his own horned Zeus......When he had noted all this and gratified his curiosity, he went to the temple of Melkart and there called loudly upon the leader of the stars in mystic words:

"Herakles, lord of fire, prince of the universe!"

According to Nonnos, Herakles "enjoyed a feast,...touched nectar and ambrosia: why not indeed, if he did drink sweet nectar, after the immortal milk of Hera?" By drinking Hera's milk Herakles became her fosterson. In the Louvre Museum is depicted a sculptured scene where, presumably Herakles, is shown drinking from Hera's milk.

Then he spoke to Melkart in words full of curiosity:

The Phoenicians in History and Legend

"Inform me, what god built this city in the form of a continent and the image of an island? What heavenly hand designed it? Who lifted these rocks and rooted them in the sea? Who made all these works of art?......Who mingled island with mainland and bound them together with mother sea?"

Thus spoke Dionysus and Herakles satisfied him with friendly words:

"Hear the story, Bacchus, I will tell you all. People dwelt here once with father Time, bred along with them, saw the only agemates of the eternal universe, offspring of the virgin earth………by indigenous art built upon foundations of rock a city unshakable on ground also of rock. Once on their watery beds among the fountains, while the fiery sun was beaten the earth with steam, they were resting together,……Now I cherished a passion of love for that city; so I took the shadowed form of a human face…and spoke to them my oracle in words of inspiration:

"Shake off idle sleep, sons of the soil! Make me a new kind of vehicle to travel on the brine."

Then he proceeds to instruct them on how to build a ship "the chariot of the sea, the first craft that ever sailed,…………Have a tiller as guide for your craft, to steer a course and drive you on the watery path…………until you come to the fated place, where driven wandering over the brine are two floating rocks, which Nature has named the Ambrosial Rocks."

"On one of them grows a spire of olive, their agemate, selfrooted and joined to the rock, in the very midst of the waterfaring stone. On the top of the foliage you will see an eagle perched, and a well-made bowl. From the flaming tree fire spits out wonderful sparks, and the glow devours the olive tree all round but consumes it not. A snake writhes around the tree with its highlifted leaves, increasing the wonder both for the ears and the eyes. For the serpent does not creep silently to the eagle flying on high, and throw itself at him from one side with a threatening sweep to envelop him, nor spits deadly poison from his teeth and swallows the bird in his jaws;…………"the flame does not spread over the branches of the tall trunk and devours the olive tree, which can not be destroyed, nor withers the scales of the snake, close neighbour, nor does the leaping flame catch even the bird's interlaced feathers. No, the fire keeps to the middle of the tree and sends out a friendly glow…You must catch the wise bird, the flying eagle agemate of the olive, and sacrifice him…pour out his blood on the sea-wandering cliffs,…Then the rock wanders no longer driven over the waters; but fixed upon immovable foundations she will be united to the free rock.

Found upon both rocks a builded city, with quays on two seas, on both sides"

"Such was my prophetic message. The Earthborn awaking were stirred and the divine message still rang in their ears………As the sage bird was sacrificed, the blood of prophecy gushed from the throat newly cut, and with those divine drops rooted the seafaring rocks at the bottom near Tyre on the sea," "There, Lord Dionysus, I have told you……how the Tyrian breed of your ancestors sprang out of the earth."

According to Philo of Byblos, Oossos found the rocks already there and dedicated them to "fire and wind" and in addition sprayed them with blood. This dedication was already a form of preparation when a temple was to be built; such as the temple that would later be occupied by EL and Melkart. The Phoenicians kept this tradition until the foundation of Cadiz (Spain) where the temple was also decorated with an olive tree, two large rocks and a fountain. Furthermore, the Phoenicians disseminated throughout the Mediterranean timber, wheat, oil, wine, spices and perfumes. Of course, the legendary cedar is also well known to have been sold to the Egyptians. It was used by the pharaohs since the Second dynasty and has been found in their tombs, the oldest one has been located inside the pyramid of Senefru (c.2650 BC) and in Egyptian monuments dating to about 1400 BC. The Phoenician ships also appear engraved, half-moon in shape, with both stern and bow, even in Babylon. Around 700 BC in the palace walls of Sennacherib bas-reliefs show Phoenician biremes, equipped with defensive weapons, with an upper deck occupied by passengers and rowers in the lower deck.

The Phoenicians played a remarkable role transmitting the Near Eastern techniques and customs throughout the Mediterranean sea to the West. They had abundant wood used for fuel and shipbuilding, they appear to have been the first people who ever navigated following the stars, beyond the sight of land, who traveled in winter time and sailed at night.

They extended their domains in early times to Spain especially the Balearic islands such as Ibiza and to Cadiz, the westernmost outpost in the 12th century BC. Concerning Gades role in phoenician trade, it should be mentionned its relation to Tartessus. A subject of controversy has been the location of Tartessus: the Phoenicians brought from there all sorts of metals such as silver, gold, tin, and minerals. The biblical Tartessus is not the city by the same name of more modern writers, especially Greeks. Modern scholars now place in the southern half of the Iberian peninsula the region of Tartessus with Cadiz as its capital. This area was celebrated by its riches in silver, gold, tin and all sorts of alloys. It was a vast region comprising parts of today's modern Spain such as Andalucia, Extremadura, Catalonia and even part of Lusitania. The Phoenicians, furthermore, obtained their ivory from an area of India known by the same name but unrelated to the Tartessus described by other writers. Apollodorus in "The Library" describes it as a region where two characteristics were present, i.e. "The existence of a river named Tartessus and the presence of abundant silver in it". Some writers after him described this area as "Tartessus, city of Iberia, named after the river that flows down from its mountain rich in silver, the river also contains large quantities of tin". Abundant archeological artefacts found along the southern part of Hispania are now proof that this area was visited first by Phoenicians and later on Carthaginians. Indo-European people were also attracted by the riches of the area and came over in search of a better life. The Greeks would later compete in the profitable business of exploitation of the mines as would the Romans much later. During the period of exploitation of the silver of Sierra Morena, the metal was first exported to Tartessus (modern Cadiz) and from there according to Diodorus Siculus (LIBRARY OF HISTORY,V: 35) "the Phoenicians would export silver to Greece, Asia and all other people".

This commerce was of great benefit to the small kings of the area. The best known of them all is the one mentioned by Herodotus (HISTORIES, I: 160-165) as "Arganthonius (670-550 BC), the king that lived to the age of 120 years and maintained the control of his government for 80 years. The meaning of his name was "the Silver King". Concerning his longevity there are several, not necessarily coinciding, opinions: while some writers such as Anacreonte, his contemporary, and Strabo, accept the existence of such a man as only one person; others argue that there were several, perhaps three, kings by the same name, thus creating some sort of a dynasty.

The Phoenician presence in Iberia lead to the establishment of several colonies. Because of their commerce and colonies their people became engaged in business, especially in the mines of the southern part of Iberia and near Granada. This gave rise to important economic and social transformations. Although politically monarchy was the most common form of government, the commerce was of more benefit to the higher classes of their society. However, Tartessus did not possess a high degree of culture. The initial phoenician influence extended with the passage of time to the whole Southern part of Hispania. This influence gave rise especially to the acquisition of new technology in metalurgy, in ceramics, the introduction of new gods (Astarte), the usage of metals such as iron and food products such as oil and wine.

The influence of the Phoenicians in the West and the transfer of their culture was the result of commerce based on the exchange of all sorts of products for minerals, particularly silver and other metals, existing in abundance in ancient Tartessus. The Phoenicians came in search of gold, silver, iron and tin and brought in exchange not only leather articles, oil, wine and slaves but their new writing and their religious and funerary habits: they introduced cremation, the use of ceramics, new weapons such as shields, spears, the art of painting with various colors, gods and goddesses (Astarte, Tanit, Reshep, Baal, Melkart and the rituals of Adonis). In addition they brought new techniques for working on jewelry and ivory, the extraction of metals, the purple dye and even domesticated animals.

In addition the Phoenicians seem to have been the founders of Lisbon and although legend has it that Ulysses founded that city, historians disagree and assign its foundation to the Phoenicians.

The Phoenicians attempted to keep their competitors, the Greeks, away from their western domains in order to control their monopoly of gold, silver and copper. The location of the mines was at the mouth of the river, known years later as Guadalquivir.

They also established colonies in Malta and Sardinia and eventually they came in contact in the Italian peninsula with the Etruscans, with whom they developed lasting relations. Besides, they appeared to have had trading posts by the eight century BC in Ischia, western Sicily and probably in Capua at the time when this area was the main outlet of the Etruscans to the sea. They shared with the Etruscans their thirst for luxury and love for gold and silver. The Phoenicians bought silver from Asia Minor and copper from Cyprus, tin from Cornwall which they needed with copper to make bronze. The Etruscans imported initially wine and olive oil from Phoenicia. Later their own highly fertile volcanic soil was applied to the cultivation of the olive and vine. The Phoenicians helped the Etrurians acquire from them aesthetic ideas and learn the art of mining metals and also the art of working on gold. The rich Etruscans wanted gold from the Phoenicians in exchange for their copper and iron. They also bought from them ivory and especially glasswork.

But the greatest phoenician asset given to other Mediterranean cultures was the Alphabet that in the first place the Greeks, later the Etruscans and after them the Romans learned from them. The

Phoenician alphabet was to be used ever since by all people in the West.

The Phoenicians shared with the Etruscans somewhat the same attitude concerning the idea of an afterlife. Etruscan tombs were quite lavish and depicted on their walls scenes of festivity and banquets: to them death was nothing else than a perpetuation of life. Other characteristics that some writers have attributed to both Phoenicians and Etrurians included the idea, that they were cruel in war and lived luxuriously and extravagantly in peace times. The reality may lie somewhere in between. Furthermore they were accused of liking orgies and that their women were promiscuous. The fact of the matter is that the Phoenicians practiced to a certain extent, as discussed elsewhere, temple prostitution, a custom quite widespread through antiquity and since Egyptian times also observed in Phoenicia.

Examination of archeological finds between 1956-1964 AD in the Etruscan sanctuary of Pyrgi near the ancient port of Caere revealed a close relationship between Phoenicians and Etruscans: two temples were found dedicated to the goddessess Astarte-Uni and Apollo-Suri dating from the first half of the 6th century BC. Hidden near one of the temples three plaques in gold with Etruscan and Phoenician inscriptions, have been found: the main text, in parallel versions, was inscribed by orders of Thefarie Velianas, king of Caere. Sacred prostitution was apparently practiced here and more evidence of the relations between these two people has been located in Sardinia, which was mainly occupied by the Etruscans but also served as place of business for the Phoenicians.

It is to be noted that a millennium later, the African Canaanites (or Carthaginians) preferred to avoid war. but occasionally engaged in wars such as what they did during the battle of Alalia that took place in the Thyrrenian sea against the Greeks. As a result they achieved an alliance with the Etruscans, after which the Etruscans remained in control of Corsica. They possessed a gross rudimentary phoenician mythology that originated at Ugarit and was described by Philo of Byblos.

CIRCUMNAVIGATION OF AFRICA

The information that has come to us relates two trips made by the Phoenicians around Africa during ancient times: the first performed by the Eastern Phoenicians, commissioned by the pharaoh Nechos of the Twenty-Sixth Dynasty and the second one by the Carthaginians on their own, under the leadership of Hanno.

The first such trip would take the Phoenicians around Africa navigating southward from a starting point in the Red Sea that separates Egypt from the Arabian peninsula and would take almost three years to complete. They proceeded south and when running short of supplies would stop, plant crops that once collected would allow them to resume their navigation as soon as the conditions became favorable. They would turn around the southern part of the continent and head towards the pillars of Hercules (Herakles). Thus only during the third year after their original departure would they reach the entrance to the Mediterranean sea and return to Egypt. Considerable speculation was motivated by the Phoenicians navigators reporting the sunrise to their right during their voyage of return. Herodotus, who tells us the story, most probably was misled by the limited knowledge the Greeks of his time had of the geography of the Earth and the navigators assertion applied to this observation after having turned around the southern tip of the continent of Lybia, as it was known to them at the time.

The second trip, undertaken this time by the Carthaginians over a century later, would be in the opposite direction under the leadership of Hanno. This general, whose figure remains shrouded in secrecy, navigating westward, after passing the narrow Gibraltar strait (Heracles pillars) would head south to the lower end of Africa and return northward by way of the Indian Ocean. However, the recorded evidence indicates that such a trip was never completed. Some evidence suggests that Hanno never did quite navigate far enough to reach the southern end of Africa. He may have stopped about what is now Guinea and then returned along the western side of Africa to Gibraltar and back to Carthage.

Pliny the Elder in his NATURAL HISTORY (Book V, chapter I, pp. 223) when dealing with the exploration of the West coast of Africa, says that

"There were also extant some notes of the Carthaginian commander Hanno, who at the most flourishing period of the Punic state was ordered to explore the circuit of Africa. It is Hanno whom the majority of the Greek and Roman writers have followed in the accounts that they have published of a number of cities founded by him there, of which no memory or trace exists, not to speak of other fabulous stories".

Hanno's notes referred to here were written in Punic and are still extant in a Greek translation. We transcribe them here based on the extant Greek version.

THE PERIPLUS OF HANNO, GENERAL OF CARTHAGE

Along the Western coasts of Lybia, beyond the Pillars of Hercules, document deposited by himself in the temple of Kronus (Saturn).

"The Carthaginians ordered Hanno to navigate beyond the Pillars of Hercules, and to found new Lybio-phoenician cities. Hanno was heading a fleet of sixty ships, containing 30.000 people, both men and women, food and other necessary provisions."

"After having navigated during two days beyond the Pillars of Hercules, we founded the town of Thymiaterium, overlooking a vast plain. From Thymiaterium and always navigating westward we found a promontory of Lybia named Soloe, covered by heavy woods: we there and then erected an altar to Poseidon (Neptune)."

"From the Cape Soloe, after navigating half a day towards the East, we arrived to a small lake near the sea. It was full of large trees and we saw a large number of elephants and other wild animals on the shores." This is most likely Cape Spartel.

The Periplus was most likely not published as an inscription or on a tablet and the text that has come to us is likely an abstract of what the Carthaginian general described. It is not the original text written by Hanno or a copy of a Carthaginian inscription but most likely a free version in Greek, modified over the years by other writers and commentators. The extant copy in Greek was probably modified over the years by numerous scribes.

"After another day of navigation beyond this lake, we founded several cities next to the sea: Caricus murus, Gitte, Acra, Melitta and Arambys. Following our route we arrived to the large river Lixus, that comes down from Lybia. The Lixite nomads fed their animals on the shores of the river. We stayed among them for awhile and established friendship with them. Above this people and in the interior of the land live wild Ethiopians, whose country is full of wild animals, contains high mountains where the Lixus river appears to take origin, according to the information we received. They added that in these mountains live Troglodytes, extraordinary men, capable of running at great speed, greater than the speed of horses."

"After having taken interpreters from the Lixites, we followed during two days, an uninhabited coast. Then Then going East during one more day of navigation, we found within some sort of a gulf, a little island that we named Cerne, in which we established a colony.

In Cerne we compared the route that we had done since our departure and following a straight line we reached the conclusion that this island was located, opposite to Carthage, in relation to the pillars of Hercules, because our navigation in days from Carthage to the Pillars and from the latter to Cerne, were similar."

The precise location of Cerne has been the topic of considerable controversy among the ancient writers: given the fact that it seems the only visitors to this island were Hanno and Polybius it is likely that this is most probably the small island of Fedal: Hanno chose to stay there despite its little size (about one kilometer in diameter) because it offered a secure place to stay slightly away from the continent. There is a precedent for this: the Phoenicians founded Cadiz at a short distance from continental Europe and at the end of a peninsula to be safe despite the fact that they had to go far to collect potable water for their needs; this is also true of Tyre that was re-founded on an island a little away from the continent in order to avoid the constant harassement of the people from the neighbouring areas.

Polybius placed Cerne facing the Atlas mountains: this is of no help considering that most of the African coast from the entrance beyond the Pillars exhibits high mountains detached from the main peaks of the Atlas. Hanno placed it at the same distance because it took him the same amount of time to go from Carthage to the Pillars of Hercules and from there to Cerne, despite the different navigational situation and for lack of better or more exact measurements other than days of navigation.

And now let us get back to Hanno's description:

"From Cerne we traversed the mouth of a great river named Chretes, and we arrived to another small lake which contained three small islands, each one larger, however, than Cerne. We went across this small lake after one day of navigation. Here the lake was surrounded by high mountains and inhabitated by savages,wild men, dressed with skins of beasts. They attacked us with large stones and forced us to retreat. Following this incident we entered into another great river, large and wide, full of crocodiles and hyppopotamuses. From there we returned to Cerne' and from......"

Some writers have attempted to explain this portion of Hanno's voyage taking him to Senegal and returning later to Cerne. There is no need for such trip since most large African rivers at that time contained large animals that modern civilization has brought to almost total extinction. Some writers consider the big river Chretes as the Senegal and place Cerne near the mouth of this river.

"From Cerne we continued south for almost twelve days along the African coast inhabited by Ethiopians that appeared frightened by our presence and would escape when we attempted to approach them. The language of this people could not be understood by our Lixite interpreters."

The African coast described here corresponds to that of the kingdom of Morocco, whose inhabitants are dark-skinned: ancient writers would call Ethiopians most individuals with dark skin either brown or black. That was occasionally the case with Indians or other people from Asia.

"The twelfth day we arrived to big mountains covered by very large odoriferous trees of various colors. We spend two more days to turn the cape formed by these mountains and found ourselves within an immense gulf that ended in a large plain. During the nights we could see along the coast a great number of fires, both large and small. After changing and providing ourselves with new water reserves, we followed for five more days along the coast of this gulf."

The high mountains described here are those of Cape Verde where the peak of the Atlas mountain ends in abrupt fashion and makes navigation sometimes hazardous and the gulf that follows that was named centuries later by the Portuguese navigators Sainte-Croix could have been the mouth of the Gambia river. Leo, the African, designated it with the name of Garguessem, and described it as surrounded by an extremely fertile territory.

"Continuing our trip, we soon arrived to another large gulf: the cape at its entrance was named by our interpreters, the Horn of the West. This gulf contained a large island and within it a salt water lake with a smaller island inside. We descended here. During the day we perceived that the fires observed at night were contained in the forest and were brilliant at night, we heard a large number number of noisy sounds of flutes, cymbals and drums, mixed to the frightened noise of the local inhabitants, obviously scared by our presence."

"We in turn became quite concerned and decided to leave the place as quickly as possible. We continued along a coast full of odors and burning fires, and we could see torrents of fire that precipitated themselves into the sea. The land was so hot and burning to the point that we could no longer tolerate the heat of the sand in our own feet. We left this place as soon as we could and during four more days of navigation, the land seemed to us covered by flames all night long. In the middle of this fire we perceived a much larger one, which seemed to reach up to the stars: but during the day we could only see a high mountain known as Theon Ochema or the Chariot of the Gods. After having passed these torrents of fire, we navigated three days and arrived to another Cape which formed the entrance to another gulf: we named this cape The Horn of the South."

The Carthaginian Admiral, after passing the gulf named years later by the Portuguese navigators Saint-Croix, arrived to its end: the Cape of Agulon. The new gulf found immediately after is located between the Cape of Agulon and the Cape of Nun, bordered by mountains along the coast after the little river named Sus. The island with the small salt water lake was probably just low-land covered by the sea. The nocturnal fires were probably signals sent by the natives to each other to let them know of the presence of foreigners with large numbers of ships, exploring their land which naturally terrified them. Concerning the extreme heat of the sand next to the continent described by Hanno where no one could rest their feet, probably never existed and this was added more recently by the Greeks and belong to the fables added by these writers to the classic description of Hanno. According to Pliny (NATURAL HISTORY: Book V, Chapter 1 and Book VI, Chapter 35) who wrote about the surroundings of Theon Ochema, instead of describing it as uninhabitable, Pliny says on the contrary that he observed "hills covered by enchanted trees, typical of the southern extreme of the mount Atlas". It is however impossible today to ascertain if an old volcano, now extinguished, ever existed there in that part of Africa. Some writers adopt the view that Hanno saw the Camerun mountains up to 13,500 feet that contain a high volcano, more closely resembling the **Chariot of the Gods**. The Carthaginians, however, were quite familiar since ancient times, with the eruptions of the Etna in Sicily, and would hardly be frightened by the view of a new volcanic eruption.

Let us continue with Hanno:

"Within this gulf existed another island similar to the previous one. It contained a lake within which another island was located: this one was inhabitated by ferocious beings: the females were more numerous than the males: they had hairy bodies and our interpreters named them Gorillas. We could not catch any male because they could escape between the precipices and defended themselves by throwing stones. But we were succesful at capturing three females: they were dificult to maintain prisoner: would bite and break their liens. We decided to sacrifice them and bring their skins back to Carthage. Because of our lack of provisions we decided to discontinue navigating any farther." Here ends the description of Hanno's Periplus.

Following Cape Nun it is believed that Hanno stopped next to the river of the same name: the wild people he describes were probably Orang-gutans that he thought were humans, because they lived in small groups, giving the appearance of primitive societies. They would occasionally defend themselves by throwing stones and were used to fight back when confronted by foreigners. It is thought that Hanno did not go beyond this point: with the ancient instruments and large numbers of people and ships, his, was a great accomplishement for his time. Two thousand years had to pass before Portuguese navigators would succeed in going around Africa to India.

PHOENICIANS IN AMERICA (800 BC)

"He who understands how, may himself obtain information about hidden truths"
(Phoenician proverb, translation of Barry Fell)

This is an Iberian inscription found in 1838 AD, at a depth of 60 feet in a burial mound at Grave Creek, West Virginia. (The language of the tablet is Punic (Phoenician), written in the Iberian alphabet used in Spain during the 1st millennium BC. Several other artifacts with inscriptions in stone have been found in Maine, New Hampshire, Vermont and Rhode Island. One of the oldest inscriptions collected in the USA exists today only as a latex mold obtained at Manana Island, near Monhegan Island, 10 miles from the coast of Maine that reads from right to left:

L NG B T B FNC C D H H L B D, to be translated
"Ships from Phoenicia, cargo platform.."

This is recognized now as a variety of the script used by Phoenician speakers in Southern Spain during the 1st millennium BC. Scholars such as James Whittall and Barry Fell visited a location where multiple caves existed, some of them with inscriptions, in North Salem, New Hampshire, now known as Mystery Hill. There exists here a complex of stone-slab chambers and associated henge stones oriented according to the sun setting behind certain stones on the days of the equinox and the summer and winter solstices. Some chambers contained massive stones such as the one known as **The Table of Sacrifice**. This one is somewhat reminiscent of similar stones found at Byblos and still visible today in that city, the ancient capital city-state of Phoenicia. In Cambridge, MA, samples obtained between 1960-1971 have been examined with radio-carbon determinations of charcoal samples obtained at **Mystery Hill** which indicate that the site was occupied towards the 2d millennium BC. An examination of the site disclosed one of the chambers that seems to have been dedicated to the Phoenician god Baal. One of James Whittall's most important finds was a triangular dedication tablet in what may have been a winter solstice noon observatory. The tablet contains an inscription in Iberian Punic script that translates from right to left:

"To Baal of the Canaanites (Phoenicians), this in dedication".

Soon these and other scholars have found dozens of similar inscriptions in central Vermont that indicate that Phoenician mariners were frequent visitors and were welcome to worship and allowed to make dedications in their own language. The antiquity of Mystery Hill has been now dated to 800-600 BC based on the style of the Phoenician inscriptions found. The available evidence indicates that

Phoenicians sailors were visitors to these sites in New England and were allowed to conduct affairs of their own.

The Iberians and the Celts in ancient times kept warring among themselves and according to Diodorus Siculus (THE LIBRARY OF HISTORY, Book V: 32-36) eventually made peace and by intermarriage became known as Celtiberians. From iron in their mines they learned to develop and use steel for their daily utensils and their weapons. They were careful and clean in their ways of life with one single bizarre exception: they consistently used their own urine to bathe the body and wash their teeth, under the belief that this custom helped maintain the care and healing of the body.

"Towards malefactors and enemies the Celtiberians are cruel, but towards strangers they are honourable and humane......The most valiant among the Celtiberians are the Lusitanians who are able to protect their bodies in battle unusually well......but when it comes to enduring the hardships of a stiff fight they are inferior to the Celtiberians."

The silver mines of the Celtiberians are the most abundant and most excellent known sources of silver and from it they obtain great revenues. Diodorus tell us of a great fire in the Pyrenees mountains that extended between the Mediterranean and the Atlantic sea and that "raged continously day after day and the surface of the earth thus rendered the land rich in iron with the melted byproduct from which were formed many streams of pure silver. Since the natives were ignorant of the of the use of silver, the Phoenicians, as they pursued their commercial enterprises, purchased the silver in exchange for wares of little if any worth. By transporting this silver to Greece and Asia and to all other peoples, the Phoenicians acquired great wealth. The results was that the Phoenicians, in the course of many years prospered greatly,…and founded many colonies in Sicily, Sardinia, Lybia and Iberia."

Eventually the Celtiberians "having come to know the peculiar qualities possesed by silver, sunk notable mines, and by working the most excellent and abundant silver to be found, they received great revenues".

By the 8th century BC the Phoenicians had come to the area of the Guadalquivir river in Andalusia in Spain where silver mines were abundant. They had established trade with the native miners who most likely were Celtiberians or Basques. The region was named in Greek Tartessus and appears to have been forgotten for almost two-three centuries. This was so because the Phoenicians since their initial exploration of the West, which included the foundation of Cadiz, kept secret their marine routes in order to carry on their business without competition, especially from the Greeks. The language spoken has now been translated and accepted as a dialect of Phoenician. The first Tartessian inscription discovered in America is engraved on a rock on the seashore of Mount Hope Bay, in Bristol, Rhode Island. It was discovered in 1780 but forgotten and even lost for a certain time: it has been vandalized and distorted with graffiti but an unretouched photograph of the original was preserved by Whittall and can be read in Tartessian Punic:

The Phoenicians in History and Legend

"Voyagers from Tarshish, this stone proclaims".

It thus appears that the inscription may have been made by merchants arriving periodically in New England such as the Phoenicians who have left inscriptions in Monhegan Island, off the coast of Maine. This business probably went on for a couple of centuries: this is illustrated by letters from the traders that have been written on metal sheets in elegant style and signed by the partners with a different and less elaborate style.

It is well known that when access to the Mediterranean markets in Eastern Phoenicia became limited, especially by the Greek competition, they used their recognized expertise as mariners and passing the Pillars of Hercules, kept secret their routes of commerce with the West, obtained copper and tin to make bronze; supplied these materials to Britain and Gaul and brought fur and leather that they appear also to have exported as far east as India.

Finally one the most remarkable finds proving the existence of numerous travelers from Phoenicia and Carthage to America was found in the excavations of the ancient Mayan city of Comalcalco, located on the coast of Tabasco. Here the Mexican archeologist Ponciano Salazar carried out excavations under control of the National Institute of Anthropology and History of Mexico and together with numerous artifacts he found what has been determined to be an ancient Carthaginian calendar dating to the end of the first millennium BC or beginning of the first AD: the calendar shows 12 succesive full moons, each moon matching 4 subdivisions (weeks of 7 days) but instead of 48 weeks the calendar consists of 50 weeks. Each month is designated, from right to the left, with the initial letter of the name of the month in the Neopunic alphabet, beginning with the month of Tishrin, at the September equinox. It contains the 12 months in the following order: Heshvan, Kislev,…Adar,…Nisan,…Iyar,…Tammuz,…Eb,…and Eilul. Some of these names are still preserved in current use in the Arabic language spoken today.

During the last quarter of the 20th century, puzzling ancient inscriptions have been found in the Eastern parts of the United States, Canada and Ibero-America. The inscriptions are written in ancient Mediterranean and European languages using alphabets dating back far over three millennia. These inscriptions speak of the presence of Celts, Basques and Phoenicians, in America. About three thousand years ago Celtic mariners appear to have crossed the North Atlantic Ocean and colonized North American sites. They came from Spain and Portugal via the Canary Islands taking advantage of the course of the winds from from the East to the West. Following them came the Phoenician traders from Cadiz and Andalusia who spoke the Punic tongue and used the Punico-Iberican script. Basques and Lybian visitors came to Pensylvannia, reached the gulfs of the St Lawrence river and gulf of Mexico, became intermixed with the Amerindian tribes and taught them the ancient tongues of Phoenicia and North Africa. The Celtiberians settled near the mouth of the rivers of New England from Maine, Vermont and New Hampshire to Conneticut.

Until recently, all Amerindian languages have been considered as indigenous products of the New World and the abundant Phoenician, Carthaginian and Old World elements of their vocabularies have passed undetected. However, the findings of numerous inscriptions and artifacts in Arkansas, Oklahoma and Colorado have led scholars during the past two decades, with the help of the American Epigraphic Society, to study the ancient inscriptions and pictorial representations. This material has led to the conclusion that Celts in America practiced Phallic cults that had dissappeared from Europe with the advent of Christianity. An American inscription engraved in a stone tablet was found buried 60 feet into the ground at Grave Creek, West Virginia. The inscription was written in Punic (Phoenician), the form of the alphabet used in Spain during the first millenium BC. The alphabet of the tablet was deciphered by Spanish scholars. The Grave Creek inscription has been published by the Epigraphic Society. The inscription was most likely a part of a longer astrological document. The different American inscriptions found throughout have been translated with the help of European scholars and range from the language spoken at Tartessus in Southern Spain to the Celtiberian and Punic of Carthage.

More inscriptions were eventually found by Barry Fell and James Whittall in Mystery Hill, New Hampshire, as mentioned earlier, dedicated in Celtic Ogam to the god Bel, the sun god of the Celts, long suspected to be the Phoenician Baal. Dozens of inscriptions were further found in central Vermont: it became clear that Phoenician mariners had been welcome visitors to this area, permited to worship in the Celtic sanctuaries and allowed to make dedications in their native tongue. The style of their inscriptions suggests that they had visited the area between 800-600 BC.

Some scholars have argued, after translations of some of the Tartessian inscriptions found in America, that it is highly probable that the American Celts were brought here by the Phoenicians who wanted to interest them in mining the American natural resources for their own profit.

The periodic arrival of Phoenician ships on the New England coast is attested by Ogam inscriptions on Monhegan Island, off the coast of Maine. Commercial transactions have been found described in metal sheets showing descriptions of ships traveling from Tarshish, Spain to Italy. They are written usually in Phoenician mixed with Greek vowels, similar to other inscriptions of a religious character dedicated to Astarte in gold laminae, dating back to 500 BC, found in the Etruscan country, described elsewhere here.

The men from Tarshish that came to eastern North America comprised Celts, Basques and Phoenicians. They brought a language that represented the Tartessian manner of writing Phoenician. The oldest and first authenticated find of an engraved Phoenician tablet in an American archeological site was a Tartessian inscription found in 1838. This tablet was excavated from a burial chamber at the base of Mammoth Mound in Moundville, West Virginia. This historic tablet was named tablet of Tasach, inscribed in the Phoenician Punic tongue used in Iberia. Other inscriptrions include the Pontotoc stele, found in Oklahoma, that depicts the Sun rays descending upon the Earth: to the left of it the Iberian Punic letters spell "Start of Dawn" and to the right "Dusk". To the right of the stele there is a crescent-shape of the Moon. The American version is believed to date to about 800 BC. In Ogam script, typical of Celtiberians, there is also a segment of the Hymn to Aton, dating to the pharaoh Akhenaton times (13th century BC), reading partially:

"When Baal-Ra rises in the east the beasts are content and when he hides they are displeased".

Phoenician (Punic) colonists left also inscriptions found in Davenport, Iowa, that took 60 years to translate, once it was realized they were written in Iberian Punic. The Tartessian inscriptions of Andalusian texts and those found in Virginia and Ohio were for a longtime considered to represent an unknown language. Just a quarter of a century ago these inscriptions have been found to be reading from right to left in Phoenician characters a Creation story. Several inscriptions found in Pennsylvania and in the Southwest, among the Pima Indiasns, also record the Creation of the Earth, the Sun and the Moon in Iberian Punic. A comparison made by B. Fell of the scripts used about 800 BC in Phoenicia proper with the ones used by Phoenician settlers in Spain and those of the Phoenician colonists of Iowa, reveals an almost identical alphabet. The Pima Indians also described the Creation of the Earth, Sun and Moon in their inscriptions and have kept a verbal tradition about these events, as well.

A location with religious connotations was found at South Woodstock, Vermont: it consists of a temple to the Celtic goddess BYN. It is oriented in such way that the sunrise on December 21-23 is seen only by a person standing at the altar. The motion of the sun is relatively slow at the time of the solstice but for the equinocial times it moves faster and the sun is seen only on one day.

In the ceiling of this temple the idealized figure of the godess of fertility Tannit, from Sarepta, Phoenicia, which was adopted by Carthage is clearly depicted. Ten miles to the north of the temple another representation in the form of a stylized Phoenician symbol of Tannit was found. The suggestion has been made that this temple was visited by Celts and Phoenician visitors from Tartessus who had sailed up the Conneticut River to trade in the Woodstock area. Another image of Tannit was found carved on the Cimarron cliffs of Oklahoma that was identified as Iberian Punic script.

CHAPTER EIGHT

MESOPOTAMIA & ASSYRIA

The Mesopotamians were the originators of the legends about the flood and about the creation of the world that were eventually accepted in the West. The Akkadian cuneiform system of writing, invented by them, became the **"lingua franca"** which was used to transmit a great deal of ancient knowledge, now well known in the West. Phoenicia, located between Egypt and Mesopotamia, since the 3d millennium, felt by pressure the influence of both countries and cultures. The phoenician city states used their own products through extensive trade and this was often the reason why foreign powers such as the Mesopotamians not only desired but on many occasions attempted to take by force anything they liked. In addition, they would threat their inhabitants with deportation unless they paid heavy taxation. This would allow their conquerors to get the phoenician riches. However no military pressure was used until the power of the Egyptians and Hittites empires declined.

Ashurnasirpal, Shalmanesser III, Tiglath Pileser III, Sennacherib, Ezzar'Haddon and Nebuchadnezzar all came to Phoenicia in their campaigns between the 11th and the 6th century BC until the fall of Niniveh in 612. The main objective in their conquests was financial:

they accomplished this successfully by dominating most of the city-states of Phoenicia at one time or another and demanding tributes that included not only gold and silver, precious stones, ivory and ebony but, from time to time, the wives and children as well as the palace personnel serving the local kings of the city-states. They also occasionally destroy the places if any resistance was offered. Finally in 538 BC the Babylonian empire collapsed and power was taken by the Persians.

Tiglath-Pileser I (1114-1076 BC) claims to be the first invader of Phoenician territory and collected tribute from the coastal city-states before returning to Assyria. The next incursion of the Assyrians would not take place until Ashurnasirpal the II came in 877 BC and then, after claiming to have cleansed his weapons in the Mediterranean sea, also collected considerable tribute from the coastal city-states, especially Tyre, Sidon, Byblus, Aradus and other smaller localities. Most of the inhabitants gave him gold, silver, tin, copper, linen, ivory, ebony and even monkeys. He returned to his country and does not appear to have come back.

The son and successor of Ashurnasirpal, Shalmanaser the III, (858-824) came back to visit the land of the "twelve kings by the sea" and at Nahar-el-Kalb, it is believed, he left a stele describing his conquests which has been erased by time and can no longer be seen. The most important battle that he fought was at Karkar, against the Aramean coalition of states, including Ben-Haddad of Damascus and Ahab, king of Israel, which at the time was under Syrian control. The results of the battle were indecisive but the Aramean king was weakened considerably. Thus Ahab revolted against him and was killed in battle. Celebrating the death of Ahab and disintegration of Israel, Mesha, king of Moab, left the well known inscription on the Moabite stone: the script resembles the Phoenician script of the sarcophagus of Ahiram of Byblos. Its text has been briefly translated in another part of this writing. Shalmanaser however returned later on the 21th year of his reign on 842 BC and received nominal submission of the Phoenician cities. This he described as follows:

"In the eighteenth year of my reign I crossed the Euphrates for the 16th time...Countless cities I destroyed, I devastated, and burned with fire. Their spoils, I carried off...I then received tribute from the people of Byblos, Tyre and Sidon."

After his death the conquered lands revolted and became again independent. His successors fought among them for control of his kingdom and although the Phoenician cities paid tribute they were allowed to continue with their commerce. Tyre seems to have prospered considerably thus becoming the principal city of Phoenicia.

Not until 744 BC a powerful figure emerged in Assyria, Tiglath Pileser the III, who decided to reconquer, unify and consolidate his empire. He appears to have come to Byblos and received tributes from Shipit-Baal around 740 BC. His main policy consisted in the deportation of people from one area to another, dispersion of ethnic and religious groups in such a way as to avoid their re-unification, and thus he was successful in achieving centralization of his government. The policy of deportation affected especially the people of Israel and Palestine but did not affect the Phoenicians.

This situation remained unchanged until the advent of Sennacherib (704-681) who attacked and defeated Egypt and Sidon. In this instance, the king of Sidon fled to save his life. He was then replaced by Ethbaal who did not refuse to pay tribute and his example was followed by Byblos and Aradus. Generally Byblos followed a policy of paying tribute but continued to remain free to carry on their commerce.

The next Assyrian king who came to Phoenicia was Ezzar'Haddon (680-669 BC). He first attacked Abdi-Milkutte of Sidon and executed him after he lost a battle. Ezzar'haddon then deported the inhabitants of Sidon to Assyria to do forced labor in the construction of his royal palace. The measure motivated the submission of the other city states that fearing deportation decided not to to resist and fight. Ezzar'haddon easily took all the Mediterranean states from the Hittite territory to Egypt advancing all the way to Memphis. He sent a considerable amount of cedar wood to Niniveh to build his palaces using the deported population of the Mediterranean coast and Cyprus as laborers. He left one of the extant stelae on the mouth of the Dog river detailing the extent of his conquests and even explaining that he deported from Egypt physicians, divination experts, smiths of all sorts and plundered the contents of the royal palaces.

The Phoenicians in History and Legend

This is one of the few stele legible today beside one of three left by Ramessess the II.

But Ezzar'Haddon died and the year following his death the Egyptian king Taharka revolted, forcing his successor Ashurbanipal (668-633 BC) to undertake another campaign against Egypt using ships and materiel from Phoenicia vassal states. He conquered not only Tyre but Byblos and Aradus. Although initially the Assyrian kings treated the Phoenician cities mildly they gradually became more demanding, tyrannical and cruel. Finally the combined attacks of Persians and Babylonians led to the collapse of the Assyrian empire with the fall of Niniveh in 612 BC. Now the Phoenicians regained their independence without revolt. But this was a short lasting event because Babylon soon claimed control of the prior Assyrian possessions.

At this point in history Babylon on one side and Egypt on the other, were in a position to claim control of the coastal city-states. (Herodotus, HISTORIES: 4:1; 2:157; & 4:42).

In 605 BC Nebuchadnezzar, son of the king of Babylon, led his army against Egypt which was governed by Nechos, the pharaoh who commissioned the circumnavigation of Africa, by the Phoenicians. The army of Necchos faced the Babylonians at Karkemish on the Euphrates and was soundly defeated by Nebuchadnezzar who pursued the pharaoh all the way to Egypt but, unfortunately for him, at this moment he received the news that his father had died back home. Thus he returned in a hurry to Babylon because the problem of succession to the throne of his father was now under dispute.

Having experienced the strenght and power of the Babylonian army, Egypt now sought allies in Phoenicia and Judea and encouraged an alliance between Tyre and its neighbors under the leadership of Ithobaal, King of Tyre. They revolted against the Babylonian Nebuchadnezzar but he returned and victory after victory submitted the revolted city-states. Although Tyre resisted a siege that lasted 13 years, one of the longest in recorded history, before they finally capitulated. Nebuchadnezzar left at least two stelae speaking of his campaigns: one at the source of the Orontes river in northern Phoenicia and the other at the mouth of the Dog River near Beirut. Craftmen from Byblos seem to have been working for Nebuchadnezzar during his building of the royal palaces in Babylon mainly of cedar wood brought from Phoenicia and transported along difficult roads all the way to the Euphrates along which it would be sent to Babylon.

In Sidon, where Assyrians and Babylonians remained for several centuries and where they used to have their place of retirement and vacations, many sarcophagii with phoenician inscriptions were unearthed during the beginning of the 20th century AD and now repose in several Museums around Europe. They are of interest not only because they are a reflection of the riches of their occupants and opulent way of life but because of their numerous interesting inscriptions revealing the evolution of the Phoenician language. Several examples are given here:

Phoenician inscription on the sarcophagus of King TABNIT (end of 6th century BC.) Istambul Museum.

"I, Tabnit, priest of Astarte, king of Sidon, the son of Eshmun'azzar,...am lying in this sarcophagus. DO NOT, whoever you are, do not open this sarcophagus and disturb me, for no silver, gold or jewelry has been given me. Only I am lying in this sarcophagus. DO NOT OPEN IT and do not disturb me, for such a thing would be an abomination to Astarte. But if you do open it......MAY YOU NOT have any seed among the living under the sun and no resting place under the shades".

Inscription on the Sarcophagus of ESHMUN' AZZAR from Sidon (now in the Louvre Museum, 22 lines of text in Phoenician, the longest in existence): photo from the Louvre Museum, Paris, year 2000.

"...In the year 14 of the reign of Eshmun'azar, king of Sidon, the son of king Tabnit, spoke as follows: I have been snatched away before my time, the son of a number of restricted days......I am lying in this casket and this grave, in a place which I myself built. Whoever you are, ruler or ordinary man, you may not open this resting place and search in it for anything....................for any ruler or any man who shall open this resting place......and carry me away...may he not have a resting place within the shades nor he be buried in a grave and may he not have a son and seed to take their place, and may the holy gods abandon him...for I Eshmun'azar, king of Sidon, the son of king Tabnit, king of Sidon, and grandson of Esmun'azar, king of Sidon......We are the ones who built houses for the gods of Sidon in Sidon-by-the-sea, houses for the Lord of Sidon Ba'al and Astarte......the gods gave us the lands of Dor and Joppa, the mighty lands of Dagon, which are in the plains of Sharon,...for the important deeds which I did. We added them to the borders of the country so that they would belong to Sidon forever......"

Inscription on the stele of YEHAWMILK, found in Byblos ~ 4th-5th century BC (Museum of Louvre).

"I am Yehawmilk, king of Byblos, son of Yeharba'al, grandson of Urimilk, whom the Lady of Byblos made King...I have made for my mistress, the Lady of Byblos, this altar of bronze...I Yehawmilk made this temple for my mistress the Lady of Byblos...I have called my mistress, the Lady of Byblos...She heard my voice and treated me kindly. May the Lady of Byblos bless and preserve Yehawmilk and prolong his days and years for he is a righteous king. May the Lady of Byblos favor him in the eyes of the gods and in the eyes of his people. If any ruler or ordinary man may continue to do work on this altar, this engraved work of gold and this portico, his name should be placed next to mine, Yehawmilk, king of Byblos…If you do not put my name with yours or if you remove the temple from its place…may my mistress, the Lady of Byblos, destroy you and your seed before all the gods of Byblos".

CHAPTER NINE

THE PERSIANS

For about two centuries the Persians dominated Phoenicia, starting with Cyrus (550-530 BC) who was followed by Cambyses, Darius, Xerxes and Artaxerxes.

From Sidon during the Persian period we have the coinage of the fifth and fourth century BC and the temple of Eshmun. From Byblos we have the reconstruction of the Temple of Ba'alath and the well-known inscription on the stele of Yehawmilk describing the changes in the Temple. Tyre seems to have occupied a position secondary to that of Sidon during this period.

When Cyrus felt secure in the throne of Persia he looked to the West and decided to expand beyond Asia Minor. He decided to march through one thousand miles of lands that where mostly under the control of Babylonia to face the existing alliance between the kings of Lydia and Babylon as well as the pharaoh Ahkmose II of the 26th Dynasty: he took Sardis in 546 BC and entered Babylon in 538 BC. He issued orders to protect the Temples as well as personal properties. During Cyrus campaings his armed forces were engaged in the northeast and the Phoenicians remained relatively independent. Regarding this Herodotus says:

"Among the Ionians only the Milesians were sheltered from danger for they had made a treaty with the Persians, thus the islanders had nothing to fear; for the Phoenicians were not yet subjects of the Persians nor were the Persians shipmen. The people of Asia were then cut off from the rest of the Ionians......The whole Hellenic race was then but small...and the least well regarded was the Ionian stock, because except Athens they had no other great city". The Egyptians also were still unconquered.

In 529 BC Cyrus died and his son Cambyses succeeded him. Cambyses needed the the help of the Phoenician city-states, with ships and crews, if he wanted to face and conquer Ahkmose the II, who in the meantime had taken possesion of Cyprus from the Phoenicians, thus adding greater strenght to his naval forces with the Cypriots on his side. He struck a deal with them in which the city-states placed their naval forces under the Persian king while he allowed them to continue with their own affairs and free to keep their own kings.

Thus the Phoenician participation with their naval fleet under Cambyses was done as alliance, not as servants. The Persian fleet according to Herodotus (HISTORIES; III: 17-20), was greatly strengthened by the Phoenicians, whose kings commanded their own ships.

Herodotus states:

"Cambyses planned three expeditions, first against the Carthaginians (now a naval power on their own, although descendants of Eastern Phoenicians). He would send a part of his fleet, against the long-lived Ethiopians, under the pretext of bearing gifts for the Ethiopian King, he first would send spies who spoke the language to see what truth there was in the story of the existence of a Table of the Sun, where meat was preserved and served for all those who needed to eat, and the third part of his army against the Ammonians".

While this was taking place the Persian King directed "his fleet against the Carthaginians. But the Phoenicians would not consent; for they said they were bound by a strict treaty, and could not righteously attack their own sons; and the Phoenicians being unwilling, the rest were of no account as fighters. Thus the Carthaginians escaped from being enslaved by the Persians; for Cambyses would not use force with the Phoenicians, seeing that they had willingly joined the Persians and the whole fleet drew its strenght from them".

The kings of Byblos since the 4th century BC were free to mint their own coins using their alphabetic letters. In the stele of Yehawmilk the king is dressed in Persian attire and similar apparel is seen on the coins from Sidon. The Persian king had a royal residence and a park (**paradeisos**) in Sidon. (Diodorus:16,41). Also as Diodorus tells us Tyre, Aradus and Sidon founded the city of Tripolis by the 4th century BC.

Following Cambyses' demise in 521 BC, Darius came to power. He intended to expand his empire and first put his eyes on Greece. At the beginning of his reign he developed an extensive system of communications by creating trade routes in the form of royal highways connecting many regions of the empire.

Darius feared that within his vast empire the more distant provinces may rebel, thus he created a system of satrapies, a total of twenty, to divide power and collect revenues from Asia all the way to India. The Persians themselves were free of taxation and the Arabians because they let Cambyses pass through their country on his way to the conquest of Egypt. As time went on Darius also collected from the islands and the dwellers in Europe as far as Thessaly. Phoenicia was united with Syria, Cyprus and Palestine as the fifth satrapy which was taxed lower than other regions. Under his rule a vast administrative system was developed. The Phoenician cities benefited by these trade routes that were safe and convenient means of transportation.

Darius also established a general coinage system throughout the empire. The coins were first made of gold of the greatest possible purity although crudely manufactured. Later silver coinage was minted especially by the governor Aryandes of Egypt. In Phoenicia this is the time that Yehawmilk of Byblos started costly reconstruction and remodeling of the Temple of Ba'alath. The distinctive Phoenician coinage started in the middle of the 5th century at Tyre while Sidon and Byblos followed somewhat later. Despite the conquest of several islands of the coast of Asia Minor and the establishment of a Persian satrap in Lydia, two Greek tyrants interrupted the peace by creating a rebellion against Darius power. Darius requested from the Phoenicians the assembly of a fleet of ships that transported troops from Cilicia to Cyprus and anchored them in the bay opposite Salamis: This was the first naval encounter between Phoenician and Greeks and ended with a defeat of the Phoenicians but the Greeks lost the land battle to the Persians. Darius then proceeded from the conquest of Cyprus to attack Ionia. While the Phoenicians began to enjoy a period of peace, Darius now wanted to add Greece to his large empire. During the three generations comprising the reigns of Darius, his son Xerxes and his grandson Artaxerxes, Greece suffered more misery than in the twenty generations before Darius was born. He marched though Thrace and Macedonia with his mind set to punish Athens.

According to Herodotus (III: 136) Darius had already sent an exploratory expedition under the direction of a Greek physician, allied with the Persians, departing from Sidon, to explore the conditions along the coast of Greece all the way to Taras in Italy. The Phoenicians supported the enterprise because the Greeks were already their contenders in trade around the Mediterranean basin. Under the Persian general Mardonius in 492 BC the Greeks suffered heavy loses when their ship were destroyed in the naval battle of 494 BC near

Miletus. With six hundred Phoenician and Cypriote ships, the Persians defeated the Ionians and the Phoenicians conquered other islands of the Aegean Sea. According to Herodotus, "the Persian fleet spent the winter at Miletus. The following year it put again to sea and without difficulty took the islands off the Asian coast including Lesbos....The Persians also took the Ionian towns on the mainland...The threats which the Persian commanders had uttered against the Ionians were now carried into effect: the best-looking boys were chosen for castration and made into eunuchs; the most beautiful girls were dragged from their homes and sent to Darius' court, and the towns themselves burnt to the ground including their Temples. He then proceeded to take all the places on the European side of the Hellespont. The people of Byzantium instead of awaiting the attack of the Phoenicians by sea, abandoned their home and fled to the Black Sea coast where they established themselves. The Phoenicians after destroying by fire the places they had taken only left intact Cyzicus, for the people of this town had already submitted to Darius. Until this period the man in absolute power was Miltiades, the son of Cimon. When he heard that the Phoenicians were in the neighborhood he decided to head for Athens after shipping his personal property. He sailed down the Black Sea but was met by the Phoenicians. He managed to escape but his oldest son, Metiochus, was captured and taken to Darius, for the Phonicians thought they had caught a great prize. But Darius, the king, treated him with great liberality and far from doing to him any harm, Darius presented him with a house, a property and a Persian wife, by whom he had children, who lived like

Persians. His father Miltiades, in the meantime, had reached Athens safely……"

The following spring Darius superseding all his senior generals sent Mardonius, a young man who had recently married one of Darius daughters, in charge of a large contingent of troops, both military and naval, under his command along the coast. He reached Cilicia and continued with his army by ship along the coast with the fleet towards the Hellespont. When he arrived in Ionia he astonished everyone: he suppressed the despots of all the Ionian states and set up democratic institutions in their place. From the Hellespont he began his march through Europe with Athens as his main objective. He then took Thasos and Macedonia and added them to Darius' empire. However in attempting to pass around the promontory of Mount Athos he was caught by a northerly gale which destroyed his ships. A great many of them were driven ashore and wrecked at Athos. While the disaster at sea occurred the troops on land under Mardonius command suffered heavy losses by a Thracian attack. The combination of these losses induced Mardonius, who was himself wounded, to begin a retreat and returned to Asia. It was the year 492 BC.

Herodotus continues: "The following year Darius heard of a possible revolt being planned by the people of Thasos and sent an order to dismantle their defences and reserves but the islanders who were rich mainly because of their gold mines had a different idea. The gold mines were said to be the most important source of revenue for the islanders. The most remarkable were those discovered by the Phoenicians who came with Thasus, the son of Phoenix, to colonize the island, on the southeastern side of Thasos, facing Samothrace. A whole mountain had been turned upside down in the search for gold. They, however, decided to obey Darius' orders, pulled down their fortifications and returned their fleet."

Subsequently the Persians were defeated at Marathon in 490 BC. The young general Miltiades had escaped twice from being killed: once by the Phoenicians who brought him to Darius and later when under trial for accusation of running an unconstitutional and despotic government, he was absolved and elected a general by the people. Herodotus tells us how everything happened:

"Upon the approach of the Persian army the opinions in Greece were divided between the generals who favored surrender and submmision to the Persian yoke because their forces were too small vis-a-vis the enemy and they did not stand a chance of success or fight against Darius. The others wanted to oppose the enemy. Miltiades belonged to the latter group, his opinion prevailed and after convincing Callimachus they decided to face the enemy. "At the chosen moment the Athenian army moved into position for the upcoming struggle but by the effort to extend the line to face the Persian front their center was weakened. The Athenians, however, advanced at a run towards the enemy......The Persians seeing the attack developing prepared to meet it, thinking it was suicidal madness for the Athenians to risk an assault with such small force, rushing in with no support from either cavalry or archers...Nevertheless the Athenians came on, closed with the enemy all along the line, and fought in a way not to be forgotten. They were the first Greeks, according to Herodotus, to charge at a run, and the first to look without flinching at the Persian dress and men who wore it, for until that day came, no Greek could hear even the word Persian without terror. The struggle at Marathon was long drawn out. In the center, held by the Persians themselves, the advantage was with the foreigners, who were far succesful at breaking the Greek line and pursue the fugitives inland from the sea; but the Athenians and their allies on the wings were victorious. Having got the upper hand they left the defeated enemy to escape and regrouped their wings into a single unit, they turned their attention to the Persians who had broken through the center. Here again they were triunphant, chasing the routed enemy and cutting them down until they came to the sea...The Athenians however lost three generals and secured seven ships; but the rest got off with the Persians aboard them...............In the battle of Marathon some 6400 Persians were killed while the Athenians losses were only 192. When the captured ships were searched it was "discovered, in a Phoenician vessel, a statue of Apollo, overlaid with gold. It was decided to return it to the place that it had been stolen from: the Temple of Delos. It did however wander for many years until the Thebans themselves, advised by an oracle, brought it back twenty years late".

Although the characters were obviously different, Marathon would remind historians of the battle of Cannae, where Hannibal defeated the Romans with a totally distinctive strategy.

When Darius heard the news about the defeat of his army at Marathon he became greatly angered, more so since their victory at Sardis made him more desirous of sending an expedition against Hellas. He sent messengers to all cities commanding the equipement of an army, charging each to provide much more than they had before provided of ships, horses and provisions and vessels of transport. Asia was shaken for three years (489-487 BC), the best men being enrolled for service againt Hellas…In the 4th year the Egyptians, whom Cambyses had enslaved, revolted from the Persians; thus forcing Darius to send expeditions against both. While Darius was making his preparations against Egypt and Athens, a great quarrel arose among his sons concerning the matter of succesion because according to Persian law he had to designate an heir before his army marched to war. Darius had three sons by his first wife and four by his second wife, a daughter of Cyrus, after he became king. Thus both of the eldest sons claimed their right to rule. Xerxes, by his second wife, had been born after Darius was king; therefore he said that it was neither reasonable nor just that anyone other than he should have the royal prerogative; and cited as an example the custom of Sparta for in

Sparta it was customary that the first son born after their father became king should succed his father. To him and no other should fall the succession to the kinship. Darius judged this plea to be just and declared him heir; but a year after the revolt of Egypt, death came upon Darius in the midst of his preparations for war: he had reigned for thirty six years. Following Darius death he was replaced in the throne by his son Xerxes in 485 BC.

Xerxes was initially by no means eager to march against Hellas; he first wanted to reconquer Egypt. But Mardonius, who was Xerxes' cousin and son of Darius sister, and had more influence over the king than any other Persian reasoned this way: "Sire, the Athenians should not go unpunished for their deeds, but my counsel is that after you have tamed the insolence of Egypt, lead your armies against Athens, that you may have fair fame among men and that all men may in time to come, beware of the fate of those who dare to invade your realm".

Xerxes was now determined to accomplish what his father had not been able to. He assembled the greatest of all expeditions recorded in ancient times. From all regions of his empire he recruited fresh forces. The Phoenicians again provided a substantial cooperation in military, naval and civil engineering. Following the tragedy at Mount Athos suffered by the armies of his father, Xerxes decided to join Athos with the mainland.

Herodotus, HISTORIES: (VII: 23 & 44; 89-95; 100, & 128) describes the events:

"First of all for about three years he had been making the preparations regarding Athos......All sorts and conditions of men in the army were made to dig a canal: this Athos is a mountain great and famous, running out into the sea and inhabited by men. At the mountain's landward end, it is in the form of a peninsula, and there is an isthmus...In this isthmus, which is at the end of the Athos, there are several Greek towns and it was now the Paersians' intent to make them into an island and not mainland towns: the foreigners started to dig dividing up the ground among their several nations......When the channel had been digged to some depth, some stood at the bottom of it and dug, others took the stuff as it was digged out and delivered to yet others that stood higher on stages and they again to others until they came to those that were the highest; these carried it out and cast away. With all except the Phoenicians the steep sides of the canal broke and fell, thereby doubling the labor......But the Phoenicians showed then the same skill as in all else that they do; having taken in hand the portion assigned to them, they started to dig as to make the topmost span of the canal as wide again as the canal was to be, and narrowed it ever as they wrought lower, until reaching the bottom where their work was of the same span as what the rest had done.

There is a meadow nearby, where they then made a place for buying and marketing......Once Xerxes had this work accomplished,

The Phoenicians in History and Legend

for the bridges he charged the Phoenicians and Egyptians with the making of ropes of papyrus and "esparto grass" imported from Spain by the Phoenicians. He then stored the provisions for his army in such places as enquiry showed to be the fittest, bringing all his provisions from all part of Asia in vessels of merchandise and transport.

On his way to Hellas, Xerxes was followed by one thousand spearmen of the best and noblest blood of Persia, after them a thousand chosen Persian horsemen and after ten thousand footmen, chosen out of the rest of the Persians. After this he prepared to march to Abydos while his men were bridging the Hellespont from Asia to Europe. It was here, near the Hellespont, that the Athenians under Xanthippus had taken the Persian governor of Sestus and crucified him alive.

Beginning then from Abydos he asked the Phoenicians and Egyptians to build bridges. But no sooner these had been done a great storm swept down and broke and scattered all the work, causing great anger to Xerxes………………When the bridges and the work at Athos were ready…and the canal itself reported now to be perfectly made, the army then wintered. When Xerxes learned that the Hellespont had been bridged and the canal had been dug through Athos he left Sardis and made his way toward the Hellespont, he arrived at Abydus and personally led his army over the bridge into Europe. At the beginning of the spring, Xerxes decided to march from Sardis to Abydos. The entire army passed followed in the end by Xerxes himself on a chariot pulled by Median horses. He rode out of

Sardis and passed later thruogh Lydia until he came into the territory of Ilium, with mount Ida on their left. When the army passed by the river Scamander, Xerxes ascended to the citadel of Priam, having a desire to view it; and having viewed and enquired about all that was there he offered in sacrifice one thousand cattle to Athene of Ilium……

When Xerxes had come to the midst of Abydos, he desired to see the whole of his army; and this he could do because a lofty seat of white stone had been set up on a hill,…built by the people of Abydos at the king's command. There Xerxes sat and looked down on the seashore, viewing his army and his fleet and as he viewed them he had the opportunity to see the ships contend in a race. They did so and the Phoenicians of Sidon won it; and Xerxes was pleased with the race and his army.

But when he saw the Hellespont hidden by his ships and all the shores and plains full with men, he declared himself happy but shortly thereafter he began to weep. Asked by his uncle the reason for his change of mood, he replied:

"I was moved to compassion, when I considered the shortness of all human life, seeing that of all this multitude of men not one will be alive a hundred years hence".

Having thus spoken, Xerxes next sent for the most notable among the Persians and when they were present he said:

"I have assembled you to make this demand, that you bear yourselves bravely and never sully the great and glorius former achievements of the Persians; let us each and all be zealous, for this is the common advantage of all that we seek. For this cause I bid you set your hands to the war with might; for as I am assured, we march against valiant men, whom if we overcome, it is certain that no other human host will ever withstand us. Now let us cross over, having first prayed to the gods who hold Persia for their allotted realm".

The entire day after the preparations for the crossing, they waited to see the sunrise, burning all kinds of incense on the bridges. At sunrise Xerxes poured a libation into the sea, praying to the sun that no such accident should befal him to prevent him from suduing Europe should he reach its farthest borders.

After the prayer he cast into the Hellespont, a golden bowl and a Persian sword (scimitar). This done they crossed over, the foot and horses by the bridge nearest to the Pontus, and the beasts of burden and the train of service by the bridge over the Aegean. The ten thousand Persians wearing garlands, and after them the mixed host of diverse nations. After this they took three more days to cross first the horsemen with their spears reversed, then the sacred horses and the sacred chariot, then Xerxes himself, the spearmen and a thousand horses and finally the rest of the host. Some historians claim that

Xerxes was the last of them all to cross. In the meantime the ships crossed to the opposite side. Having passed over to Europe, Xerxes viewed his army crossing under the lash, seven days and seven nights, with never a rest.

A tale is reported by Herodotus that once Xerxes had crossed the Hellespont, a man of the Hellespont cried:

"O Zeus, why have you taken the likeness of a Persian and changed your name to Xerxes, leading the whole world with you to remove Hellas from its place? Your mightest could have done that without these means.".........

Xerxes army contained people from all nations: Persians, Medians, Hyrcanians, Babylonians, Assyrians, Bactrians, Indians, Arians, Caspians, Arabians, Ethiopians, Egyptians, Lybians and a host of others. The Persians, Medians, Indians, Lybians, Caspians and Arabians were alone the only nations to have riders. The number of horsemen was shown to be eighty thousand, besides the camels and the chariots.

The number of triremes was shown to be twelve hundred and seven; those that funished them were: first, the Phoenicians with the Syrians of Palestine furnished three hundred, their men were equipped with helmets on their head in the Greek fashion. These Phoenicians dwelt in old time by the Red Sea. The Egyptians furnished two hundred ships, the Cyprians a hundred and fifty ships, the Cilicians one hundred ships, the Lycians fifty, the Dorians of Asia thirty, the Carians seventy ships, the Ionians a hundred......There were fighting men of the Persians and Medes on all ships.

The best sailing ships were furnished by the Phoenicians, and among them by the Sidonians. These, like the ones among them that were ranked in the land army, had their native leaders in command of their contingents. Those from other nations came not as generals but as slaves. Of those that were on shipboard the most famous after the Persian admirals were Tetranmestus of Sidon, Matten of Tyre and Merbalus of Aradus among the Phoenicians. Of the other captains it is remarkable to mention Artemisia, who greatly marveled, because being a woman she went before her army against Hellas since her husband had died and left her with a very young son. She was half from Halicarnasus and half Cretan and only provided five ships. Her ships were reputed the best in the whole fleet after the ships of Sidon; and Xerxes gave her opinion a great deal of weight.

Xerxes then had a desire to ride through and view his army: riding in a chariot he past the men of each nation, he questioned them and his scribes wrote all down, until he had gone from end to end...This done Xerxes left his chariot and boarded a ship from Sidon; sitting under a golden canopy he was carried past the prows of the ships, questioning them in a similar manner as he had done with the army and making the answers to be written down. He then passed in front of the ships loaded with their men and captains……Having gathered information about the valor of the Greeks,……Xerxes marched with his army through Thrace towards Hellas.

Finally arriving in Thessaly he saw the mountains Olympus and Ossa with the river Peneus flowing in a narrow pass between them, he was taken with a desire to view the mouth of the river Peneus, because he had in mind to march by the upper road through the highland people of Macedonia…Embarking then in a ship of Sidon, wherein he always embarked when he had such business at hand, he made a signal for the rest to put out to sea, leaving his land army where it was. Thessaly was in ancient times a lake, surrounded by exceedingly high mountains and several rivers which joined in a single one before entering into the sea. The Thessalians say that Poseidon made this passage and this is a reasonable belief for those who think that Poseidon is the shaker of the earth and that rifts made by earthquakes are the god's handiwork. Xerxes marveled at the sights of the Thessalian land and thought them wise for joining his forces to avoid destruction of their land. In this he was mistaken. He was delayed for many days in this part of the country for a third part of his army was clearing a road over the Macedonian mountains…and several Greek people, especially the Thessalians, made tributes to him. To Athens and Sparta, Xerxes sent no heralds to demande any tributes because his father Darius had not been succesful in a previous similar enterprise………The professed intent of the king's march was to attack Athens but in truth all Hellas was his aim.

On their side the Thessalians did not submit to Persia until they heard that their army was about to cross to Europe, they then sent delegates to demand delegates from other Greek towns help to defend the passage past Mount Olympus because they felt themselves incapable of facing the Persians alone. The Greek answer was to send an army by sea to Thessaly to defend the pass. Between Mount Olympus and Mount Ossa ten thousand Greek infantry, reinforced by the Thessalian cavalry, took up their position. But advised by the Macedonians not to face the Persian army they decided, when learning that there was another way into Thessaly through upper Macedonia, the way that Xerxes in fact took, they no longer hesitated and whole-heartedly worked in the Persian interest. The Greeks, on their part, upon their return to the Isthmus discussed the situation and the proposal which found most favour was to guard the pass of Thermopylae. They knew nothing as yet about the mountain track by means of which the men who fell at Thermopylae were taken in the rear and learnt about it only when informed by the people of Trachis. The pass through Trachis into Greece is at Thermopylae fifty feet wide, both east and west of Thermopylae, it is still narrower. The Persian fleet and the army advanced without any loss as far as Thermopylae. Xerxes reached Thermopylae at the head of an army consisting of **over five million men** without counting the eunuchs, the soldier's wives and the female cooks......From Thessaly Xerxes went on into Malis, following the shore of a bay, flat and braoad in one part and surrounded by a chain of lofty and trackless mountains, that enclosed the whole territory......Xerxes was lying with his force at Trachis in Malian territory in control of all the country northward while the Greeks occupied the pass known as Thermopylae and the whole mainland to the south: they counted over five thousand men. Herodotus says: "There was no cause for alarm, after all it was not a god who threatened Greece, but a man, and there neither was nor ever would be a man who was not born with a certain degree of misfortune. The present enemy was no exception: he too was human..."

The contingents of the various states were under their own officers, but the most respected was Leonidas the Spartan, from the family of Heracles, who was in command of the whole army............The Persian army was now close to the pass, and the Greeks, suddenly doubting their power to resist, held a conference to consider the advisability of retreat. Some felt indignation at the suggestion to retreat, Leonidas gave his voice for staying where they were and proposed sending an appeal for reinforcements to the various states of the confederacy, as their numbers were inadequate to cope with the Persians.

While the Greeks were discussing their strategy on how to resist the Persian army, Xerxes sent a man on horseback to ascertain the strenght of the Greek force. The Persian rider approached the camp and took a thorough survey of all he could see. The people he observed happened to be the Spartans, some of them were stripped for

The Phoenicians in History and Legend

exercise while others were combing their hair. The Persian man watched this with astonishment and then rode quietly off. Xerxes was bewildered when he heard the story, namely that the Spartans were preparing to die and deal death with all their strenght and yet what they were doing seemed to him merely absurd. Darius sent Demaratus to watch and report to him what the behaviour of the Spartan meant. He reported back that it is common practice of the Spartans to take care of their hair even before facing battle but I assure you that if you can defeat these men and the rest of them that are still at home, there is no other people in the world who would dare to stand firm and lift a hand againt you. You have to deal now with the bravest men of the finest kingdom in Greece. Four days Xerxes waited to see if the enemy would retreat until he was seized with anger and sent forward the Medes first and later the Persian troops known as the King's Immortals; all day the battle continued with even results; both had losses on their sides and a third day of fighting did not resolve the battle. Then Xerxes having no idea of how to deal with the conflict until a man from Malis came to inform the king of the existence of a track which led over the hill to Thermopylae.

The existence of the track was known to the local people and this was then the mountain track which the Persians took; they marched throughout the night. By early dawn they were they were at the summit of the ridge, near the spot where a thousand men stood on guard to watch the track, for they had volunteered for their service to Leonidas. The ascent of the Persians had been concealed by the oak trees that covered the hills and only because there was no wind suddenly the Phocian guards saw the Persian troops who were surprised at the sight of troops preparing to resist: the Persian arrows flew thick and fast and made the guards withdraw to the highest point of the mountain where they feared destruction; however the Persians ignored them and passed along the descending track with great speed. In the middle of the confusion which arose at the approach of the Persians from the hills the army under Leonidas split: some wanted to stay while others wanted to escape. Leonidas appears to have dismissed the troops that he felt had no heart for the fight but at the same time honor forbade him to go and thought it unbecoming for the Spartans under his command to desert the post that they had originally come to defend. Thus it appears that the confederate troops, by Leonidas orders, abandoned their posts and left the pass. The Thespians refused to desert Leonidas and remained with his men and died with them. The morning after Xerxes poured a libation to the rising sun and waited until it was well up before he began to move forward………As the Persian army advanced to the assault, the Greeks under Leonidas, knowing that they were going to their deaths, went out into the wider part of the pass much further than they had gone before, put forth all their strenght and fought with fury and desperation. In the course of that fight Leonidas fell, having fought most gallantly, and many distinguished Spartans with him…Among the Persian dead, too, were many men of high distinction including two brothers of Xerxes……Of all the Spartans that fought valiantly the greatest signal of courage was displayed by the Spartan Dieneces.

It is said that before the battle he was told by a native that when the Persians shoot their arrows, there are so many that they hid the sun. He responded: "This is pleasant news, if the Persians hide the sun, we shall have our battle in the shade"..................

After the encounter, Xerxes went over the battlefield to see the bodies and having been told that Leonidas was king of Sparta and commander of the Spartan force, he ordered his head to be cut off and fixed on a stake...This supports the opinion that while Leonidas was alive, King Xerxes felt fiercer anger against him than against any other man; for normally the Persians, more than any other nation, honour men who distinguish themselves in war and bury them with great honours.After the disaster at Thermopylae the Persians advanced devastating by sword and fire several areas.

The army of Xerxes was now divided: one division, the stronger and more numerous, proceeded with Xerxes towards Athens after entering Boeotia...The other division directed itself towards Delphi, keeping Parnassus on their right, they advanced detached from the main body of the army for the special purpose of plundering the Temple at Delphi and bring its treasures to Xerxes. The news of the approach of the Persians brought great consternation at Delphi and in the middle of their terror thay asked their God's oracle whether they should bury the sacred treasures or get them out of the country. He responded that they had no reason to panic since they were able to defend themselves on their own...Just as the Persians came to the Temple of Athene, thunderbolts fell on them from the sky and large rocks, torn from Parnassus came crashing down and killed a large number of them. In panic the Persians try to fly but were attacked by the Delphians causing a great slaughter. The Persians who escaped with their lives made it straight for Boeotia. The Greek fleet, at the Athenians' request, stopped at Salamis. They had expected that the full strenght of the Peloponnesian army would concentrate in Boeotia to hold the Persian advance but they had something else in mind, namely they proceeded to fortify the Isthmus in order to protect themselves, while the rest of Greece might take its chance. The Athenians returned to their harbours and advised their people by a proclamation that every citizen should get the members of their household to safety. The Greeks war fleet consisted of 378 warships without counting the light galleys.

The commanders of the various contingents met at Salamis and the general feeling of the council was in favour of sailing to the Isthmus and fighting in defense of the Peloponnese, on the grounds that if they were beaten at Salamis they would find themselves blocked up in an island, while if disaster overtook them at the Isthnus, they could find refuge among their own people. While the discussion was still in progress a man arrived with the news that the Persians had enetered Attica and set fire to the entire country. The march from the Hellespont to Attica had taken the Persian army three month and one more month in the actual crossing of the strait. The Persian arrived to Athens and found it abandoned......

The Persians occupied the hill which the Athenians called the Areopagus, opposite the Acropolis, and began the siege. After a lenghty resistance, the Persians found a place where the ascent was so steep that no guard had been set, because it was thought not possible that any man would be able to climb it; but some soldiers managed to scramble up the precipitous face of the cliff. When the Athenians saw them on the summit, some leapt from the wall to their death, some sought sanctuary in the temple and the Persians made it up for the gates, flung them open and slaughter the ones in the sanctuary. They stripped the temple of its treasures and burnt everything in the Acropolis. Xerxes was now absolute master of Athens.

Meanwhile at Salamis the news of what had happened at the Acropolis were so disturbing that some commanders decided to sail in immediate flight. Some stayed and passed the resolution to fight in defense of the Isthmus.

Once the conference was over and the various commanders had returned to their ships, Themistocles was informed that if they sailed to the Isthmus and abandoned Salamis there existed the danger of the alliance breaking up if they left Salamis. He went immediately to the commander-in-chief and asked him to call the various commanders to another conference.

Before this new gathering, Themistocles spoke:

> "it is in your power to save Greece if you take my advice and engage the enemy's fleet here in Salamis instead of withdrawing to the Isthmus. If you fight there it will be at your disadvantage to fight in the open sea with smaller ships and lesser numbers than the enemy's. If we fight here at Salamis

we shall be in narrow waters and fighting in a confined space will favor us while the open sea favours the enemy. If we beat them at sea in this confined space the Persians will not take Salamis or other towns and will retreat in disorder.

The Corinthians then opposed Themistocles accusing him of having no country because Athens was in Persian hands. He responded "as long as Athens has two hundred ships we have a country, if you refuse my advice, we will pack our families and go to Italy".

The commander-in-chief realized that without the Athenian contingent his strenght will not be adequate to offer battle and decided to stay at Salamis following the suggestion of Themistocles and fight it out right there. The Persian sailors then returned and according to Herodotus "both by land and sea the Persian forces were just as strong at the time of their entry into Attica as they had been at Thermopylae, because despite their losses at the storm, Thermopylae and Artemisium, the re-inforcements they received compensated their prior losses. The further Xerxes advanced into Greece, the more peoples followed him". When the rest of the Persian troops arrived at Phaleron, Xerxes paid a personal visit to the commanding officers to hear their opinions;…the rulers of states and commanders of squadrons were summoned to appear before him. They took their seats according to the precedence which the King had assigned them: the lord of Sidon first, the lord of Tyre second, and so on in their order. Then Xerxes sent Mardonius to ask the opinion of each one about giving battle at sea, beginning with the lord of Sidon. The answers were unanimously in favour of engaging the Greek fleet with one single exception: Artemisia. This woman responded:

> "Tell the king for me, Master, spare your ships and do not fight at sea, for the Greeks are as far superior to us in naval matters as men are to women…What pressing need do you have to risk further actions at sea? Have you not taken Athens, the main objective of the war? Is not the rest of Greece in your power?……Let me tell you how I think things will go now with the enemy; if you are not in a great hurry to fight at sea, if you leave the fleet in the coast where it now is, then whether you stay here or advance into the Peloponnese, you will easily accomplish your purpose. The Greeks will not be able to hold out against you for long: their forces will soon disperse, break up and go home. I hear they have no supplies in the island where they now are, and the Peloponnesian contingents………will hardly like the idea of fighting in defence of Athens". If, on the other hand, you rush into a naval action, my fear is that the defeat of your fleet may involve the army too………"

The king was highly pleased with Artemisia' comments but his orders were that the advice of the majority should be followed.

The orders were now given to put to sea, and the ships proceeded towards Salamis, where in the evening they took their respective positions......The Greeks were in a state of acute alarm, especially those from the Peloponnese, for waiting at Salamis to fight for the Athenians, the Persian army was that very night on march from the Peloponnese.

The Greek commanders were now in trouble: they did not know that the enemy ships had blocked their scape at both ends of the channel, thus being forced to fight there whether they liked it or not. At this point there came an Athenian by birth, Aristides, who had been banished from Athens by popular vote. He asked to see Themistocles who was no friend of his but actually his greatest enemy. Aristides knew of the anxiety of the Peloponnesian commanders and their intention to withdraw toward the Isthmus but he addressed Themistocles in these terms:

"At this moment, more than ever before, we should be rivals, to see who can do most good to our country: because no matter what the Peloponnesian say, I have seen with my own eyes that they can not withdraw from Salamis, because our fleet is surrounded". Themistocles believed him and responded "It is your turn to take them the news yourself; if they believe you good and well and if they don't, it is no odds for if we are surrounded, escape is no longer possible."

Aristides reported to them how the entire Greek force was surrounded but many of them did not believe him until a Greek ship which had been part of the Persian fleet deserted and brought them similar news. The Greeks now believed him and had a round number of 380 ships. Themistocles was chosen to address the fleet and emphasized the advantages of fighting for life and fortune.

The two fleets now were facing each other: the Athenian squadron found itself facing the Phoenicians, who formed the Persian left wing; the Lacedaemonians faced the ships of Ionia fighting in favour of Persia: the greatest part of the Persian fleet suffered severely in the battle; the Greek fleet worked together as a whole, while the Persians had lost formation, were no longer fighting with a plan, however, they fought well all that day.

Remarkable in the battle was Artemisia who being under attack by an Athenian trireme and finding escape impossible she ran over with her ship and sank one of the Persian ships: seeeing this the Greek ship thought Artemisia was fighting on their side and abandoned the pursuit; she escaped with her life and raised in Xerxes esteem for he was told

"Do you see my lord, how well Artemisia is fighting? She has sunk an enemy ship". Xerxes asked if it was really Artemisia and he was told there was no doubt.

He then is said to have exclaimed "My men have turned into women, my women into men".

Among those killed was a son of Darius thus brother of Xerxes. Evidently a great confusion existed during this battle: some Phoenicians who had lost their ships came to Xerxes and attributed their loss to the Ionians traitors…But while they were talking a ship from Samothrace sank an Athenian ship but in turn was hit by another. When they were sanking the men in the Samothracian ship, armed with javelins, cleared the deck of the attacking vessel, leapt aboard and captured her. When Xerxes saw the Ionian ship do such a fine job, he turned to the Phoenicians and in extreme anger ordered that they be decapitated because of treachery. The remainder of the Phoenician commanders, upon seeing what happened to their compatriots, first reached port in the coast of Attica and then, when night fell, set sail for Asia returning to their states of origin.

After the battle the Greeks towed over to Salamis all the disabled ships, fully expecting that Xerxes will use his remaining ships to make another attack. However, Xerxes when he realized the extent of the disaster, feared that the Greeks might sail to the Hellespont and break the bridges thus leaving him isolated in Europe. He laid his plans to escape and sent his messengers to Persia with the news of his defeat.

Mardonius could see that Xerxes took the defeat at Salamis very hard and guessed that he was determined to get out of Athens. Thus Mardonius addressed Xerxes, "My lord, I beg you not to take the recent events too deeply at heart. No one of those people who now imagine that their work is done, will abandon their ships to fight at land, thus I suggest an immmediate attack on the Peloponnese………None of the reverses that we have suffered are due to us, you can not say that we the Persians have on any occasion fought as cowards. Why should we care if the Egyptians and Phoenicians and Cilicians and Cyprians have disgraced themselves? Listen then to what I propose: go home, if you have made up your mind, with the greater part of the army, and I will make it my duty with 300.000 picked troops, to deliver Greece to you in chains". Xerxes summoned a conference and during the debate sent for Artemisia to take part in the discussion.

Xerxes explained Mardonius proposal to her and she replied: "My lord, it is not easy to give you the best advice…but I think that you should yourself quit this country and leave Mardonius behind with the forces he is asking for,……While you and yours survive the Greeks will have to run a painful race for their lives and land…Mardonius is only your slave: if he were to lose, the Greeks will not derive any pleasure by defeating him, while you will be going home with the main objective of your campaign accomplished, for you have burnt Athens".

Xerxes was pleased with her advice and sent her to Ephesus with several of his own bastard children that he had brought along in his campaign and to look after his children he sent his chief eunuch, Hermotimus. He had been castrated according to Herodotus "by a certain Panionius, a man who made his living by the abominable trade of castrating any good-looking boys he could get hold of".

Hermotimus, nevertheless had a certain share of luck, for sent to serve Xerxes, the King came lo like him and made him the most valued of his eunuchs. When Xerxes was in Sardis and preparing to lead his Persian army against Athens he sent Hermotimus on business to the part of Mysia called Atarneus where he happened to meet Panionius. Perceiving who he was, he held long and friendly conversation with him:

"It is to you, he said, that I owe all my prosperity, if you will bring your household and dwell here, I will make you prosperous in return"; with more promises he managed to convince Panionius who accepted his offer gladly; Panionius then brought his wife and children with him to Sardis, where Hermotimus had been so succesful.. When he got there Hermotimus told him: "No man ever earned his living by a viler trade than you. What harm had I ever done to you or your forefathers that you should have made me a nothing instead of a man?…You thought that the gods will have no knowledge of such behaviour but their just law and for your vile crime have delivered you into my power. Now you shall be content with the fullness of that justice which I will execute upon you". He then ordered him to castrate his own four sons and then had them castrate their father.

The Phoenicians in History and Legend

A few days after the battle of Salamis, Xerxes' army began its withdrawal, marching into Boeotia. Mardonius decided that now it would be better to winter in Thessaly and make his attempt into the Peloponnese the following spring. Xerxes made his way by forced marches to the Hellespont. He reached the crossing in forty-five days but lacking provisions and his army ill with plague and dysentery many died. He appeared to have returned to Asia mainly by land. Mardonius went back to Greece and following several proposals to the Athenians that were rejected, he finally engaged the Lacedaemonians in Plataea. Mardonius himself, riding a white horse inthe battle and surrounded by a thousand of his picked men who were the flower of the Persians, foght the hardest. So long as Mardonius was alive the Persians stood their ground and defended themselves overthrowing many Lacedaemonians; but when Mardonius lost his life and his guards fell, then the rest of them also yielded. That day the Spartans gained from Mardonius their full measure of vengeance for the slaying of Leonidas. The body of Mardonius disappeared the day after the battle; and although it is unclear how or who took it, it is believed that his body was most likely buried.

Years later, having being king for over twenty years, Xerxes will be the victim of a royal plot and will be assassinated while sleeping (465 BC) by a man in whom he had placed his entire trust, named Artabanus, captain of the royal body-guard, with the help of Mithridates, the eunuch, who also had the trust of the king. Xerxes first son Darius would be killed but his second son, Artaxerxes, would escape with his life and having taken vengeance upon the slayer of his father, took over the kingship of the Persians and ruled for forty-three years. Artaxerxes achieved a peace treaty with the Greeks although the terms of such treaty are the subject of controversy among the historians of the period. He was succeeded in the throne first by his son Artaxerxes II (405-359 BC) and later by Artaxerxes III (Ochus) 359-338 BC.

Artaxerxes III will return to the idea of recovering Egypt and the rest of the Middle East. On 344-343 BC he will organize an expedition towards Egypt with great success and end up in absolute control of Egypt, Phoenicia and Cyprus. These events appear to have been preceeded by an unsuccesful attempt by Artaxerxes II to conquer Egypt but having been defeated, he remained inactive and although he would send armies and generals he usually failed.

Things remained peaceful but when the Phoenicians and the people of Cyprus decided to revolt against the Persian yoke, Artaxerxes became enraged and decided to make war upon the insurgents. To begin with he decided to carry on his campaign personally, he rejected the use of foreign generals and organizing a powerful army advanced towards Phoenicia first. His army was made with great provisions of arms, missiles, food and forces: he assembled three hundred-thousand foot-soldiers, thirty thousand horsemen, three hundred triremes, five hundred merchant men and other ships to carry his supplies.

In Phoenicia there was an important city named Tripolis that had been founded by Tyrians, Sidonians and Aradians. This city enjoyed the highest repute because that was the place where the Phoenicians held their common council and deliberated on matters of supreme importance to them. Since the satraps of the Persian king lived in Sidon and abused insolently their power, the Sidonians decided to revolt from the Persians and convinced the other Phoenicians to make a bid for independence. They sent ambassadors to the Egyptian king and persuaded him to accept them as their allies. Because Sidon was distinguished for its wealth and its citizens had amassed great riches from their shipping, many triremes were quickly outfitted and a multitude of mecenaries gathered; besides arms, missiles, food and other materials necessary for war. The first hostile act was the cutting down and destroying the royal park **"paradeisos"**, in which the Persian kings were used to take their recreation; next they burned the supplies of the Persian horses, which had been stored up by the satraps in preparation for war and lastly they arrested all Persians of insolent behaviour and proceded to chastise them with their vengeance. Artaxerxes, who was now in Babylon, being apprised of the rash acts of the insurgents, issued threatening warnings to all the Phoenicians and in particular to the people of Sidon. The King departed Babylon after assembling his infantry and cavalry forces, immediately assumed command of them and advanced against the Phoenicians. While he was still on his way, the satraps of Syria and Cilicia, having joined their forces, opened the war against the Phoenicians.

Tennes, the King of Sidon, with the help of four thousand Greek mercenaries acquired from Egypt under a general known as Mentor the Rhodian, and other citizens of his own state engaged the satraps army, defeated them and drove the enemy out of Phoenicia.

The citizens of Cyprus, where many Phoenicians lived and had established bonds of trade, immediated revolted as well against the authority of the Persians. Under these circumstances Artaxerxes army advanced against Sidon and Phoenicia. The ruler of Sidon, Tenes, after his initial victory had second thoughts. When he was informed of the great size of the Persian army he thought that the insurgents were incapable of fighting against it and decided to provide for his personal safety. Accordingly, without the knowledge of the people of Sidon, he sent the most faithful of his servants to Artaxerxes, with the promise that he will betray his people and turn in the people of Sidon to him, and assist him in conquering Egypt because of his knowledge of the landing places in the ports of the Nile. The Persian King was delighted with an offer of this sort. He sent, however, messengers to the people of Athens and Sparta requesting support for his campaign against Egypt: they replied that although they considered Persia their friend they were not willing to send troops against Egypt. However other Greek cities and ports of Asia Minor assembled troops to the point that they ended with a total of ten thousand Greek soldiers as allies of the Persians. With this contingent in his service, Artaxexes traversed Syria and arriving into Phoenicia encamped near Sidon. Tennes who had promised to surrender Sidon did not ask his people to make preparations of any sort to resist and confessed to Mentor the

Rhodian his intentions and plans of betrayal. Mentor marched with a contingent of five hundred of the most important citizens of Sidon, pretending that he was going to a common meeting of the Phoenicians. He then took the one hundred most distinguished in the role of advisors and delivered them to Artaxerxes. The Persian King had the One Hundred shot as instigators of the revolt and then summoned Tennes to appear before him and asked whether he was going to deliver the city to him because he wanted to overwhelm the Sidonians with a merciless disaster and strike terror into the other cities by this punishment. The five hundred citizens carrying supplicant branches were then delivered by Tennes to Artaxerxes who executed them. He then was taken into the city of Sidon by Mentor the Rhodian. Once the Persians were in absolute control, the King believing that Tennes was no longer of any use, put him to death. This is the way Tennes paid for his treason to his state. A modern historian has stated that "Tennes was cynically executed by Ochus while Mentor with equal cynicism was taken into his service" for the upcoming Egyptian campaign. The citizens of Sidon gave an example of Phoenician bravery when before the arrival of Artaxerxes they burned all their ships to avoid anyone escaping or joining the enemy, then shut themselves in their houses with their women and children while the fire consumed them. It has been claimed that about forty thousands people, including servants, perished in the fire. After the disaster had befallen the Sidonians and the whole city and its inhabitants obliterated by fire. The richness of the city was such that melted by the fire, a vast amount of silver and gold were found. The

Persian King sold the funeral pyre for many talents. The rest of the phoenician cities, panic-stricken, surrendered to the enemy without resistance. Artaxerxes proceeded with his army into Egypt and after having submitted the entire country, he demolished the walls of the most important cities. By plundering shrines he gathered a vast amount of silver and gold and carried off the inscribed records from the ancient temples which later on were returned to the Egyptian priests in exchange for huge sums of money by way of ransom. Artaxerxes rewarded the Greeks who had accompanied him in his campaigns and after installing a new satrap in Egypt, he went with his army to Babylon.

CHAPTER TEN

GREECE AND ROME IN PHOENICIA

By the year 336-335 BC, Philip of Macedon, partly because of his success in the battlefield and in part because of his diplomatic skills had united all Greece under his command. He raised his native Macedonia to the highest level of power over the other Greek States and proposed to their leaders to attack Persia, anxious to pay back a visit to Persia, the country of Darius and Xerxes, to punish those who had burned Athens and profaned the temples. Under the pretext of liberating the predominantly Greek cities of Asia Minor from Persian domination he convened a general congress at Corinth. There he spoke about the war against the Persians and by raising great expectations he won the delegates es to his cause. Philip consulted the oracle and although the news were not favorable, he thought that the gods supported him in the conquest of Asia. Straightway he set in motion plans for lavish sacrifices to the gods at the wedding of his daughther Cleopatra, whose mother was Olympias. He had decided to give her in marriage to Alexander, king of Epirus, Olympias's maternal uncle. While the preparations for the campaign against Persia were under way, Philip attended a state banquet preceded by a parade with the statues of the twelve gods to which a statue of himself enthroned among them was added.

Philip of Macedonia will lose his life at the zenith of his power as the indirect consequence of a homosexual quarrel among the high members of his court and his bodyguards. Some historians have speculated that these events were the result of a wider conspiracy in which even his son Alexander may have been involved. It is not necessary to emphasize that during this historical period sexual predilections and orientation were highly tolerated and also quite common, especially among the higher classes of the Greek society. The events that led to king Philip's death have been thoroughly described, among others, by Plutarch and Diodorus Siculus.

Diodorus Siculus has described how it happened:

"Every seat in the theatre was taken when Philip appeared wearing a white cloak, and by his express orders his bodyguard held away from him and followed only at a distance, since he wanted to show publicly that he was protected by the goodwill of all the Greeks, and had no need of a guard..." Philip walked between the two Alexanders, his son and his son-in-law, convinced that everyone's support was on his side and ignorant that a plot against him was in the making.

Diodorus continues:

"There was a Macedonian named Pausanias…who was a bodyguard of the king and was beloved by him because of his beauty. When he saw that king Philip was becoming of enamoured of another man (also named Pausanias like himself), he addressed him with abusive language, accusing him of being a hermaphrodite and prompt to accept the amourous advances of any other who wished…**Unable to endure such an insult, the other Pausanias kept silent for the time but…decided to bring about his own death voluntarily and in a spectacular fashion by stepping in front of king Philip during a battle, a few days after, with the king of the Illyrians…and receiving in his body all the blows directed at king Philip.**"

"The incident was widely discussed until Attalus, an influential member of the court inner circle, invited the Macedonian Pausanias to dinner. When he got him drunk and unconscious, he handed his body over to the muleteers to be abused in drunken licentiousness. As soon as he recovered from his drunken stupor and, deeply resenting the outrage to his person, Pausanias denounced Attalus before the king……King Philip shared his anger at the barbarity of the act but did not wish to punish Attalus who besides being a valiant soldier, had already been selected as general of the advanced force being sent into Asia. The king tried to calm the anger of Pausanias the Macedonian giving him substantial presents…"

"However, Pausanias nursed his wrath, and yearned to avenge himself, not only on the one who had done him wrong but also on the one who failed to avenge him….Pausanias was determined to act under the cover of the festival, thus he posted horses at the gates of the city and came to the entrance of the theatre carrying a Celtic dagger under his cloak. When Philip directed his attending friends to precede him into the theatre, while the guards kept their distance, Pausanias saw that the king was left alone, rushed at him, pierced him through the ribs, stretching him out dead…He ran to the gates as one group of the bodyguards hurried to the body of the king and others went in pursuit of the assassin…They caught and killed him with their javelins."

Speculation has existed that Pausanias was executed inmmediately in order to silence him before he could uncover other co-conspirators. Other historians such as Plutarch and Arrian mention the suspicion that included as possible co-conspirators even his daughter Olympias and her brother Alexander. We will never know.

King Philip was succeeded by a young man, aged twenty, who history will prove to be the most illustrious commander of all times: his son Alexander. The young commander immediately proceeded to execute several individuals who were supposed to have been involved in the conspiracy that ended his father's life. Alexander was a descendant on his father's side from Heracles and on his mother's side from Achilles. However he could not count on the general support that his father had while still alive; thus he was compelled to convince all the Greeks that he was their best man: he used diplomacy but also force when necessary. Once his power was consolidated the young commander decided to pursue what his father had planned for the invasion of Asia.

Alexander crossed the Hellespont, entered Asia Minor and appeared in Cilicia after passing the Taurus Mountains, the ancient home site of the Phoenician gods El, Baal, Ashoreth and Anat.

The young Alexander, despite his age, had already seen the horrors of war fighting next to his father against the coalition of Beoetia and Athens and had distinguished himself for his valour and swiftness of action. In Athens the death of Philip was received with rejoicing, and the Athenians were not ready to concede the leading position among the Greeks to Macedonia. Thus after his father's death when some Greek city states were not willing to give him the command of all Greek forces, he decided to coerce them if not by diplomacy then in the battlefield. He first had to deal with the Thessalians and later proceeded to subjugate with his army the Boeotians. After this he proceeded to Corinth where he called an assembly of delegates who concluded by naming him Plenipotentiary of the Greeks. He then asked them to join him in an expedition against Persia seeking satisfaction for the offences which they had committed against Greece.

After defeating the Thebans and destroying their city, Alexander went back to Macedonia to prepare his forces for the invasion of Asia.

Once lavish sacrifices were made to the gods, Alexander advanced with his army to the Hellespont and took his army from Europe to Asia.

According to Diodorus "he personally sailed with sixty fighting ships to the Troad, where he flung his spear from the ship and fixed it in the ground. He then leapt ashore himself the first of the Macedonians, signifying that he received Asia from the gods…He visited the tombs of the heroes Achilles and Ajax, honored them with offerings…and proceeded to count his forces. The infantry consisted of twelve thousand Macedonians, seven thousand allies and five thousand mercenaries…in addition to seven thousand others, making up a total of 32.000. His cavalry counted fifty-one hundred. These were the men who crossed with Alexander to Asia."

Alexander began his march out of the Troad and came to the sanctuary of Athena, where he made splendid sacrifices and dedicated his own armour to the goddess. Memnon, the Rhodian, was commanding the Persian forces. He proposed to send naval and land forces across to Macedonia and transfer the impact of the war to Europe. He failed to convince the leading Persians who considered this measure an insult to their own dignity. Subsequent events proved that Memnon had been right but upon the rejection of his advice, he proceeded to face Alexander by the river Granicus. In the ferocious battle that followed the Macedonians routed the Persians but not without considerable danger.

"The Persian satrap, son-in-law of Darius, a man of superior courage, hurled himself at the Macedonian lines with forty of his companions...As the force of his attack seemed dangerous, Alexander turned his horse toward the satrap and rode at him. To the Persian, it seemed as if this opportunity for a single combat was god-given. He hoped that by his individual gallantry Asia might be relieved of its terrible menace, the renowned daring of Alexander arrested by his own hands, and the glory of the Persians saved from disgrace." In the battle that ensued "Alexander drove his lance squarely into the satrap's chest. The point of the lance snapped off against the breastplate, the Persian drew his sword and drove at Alexander but he recovered in time to thrust at the man's face...the Persian fell...The total of the Persian infantery killed was more than ten thousand, two thousand of the cavalry and twenty thousand were taken alive. By common consent the palm for bravery went to Alexander".

General Memnon and some Persian suvivors had taken refuge at Miletus: Alexander attacked them and forced the remainder to either surrender or flee. Alexander treated the Milesians kindly but sold all the rest as slaves. Furthermore, Alexander then sent back the Athenian contingent of twenty ships and dismissed the rest of the fleet: Alexander's decision was sound since he judged that the Macedonians would fight more desperately if he deprived them of all hope of escape by flight. Almost two thousand years later Hernan Cortez, the Spanish conqueror of Mexico, would use the same strategy by burning his ships off the coast of Mexico, and forcing his troops to advance with him to achieve the conquest of the Aztecs.

After the capture of Miletus, the bulk of the Persians and mercenaries, as well as the most enterprising of the commanders, concentrated their forces at Halicarnassus. Memnon sent his wife and children back to Darius and was then made supreme commander of the Persian army.

Both armies then confronted each other in the siege of Halicarnassus with loses on both sides and finally Memnon gave orders to abandon the city in flames. The next day Alexander learned what had taken place and decided to raze the city and surrounded the citadel with a formidable wall. Alexander with some of his troops, then overran the littoral as far as Cilicia, taking many cities on his way.

In 333 BC Darius sent money to Memnon and appointed him commanding general of the whole war. Unfortuntely for the Persians Memnon fell ill and died from an illness not well defined. Darius after mutiple considerations decided to take personally the command of his army and summoning his forces from all directions, ordered them to go to Babylon. There 400,000 men and 100,000 cavalry were assembled.

Alexander in the meantime fell ill either from fatigue or from swimming in a cold river but recovered promptly after medical intervention. Alexander's mother wrote to him at this time warning him to be alert and trust no one even his own bodyguards.

Upon his recovery he learned that Darius had left Babylon with his wife, children and his mother and advanced with his army in the direction of Cilicia and soon reached a location a few days away from him. Alexander then sent Parmenion with a body of troops to seize the gates off the Taurus Mountains. Darius learning that Alexander was holding the passes and thinking that he would never dare to fight in the plain, made his way quickly to meet him. The people of the country with little respect for the Macedonians and impressed by the great numbers of the Persian army proceeded to bring food and other supplies to them.

Thus both armies reached Issus, a large city. Alexander upon learning of the proximity of the Persians thought this an opportunity provided by the gods to destroy the Persian power in a single victory. With the cavalry in the front, he ordered the infantry phalanx to remain in reserve behind it. He himself advanced at the head of the right wing with the best of the mounted troops and with the Thessalian army on the left, to the encounter with the enemy. The trumpeteers on both sides sounded the signal of attack: Alexander cast his glance in all directions anxious to see Darius and once he identified him, drove with his cavalry at the king himself. By now the rest of the cavalry on both sides were engaged and many were killed as the battle raged undecisively. The brother of Darius, Oxathres, seeing that Alexander was riding towards his brother, with the best of his horsemen threw himself against Alexander and took up the fight directly in front of Darius, inflicting and suffering multiple casualties. But the Macedonians were superior and soon the horses of Darius chariot became unresponsive to their bridles; Darius himself was forced to catch the reins and decided to escape......It has been speculated that Darius only wanted to regain control of his horses to continue fighting but his troops thought otherwise and decided to escape. Seeing the King in this state the Persians with him turned to flee, the whole Persian cavalry was soon in full retreat and promptly reached safe territory.

The infantry continued the battle but soon retreated through difficult territory where many of them died in the narrow passes of the whole countryside which soon was covered with bodies.

When night fell the Macedonians gave over the pursuit and turned to plunder: gold, silver, and large numbers of rich dresses from the royal treasure were all taken with the wives. The ladies of the royal house, friends and relatives had accompanied the army according to an ancestral custom of the Persians. "The lot of these captured women was pathetic in extreme" says Diodorus Siculus...... What particularly moved to tears of pity those who saw it was the family of Darius, his mother, wife, two daughthers of marriageable age and a 6-year-old son. Alexander participated for a while in the pursuit of the enemy troops but finally gave up and returned to his camp towards midnight. Having dispelled his weariness in a bath, he turned to relaxation and to dinner. The women were informed of Alexander's return and believing Darius dead started with a great outcry and lamentation. The king then sent one of his friends to inform the women that Darius was alive and that he would respect their rank and give them proper consideration. As they heard the good news, the captive women hailed Alexander as a god...At daybreak he visited them, promised the mother of Darius her royal jewelry, restored her to her previous dignity and proper honors. He promised to provide for the marriage of her daughthers and to raise the boy as his own son. As to the wife of Darius, he said that he would see that her dignity should be maintained and that she would experience nothing inconsistent with her former status.

Darius in the meantime returned to Babylon and after gathering the survivors of the Issus battle sent three letters to Alexander proposing a peace treaty with cession of all territory west of the Euphrates, release of the captives in exchange of his daughthers and additionally he offered either 10.000 or 30.000 talents, according to various sources. One letter was sent after the Issus battle, another after the capture of Tyre and the third was perhaps an embassy after Alexander's return from Egypt, in consideration of the treatment Alexander had given to Darius's queen. Alexander rejected all offers from Darius.

After the battle of Issus Alexander buried the dead including those Persians who had distinguished themselves by courage. Then he offered rich sacrifices to the gods and marched towards Egypt. As he came through Phoenicia he received submission of all the coastal city states with the exception of Tyre.

At Tyre, Alexander expressed the desire to sacrifice to the Tyrian Heracles but the people barred him from entering the city. Some sources claim that it was the time of the great annual festival to the god and the Tyrians felt that to allow Alexander to sacrifice at this time would have meant acknowledgeing his sovereignty. Others say that the Tyrians offered to let him sacrifice at the temple of the Heracles of Palaetyrus, the mainland portion of the city but not on the island. This temple of Heracles at Tyre was the most ancient temple to the god (Melkart), described by Herodotus. Alexander became angry and threatened to resort to force, but the Tyrians preferred the prospect of a siege. They would draw Alexander into a protracted and difficult siege because they had confidence in the strenght of their island and their military forces. Besides they counted on receiving reinforcements from Carthage, a colony of Tyre. The king knew that the city could hardly be taken by sea because of the fortified walls one hundred and fifty feet high and because he possessed a powerful fleet. From the land it was even more difficult because the island was located about half a mile from the coast. Alexander was however determined to run every risk and make every effort to save the Macedonian army from bcing held in contempt by a single "undistinguished city."

Thus he decided to demolish Old Tyre and build a mole from the continent to the island. He set tens of thousands of men to carry stones to build a mole two hundred feet wide. He drafted the entire populations of the neigbouring cities that had surrendered, mainly Aradus, Byblos and Sidon, and after that the project advanced rapidly because of the numerous workers. At first the Tyrians sailed up to the mole and mocked the King, asking if he thought that he would get the

The Phoenicians in History and Legend

better of Poseidon. But as the work proceeded rapidly they voted to transfer their women, children and old people to Carthage. Then they prepared to face the forces of Alexander with their eighty ships but found difficulty because of the abundance of the labor force; they succeeded in sending some of their people to Carthage but were forced to stand the siege with most of the general population still in the city...All kinds of novel devices were fashioned by their engineers and artisans, so that the entire circle of the walls of the city including the side where the mole was being build was loaded with machines for defence. Soon the Tyrians became alarmed at the advance of the mole, thus they equipped many small vessels with with light and heavy catapults, and attacking the workers on the mole wounded many and killed not a few. Large numbers of missiles of all sorts in large numbers rained over unarmed and densely packed men; no soldier missed his mark since the targets were exposed. The missiles struck from the front and from the back, as men were working on both sides of a rather narrow structure and no one could protect himself...Alexander moved immediately to rectify what threatened to be a shocking disaster. By now the ships from Aradus, Byblos, Berytus, Sidon and Cyprus had joined him: he advanced with all speed for the harbour of Tyre to cut off the retreat of the Tyrian ships: both fleets fought with fury and determination, as the Macedonians were already nearing the entrance to the city but the Tyrians, by a narrow margin, escaped losing their whole force and got safely to the city losing only a few ships from the tail of their column.

As his siege engines drew close to the city and the capture of the city seemed imminent, a powerful north-west gale blew up and damaged a great part of the mole. Alexander was disconcerted by the forces of nature and thought of giving up the siege attempt. But driven by his ambition he sent many men to the mauntains to fell and bring back huge cedar trees. By placing them besides the mole, he broke the force of the waves. He managed to restore most of the collapsed mole and attacked the walls with his stone throwers...The Tyrians had bronze workers and machinists who made wheels with many spokes and setting them to rotate, they destroyed some of the missiles and deflected others. They caught the balls from the stone throwers in soft and yielding materials and weakened their impact. In the meantime Alexander sailed around the city and made it clear that he intended to attack the city by land and sea: by this time the causeway had reached the wall and connected the city to the mainland...When the Macedonians moved up towers as high as the walls and thus were able to assault the city defenders, the Tyrians forged great tridents armed with barbs and used these to stricke the assailants standing in the towers at close range. The barbs stuck in the enemy shields and with ropes attached to the tridents they could haul and pull them within the walls. Their victims were forced to get rid of their arms and expose their bodies to the missiles or cling to their shields and perish by falling from the towers.

The Tyrians engineered another ingenious device to attack the Macedonians; they fashioned shields of bronze and iron, filled them with sand and roasted them continously over a strong fire until the sand became red hot. They were then sent by catapults against those Macedonians fighting bravely: the sand sifted down under their breastplates and shirts, scorching the skin with the intense heat…with excruciating agony they fell into madness and died…At the same time the Tyrians poured down fire and flung javelins and stones and by the volume of their missiles weakened the resolution of the attackers. With many hands at work they kept all their engines busy and caused many deaths among the besiegers…Alexander with the dart-throwers on the wooden towers, kept up a constant fire of missiles and terribly punished the defenders of the walls. The Tyrians were bold in face of their enemies and matched the courage of the Macedonians with their own valour.

Alexander saw that the Macedonians were held in check by the resistance of the Tyrians and as it was night now, he recalled his soldiers by a trumpet call. His first impulse was to break off the siege and march on to Egypt, but he changed his mind as he reflected that it would be disgraceful to leave the Tyrians with all the glory…

According to Arrian, Alexander then spoke to his army as follows:

"My friends and allies: so long as Persia is supreme at sea I cannot see how we can march in safety to Egypt. Nor, again, is it safe to pursue Darius, leaving in our rear the city of Tyre, of doubtful allegiance and Egypt and Cyprus still in Persia's hands, especially in view of the state of Greek affairs. The Persians might again secure control of the coastal cities, when we have advanced in full force towards Babylon and Darius and with a larger expedition transfer the war into Greece, where the Lacaedemonians are openly at war with us, Athens is kept in control for the present by fear rather than goodwill. But if Tyre is destroyed, all Phoenicia would be in our hands, and the best and strongest part of the Persian navy, the Phoenician, would most probably come over to us. For if their cities are in our hands neither the rowers nor the marines of Phoenicia will tolerate dangers at sea for the sake of others. After this either Cyprus will come to our side or will be taken easily by naval attack. If we keep the sea with Macedonian and Phoenician ships, our expedition to Egypt would be easy on the very same account."

Alexander then told his commanders that he had had a dream in which Heracles was stretching out his right hand to him and taking him into the city. This, according to him, meant that they had the support of the god. Others believed this dream meant that he would evntually take Tyre, it will be with great efforts and the loss of many lives. The commanders were then convinced to continue the attack on Tyre.

Preparing all his ships for fighting, he began a furious general assault by land and sea. He saw that the wall on the sea side was weaker than elsewhere, and brought up to that point his triremes lashed together and supporting his best siege engines. Now he performed a feat of daring, hardly believable to even those who were present. He flung a bridge across from the wooden tower to the city walls and crossing it alone gained a footing on the wall,...not fearing the menace of the Tyrians......He then ordered the Macedonian army to follow him, he slew those who came within reach with his spear, and others by a blow of his sword: this put an end to the high confidence of the enemy.

Simultaneously in another part of the city, the Macedonians were able to bring down a considerable stretch of the wall; and when entered through this breach and found Alexander coming over the bridge on to the wall, the city was taken. The Tyrians kept fighting in the streets until the end: about seven thousand of them died. Alexander sold the women and children into slavery and crucified about 2000 men of military age. So, bravely, Tyre had resisted a siege of seven months...falling finally on the 29th of July 332 BC.

He installed as King of Sidon a man named Abdalonymus, a phoenician name (**'bd 'lnm**) meaning "Servant of the gods". He was placed in the position formerly occupied by Straton who was deprived of his throne. The new king became a friend of Alexander and took over the kingdom, an instructive example of what Fate can achieve. Some scholars speculate that this king was the owner of the Sarcophagus of Alexander found at Sidon (now in the museum of Istambul), where it was taken from during the Ottoman empire. It is well known that the Turks occupyied the city many centuries later, until the 19th century AD. The mention of King Straton shows that this later incident must have happened at Sidon, not Tyre.

Alexander advanced towards Egypt and on his way there he took Gaza by siege and later on, after fixing the affairs of Gaza, proceeded to Egypt where he was received without resistance. Alexander then went to the Temple of Ammon: he consulted the oracle who told him that he will conquer the rest of the earth, something which pleased him considerably.

He decided to found a great city in Egypt, and left orders to the men staying behind with this mission to locate the city between the marsh and the sea. He himself designed the new city and laid out the streets skilfully, ordering that the city should be called after him Alexandria. It was approximately 331 BC.

Alexander then returned to pursue Darius in Northern Syria where he received another embassy sent by Darius, this time offering him all the territory west of the Euphrates, thirty thousand talents of silver and the hand of one of his daugthers. Alexander met then in council with all his high commanders and urged them to speak freely on the matter. No one dared to say anything with the exception of Parmenion, who said: "If I were Alexander I would accept the offer and make a treaty".

Alexander cut in and said: "So would I, if I were Parmenion".

Hastily Alexander went through el-Bekaa and the Orontes valley, passed the Euphrates, traversed Mesopotamia from the North to the East and finally passed the Tigris, above the site of Niniveh. In the plain near Arbela he defeated the army of Darius who himself managed to escape to Ecbatana. After the battle Alexander buried his own dead and entered Arbela but not liking the pollution of the unburied enemy bodies, he moved to Babylon, where he was received lavishly. He stayed there for about a month.

Alexander then advanced in the direction of Persia sending the main group of his forces ahead while he went with a smaller contingent through the passage known as the Susian Rocks. Here there was a large Persian army of over 25.000 infantry and three hundred cavalry. Alexander then advanced with his forces through narrow defiles in rough country, without opposition. The Persians allowed him to proceed along the pass for some distance, but when he was about halfway through, they suddenly attacked him with huge boulders,which falling upon the ranks of the Macedonians killed many of them. Many of the enemies threw javelins from the cliffs into the crowd, killing many more. The Persians killed many and injured not a few. Alexander was helpless to avert the suffering of his men, many were slain and disabled. Thus he recalled his soldiers and decided to withdraw from the pass to a safe distance. Once in a safe place he began to inquire whether there was another way to bypass the Persian forces. A Lycian prisoner was found who knew the country well and offered to help leading the forces through a path concealed by bushes which led to the rear of the Persians guarding the pass: under his direction Alexander did make his way over the mountain at night and through deep snow. He then attacked from the rear and defeated the Persian army. The way was now open to Persepolis. Once there he gave it over to his Macedonian soldiers to plunder all except the palaces. As the capital of the kingdom it was the richest city under the sun but after the plundering it exceeded all others in misery. When all this was over Alexander went after Darius.

The Persian king wanted to face Alexander at Bactria but in the course of his flight he was seized and murdered by Bessus, the satrap of Bactria. When Alexander arrived with his cavalry he found Darius dead. Some writers state that Alexander found Darius still breathing and promised him to pursue Bessus and punish him. Plutarch tells us that Alexander found Darius still alive and covered him with his own cloak. He gave him a royal funeral.

When Alexander arrived at Hyrcania, he was met by the queen of the Amazons, named Thalestris. She was remarkable for her beauty and strenght and arrived with an escort of three hundred Amazons in full armour. Alexander marvelled at the unexpected arrival and dignity of the women. When he asked Thalestris the reason for her visit, she replied that it was for the purpose of getting a child. He had shown himself to be the greatest of all men with his achievements and and she was superior to all women…so presumably the offspring of such outstanding parents would surpass all other mortals in excellence. The king was delighted and granted her request. He consorted with her for thirteen days, after which he gave her fine gifts and sent her home with honours. Historians hold differing opinions about the veracity of this event in the life of Alexander: some favor the fact described and others not only deny the existence of the Amazons but, of course, the truthfulness of the story.

Arrian describes the incident of the Amazons' visit to Alexander in a somewhat different manner: "The satrap of Media sent Alexander as a gift one hundred women…equipped like cavalry troopers". According to the story Alexander sent them away from the army, in order to avoid any outrage from the Macedonians or the barbarian troops……He told them to inform their queen that he would come to see and have children by her. Both Aristobulus and Ptolemy deny the existence of the Amazons……Following a brief discussion, Arrian concludes: "And yet I do not think it credible that this race of women ever existed…"

Alexander then decided to adopt many of the customs of the Persian kings, began to dress like them and added concubines to his retinue in numbers not less than the days of the year and outstanding in beauty as selected from the most beautiful women of Asia. They paraded in front of his sleeping place so that he might select the one with whom he would lie every night.

Alexander continued with his army and in his advance encamped near the Caucasus, where he was shown the legendary rock, in which the cave of Prometheus was located and pointed out to him by the natives, as well as the nesting place of the eagle of the legend. Some historians reject again the existence of the mythological place.

He plunged towards Kabul in Afganistan and after passing the mountains he finally caught Bessus and gave him proper punishment. He then continued in his conquests, victorious in battle after battle passing through most of India, crossed the river Indus which "no one had crossed before Dionysus", (the latter are Alexander's words as quoted by Arrian). He crossed by both mouths of the Indus, and came through the Gadrosian desert, where no one had ever gone before with an army,...while the fleet had already sailed along the coast from India to Persia,...with instructions to meet him at the mouth of the Euphrates river. Alexander also held weddings at Susa for himself and the closest members of his inner circle.

Alexander, acoording to Justin and Plutarch, at this time married Barsine, daughther of Artabazus, believed later to have born Alexander a son, named Heracles. Arrian claims that Barsine was the eldest daughter of Darius. Aristobulus says, he also took another wife as well, Parysatis, the youngest daughter of Artaxerxes III. He had already taken Roxane, the daughter of Oxyartes the Bactrian. This Barsine, named Statira by most other historians (including Plutarch), would be murdered by Roxane, after Alexander's death and when Barsine was about 7 months pregnant.

Alexander advised all of his inner circle of friends to marry Asiatic women: to his closest friend, Hephaestion, he gave in marriage another daughter of Darius, sister of his own wife, for he desired Hephaestion's children to be cousins of his own. To Ptolemy the bodyguard and Eumenes the royal secretary, the daughters of Artabazus and Artonis, to Nearchus the daughter of Barsine and Mentor, and finally to Seleucus he gave Apame, the daughter of Spitamenes the Bactrian. The latter will be the only lasting marriage and she became the ancestress of the Seleucid dynasty. These weddings were celebrated in the Persian style and Alexander gave them all dowries. More than ten thousands other Macedonians married Asian women and had their names registered by Alexander's orders.

At Ecbatana Alexander offered sacrifices, held athletic and musical games, and had drinking bouts with his companions. At this time Hephaestion fell ill, his illness had run for seven days and the race-course was filled with people to witness the athletic event but when Alexander heard that Hephaestion was seriously ill, he left the course and hurried to him, but found him no longer alive.

Historians have given varied accounts of Alexander's grief on Hephaestion's death: all have related that his grief was great. Some say that the greater part of the day he lay prostrate and weeping on his companion's body…Others say that he hanged Glaucias the physician, either because of a drug wrongly given or because Glaucas did not stop Hephaestion from drinking most immoderately. Others tell us that he ordered the temple of Asclepius at Ecbatana to be razed to the ground. There is no proof that this happened. Yet others say that when Alexander was going to Babylon he found on his way a group of emissaries from Greece and after they obtained from him what they demanded he gave them a votive offering to take back to Aesculapius adding

"Yet Asclepius has not been kind to me, in failing to save for me the comrade whom I valued as much as my life".

Most authors agree that after his friend's death Alexander tasted no food for two days and took no care of his body, but lay either moaning or in a sorrowful silence; that he ordered a pyre to be made ready for Hephaestion in Babylon at the cost of ten thousand talents…and he never appointed anyone in his place……and ordered athletic and musical games far more splendid than any before…and he provided for three thousand performers to be present. This is related both by Ptolemy and Aristobulus. Ammon's oracle told Alexander to give Hephaestion the burial of a hero.

Following the funeral he departed for Persepolis. After arriving at Persepolis, which was in ruins, and resting there for a while, he decided to move on to Babylon.

When he had crossed the Tigris with his army on the march towards Babylon, Alexander was met by Chaldean seers, who drew him aside from his companions and begged him to stop his march into Babylon because they had an oracle from their god Baal indicating that his entry into the city at that time would do him harm…He is said to have responded with a verse from Euripides:

The best of the prophets is he who guesses well.

Alexander was rather suspicious of the Chaldeans……The temple of Ba'al was in the center of the city of Babylon, unequalled in size,…and Xerxes had razed it to the ground when he returned from Greece. Alexander had in mind to rebuild it, on the original foundations, others say that he wished to make it even larger than the previous one.......Aristobulus relates that Alexander did follow the Chaldeans advice in deviating from his course of entry into the city, and that he camped the first day by the river Euphrates, and the next day marched with the river close on his right, with the intention of entering from the western side, but finding it difficult for his army, decided to defy the seers' predictions.

Another story recorded by Aristobulus deals with someone named Apollodorus, one of Alexander's commanders, who after he had met Alexander on his return from India, observed that his behaviour was rather punitive and unforgiven towards those who had violated some of his orders before he departed for India. He wrote to his brother Pithagoras, who was a seer, who issued auguries from the flesh of sacrificed victims, asking about his own welfare. Pithagoras first sacrificed in regard to Hephaestion and because he could not find the liver lobes of the victim, reported back that to Apollodorus in a sealed letter from Babylon to Ecbatana. Apollodorus received the letter informing that he had nothing to fear from Hephaestion...who died the day after the letter arrived.

Apollodorus then requested his brother to prophesy about Alexander and again the response was similar: "the liver of the victim had no lobes". This time he did not keep silent and immediately advised Alexander of the ominous news. Alexander waited until he arrived to Babylon and personally asked Pithagoras what was the meaning of his prophesy. To this he responded "Something very serious may happen to you". Alexander thanked him for speaking the truth without deceit.

Another story along these lines had been recorded about Calanus, the Indian sophist: when he was going to the funeral pyre to die, he greeted all of Alexander's companions but refused to approach and greet Alexander: he told him:

"I will meet you at Babylon and greet you there".

Only after Alexander's death, this response was understood.

Aristobulus says that Alexander also found at Babylon the fleet that had sailed with Nearchus up the Euphrates from the Persian sea. In addition a fleet from Phoenicia consisting of forty seven ships had been brought to Babylon to meet him. Alexander intended to colonize the Persian Gulf, because he thought that it would become just as prosperous a country as Phoenicia.

Because nothing had happened to him despite the Chaldean's prophesy he went to visit the tombs of most of the kings of Assyria, which were built in the lakes and marsh lands. While he himself was steering a trireme, a strong breeze struck his cap and the diademe attached to it. They fell into the stream and the diademe was caught in one of the reeds which grew on a tomb of the old kings. This seemed to presage his destiny: a Phoenician sailor that had swum to fetch the diademe carried it back bound around his head instead of his hands because it would have become wet as he swam. Aristobulus says that it was the Phoenician sailor who brought the diademe to Alexander.

For his enthusiasm most historians say that Alexander gave him one talent and ordered his head cut off. For the prophets said that "the head which has worn the royal diadem should not be allowed to live". Aristobulus, however, says that the sailor was only flogged for fastening the diademe about his head. History and legend.

Alexander continued to receive embassies from many parts of his kingdom: Persia, Greece and the sacred envoys from Ammon.

Arrian describes the events of Alexander's death:

"But in fact Alexander's own end was now close. During a meeting with his commanders Alexander felt thirsty and left his royal throne. On either side of the throne there were couches with silver seats, in which the Companions of the tribunal in attendance used to sit. The Companions had all risen when the king left. A beggar passing by saw the empty throne surrounded by eunuchs standing around the throne, passed through the eunuchs and sat in the place of Alexander......When Alexander learned this the put the man to the rack to learn whether this was part of a plot. He would only say that the idea had come to him to do so". Diodorus describes the same episode.

Arrian continues: "Not many days later Alexander offered the gods sacrifices for good fortune...and then began feasting with his friends and drinking far into the night......Some have recorded that when he was ready to leave and retire to his bedroom, Medius, one of his most trusted companions at the time, met him and asked him to come and share his celebration, for it would be a merry party.

The so-called Royal Journals give the account followed by Arrian but on several points are alleged to be spurious: "He drank and made merry with Medius and then after rising and bathing, went to sleep; afterwards he dined with Medius and again drank until late into the night, and then breaking off from the party, bathed and after bathing ate a little and slept just where he was, for he already had a fever.

However, he was carried out on a couch to perform the daily sacrifices; after making the offerings he lay down in the men's appartments until dark. At this time he gave the men instructions for the upcoming voyage. Then he was carried on his couch to the river, and embarking on a boat he sailed across the river to the garden, and there again bathed and rested". For the next five days he ate little, offering the daily prescribed sacrifices, bathed and remained with a high fever days and nights. On the sixth day, "being now very ill, he still offered the appointed sacrifices but ordered the generals to wait in the court and the soldiers outside the doors. He was now extremely ill and was carried from the garden to the palace. When the officers came in he recognized them but he was speechless. He was in high fever that night and day and also the next night and day……All his soldiers longed to see him, some simply to see him still alive…and others because of rumours that his death was being concealed by his bodyguards……but the majority pressed to see Alexander from grief and longing to see their king. When the army file passed he was already speechless but greeted them all raising his head and making a sign to them with his eyes. Meanwhile the generals were in the Temple and consulted the oracle as to whether it was desirable to bring Alexander into the temple...but were told to leave him where he was: thus Alexander died. Some have recorded that when his companions asked to whom he was leaving his kingdom, he replied "To the best man". Aristobulus and Ptolemy have recorded no more than this.

"Alexander died in the hundred and fourteenth Olympiad......and according to Aristobulus he lived thirty two years and eight months; his reign lasted twelve years and eight months.

He excelled in physical beauty, in zest for exertions, in shrewdness of judgement, in love of honor and danger......He exercised the greatest self-control..."

Considerable speculation has surrounded the circumstances of his death. In modern times the illness that led to his unexpected death has been thoroughly discussed and among the multiple possibilities considered are included: Alcoholic hepatitis with fulminant liver failure; fermentation of the wine with methanol production and intoxication through formaldehyde to formate (this possibility is of interest because of the alleged absence of decomposition of the body after death); arsenic in the wine could have led in large quantities to severe hepatic necrosis; or hepatitis B with fulminant hepatitis may have occurred; perforated gastro-duodenal ulcer with peritonitis and finally typhoid fever with severe abdominal manifestations and the possible association with a Guillain-Barré syndrome. Numerous theories have circulated throughout history about the cause of his death and obviously, for lack of scientific methods during his lifetime, modern speculations are futile.

After Alexander's death, his generals attempted to obtain the choicest parts according to their strenght: Ptolemy took Egypt, Seleucus Babylonia, Antigonus the rest of Asia Minor and Antipater took Macedonia.

Control of Phoenicia shifted on and off between Antioch, Babylonia and Egypt until finally it was controlled by Ptolemy I in 283. It remained under Egyptian hegemony until 198 BC with its main city-state being Sidon: This is the time of Tabnit I and Esmun'Azzar. Their sarcophagi were found by Renan in 1855 AD together with the famous, so-called Sarcophagus of Alexander. The latter was taken during the Ottoman Empire to the Istambul museum.

The sarcophagus of Esmun'Azzar contains on its lid the longest Phoenician inscription, descibed elsewhere under the section dealing with the Alphabet. This sarcophagus of Eshmuna'Azzar, dating from the third century, rests today in the Louvre.

From 198-82 BC, Phoenicia became part of the Seleucid kingdom, under Antiochus the IV. When the Seleucid power beagan to decline, the Phoenicain city-states slowly again achieved a certain degree of autonomy: first Aradus, then Tyre and after them Tripoli, Byblos, Sidon, Berytus and Acre. Berytus and Tyre issued their own coins, sometimes in gold, with bilingual legends in both Greek and

Phoenician. But the Phoenician vitality, despite this degree of autonomy, the vitality they had exhibited since time immemorial was now quite feeble or gone.

Around 70 BC Arabian tribes of Aramean speech began to overrun the territories between Sidon and **P'ne-El** (in Phoenician "the face of god"), an area north of Batrun, devastating the fields of Berytus and Byblos in between, and generally acting as professional brigands. The instability in the area continued until 64 BC, when a Roman general, Pompey, came with a fresh army sent by the Roman Senate and restored peace. He quickly took over several regions of Asia Minor including Phoenicia. He annexed Syria, Lebanon and Palestine under the common name of Provincia Syria. Officially Phoenicia no longer existed.

Pompey proceeded to decide the successor to the throne of Judea which was under dipute between two brothers. On his way there he went through Tripoli and passing by Heliopolis (Baalbeck today) reached Damascus. Before he arrived there he had to impose authority in the region, because Tripoli, Byblos and Beirut were under constant attacks by caravan traders that went through the region overrunning the cities that were ruled by "tyrants". Pompey took energic measures against them and proceeded to behade the rulers of Tripoli, Baalback and Byblos, who were often encouraging brigandage. The Syrians from Damascus unhappy with the situation had already contacted Ptolemaeus, king of the Nabatheans, to restore order. When Ptolomaeus learnt that Pompey had already punished several tyrants by beheading them he decided to approach Pompey with a large sum of money: he gave him the sum of one thousand talents and saved his own head. For a number of years the area was in a state of turmoil and several of the Roman contenders for supreme power visited the Eastern shores of the Mediterranean sea. Julius Cesar stopped in the area at about 47 BC and addressed a decree directed to the magistrates, council and people of Sidon.

In addition, the Romans allowed Ptolomaeus to rule the region until 40 BC. He was succeeded by his son who unfortunately did not live long because Mark Antony who took his lands, put him to death. He then gave the conquered territories to his lover Cleopatra, with the exception of Tyre and Sidon because he considered these coastal city-states independent. Mark Antony, member of the second triumvirate, gave Cleopatra the territory of the Bekaa and the majority of the coastal towns as far as the Egyptian borders with the exceptions noted in 36 BC. Cleopatra intended to build a pleasure house for herself and her Roman lover on a Phoenician mountain overlooking the sea. Unfortunately this was not to happen because Octavian, the nephew of Cesar, obtained a decisive victory in the battle at Actium and then decided to push Antony and Cleopatra all the way back to Egypt, where, as it is well known, they committed suicide. The people of Palestine and Phoenicia, longing for stability and peace, welcomed the change.

Octavian was given the name of Augustus Cesar by the Senate in 27 BC, thus he succeeded his uncle. Soon the Romans realized that the Bekaa-Baalbeck region was in such strategic location that at about 16 BC Augustus had decided to station his most experienced Roman legions in Beirut and Baalbeck, thus providing the area with ample new roads with rapid means of communications. In addition they decided to build at Baalbeck the greatest temple conceived until that time: the **Temple of Jupiter Heliopolitanus**.

A period of peace and prosperity (**Pax Romana**) eventually occurred and extended until the times of Marcus Aurelius, the Stoic Emperor and Philosopher. Wealthy Phoenicians and Roman settlers began to use higher and higher places among the mountains and hilltops of Phoenicia as their residences and left their imprint in the form of Greek and Latin inscriptions, tombs and sarcophagi. During the second century AD Septimius Severus, born in Leptis, North Africa, a former Phoenician colony, married the daughter of Elagabaal and ordered the partition of the area between an eastern part (Coele-Syria) and a western portion (Phoenicia). Eventually a Phoenicia Prima and another Phoenicia Secunda emerged, as discussed elsewhere. Phoenician legends on coins began to dissappear. But the phoenician language persisted until the fith century in North Africa, under the Punic form. This in turn had infuenced the development in Spain of the Ibero-Phoenician language which spread later to the Americas, where stone inscriptions have been found that date back, according to certain scholars, to 800 BC.

HELEN, PARIS AND THE TROJAN WAR

Homer places Helen in Phoenicia before the Trojan war and scholars have long debated whether or not Helen was really taken by her lover Paris to Troy immediately following her abduction. The Homeric account appears to suggest that the lovers were forced to stay on phoenician shores, where storms had taken them, after their escape from Menelaus' quarters. Thus the Trojans did not have a Helen to return to the angry Greeks when threatened by imminent destruction. Avoiding the destruction of their city and the subsequent devastating war would have been rather simple, had she been there. But then the great poem would never have been written.

Paris persuaded Helen to leave Sparta and take off with him while her husband Menelaus was away. Some say this happened because such was the will of Zeus, in order that his daughter become famous for having embroiled Europe and Asia in war or because of his desire was to make Helen the mother of a race of demigods. For nine days Paris was the guest in the house of Menelaus and on the 10th day while Menelaus absented himself to attend the funeral of his grandmother in Crete, Helen decided to abandon her daughter Hermione and took off with Paris. The voyage of Helen with Paris to Sidon was known to Homer (Iliad VI: 289). Herodotus described how the lovers sailed from Sparta to Cyprus and later to Sidon where they were entertained by the king but Paris treacherously murdered his host and plundered his palace. Embarking with his booty on his ships, he was pursued by the Sidonians. After a bloody battle the Sidonians

The Phoenicians in History and Legend

lost and Paris succeeded to escape with several vessels. Hera sent them a heavy storm and after great tribulations Paris arrived in Troy. It does however seem that, with the consent of Zeus, Paris stole Helen and carried her to Egypt where, he left her under the custody of the Egyptian king Proteus, while Paris returned to Troy with a phantom of Helen made out of clouds. Herodotus gives a different account of these events: (Histories; Book II: 112-120): According to him as a consequence of the storm, Paris took the real Helen to Egypt, where king Proteus, infuriated by the crime of Paris banished him from Egypt but retained Helen until Menelaus arrived and thus returned her to him.

King Proteus by magic arts created a Helen that he sent with Paris to Troy while the real one stayed in Egypt. A poet named Stesichorus in the 6th century BCE appears to have been the first to create the story of the false Helen, after suffering a sudden blindness that he thought was caused by Helen. He created the theory that the presence of Helen at Troy, for which the Greeks and Trojans fought and died was a mere fantasy. The real Helen was in the meantime either in Egypt with Proteus or back in Sparta with Menelaus. It is well known that when Menelaus became aware of the abduction of Helen by Paris he managed to assemble all the Greeks to attack Troy and warned them to look for the safety of their own wives.

Proteus, according to Herodotus, was a native of Memphis who had a richly decorated sacred dwelling in a district known as the Camp of the Tyrians, because the neighborhood was predominantly inhabited by Phonicians from Tyre. They had a temple dedicated to

Aphrodite the Stranger, build apparently in honour of Helen, who Herodotus had heard lived in the court of Proteus. When Herodotus inquired about the story of Helen, the priests told him that when Paris left Sparta with his stolen bride they met with foul weather in the Aegean Sea which drove their ship towards Egypt until at last they found themselves ashore at the mouth of the Nile where a temple to Heracles existed. In this precinct whomever sought refuge and submitted to the service of the god could not be punished by his master. Several of Paris' servants decided to get him into trouble and deserted to the temple where they told the story of Helen's abduction to the priests and the warden. The latter sent a message to Proteus in Memphis telling him "A Trojan stranger has arrived here from Greece, where he has been guilty of seducing the wife of his host, then carried her off with a great deal of her husband's property, but has been forced by bad weather to land on his coast. Should he be allowed to go with the stolen goods or should they be confiscated? Proteus replied that "whomever has committed such crime against his friend should be arrested and sent to him so that Proteus could hear what he has to say for himself". Thus Paris was arrested and sent to the presence of the king: Paris could not explain to the satisfaction of the Egyptian king how and why he had taken not only Menelaus' wife but his properties as well: "You seduced your host's wife…and persuaded her to escape with you on the wings of passion…I will keep this woman and the treasure, until the Greek to whom they belong chooses to come and fetch them". This was the account the priests gave Herodotus about the arrival of Helen at the court of Proteus.

Homer knew about the wanderings of Paris and described them in The Iliad (VI: 289). Although Homer may have not used the story in all its minor details because of its lack of epic character, he does not forget to mention in his story that in the course of these events Paris brought Helen to Sidon in Phoenicia when he says:

> There were the bright robes woven by the women of Sidon,
> Whom the hero Paris, splendid as a god to look on,
> Brought from that city when he sailed the wide sea
> Voyaging with high-born Helen, when he took her home.

In the Odyssey (IV: 225-230) he also mentions

> …Drugs of subtle virtue the daughter of Zeus was given
> By an Egyptian woman,……;
> For the rich earth of Egypt bears many herbs
> Which steeped in liquor have power to cure, or to kill.

When Herodotus inquired from the priests about the truth of the Greek story of what happened at Troy, they replied what they had learned from the words of Menelaus himself: after the abduction of Helen, the Greeks sent a strong force in support of Menelaus cause,…being received within the walls of the town,…when asked to return Helen and the treasures that Paris had stolen, the Trojans gave always the same answer they had given over and over since, that neither Helen nor the treasure was in their possession, but were both in Egypt…in the hands of the Egyptian king Proteus. The Greeks laid siege to the town and persisted until it fell; but no Helen was found and they heard again the same story. Thus Menelaus was sent to Egypt to see Proteus……after his arrival to Memphis, he was well received and entertained; Helen was restored to him with all the rest of his property. Herodotus believed the story of the Egyptian priests and argues that "had Helen really been in Troy, she would have been handed over to the Greeks with or without Paris consent, for Priam would not have been mad enough to be willing to risk his own life, his children's lives and the safety of the city just to let Paris continue his romance with Helen. Furthermore, after losing many battles in their clashes with the Greeks, losing most of his children and having his city in flames. Paris was not the heir to the throne but Hector, his elder brother and a better man than he. The fact seems that if they did not give up Helen is because they did not have her; what they told the Greeks was the truth…and the refusal of the Greeks to believe it…may have come from divine volition in order that their brutal destruction prove to mankind that "great sins meet with great punishments at the hands of the gods", concludes Herodotus.

PYGMALION AND ELISHA (ELISSA, DIDO)

Elissa's great-aunt was none other than Jezebel, the queen of the Hebrews. Pygmalion (Dido's brother) came to power in violation of their great-grandfather's desire that he should share the authority over Tyre with his sister Dido. Accoding to legend King Matten, their father, reigned for twenty nine years and was succeeded by Pygmalion. Following the conspiracy against the king perpetrated by Dido's uncle-husband, Acharbas, priest of Astarte, and the reaction by Pygmalion that led to Acharbas death, Dido (Elissa) decided to abandon Tyre and found a colony in North Africa. Acharbas, high priest of Herakles, had accumulated a substantial fortune, that provoqued the greed of Pygmalion. After his uncle's death he attempted to get his fortune, only to find out that it had been hidden by Elissa. Dido then plotted to escape from Tyre and thus convinced her brother of her desire to move to her palace on the island off mainland Paleothyrus. He gladly accepted, convinced that he will inherit the fortune of Acharbas. The treasures and gold left by Dido's husband were secretly concealed aboard her ship. In the meantime she made the servants of her brother move into his presence the bags of sand that Pygmalion believed contained the riches. Once aboard she began to throw the bags into the sea because she said they contained the riches that had caused the death of her husband. Her brother did not believe her. When she sailed out to the sea, Pygmalion was going to follow her with a large fleet but dissuaded by his mother, decided not to follow her. She escaped first to Cyprus where a large contingent of her followers was further increased by one hundred virgins recruited there. These women appear conveniently to have come for the annual ritual ceremonies involving the offering of their virginity to Astarte.

Virgil describes in the mouth of Venus the flight of Dido from Phoenicia:

"From the Punic realm,…a Tyrian people, from the city of Agenor…Dido wields the sceptre -Dido, who, fleeing from her brother, comes from the city of Tyre. Long would be the tale of wrong, long its winding course, but the main parts of the story I will trace."

"Her husband was Sychaeus (Acharbas), richest of the Phoenicians in land and fondly loved by unhappy Dido; to him her father had given the maiden, yoking her to him in the first bridal auspices. But the kingdom of Tyre was in the hands of her brother Pygmalion, monstrous in crime beyond all others. Between these two came frenzy. The king, impious before the altars and blinded by lust of gold, strikes down Sychaeus, careless of his sister's love; and for long he hid the deed, and by many a pretence cunningly cheated the lovesick bride with empty hope. But during her sleep the very ghost of her unburied husband appeared to her; raising his pale face, he laid bare his breast pierced with steel, unveiling all the secret horrors of the house. Then he bids her speed flight and advises her to leave her country, and to aid her journey she can take a mass of silver and gold known to no one. Moved hereby, Dido made ready her flight and her company. Then she assembled all who felt towards the tyrant relentless hatred or keen fear; the seized the ships that were ready and loaded with gold.........They came to the place where now sit the huge walls and rising citadel of new Carthage. They bought land as much as they could encompass with a bull's hide." The legend ran that the Phoenician settlers bargained with the Libyans for as much ground as could be covered by a bull's hide. This was cut into very fine strips by the Phoenicians, which thus were able to enclose a large tract of land.

Among Dido's followers were members of the Barcus family, who would be the direct ancestors of Hamilcar and Hannibal. From Crete they would depart for their final destination in Africa where the foundation of Carthage takes place. The time, according to most sources, was during the early 9th century, about BC 814.

Years later Virgil would describe it as
"An ancient city, the home of Tyrian settlers, Carthage,...rich in wealth and stern in war's pursuits."

"This city, it is said, Juno loved above all other lands,...here was her armour and here her chariot; here should be the capital of all nations,...Yet in truth she had heard that a race was springing from Troyan blood, to overthrow some day the Tyrian powers; that from its people, kings of broad realms and proud in war, should come forth for Lybia's downfall."

The daughter of Saturn fearful of the Trojans and still remembering what happened at the war with Troy, with the cause of her wrath and her bitter sorrows still in her mind; at then seeing the remaining Trojans hardly out of sight of Sicilian land, in her quality as queen of the gods, sister at once and wife of Jove, blasts the sea with a tempest:

"In a moment clouds snatch sky and day from the Trojan's eyes; black night broods over the deep. From pole to pole it thunders, the skies lighten with frequent flashes, all forbodes the sailors instant death".

Aeneas then cries aloud invoking the help of the gods. "In the meanwhile, Neptune saw the sea in a turmoil of wild uproar, the storm let loose and the still waters upheaved; greatly troubled but gazing out over the deep he raised his serene face above the water's surface. He sees Aeneas' fleet scattered all over the sea, the Trojans overwhelmed by the waves and by the falling heavens" all of these events caused by Juno's wrath. Then he decides "to calm the swollen seas, puts to flight the gathered clouds, and brings back the sun".

Aeneas' people then look for the nearest shore and turn towards the coast of Lybia. In the coast of Libya "In a deep inlet lies a spot, where an island forms a harbour with the barrier on its sides, on which every wave from the main is broken and then parts into receding ripples. On either side loom towards heavens huge cliffs and twin peaks, beneath whose crest, far and wide, is the stillness of sheltered water; above too, is a background of shimmering woods with an overhanging grove". This is an accurate description of the location where Carthage was founded by Dido, as described by contemporary historians of Hannibal and Scipio Africanus.

Virgil continues: "Here, with seven ships mustered from all his fleet, Aeneas takes shelter; and disembarking with earnest longing for the land, the Trojans gain the welcome beach" where they share their wheat, meat and wine.

Juno fears the uncertain house and double-tongued Tyrians and instead of Ascanius, Aeneas son, she decides to send Cupid to change Dido's behaviour

"to outwit the queen with guile and encircle her with love's flame, so that no power may change her, but she may be held fast in strong love for Aeneas......Love obeys his dear mother's words and goes forth, carrying royal gifts for the Tyrians. As he enters, the queen has already, amid royal hangings, laid herself on a golden couch, and taken her place in their midst.........Above all, the unhappy Phoenician, doomed to impending ruin, cannot satiate her soul, but takes fire as she gazes, thrilled alike by Cupid and by the gifts...She then with her eyes and all her heart clings to him...knowing not, poor Dido,how great a god settles there to her sorrow......Cupid little by little, begins to efface Sychaeus, and essays with a living passion, to surprise her soul and heart unused to love......Then the queen called for a cup, heavy with jewels and gold, and filled it with wine", and made a toast that

"Jupiter grant that this be a day of joy for Tyrians and the voyagers from Troy…may Bacchus, giver of joy, be near and you O Tyrians, grace the gathering with friendly spirit".

Juno and Venus now control Dido's behaviour: "Dido herself, matchless in beauty, with cup in hand, pours libation between the horns of a white heifer,…Unhappy Dido burns and through the city wanders in frenzy,…Now through the city's midst she leads with her Aeneas, and displays her Sidonian wealth,……Dido is on fire with love and has drawn the madness through her veins. Let us then rule this people jointly with equal sovereignty".

Juno then spoke: "Aeneas and Dido plan to go hunting together in the forest, soon as tomorrow's sun rises. On them, I will pour down from above a black rain mingled with hail, sending to the same cave Dido and her companion. I will be there and link them in sure wedlock, sealing her for his own; this shall be their bridal…"

"As soon as Dawn rose and left the ocean and sunlight burst forth,…attended by a mighty throng, and clad in a Sidonian robe with embroidered border. Her quiver is of gold, her tresses are knotted into gold, golden is the buckle to clasp the her purple cloak……Aeneas himself, goodly beyond all others, advances to join her and unites his band with hers"……

"Meanwhile in the sky begins the turmoil of a wild uproar; rain follows, mingled with hail…torrents rush down from the heights. To the same cave come Dido and the Trojan chief. Primal Earth and nuptial Juno give the sign; fires flashed in Heaven, the witness to their bridal, and on the mountain-top screamed the Nymphs. That day was the first day of death......For no more is Dido swayed by fair show or fair fame, no more does she dream of a secret love: she calls it marriage".

BERYTUS AND THE SCHOOL OF LAW

This city was the seat of the most renowned school of Roman law, probably founded by Septimius Severus. The original location of the school had been forgoten for several centuries. It appears to have been destroyed by a cataclismic earthquake and tidal waves in 551 AD. Its ruins have not been discovered despite the extensive reconstruction of the city of Beirut that has followed the latest war towards the end of the 20th century AD. In its time this school of law was more important than similar schools at Athens and Alexandria. This Berytus institution had become a university with schools of law, letters and philosophy by the end of the 5th century AD. Among its most prominent figures were Aemilius Papinianus, born in Emessa and Domitius Ulpianus, born in Tyre. Papinian disapproved of the assassination by Caracalla of his own brother, named Geta. The emperor infuriated by this first deposed him and finally Papinian was beheaded by orders of the tyrant. Excerpts of Papinian's writings were included by Justinian as part of his Code: this would serve as the basis for the laws that were to rule later continental Europe. The other important figure of the law school was Domitius Ulpianus, born at Tyre about 170 AD. He held a chair at Berytus and later was called to Rome to assist Papinian under Septimius Severus. Ulpianus was also asssassinated in the imperial palace during a mutiny in the presence of the Emperor. The Justinian Code was the most complete collection of Roman law in its time, when Berytus was according to Justinian "the mother and nurse of all laws".

The city of Berytus was occupied by Greeks first and Romans later since the 2d century BC. However, hard evidence of occupation during this period was mostly lacking until the recent excavations were started a decade ago in the center of the city, following the almost total devastation left by the war during the last quarter of the 20th century AD. These excavations were initiated in order to reconstruct the city after its almost total destruction by the recent events of the civil war. These operations, conducted by international teams, have revealed an area of over 30 acres that contains archeological evidence of continuous occupation of Beirut for about five millennia since the early Bronze age.

In the northern part of the Martyrs' square of Beirut, a monumental entrance to the city of the Bronze age has been discovered. The remnants of the city walls of the Bronze Age have also been found and dated to the 18th century BC together with the monumental entrance described elsewhere. The limits of the Phoenician city have also been found and the habitats of the Persian-Hellenistic period as well as a cemetery in the regions arround the square that formerly were not known to exist. A quarter of the city of the Phoenician-Roman period has also been found with houses ornamented by mosaic scenes. A part of the Roman forum with marble arcs, finely sculpted and decorated, has also been uncovered. During the Hellenistic period Beirut is known as Laodicea of Canaan and in Greek as Laodicea of Phoenicia. During the 10th to 9th century, artifacts have been found representing images of goddesses, utensils and weapons in bronze or bone. The commercial and residential quarters were found in the streets surrounding the Martyr's square. Beirut possessed numerous thermal establishements which now have been found in close connection with the residential areas of the city.

Within an area close to the Place de l'Etoile of present-day Beirut, an ancient monumental construction has been found consisting of a great wall with terraces ornated by arcades and niches which seem to have belonged to the Forum. Within the necropolis, funerary masks in gold and ceramic artifacts dating to the 1st century BC have been discovered. The Roman city seems to have been built over the remnants of the area of Greek occupation. Under the Roman Empire Beirut was named "Iulia Augusta Felix Berytus" and given control over extensive territories to the interior and also extending to the Orontes River in the North. Latin became the official language and The School of Law became the reservoir of the greatest intellects in the Middle East. The climax of the school was reached during the 4th century and lasted until Beirut was destroyed by a violent earthquake on July 9, 551.

CHAPTER ELEVEN

CARTHAGE AND THE PUNIC WARS

The people of Carthage, Susa (ancient Hadrumentum, **hdrm** in Punic) and Kerkuane were an ethnic mixture of the Eastern Phoenicians with the autochthonous races of the area. The Phoenicians, according to recent evidence, began to explore the Mediterranean area of Africa by the middle of the second millennium BC: Lixus, a city in Morocco was founded, according to Pliny, around 1180 BC, and the sanctuary erected by the phoenicians in Cadiz occurred towards 1110 BC. In the place where the city of Lixus stands, writes Pliny, **"the Gardens of the Hesperides"** once grew, next to the temple of Herakles. (Pliny, Nat. Hist. XIX, 63). Sometime later, in 1101 BC the city of Utica was founded in Tunisia. And Pliny continues, "It appears that Utica was founded by the Phoenicians 287 years before Carthage". A cylinder seal found in Malaga, Spain, places the Phoenicians there in the middle of the second millennium. Their navigational objective was most probably motivated by the metal trade which was so much attracted the interest of the two world powers of the day, Mesopotamia and Egypt. The Phoenicians went in search of gold, copper, silver, lead and especially tin. They may have gone as far as England in order to obtain the latter.

The sanctuaries of Carthage give information concerning the character and religion of its people: in the temple of Eshmun, which could be reached only by a monumental series of steps, the wife of Hasdrubal with her children and others duiring the invasion of Carthage, chose to join them and resist but not surrender, preferred to die by fire instead of being taken prisoners in order to vindicate the honour of Carthage. Other temples existed as evidenced by Punic inscriptions dedicated to Baal, Tannit and Astarte. A temple dedicated to Apollo with a chapel entirely decorated with gold leaf was totally destroyed by the soldiers of Scipio the Africanus, as described by Polybius. The Carthaginian sanctuaries were open to all people: rich and poor, men and women, slaves and their owners.

Evidence exists that marine bases to defend the city were built by excavating the rock in order to assure protection from potential invaders and protect from the course of the winds.

The ports were used during the Punic wars and have dissappeared. Despite international efforts directed at rescuing them for history, they remain still uncovered. The Carthaginians had inherited from their eastern phoenician ancestors their love for luxury: the elegant houses along the ports were totally burned by the Romans. The phoenico-punic people left an abundant number of towns in Morocco founded by them and mentioned by Pliny. The most important were Lixus and Melilla. The later city derives its name from the Latin word for "honey", described in Greek in the Periplus of Hanno as "acxros", meaning "cape" from the Punic word **rs**. The name of Lixus was

mqm SMS, phoenician expression meaning the "abode of SMS", the sun-god worshipped by the Phoenicians.

In their earlier expansion the Phoenicians build a monumental temple to Astarte in Kition that lasted from the tenth to the fourth century BC but eventually was diminished in size and later destroyed. There remained evidence of great richness in votive offerings. The Phoenicians occupied most of the Mediterranean islands during the first millennium BC: Sicily, Malta, Sardinia and Ibiza. In Sardinia they left the important constructions at Nora where the temple of Tannit and the temple of Eshmun, dating from the 7th to the 3d century have been found.

A large inscription in the phoenician language known as the **Nora Stone** was dated as far back as the 9th century BC by Albright although other scholars disagree and believe that it can not be placed before the 6th century BC. For a long time it was considered the earliest phoenician inscription before the sarcophagus of Ahiram was discovered. The same is true of **the stele of Mesha**, king of Moab, now preserved at the Louvre Museum; dated to about 800 BC. It was also thought to represent the most ancient inscription in the phoenician tongue, before the epitaph on the lid of the sarcophagus of Ahiram was found at Byblos. At Tharros the phoenicians build a tophet in the 7th century and Doric temples which lasted until the Roman times in the 2d century.

In Spain the Phoenicians founded Cadiz, Cartagena, and Malaga. Temples dedicated to Kronos and Heracles existed in Cadiz, according to Strabo. In Ibiza they built temples to Melkarth-Reshep and to Tannit that lasted for about five centuries.

Hasdrubal, the son-in-law of Hamilcar, founded Cartagena in 221 BC but nothing of the Punic culture remained there after their defeat by the Romans and its destruction by Scipio, according to Polybius. Over the ancient city of Malaga (in phoenician designated as **melakah**), an ancient town has been newly excavated by Spanish archeologists on a hill overlooking the modern city of Malaga just recently (1996 AD).

As discussed earlier, the geography known to the Greeks in the second millennium was poor. The names of Europe, Asia and Africa were given later by the Greeks to the continents. The most commonly accepted theory supports the contention that were derived as follows: Europe was derived from the phoenician designation of Europa (according to legend kidnapped by Zeus disguised as a bull, a feature which made Kadmus come to Greece and among other things, as discussed elsewhere, he brought the alphabet). The name Lybia, first given by the Greeks to Africa, was derived from the name of the wife of Poseidon and mother of Agenor, the Phoenician king. The designation of Asia is more a topic of controversy: According to some, Asia was named after the wife of Prometheus. According to the Lydians, however, Asia was originally the name of the grandson of Manes and a tribe called Asias existed in Sardis.

The Phoenicians in History and Legend

From their native seat, the narrow strip of Asia Minor known as the land of Canaan, the earliest people who spread to the West were the Phoenicians. The Hellenes named this people Poiniki ("people from the land of the purple or land of the red men").

The Phoenicians, from the beginning of recorded history, directed their resources of courage, acuteness and enthusiasm to the development of commerce. Theirs was an advanced culture and civilization but most of their literature is believed to have been written in papyrus and has not been preserved. The arts of navigation, manufacturing and colonization, soon connected the East with the West. Through their hands gold and pearls, purple, slaves, ivory and lion's skins reached the West where they were exchanged for linen of Egypt, wine of Greece, copper of Cyprus, iron from Elba, silver from Spain and tin from England. Their religion was primitive and their worship was directed to support rather than restrain lust and the pleasures of life. Historians, however, differ in their estimation of their religious practices. From the Babylonians they learned to follow the course of the stars, there they first saw the representation of sounds in pictorial figures and it was from there also that they most likely began to become familiar themselves with the concepts of space and time.

The Phoenicians were, traditionally, peaceful people, with no political ambitions, but since ancient times were subject to the yoke of the Egyptians and Assyrians: they preferred to pay taxes than close their routes of trade. They avoided war even with their enemies: in the early great battles of antiquity that took place for the control of the western Mediterranean, in many instances, they left the fight to the Etruscans instead of facing themselves the Greeks. This was not the result of cowardice: to navigate with poor ships and weak vessels in unknown seas required great courage, tenacity and brave hearts. The many documents in Phoenician as well as in bilingual vocabularies found around the entire Mediterranean area testify to the tenacity of this singularly industrious and adventurous people. For over a millennium they controlled vast areas of the southern Mediterranean towns and cities of Europe and founded new ones through Northern Africa. The geography of the locations of various Phoenician ports reveals that very little stopped them in their advance through the seas: in the absence of navigational instruments, distance and winds were not obstacles, their ships navigated even during the night. It seems that they were the first to use the constellation of **Ursa Minor** to guide themselves in the uncharted seas. That was one of the main characteristics of these navigators: when they would advance towards the unknown, the high seas would not frighten them. On the other hand, on land they preferred to live secure in the possesion of their riches.

During the 17th century AD, Samuel Bochart was the first to place the Tartessus of the Greeks in southern Spain. The area was well known as controlled by phoenicians in their business. This view is now generally accepted by some scholars. In Herodotus, Polybius and Strabo, Tartessus is either a region of Andalusia, a mountain, a river or a city. The Greek sources emphasize the prosperity of

Tartessus and the longevity of its inhabitants: Herodotus mentions especially the King Arganthonius, who lived as king apparently for about 150 years. This point is rather controversial, as discussed elsewhere. Pliny the Elder (NAT. HIST.; IV, 22) considered Cadiz as the ancient Tartessus. Recently it has been postulated that Tarshish could be the phoenician expression of a Celtiberic name, **trt/ trs**, that became Tartessus in Greek and later on Turdestania during the Roman era.

Of all the settlements established by the Phoenicians outside of their eastern site of origin the most succesful were build in North Africa (Carthage) and Spain (Cadiz). The Carthage town was situated in a strategically ideal location: It was in a fertile ground within the richest corn district of North Africa, located in the gulf of Tunis with country houses and groves of olives, orange trees falling slowly to the sea and ending near a promontory with good anchorage for vessels and where drinkable spring water came close to the sea shores. They continued to pay rent for a long time to the natives for the land they occupied and even send money to the mother city of Tyre. But their passiveness had a limit: they saw themselves slowly infiltrated and replaced by the Greeks not only in Greece but in Italy, Sicily, Spain and even Lybia itself. The time had come for them to face the Greek competitors that soon began to act as invaders or to be totally crushed. They undertook the task of stopping the Greeks and after hotly contested wars they forced them to limit themselves to occupy the desert portion to the west of Tripoli in Tunisia. They faced the Greeks in the western part of Sicily and took control of the south-western part of the Mediterranean. Carthage could no longer remain as a mercantile center and soon re-invented the practice of hiring mercenaries. They ceased paying rent for the soil and began to cultivate the land as landlords and traders with hired laborers or by means of slaves.

The Lybian farmers began to pay as tribute a fourth part of their produce; the Nomads were then slowly driven into the desert and mountains or were obligated to recognize Phoenician supremacy. The towns occupied along the shores by other Lybiophoenicians from Hippo, Hadrumentum, Little Leptis and great Leptis began to contribute as a matter of law to the common fund with the tributes obtained from citizens who were protected by the same laws as the Carthaginians and could intermarry on equal terms. In this way the former colony became the capital of a powerful North-African domain which extended from the desert of Tripoli to the Atlantic Ocean in Morocco and Algeria. Phoenician was then written and spoken by the tribes of Nomads and the more civilized among them adopted the Phoenician alphabet. The rise of Carthage was associated with a parallel decline of Tyre and Sidon under the constant sieges by Shalmanazar and Nebuchodonossor.

The Phoenicians now controlled not only Carthage and its satellites but Cadiz and part of Andalusia in Spain where silver mines were located near Granada. They were also dominating Sardinia and a great part of eastern Sicily with Malta and other smaller islands. For the next 100 years multiple wars gave the Carthaginians the control of all of Sicily with the exception of Syracuse; the latter was under the able leaderhip of men such as Dionysius and Pyrrhus. The attempt of Pyrrhus to re-establish a Syracusan naval fleet failed and finally the Carthaginians commanded the whole western Mediterranean.

The Constitution of Carthage:

Most of the information that we have concerning this topic has come to us from Aristotle (384-322 BC) in his treatrise on Politics. The best constitutions known to him are discussed in Book II, where he compares the Constitutions of Crete, Sparta and Carthage. In section VIII he says:

> "Carthage appears to have a good constitution with many outstanding features as compared to those of other nations, but most nearly resembling the Spartan in some points…Many regulations at Carthage are good and a proof of this is……that the populace willingly remains faithful to the constitutional system and that neither a civil strife has arisen…nor yet a tyrant."

To best understand at a greater length what the Carthaginian Constitution was, it is necessary to indicate the different categories described by Aristotle.

"Tyranny is monarchy exerting despotic power over the political community; oligarchy is when the control of the government is in the hands of those who own the properties; democracy, on the contrary, is when power is under the control of those that do not possess much property and are rather poor"......"We must ascertain what are stated to be the determining qualities of oligarchy and democracy and what is the principle of justice under one or the other form of government.

For all men lay hold on justice of some sort, but they only advance to a certain point and do not express the principle of absolute justice in its entirety. For instance it is thought that justice is equality and so it is, but not for everybody but only for those who are equals; if it is thought that inequality is just, although not for everybody but for those who are unequal; the latter strip away the qualifications of the persons concerned, and judge badly. The cause of this is perhaps that most men are bad judges when their own interests are in question"...the meaning of "just" varies according to the parties concerned: the examples of wealth and freedom divide men in unequal or equal categories.

The ideal is to reach equality to a certain point that may appear quite just to both parties..."The name of aristocracy is properly given to the constitution of which the citizens are best in virtue absolutely and not merely good in relation to some arbitrary standard......When the constitution takes into consideration wealth and virtue as well as the common people, as for instance at Carthage, this is the nature of an aristocrasy"...this compares with what happens in Sparta, where

The Phoenicians in History and Legend

they take in view both virtue and the common people and with the mingling of both factors, democracy and virtue. In the constitutional government they elect their officals not only by wealth but also by goodness: this form of constitution is called aristocratic and seems to be the best. Common points between the Carthaginian and the Spartan constitutions are the Magistracy of One Hundred and Four which they both elected by merit and while the Spartans are drawn from any class, the Carthaginians are selected by their wealth instead. The selection of Kings and the Council of the Elders represent another difference i.e. this is a superior characteristic in Carthage's constitution when compared with other constitutions because the Kings are not confined to the same family and the Elders are not elected just by age but on account of merit and wealth. The reference of certain matters to the popular assembly rests on the kings in unanimous agreement with the Elders but the people also participate: they sit and listen to the decisions taken by the rulers and if they disagree they may speak against the proposals introduced, a characteristic unique to the Carthaginians and not found in other constitutions. Their constitution has democratic and oligarchic features but the Carthaginian system deviates from aristocracy in the sense that they think that the rulers must be chosen not only for their merit but also for their wealth: this system is applied to the election of Kings and Generals. The characteristics were considered a bad thing by some, because the greatest offices of the state may become available for sale and…"a state in which virtue is not held in the highest honor cannot be securely governed by an aristocracy"…A single man can hold several offices in Carthage and this is considered a distinction.

Aristotle adds: "One man, one job is the best rule for efficiency......and the lawgiver should not appoint the same man to play the flute and make the shoes". It is better for the well being of the state if a large number of individuals share different jobs and the functions are performed better and more quickly. Everyone in command except the Commander-in-Chief should have someone of higher rank over him. But the constitution being oligarchical a great wealth became dangerous and in order to avoid this danger of being wealthy, they started the habit of sending riches to their families in the mother-city of Tyre. They also adopted the habit of constantly sending out a portion of their common people to appointments in the cities. These measures were implemented in an attempt to cure the defect in their system and render it more stable.

Aristotle considered the constitution of Carthage that of an aristocracy that later switched to a democracy and then to an oligarchy. The affairs of state were carrried on by the Council of the Elders: two kings and twenty eight magistrates. This council decided on declarations of war, nominating generals and other magistrates. The generals were sort of dictators while the others acted as Judges. The council of the Elders and the magistrates were under the Corporation of the Hundred and Four Judges or simply "The Hundred". Public offices could be bought easily thus a single family notable in wealth i.e. the Mago clan, attempted once to buy all positions. This led to a change in the Constitution that required the Judges to stay in power for only one year. Some, however, stayed in power longer and even for life. Thus the designation of "Senators", given to them by some early authors.

The Carthaginian Constitution was controlled by capitalists and a middle class scarcely existed. As a consequence, a democratic opposition soon emerged. Among the states of antiquity Carthage was financially the wealthiest city of the world. They were also experts in agriculture but as a rule a Phoenician was not supposed to acquire more land than he could properly manage.

Science and Phoenician literature imitated the Greeks: when Carthage was taken years later, rich art treasures and large librairies were found that had been carried off there from Sicilian temples. Intellectual activities were also at the service of the capitalistic society. Knowledge of foreign languages was greatly appreciated and fostered. Even the laborers or slaves were supposed to be able to read and possess some degree of culture.

Gold and silver were used as money but in addition some sort of token coin money was used as currency: no other place in antiquity used this sort of currency. The Carthaginians did not consider their dependent districts equal to them: they sent overseers everywhere and taxed them with heavy tribute. Even their own subject tribes were treated as slaves of the state. Only in Sicily it appears that a milder rule was exercised and it was here that a party really friendly to the Phoenicians existed. The Carthaginian way of conducting war was far more expensive than the Roman due to the native aversion of the

Phoenicians to warfare and their extensive use of mercenaries. Only military honour and personal advantage kept together the armies of Carthage while the Romans were united by love for their fatherland. The Carthaginians experienced difficulties with their slaves and mercenaries and quite often found their paid serfs more dangerous than their enemies. The Carthaginian government always maintained its war chests full in order to be able to support their mercenaries. In matters such as ship-building they excelled over the Greeks, they were better sailors; their rowers, all of them slaves, were excellently trained and their captains were expert and fearless.

With the help of the Greeks the Carthaginians forced Pyrrhus to abandon Sicily and Italy, leaving the largest part of the island in the hands of Carthage. Ever since, Carthage regarded the affairs of Sicily as an internal matter and did not allow any outside power to interfere, treatening to go to war. Political intrigues eventually brought the Romans to Sicily in their first excursion out of the peninsula. They were succesful there against an army composed of Syracusans and Carthaginians.

In subsequent campaigns, resistance from general Hamilcar Barka inside his maritime fortresses along the coast, soon taught the Romans that it was not easy to defeat the Carthaginians, who kept the coastal towns of Sicily constantly harrassed. Carthaginian detachements landed constantly on the Italian coasts, demanded and obtained contributions from the allies of Rome and eventually paralyzed their commerce. The Romans understood that to conquer and beat the Carthaginians in the field was nothing easy.

The war for Sicily:

Forced by circumstances Hamilcar Barka, like the good and prudent leader that he was, decided to send an embassy to treat for peace because there was no reasonable prospect left of saving the troops under his command. Lutatius, the Roman commander, accepted immediately to negotiate, says Polybius, "conciencious as he was that the Romans were worn out and enfeebled by the war, he succeded in putting an end to the conflict by a treaty which contained several clauses: there shall be friendship between the Carthaginians and Romans in the following terms: the Carthaginians had to evacuate Sicily and return all prisoners to the Romans without ransom and pay the Romans in installments the sum of 2200 talents." The people of Rome did not accept these terms and insisted in doubling the indemnity and requiring the Carthaginians to evacuate all islands between Sicily and Italy. Hamilcar accepted. "Those were the terms of peace, Polybius continues, to end a war which had lasted without a break for 24 years......The Romans lost in this war about seven hundred quinquiremes and the Carthaginians about five hundred....In the longterm "the purpose and prosecution of this war was equally characterized on both sides by enterprise, a lofty spirit, and above all by ambition for supremacy. In individual courage the Romans were superior on the whole, but the General to whom the palm must be given, both for daring and for genius was **Hamilcar**, surnamed **Barka**, the father of the future Hannibal, who afterwards made war on the Romans" and has been considered by some historians as the first among all commanders in history.

The domination of Sicily, took place after multiple battles in many small wars that followed with no clear advantage to either side since 275 BC. The most inglorious occurred between 248-243 BC. It is at this time (c.247) that one man, already mentioned, emerged with a different attitude towards war and peace: **Hamilcar Barka** ("lighting" in phoenician). The family name was derived from **baraq**, a phoenician word meaning "lighting", from which perhaps the word Barcelona was also derived. His army was defective, with poor infantry and the Carthaginian government passively observed its defeats unwilling to help because the African city was then controlled by the opposing party. Hamilcar knew that the mercenaries were indifferent to any state in the conflict, thus he decided to establish himself with his forces on Mount Eryx, near Palermo, from which he could commmand the surrounding country from a fortress. He settled the mercenaries of his army with their wives and children and began to plunder the Italian coastal towns to obtain revenues. With copious supplies he maintained his soldiers satisfied, and he did not ask for any help from Carthage: the Romans could not touch him in his stronghold and even more he decided to create a new fortress at Eryx, another mountain that had at its summit the temple of Aphrodite. The Celtic deserters from the Roman army defended and plundered the temple while Hamilcar deprived the Celts of the town in the plain surrounding the temple area.

The Romans rapidly realized the situation was precarious because Hamilcar soon was in control of Sicily: the wealthy Roman citizens decided then to build two hundred ships and attacked the Carthaginians which were not strong enough and lost in battle fifty ships: Hamilcar without sacrificing his military honour signed a peace treaty. He surrendered Sicily but maintained the independence of the Carthaginian state and its territory. In the terms of the treaty the unconquered general of a vanquished army gave away the mountains that he had defended for seven years and delivered the fortressess the Phoenicians had held for at least four hundred years: the result was peace in 241 BC.

But the Roman fleet consisted to a great extent of Italian Greeks, slaves and outcasts, and the Roman victory was in reality indecisive, superficial, and in great part due to the errors of the Carthaginian enemy in conducting the war. However, in the years that followed, the Romans obtained Sardinia and Corsica, the island occupied since ancient times by the Etruscans, former allies of the Phoenicians. The Romans only occupied coastal zones in both islands. They continued their victories until taking the entire Italian peninsula.

The Carthaginians by the peace treaty lost not only Sicily but also its tribute, which were now collected by the enemy. Furthermore, they could no longer control the southern sea routes alone and lost the capacity to move freely between the Eastern and the Western Mediterranean.

After the peace of 241 BC neither the Romans nor Carthage were fully satisfied: although the Romans were not yet probably thinking of beginning the conquest of Africa, the Carthaginians could not depend on the good intentions of their enemy. As a natural reaction two parties originated in Carthage: one known as "the party of peace", supported by the aged, the feeble and the rich found their exerted power in the Council of the Elders, led by a certain Hanno, known as the Great. The other, "the party of war", was supported by the discontents who sided with the leaders of the Sicilian army such as Hamilcar and his son-in-law Hasdrubal.

The mercenary war:

After the completion of the peace treaty with Rome in 241 BC, the Carthaginians found themselves immersed in a more fratricidal war with their own mercenaries. On the conclusion of the treaty and after Barka removed his troops from Eryx, he resigned his command immediately. The command then fell into the hands of General Gesco who took the steps necessary to return the mercenaries to Carthage. This he did by embarking them in detachements and at certain intervals in order to give the Carthaginians time to pay them and send them to their native countries before the next batch would cross and catch them up. But the Carthaginians, partly for lack of money, decided to keep them in Carthage and only when the mercenaries began to commit frequent offences, night and day, the Carthaginians decided to ask their commanding officers, to withdraw them all to a town called Sicca until they could be payed in full. The mercenaries accepted this arrangement and moved with their families, started to live in a free and easy manner, a state to which they were no longer used to, with plenty of time for relaxation and leisure.

Having nothing to do they started to remember the promises of the Generals in Sicily and began to increase their demands. When a force of about 20.000 was assembled in Sicca, Hanno, the African Commander-in-Chief, came there and attempted to explain that their demands could not be met and that they must renounce to some of their stipulated wages: this lead to a spirit of disension and sedition, the soldiers began to hold constant meetings. Polybius says: "As they were neither all of the same nationality nor spoke the same language, their camp was full of confusion, tumult and turbulence." As this climate of confusion, anger and passion became the rule the main result ended in a mixture of discontent and human wickedness. It became extremely difficult to communicate with them and address them as a group because no general could speak so many languages. Polybius continues: "some of these troops were Iberians, some Celts, some Ligurians, some from the Balearic islands, many Greek half-breeds, slaves and deserters, and the largest portion consisted of Lybians." Hanno continued to attempt to communicate with them through their officers but unsuccessfully.

"At lenght refusing to treat with Hanno, distrusting their divisional officers and highly indignant with the Carthaginians, they marched on the capital and encamped in its neighborhood at the place called Tunis."

The Carthaginians now realised that they had committed two great mistakes: one was collecting a large body of mercenaries in a single place and second to let the mercenaries live with their families who they now could not use as hostages. The mercenaries continued to add new claims to their previous ones and finally "the Carthaginians promising to concede everything in their power agreed to refer the disputed points to the general who had been their commander in Sicily: Hamilcar Barka. But the mercenaries did not accept him, believing that this state of affairs was his fault because he had resigned his command voluntarily. Instead they decided to name Gesco, who had payed more attention to them in Sicily. Upon his arrival to Tunis, Gesco, bringing the money, met with officers first and later with the troops: finally he payed off each nationality separately.

Then two men, a former Roman slave named Spendius and a Lybian freeman called Mathos, decided to break off the negotiations with the Carthaginians and instigated the Lybians to revolt because they had not yet being paid: the soldiery began to plunder the personal effects and the money chest of the Carthaginians and to abuse Gesco and his entourage personally: it was the year 240 BC and the war started. Mathos with his Lybians put siege to Carthaginian cities such as Utica. The Carthaginians unaccustomed to this set of circumstances appointed Hanno as commander in the hope that he would succed in putting down the revolt but Mathos, joined by seventy thousand Lybians cut the peninsula of Carthage making it impossible for the inhabitants to attempt to acquire supplies.

Hanno had experience in matters of policy but in the battlefield lacked experience and energy. Having failed in several attacks against the mercenaries, the Carthaginians called to rescue them none other than Hamilcar Barka.

Polybius describes his return as follows:

"With seventy elephants and about 10.000 men, Hamilcar, in his very first expedition, struck terror into the enemy by the unexpectedness of his attack, cowing their spirit, raising the siege of Utica, and showing himself worthy of his past exploits and of the high expectations of the populace…On the neck of land connecting Carthage to Africa there were several difficult passes and a river controlled by Mathos…thus Hamilcar seeing all the obstacles, after passing in review every means and every chance of surmounting these difficulties, devised a plan: he had noticed that when the wind blew strongly from certain quarters the mouth of the river became shallow just where it fell into the sea. He therefore prepared his forces ready to march…and when the right time came he left Carthage at night, crossed the river and at daybreak had his army all across……Both those in the city and the enemy were taken by surprise: Spendius, upon learning what had happened, put his two forces in movement and tried to meet them in the plain. As soon as they advanced, thinking that they had caught the Carthaginians in a trap, they attempted to engage the enemy.

Hamilcar was advancing with the elephants in front, followed by the cavalry and light-armed troops and last all the heavy-armed. When he realised the enemy was advancing in suchhaste, he reversed the order of his troops. He told those in front to retire at all speed......The Lybians and mercenaries thinking that the Carthaginians were afraid of them and retreating, broke their ranks and attacked vigorously. But the cavalry wheeled around again and faced the Lybians, followed by the remainder of the Carthaginian army coming up, the enemy was so surprised that they at once turned and fled panic-stricken, collided with with their comrades,...the larger number were trampled to death, the cavalry and elephants attacking them at close quarters...Hamilcar succesful in this fashion, traversed the rest of the country winning over some towns and taking others by assault: this restored some confidence and courage to the Carthaginians." Mathos, in the meantime, sent messages to the Numidians and Lybians asking for help and Spendius managed to maintain about 2000 men. Fate came to help Hamilcar, who had established his camp in a plain surrounded by mountains, when a young Numidian of high rank and full of martial spirit named Naravas, came to offer his help, out of his admiration for Hamilcar, with a fresh army of 2000 more men.

Under these circumstances and with the new reinforcements Hamilcar offered battle to the enemy. Spendius and the Lybians were defeated by Hamilcar in the plain and lost ten thousand killed and 4.000 prisoners. Hamilcar gave permission to the prisoners to either join his army or to go free but threatened them that if they were caught again fighting against Carthage they would be given inevitable death. Mathos and Spendius, apprehensive of the effects of Hamilcar's leniency with the prisoners, allowed the torture and death of Gesco and his friends who had been taken at Tunis.

The Carthaginians with great indignation sent messages to Hamilcar and Hanno to come and avenge the unfortunate victims. The mercenaries were thus displaying such brutal behaviour that Hamilcar asked Hanno to join him in order to put an end to the war but Hanno quarreled with Hamilcar and, subsequently deposed by the soldiers, left Hamilcar as the supreme commander. He was joined by another general named Hannibal, sent from Carthage with an army and together with Naravas they intercepted the supplies sent to Mathos and Spendius. The mercenaries then resorted to cannibalism and finally Spendius and the Lybians proposed peace to Hamilcar: he accepted on condition that he be allowed to retain ten prisoners of his choice. By this means the Carthaginians got into their control Spendius and the other pricipal leaders.

As Polybius describes it:

> "The Lybians upon learning of their officers arrest and ignorant of the treaty, thought they had been betrayed, rushed to arms but Hamilcar surrounded them (more than 40.000) and cut them to pieces. In subsequent events Spendius was crucified facing the armies of Mathos and in battle Hannibal was taken prisoner and crucified alive by the Lybian opposing army".

The situation had become such that Carthage sent a commission of thirty senators with Hanno to convince the generals to reconcile their differences for the well being of Carthage: they did agree and finally decided to meet Mathos forces in a general battle to finish the war: the Carthaginians gained the victory, most of the Lybians fell in battle or escaped but Mathos himself was made prisoner. The rest of Africa at once submitted to Carthage."

Polybius concludes:

> "This Lybian war, that had brought Carthage into such peril, resulted not only in the Carthaginians regaining possession of Lybia, but in their being able to inflict exemplary punishment on the authors of the rebellion......This war had lasted for three years and four months, and it far excelled all wars…in cruelty and defiance of principle".

The seizure of Sardinia by the Romans then inspired the brighter minds in Carthage to support the Barkas despite the attempts of the opposition to follow the Romans: the government named Hamilcar the full Commander-in-chief with absolute powers that only the popular assembly could reverse. However, to form an army he needed not only the officers from the cultivated class but the common citizens who could be kept loyal only with money more than enthusiasm. In order to defeat and deceive his enemies and keep a few well-disposed minds in Carthage satisfied, he decided to move to Spain in search of the means to carry a foreing defensive attack in case of need. Thus inmmediately after the mercenary war he departed for Spain. Along the coast he went with the army and his elephants and by his side sailed the fleet under the command of his son-in-law Hasdrubal. After Hamilcar's death, because his eldest son Hannibal was still a child, according to Livy, "the supreme command was given to Hasdrubal for about eight years. It was his youthful beauty that won for him in the first instance the favour of Hamilcar, who subsequently selected him, no doubt for other than his mental qualifications, to be his son-in-law". What Hamilcar personally did in Spain is not well known but it must have been remarkable because a generation later, Cato the Elder, not an admirer of the Carthaginians, did say that no king was worthy of being compared with Hamilcar given his accomplishements as a soldier and statesman until he met his end in the battlefield: he had converted the southern and eastern coasts of Spain into a Carthaginian kingdom. The prisoners of war were incorporated into the Carthaginian army and the mercenaries grew attached to the good phoenician lifestyle rather than motivated by patriotism. The constant battles with the brave Iberians and Celts slowly built a powerful infantry which ended by co-operating with the Numidian cavalry. After Hamilcar's fall, Hasdrubal, for the eight years that followed made great progress: agriculture and mining in the region became highly productive: Hasdrubal founded in Spain Cartagena **("new Carthage")**. The silver mines found nearby were source of riches to the point that commerce and manufacturing flourished, the army was supported and revenues remained available in quantities sufficient to be sent to his native Carthage.

The progress of Hamilcar in Spain kept the Romans concerned to the extreme of demanding from Hasdrubal after the death of Hamilcar, to confine himself to the Ebro and not to approach the Pyrenees, which the Romans were occupying in the event that a war with the Spanish Carthaginians became necessary. When in the year 220 BC Hasdrubal died at the hands of an assassin, the Carthaginian officers of the Spanish army elected unanimously to succeed him the eldest son of Hamilcar, **Hannibal. (Hanni-ba'al,** grace of Ba'al, in Phoenician).

HANNIBAL: Livy says: (Book XXI pp.7 & following) "There could be no question, for Hasdrubal's successor, that the choice originating from the soldiers; who immediately bore young Hannibal into the praetorium and with loud and universal acclamation hailed him general; provided that he obtained the ratification of the senate. The approval of the commons followed immediately but Hanno, the leader of the other faction, gave a sounding speach against the succesion…A few and, these included the best men in the senate, supported Hanno, but, as often happens, the larger party prevailed over the better."

Hannibal's choice, continues Livy, with the obvious bias of a Roman, "won the favour of the entire army. The old soldiers thought that Hamilcar had been restored to them as he had been in his youth; they beheld the same lively expression and piercing eye, the same cast of countenance and features. It was 221 BC and Hannibal "soon brought it to pass that his likeness to his father was the least consideration in gaining him support. Never was the same nature more adaptable to things the most diverse: obedience and command. And so no one could not readily have told whether he was more dear to general Hasdrubal or the army. When any bold or difficult deed was to be done, there was no one whom Hasdrubal liked better to entrust with it, nor did any other leader inspire his men with greater confidence or daring. To reckless courage in incurring dangers he united the greatest judgement when in the midst of them. No toil could exhaust his body or overcome his spirit. He was equally tolerant of heat and cold. His consumption of meat and drink was determined by natural desire, not by pleasure. His times of waking and sleeping were not marked off by day or night: what time remained when his work was done he gave to sleep, which he did not court with a soft bed or stillness, but was seen repeatedly by many lying on the ground wrapped in a common soldier's cloak among the sentinels and outguards. His dress was in no way superior to that of his fellows, but his arms and horses were conspicuous. Among horsemen and foot soldiers he was no doubt the first, first to enter battle and last to leave it when the fighting had begun. "These admirable qualities of the man were equalled" and here comes again the Roman patriot and historian, "by his monstrous vices: his cruelty was inhuman, his perfidy worse; he had no regard for truth and none for sanctity, no fear of the gods, no reverence for an oath, no religious scruple. With this endowment of good and evil he served for three years under his brother-in-law Hasdrubal, omitting nothing that should be done or seen by one who was to become a great commander".

Hamilcar after being victorious in the Lybian mercenary war decided to seek resources in Spain to be used against Rome that had imposed upon them unreasonable conditions following the Carthaginian defeat in Sicily. Before departing for Spain, although the story is probably spurious and legendary, Hamilcar had told his eldest son, then nine year-old, to swear at the altar of Baal, the phoenician god of war, eternal hatred of the Romans. This story, according to Polybius, was told by Hannibal to Antiochus when after the second Punic war he was staying as his guest and Antiochus was leaning towards releasing him to Rome. Although Hannibal spent his youth at the camp, he became an excellent runner and a fearless rider and had time to acquire the culture that was the rule in people of his class and rank. He became so proficient in Greek under the tutorship of a Spartan that he was eventually capable of composing state papers in that language. As he grew up he entered the army of his father and followed him in battle; later he commanded the cavalry under his brother-in-law Hasdrubal and distinguished himself for personal bravery and his talent as a leader. Now his comrades had given him the command to do what his father first and his brother-in-law after, had not been able to accomplish: the conquest of Rome.

Some contemporaries of Hannibal tried to cast stains of various sorts on the character of Hannibal, as described by Livy, that did not diminish his qualities: he was accused of cruelty, meanness and proneness to anger: characteristics that more properly belonged to some of his lieutenants. Most historians, however, present of him a noble image that combined discretion and enthusiasm, caution and energy as well as the inventive craftiness that was part of his phoenician heritage: he studied his antagonists with great care, he was a genius in strategy and a gifted statesman; the power he exerted over men was unparalleled in the history of warfare as shown by his incomparable command of an army consisting of many men from many countries and races and speaking multiple languages.

Immediately after his nomination he decided to attack Rome before Rome itself began the war in North Africa, his homeland. But the party in Carthage did not share his desire to start a new war against Rome: the former enemies of his father were not inclined to allow him, a young commander in Spain, to start an attack that they considered unjustified. Hannibal had started to make preparations for his attack on Rome and the defense of both his bases in Spain and his own homeland in Africa.

Hannibal by then had decided to spend the winter of 219-218 in Cartagena where by a generous partition of the booty, says Livy "he confirmed them all, both citizens and allies, in their allegiance to himself. In the spring he pushed towards Hermandica, now the site of modern Salamanca. After obtaining considerably booty he felt in danger because of the opposition of several local tribes which had formed an alliance against him. Had he attacked them, he may have suffered a defeat. Thus he decided to encamp on the bank of the river Tagus and waited for the enemy to settle for the night......"The allied tribes numbered about 100.000 men but Hannibal ordered his cavalry to charge when they saw the tribes entering the stream while keeping 40 elephants along the bank......The meeting in midchanel was no equal conflict since he attacked the footmen with his cavalry...a great number of them perished in the stream while the others were trampled down by the elephants."

"The rearmost were trying to retreat to their bank in search of safety...when in the middle of great panic Hannibal entered the stream in a fighting column, driving them in confusion, laid waste their fields and a few days later received their surrrender. Now the Carthaginians controlled everything south of the Ebro except Saguntum." Hannibal provoked on several instances the city of Saguntum, an allied of Rome, until finally accusing them of transgression of a treaty with the Torboletes, subjects of Carthage, he sent notice to Carthage of his intentions to defend them and before waiting for a response of approval he attacked Saguntum: they defended themselves in the eight month siege with incredible energy but, without help from Rome, they finally succumbed.

Polybius says: (Book III, Para, 14-15, pp. 35-37) "The Saguntines sent repeated messages to Rome…alarmed for their own safety. The Romans, who had more than once paid little attention to them, sent on this occasion delegates to report on the situation. Hannibal at the same time, having reduced the tribes he arrived with his forces to winter at New Carthage,…Here he found the Roman delegates, to whom he gave audience and listened to their present communication. The Romans protested against his attacking Saguntum, which they said was under their protection, or crossing the Ebro, contrary to the treaty engagements they had established in Hasdrubal's time….Hannibal, in his answer to the delegates affected to be guarding the interest of the Saguntines and accused the Romans of having a short time previously commited acts of cruelty, during a party quarrel at Saguntum and when they were called in to arbitrate, the Romans unjustly put to death some of the leading men. "The Carthaginians, he said, would not overlook this violation of good faith for it was from old the principle of Carthage never to neglect the cause of the victims of injustice…The Romans delegates, clearly seeing that war was inevitable, went to Carthage to convey the same protest to the Government there."

When the Saguntine spoils reached Carthage, patriotism was suddenly aroused and when the Roman embassy arrived there asking for the surrender of their general, they were met with disdain: the war against Rome had begun in 219 BC.

The army to depart from Spain consisted of 120.000 infantry men, 16.000 cavalry, 58 elephants and 50 quinquiremes, most of them manned. The troops consisted mainly of Carthaginian subjects called out for service, Lybians and Spaniards, and no mercenaries. To express his trust and confidence he gave them a leave of absence for the whole winter and promised, under oath to the Lybians, the citizenship of Carthage, should they return to Africa victorius. He sent 20.000 men to Africa and left for the protection of Spain 15.000 men behind under the leadership of his own younger brother Hasdrubal.

He secured the communications between Spain and Africa and switched his troops away from their original site of origin; assured that 20 quiquiremes with 1000 men will depart from Africa to the west coast of Italy and with the main army he personally departed for Italy. Why the invasion was planned by land and not by sea has been a subject of discussion by historians: it is believed that in his choice weighed the fact that he counted on being able to recruit men from all the tribes on his way who were struggling for independence from Rome; he concluded treaties with several of them and set out from Cartagena to the Ebro in the spring of 218 with 90.000 infantry men, 12.000 cavalry; about two thirds Africans and one third Spaniards, and 37 elephants more to impress the Gauls than to use them in war. He informed his soldiers of the alliances that he had made, the resources and the object of the expedition; thus infusing confidence in their leader. The Romans on their part had half a million soldiers, their cavalry was less numerous and less good than the Carthaginian but they counted with a fleet of 220 quinquiremes.

They would have wanted to decide the beginning of the war in Africa but were forced by the events to face Hannibal in Europe. The country between the Ebro and the Pyrenees was still free and allied to Rome. The second consul Publius Cornelius Scipio was ordered to the Ebro but instead decided to put down an insurrection on the valley of the Po, and prepare new legions for Spain.

This gave Hannibal the advantage of advancing across the Ebro and although he met with resistance by the natives with the loss of a fourth of his army he reached the Pyrenees. Arrived there he sent home a portion of his troops thus giving his soldiers confidence in their general's decision. With 50.000 infantry and 9.000 cavalry he easily crossed the Pyrenees and then took the coast route through Celtic territory and did not meet resistance until the end of July, upon arriving at the Rhone, opposite to Avignon. When the consul Scipio on his way to Spain learned that Hannibal had not only crossed the Ebro and the Pyrenees, he then decided to change his plans and face the Carthaginian at Avignon. However he again lost time in preparations and when he arrived there Hannibal had passed several days earlier the Rhone and was on his way to the Alps to accomplish one the most remembered events in history: the passage of the Alps. Hannibal passed with cavalry and elephants across the longest route but the one that helped him best because he had allied tribes on that side and the chain of the higher Alps was the broadest, fertile and most populated of the Alpine valleys and he knew this had been the great military route since the earliest times from the Celtic to the Italian territory. With great dexterity Hannibal himself on the crossing was helped by one of the most important Celtic chiefs: He escorted the Carthaginians not only through the plain but also supplied them with provisions and arms, clothing and shoes for the soldiers. Hannibal had to encamp at the foot of the mountains until after sunset because of the enemy's presence in the form of natives and when night fall came and the Celts dispersed to their houses in the nearest town he passed by night. He faced troubles in the descent similar to those in the ascent because it was already September, it had started to snow and the snow in the descent was melting and slippery: Hannibal encamped at the top of the mountain with the cavalry, the baggage and the elephants and had to wait 4 days until finally the route was cleaned and he could advance and meet the infantry which had passed earlier.

He went though the valley of the Doria where the inhabitants were allies of Carthage and where they rested to recover. Had the Romans waited for him with an army at a point near Turin the Carthaginians would have had a really difficult time. But again the Romans were not there. The passage of the Alps had been achieved but at a heavy cost: Hannibal had lost more than half of the army he had after passing the Pyrenees in the conflicts, marches and inconviniences crossing the rivers. He now counted only 20.000 infantry (three fifths Lybians and two fifths Spaniards) and 9.000 cavalry, attesting the great competence of the Numidian army. The passege of the Alps would be remembered by history better that the battles of Lake Trasimene and that of the plains of Cannae.

The presence of Hannibal's army on the Roman side of the Alps changed completely the plans of Rome: they recalled Publius Scipio but when he arrived in the valley of the Po he was confronted with Hannibal's reconnaissance army: the Roman losses were considerable, the consul himself was seriously wounded and would have died were it not because his son of only 17 years of age took over and rescued him from the ranks of the enemy. In the meantime the second army joined the remnants left in the valley of the Po lead by Sempronius who now held the command of an army of 40.000 Romans. Hannibal knew this man and to provoke him he proceeded to waste the Celtic villages that had remained faithful to Rome. This brought a conflict between the cavalries and Hannibal allowed the Carthaginians to be followed by the Romans who were foolishly pursuing them to the swollen river Trebia (it was December). Suddenly the cavalry halted: the Roman vanguard found itself facing Hannibal's army in a place chosen by himself: despite ferocious resistance the Romans infantry and cavalry finally gave up when the elephants entered the battle and a Carthaginian army of 1.000 infantry men emerged behind enemy lines under the command of Mago, Hannibal's youngest brother, breaking the rear ranks.

The first Roman division, however, 10.000 men strong broke through the Carthaginian line inflicting heavy damage and escaped.

The remaining army was slaughtered by the elephants and light enemy troops while attempting to cross the river. The battle of Trebia represented a heavy loss for the victors too: many veterans died of disease and Hannibal lost all the elephants. Tiberius Sempronius escaped alive with a small cavalry escort and managed to reach Rome.

Hannibal did not bother himself following the enemy in the inclement weather and decided to stay and organize the Gallic insurrection: more than 60.000 foot soldiers and 4.000 horseman are believed to have joined his army.

The Roman senate decided to fortify its northern frontier, ordered the troops from the fortresses on the Po to join the forces from the north and wait for the favorable season to descend into the valley of the Po. But Hannibal had no intention to defend the valley, he knew his men and knew the Roman infantry. Despite the brilliant battle of Trebia, Hannibal knew that his foot soldiers were inferior to the Roman legionaries: the single element that Hannibal had to throw into the scale of so many disadvantages was his military genius. The Roman soldiers remained superior to his own in the very same way that he was far superior to all the Roman commanders.

Before attempting to cross the Apenines he ordered all the Roman prisoners to be separated and loaded them with chains as slaves while the Italian allies were released without ramson and charged to spread the news at home that the war was against Rome and not against Italy. The passage of the Apennines took place without any difficulty at a point as distant as possible from the enemy but the plains of the Arno in Tuscany were flooded by the melting snow and the spring rains: the suffering was great and many soldiers contracted diseases including Hannibal himself who lost an eye from disease. According to Polybius "the entire army suffered much, mainly from lack of sleep while they had to march through water for 3 consecutive days and nights; the Celts suffered the most, many animals died in the mud and Hannibal himself was riding in the only remaining elephant of the 37 that had passed the Alps". This appears to have been the only Indian elephant that Cato the Elder, would refer to later. Gaius Flaminius mistaken by his blind love of the common people, his bitter hatred of the nobility and his own belief of being a military genius was re-elected consul and convinced the people that only he could defeat Hannibal. In contrast Hannibal instead of attacking him, passed by him and led the Celts and his own cavalry to pillage the country all around, the entire rich plains of Tuscany, rich in grain and cattle were victim of this furious army which took villages, animals and crops in the warm days of early spring.

This aroused the indignation and complaints of the people towards their hero Flaminius who had promised to liberate them forever. The Etruscans, former masters of the land and ancient friends of the Phoenicians, resented the dominance of their land by the Romans and might have considered the Carthaginian closer to them in blood and culture than the Romans. Flaminius, disregarding the advise of some of his officers to wait for his fellow consul Servilius, set off in pursuit of his enemy while Hannibal prepared his army and waited for him on

Lake Trasimene. He selected his battle field: a narrow passage between two steep mountain walls, closed at its outlet by a high hill and at its entrance by the Trasimene Lake. Hannibal approached the lake by a defile known as "Malpasso" where in the misty waters of Trasimene the images of two little islands, Isola Minore and Isola Maggiore, appeared projected on the right side. To the left of him was the valley of the river and once through the narrow entrance he could see the valley of Tuoro.

Here immmediately visible to the Romans he stationed a large part of his army. Thus the lake shore provided the bottom and the hills to the north, east and west the enclosing sides. On the East side Hannibal located his best troops, the Africans and the Spaniards. On the Western slopes which would be on the left flank of the Romans, Hannibal placed the Gauls and the Carthaginian heavy cavalry and on the East in flat ground below the hills were his light troops. That was it. Hannibal only had to wait until the Romans entered through the defile and once in place he would drop down the slopes the Gauls and the cavalry, taking the Roman legions on their left flank and closing the road behind them.

Flaminius arrived near the lake at night and encamped to the west outside Malpasso, to wait for dawn. All historians who have written about this battle concur that it was a misty morning, and the damp air was hiding the lake and lying thick over the river valley. Flaminius was very eager to start before Hannibal could advance further towards Rome and gave the orders to advance. Hannibal waited until the Roman troops were in contact with his own, then the trumpets sounded: from the western slopes down came the Gauls and the cavalry closing the passage.

Livy says:

"the onset was sudden and unforseen and the mist lay thicker on the plain, the attacking columns had been clearly visible from the hills and did therefore deliver their charge simultaneouly".

Held in the front and taken from the front and rear, the Romans had no time to align themselves: then the Gauls, the cavalry and the Numidians attacked again and again, killing the Romans on the spot: while the advanced ranks fought their way up towards the Carthaginians, the main body of the army and the rear were cut down. Livy continues, "It was not an ordered battle, neither the vanguard nor each soldier kept to his legion". They were massacred.

Polybius said:

"there fell in the valley about fifteen thousand of the Romans, unable to fly or to quit the ranks". The consul was killed by a Gaul who recognised him from his armour. The remnants of the army were crushed by the Spaniards, Gauls and Africans. Some 6.000 men escaped to higher ground where they could see the devastated Roman army.

The following day they were captured by the Numidian horsemen. Hannibal ordered a search for the body of Flaminius to give him proper burial but he was never found. About 15.000 men died and 15.000 were made prisoners from the Roman side. Faithful to his practice Hannibal liberated the allies of Rome and kept the Romans as slaves. The Carthaginians lost only 1.500 troops. The magnitude of the disaster was such that when the news reached the highest Roman magistrate, with approval of the senate, he announced to the people:

"There was a great battle and we were totally defeated". Rome was in such state of shock that they did what according to Livy "had never been done before, they decided by popular election to create a dictator and the choice fell upon Quintus Fabius Maximus: he was given authority to break down the bridges over the rivers Arno and Tiber and to fight for Rome since they had not been able to save Italy". Fabius belonged to one of the most illustrious Roman families: one of his ancestors had been made consul on three occasions in the 5th century BC and he was respected by the aristocracy and by the populace.

All Etruria was lost and Hannibal could now march on Rome. But the Carthaginian leader was more farsighted than Pyrrhus had been. Instead of marching on Rome, Hannibal marched through Umbria, devastating the Roman farmhouses of the territory and halted on the shores of the Adriatic to rest his army during the finest season of the year. His soldiers were given fresh fruit and oil to heal their scorbutic lesions due to vitamin C deficiency and the horses were treated with good food and rubbing alcohol for their bodies. He had thus far defeated all Roman commanders but had made no allies: he knew well that his army was, compared to the Roman legions, relatively small. Quintus Fabius was re-inforcing the Roman army and following south but did not have the slightest desire to make the same mistake of his immediate predecessor. He was not going to attack and preferred to gradually weaken and starve the enemy's army.

Knowledgeable about Fabius' plans, Hannibal passed by the Roman army and marched over the Apennines into the heart of Italy, then turned towards Capua, the second largest city after Rome, in the hope to acquire their friendship but was once again dissappointed. According to Polybius "Hannibal had decided to move from the east to the south-west in the hope to acquire through their seaports a means of communication with Carthage while terrorising the major cities into deserting the Roman alliance".

The present Capuans were descendants of the old mercantile Greek citizens and had never forgotten their hatred of their competitors, the Phoenicians, and their descendants, the Carthaginians. Hannibal then went towards Apulia and since nowhere did he meet serious opposition, he selected the flat district of northern Apulia, rich in grain and grass, to establish his winter quarters.

In the meantime in Rome Marcus Minucius, temporarily in command in the absence of Fabius, kept the Carthaginian soldiers busy, drove them back from their advanced positions and provoked a wave of discontent in the Roman people because while Fabius advised prudency, the enemy had laid waste all central Italy without opposition beneath the eyes of a Roman army of equal numbers. It was in their favor that the Italian allies were still on the side of Rome despite Hannibal demonstration of the superiority of the Phoenicians but for how long will this last? The populace in concert with the discontent soldiers revolted and led to a division of the command between Minucius, former lieutenent of Fabius and Fabius himself.

Thus the Roman army was once more divided and placed under two notoriously different leaders. While this was happening in Rome, Hannibal had been so successful that his army spent the winter without complaint in Apulia. It was the national hatred against the Phoenician hero that kept Rome safe: the majority of the senate finally decided to depart from a behaviour that was slowly ruining the state.

They decided to equip an army of eight legions, such as Rome had never done before, and in order to please the multitude, in 219 BC, they elected two new consuls: Lucius Aemilius Paulus, from a patrician family and a good military record as successful commander of the Illyrian war, and Gaius Terentius Varro, a plebeian of ultrademocratic opinions who had gained popularity by his defamatory opposition to Fabius, in short, according to Livy "an incompetent man of the popular party".

Until the spring of 216 BC the Carthaginians remained at the camp of Geronium and the two armies stayed in face of each other without any significant real action. Fabius term expired and the

Romans selected temporarily Servilius and Regulus. Things had not gone quite well for the Carthaginians and Hannibal: his brother Hasdrubal had been pushed back to the Ebro for the winter, he had received no reinforcements from Carthage, Rome was still controlling the Mediterranean sea and Hannibal had not received any single ally.

Rome, however, had changed the system of dictatorship and had reverted to the dual consular system by electing Paulus and Varro. Finally, in the spring of 216 BC Hannibal decided to move out in search of supplies and marching to the south crossed the river Aufidus and descended upon the town of Cannae, located on a hill and one of the original Roman grain depots. From there he could continue to take the early corn of Apulia. Servilius and Atilius were still acting consuls and had no intention to face Hannibal on their own thus they continued to follow him at a safe distance, drawing their supplies from depots far away because they have been deprived of the others by Hannibal. The Roman senate was determined to go against Hannibal: all segments of the population shared the same desire. For the pride of Rome and to maintain the respect of their allies it became essential to annihilate the invaders. According to Polybius the legions under Servilius plus the new ones under Paulus and Varro numbered a total of eight. Livy believes there was a total of 45.000 to 60.000 men without including the cavalry. Polybius cited at least 40.000 men from Rome and a similar number from their allies thus about 80.000 infantry and 6.000 cavalry that went to face Hannibal at Cannae. Hannibal had 40.000 infantry and 10.000 cavalry.

Hannibal had first encamped to the south of the hill of Cannae but before the arrival of the Romans, he moved his troops across the Aufidus and set up a new camp on the west bank of the river. The first day the two armies came in sight of one another Aemilius Paulus was in command and realising that the land ahead favored the cavalry of the enemy, advised Varro of the situation but Varro dissagree and the following day, having the command, he decided to take the legions down to the Aufidus and face Hannibal across the plain.

Terentius Varro did not want any advise and talk about moving to a hilly ground only made him more determined to come down to the plain. Thus the whole Roman army was moved to the west bank of the Aufidus but a small contingent was sent to establish a smaller camp on the eastern bank of the river. The following day Paulus was in command and "realised that the Carthaginians may have to move their camp in order to obtain supplies" and Hannibal, now on the far side of his supplies, sent the Numidians to harass the Roman watering party on the east bank of the river. The Romans became nervous when they saw the Numidians denying them their water supplies. The hot summer had set in, it was June, and water was quite important.

In addition, the wind shifted to the south and a sirocco began to blow a film of dust and moisture over the newer Roman legions which began to sweat under their heavy armour as the sun rose. Hannibal's veterans, used to the intemperances of the climate, could not care less. On their fourth day of facing each other Varro was in command and soon after sunrise began to move his army out of both camps, he crossed the river and joined the east bank forces. This was a smart move: the watering place and the granary buildings were on that side which also was somewhat hilly and difficult for the cavalry. When Hannibal saw the Roman move he sent his light-armed troops across the river and knew that the main body of the Roman army was now ready for battle: he had been waiting for this moment since Lake Trasimene.

Hannibal's main body of his army crossed the river in two places and he began to arrange them according to his tactics: below the hill of Cannae he put the Numidians on his right flank so that they could use the open country and the Spaniards and Gauls on his left next towards the river. Next to them he placed half of his African veterans. In the center he put the main body of his troops of Spaniards and Gauls, that he was to command himself with the help of his younger brother Mago. Hasdrubal commanded the Carthaaginian left and Hanno the right with the great African commander Maharbal leading the Numidian horses. Paulus commanded the Roman cavalry while Varro led the allied cavalry and Servilius commanded the Roman center of the legions.

Because the numerical superiority of the Romans was clear to every observer, Plutarch says, that a man named Gisgo told Hannibal,

"It is astonishing to see such great number of men" and Hannibal responded: "yes Gisgo, you are right but you have not noticed something."

What is that?, replied his officer.

And Hannibal said: "In that great number of men opposing us there is not a single one named Gisgo."

The tension broke in laughter among the soldiers listening to the conversation of the Carthaginian leaders.

The sun was already high in the sky and hitting the Romans in their face and the Carthaginians in their back. "The sirocco, Livy said, began to blow clouds of dust steadily on the face of the Romans and their allies. Silence now preceded the storm of the battle about to begin. When the armies started to move the Carthaginian center formed a crescent with the cusp drawn forward, composed mainly by the Spaniards and Gauls, leaving the heavily armed Africans as reserves on both wings and projecting like dark shadows. The real battle started next to the river between the Spanish and Gallic horsemen and the heavy Roman cavalry.

Livy describes that

"both parties pushed straight ahead and their horses next to each other, the riders started to grab their enemies and pull them from their seats to the ground: the Romans were no match for the enemy and the struggle was soon over, the defeated Roman cavalry turned and fled".

The heavy cavalry of Hasdrubal went through the gap left by the collapse of the Roman right wing. Aemilius Paulus, still unharmed, placed himself at the head of the legionaires. The Numidian right was now attacking the allied Roman horsemen and soon were pursuing them as they scattered. Among those who fled soon enough was Gaius Terencius Varro. In the meantime the main bodies of the infantry collided with each other and the Roman legions pushing forward soon formed an indentation in the cusp of the Carthaginian crescent.

The legions began to pour in behind one another but the Africans on either side stood like iron walls because they had not really begun to fight. The Roman legions continued to drive Hannibal's center and penetrated so far that soon the African infantry on the wings enclosed them. In the heat of the battle "Paulus fell with terrible wounds." In the meantime, Hasdrubal, with the heavy cavalry, had destroyed the Roman right wing and turned around behind the Roman legions and attacked the allied horsemen, already in disarray, in flight before the Numidians, completing the collapse of the Roman left wing.

The double enveloping of Hannibal's tactics was now complete: while the Roman infantry was still fighting ferociously with the Spaniards and Gauls of Hannibal, Hasdrubal had returned and attacked the Roman infantry by the rear and now the Romans were totally encircled and stricken by the surrounding wings of the Africans. It was the most bloody afternoon in the history of warfare. The actions of Hasdrubal were essential: Hasdrubal after having completed the defeat of Paulus, turned around, re-arranged his cavalry and attacked the center of Varro's cavalry, already almost defeated by the Numidians. Scattered by the double attack, Hasdrubal leaving the pursuit of the fugitives to the Numidians, arranged his squadrons for the third time and led them against the rear of the Roman infantry that was fighting against Hannibal and Mago: this last charge proved decisive: the entire army was annihilated in the field completely.

Livy and Plutarch gave a total of about 50.000 Romans dead, Quintilian gives 60.000 and Polybius 70.000 Romans dead. The Carthaginians lost about 5.500 men and 200 cavalry. The Consuls Paulus, Servilius, Atilius and Minucius were all killed.

Eighty members of senatorial rank and 29 military tribunes died on that day. But of the surviving infantry that managed to escape one of the military tribunes is worth naming, Scipio the younger, later to be known as Scipio Africanus, who had followed closely the military exploits of Hannibal and eventually would defeat him in Africa, thus helping change the course of the history of the West.

Terentius Varro escaped and made it to Rome where he was received with understanding and flexibility. Polybius comments: "A few escaped to Venusia, among them being the Consul Gaius Terentius, who disgraced himself by his flight and in his tenure of office had been most unprofitable to his country." Had he been a Carthaginian commander his fate would have been crucifixion. The 10.000 men that had been left to guard the adjacent Roman camp and seize the remaining Carthaginians in case of defeat were now rounded up: two thousand were killed and the rest made prisoners.

Hannibal, as it was his custom, tried to reclaim the bodies of his antagonists but only that of Aemilius Paulus was found: he was buried with honours. Many officers among the Carthaginians felt that the moment had come to march on Rome: Maharbaal, the cavalry commander, apparently told Hannibal "In five days from now, you shall dine as victor in the Roman Capitol". Hannibal replied that he had to reconsider this suggestion and Maharbal, according to Livy, said: "The gods give a man many gifts but not all. You know how to obtain victories but not how to use one".

Hannibal did not respond, he knew he had an army not large enough to put siege to Rome and to take it easily by starvation.

According to Polybius "after Cannae the Carthaginians became masters of the Italian coast: towns and cities invited Hannibal to come in".

This time Hannibal did not immediately allow the Roman allies who were made prisoners to go home, he requested through a delegation sent to Rome a ramson for the prisoners at a price 50% higher than that of the allies but Rome refused to pay a ramsom: they expected their soldiers to die fighting for Rome and never surrender. Fabius Maximus once more took care of the morale: public mourning was forbidden and rumor and gossip were eliminated by the imposition of silence in all public places. Most of the south abandoned the Roman confederacy to join Carthage except the Latin colonies and the Greek cities that maintained their allegiance to Rome.

Hannibal needed now men and money if he intended to besiege Rome: despite his brilliant victories in the North, at Lake Trasimene and finally under the hill of Cannae, Rome had refused to surrender. His brother Mago had gone to Carthage to take the good news and ask for help but another Hanno, traditional family enemy of the Barkas, prompted objections against sending Hannibal any assistance, especially in the form of trained North African infantry and cavalry.

In contrast, the Carthaginians thought that now it was the best time to make peace. The decision was eventually overruled and it was decided that Hannibal should be sent substantial re-inforcements: 20.000 men were supposed to come from Spain while from Carthage immediately 4.000 horses and 40 elephants were to be dispatched. The most secure re-inforcements should come from Spain but the situation there was not good at all: Gnaeus Scipio first defeated Hanno and later with the help of his brother Publius he crossed the Ebro and advanced towards Saguntum. Hasdrubal in the meantime tried to pass the Pyrenees with an army sent from Africa but was opposed at the Ebro and totally defeated. The tribes of the Celtiberians and other smaller tribes joined the Scipios and in Spain, Hasdrubal was having a hard time maintaining control all the way to the Guadalquivir.

The brothers Scipio had taken control of the Spanish coast and pushed Hasdrubal south of the Ebro. The alliances between the Carthaginians and Macedonia and Carthage and Syracuse had not been successful but Capua and most communities of lower Italy passed over to Hannibal. However some opposition persisted in Capua against breaking their alliance with Rome and Hannibal was forced to make certain prominent opponents prisoners and sent them to Carthage.

The southern Greek and Latin colonies remained attached to Rome. In addition, the war in Campania did not go well and Hannibal was reduced to the defensive by the remaining Roman armies: if he was to accomplish his original objectives he needed help from Carthage, from Cartagena, Sicily and Macedonia. But help from home was not coming. The Scipios were victorious on the Ebro, Guadalquivir and Andalusia and Himilco and Hippocrates sent in from Carthage failed in the siege of Syracuse. Marcus Marcellus, an old experienced commander, remained in Syracuse while Himilco, Hippocrates and the Africans troops were dying with epidemic fevers and pestilences. Following these events Marcellus allowed the Romans to pillage the city and even put to death the respected mathematician Archimedes.

Sicily seemed lost for the Cathaginians despite the fact that the town of Agrigentum was under Phoenician control. The lack of support from Carthage fostered by the enemies of Hannibal forced him, commander-in-chief, to enter into negotiations with the Romans: this was a most unfortunate decision, they delivered Agrigentum. The Phoenician garrison in town was put to death by the Romans and the citizens were sold into slavery, it was the year 214 BC.

While Hannibal obtained a victory in Tarentum, giving him an excellent port on the coast, Phillip of Macedonia first made peace with the Greeks and later with Rome in the years 206-205. The Scipios had been thus far successful in Spain and found an ally in Western Africa in a powerful prince of Oran and Algiers by the name of Syphax. The threat from this man to the Lybian subjects of Carthage forced Hasdrubal himself to go to Africa with the Spanish troops; this provoked an African rival of Syphax named Massinissa to go against him and after defeating him inflicted a cruel vengeance on the rebels.

These events allowed Hasdrubal to return to Spain with considerable re-inforcements and with Massinissa and his men. The brothers Scipio who had been, in the absence of Hasdrubal, plundering the Carthaginian territory found themselves attacked now by three African armies under Hasdrubal Barka, Hasdrubal the son of Gisgo and Mago. The Romans were forced to take 20.000 Celtiberians under pay to defend themselves: Gnaeus opposed Hasdrubal Barka but then the Spaniards refused to fight against the Carthaginian and Gnaeus was forced to retreat. Publius found himself assailed by the two other armies under Hasdrubal Gisgo and Mago and Massinissas' horses: against these forces the Roman brothers were defeated and killed; their bodies were not found.

All Spain south of the Ebro was now in Cathaginian hands: the Roman senate learned from Utica that Carthage was preparing to send an army over the Pyrenees with Hasdrubal and Massinissa and decided to pay more attention to her affairs in Spain. They decided to select a new general and although for a longtime none wanted to take the task, a new man offered himself to take it: he was 26-year-old, Publius Scipio, the son of the general who had died in Spain. The young man had saved his father from being killed in the battle of Ticinus and was at Cannae among those officers that had survived and escaped. History will remember him as Scipio Africanus.

Scipio offered himself in the absence of anybody better for the post of danger: history will record that he gained battles and conquered territories but as a politician he was not that brilliant. Scipio the younger went to Spain in the year 210 BC and fortunately found the three Carthaginian commanders away, at laest at 10 days of distance from Cartagena. With his army of 30.000 men he surprised the garrison of only 1.000 men guarding the capital, and a combined attack by land and sea made him promptly victorious, in one day he took the Carthaginian capital of Spain. Fate had been on his side and after this marvellous victory, the Roman citizens felt they had made the right choice. The Spaniards on both sides of the Ebro decided to accept Roman protection; Scipio spent the winter of 208 re-arranging his army and finally marched towards Andalusia. He had a clash of no consequence with Hasdrubal Barka. Hasdrubal retained his possessions: he retained his chest, the best of his troops, went through the western passes of the Pyrenees and reached Gaul before the winter season, which he chose to spend there. In the meantime, the

Phoenicians with a main army composed of Spaniards were defeated by Scipio.

While Hasdrubal was in Gaul, Mago went to pass the rest of the season in Cadiz, the last remnant of the Carthaginians in Spain. Carthage ordered Mago to join his brother in Italy, thus after 13 years he left the Spanish soil. The war had ended in Sicily, Greece and Spain; thus the struggle then continued only in Italy. On the year 212 BC Hannibal took Tarentum and with his best troops he went to Campania and Capua, now occupied by the Romans, which did not capitulate.

He decided finally to march towards Rome with the intention of inducing the Romans to leave Capua and thus break up the blockade. But he really did not intend to take Rome nor could he and after a short stay he departed while the Romans saw in his departure a miraculous intervention of the gods. Hannibal continued to defeat commanders such as Publius Galba but lost most of his cities such as Tarentum and Capua, where the Romans committed great atrocities: sold the citizens into slavery, confiscated the estates of the wealthy, took officers and magistrates, Capuans and Phoenicians, and beheaded them in the public market place. The Roman behaviour has been intrepreted by historians and commentators as typical vengence exerted against the Capuans for the long rivalry they had sustained with Rome.

Hannibal had lost little by little his most important acquisitions when Marcellus was elected consul for the year 208: unfortunately the brightest commander of the Romans during a routine reconnaissance was surprised by the African cavalry and in the encounter that followed he was wounded and killed. The Romans by now were suffering from the heavy burden of the long war, their allies were also tired and all of these communities although not united by themselves or under Hannibal command informed the Romans that they would not continue their contributions and their soldiers; a conspiracy among the Etruscans in favor of Hannibal was uncovered and news arrived that Hasdrubal was on the Italian side of the Alps. Volunteers from Etruria and Umbria joined the Carthaginians and Rome was again facing the prospect of a continuation of the war against the two elder sons of Hamilcar Barka. Fate however would decide otherwise: Claudius Gaius Nero with his forces managed during the night to join those of his fellow consul Marcus Livius.

The historian Livy says that the following morning
"Hasdrubal decided to take a look at the Romans with a few horsemen and noticed that among the enemies old shields there were new ones and supected that new troops had arrived: he sent then some of his men around the Romans to check if new tents had been erected and they reported back that nothing unusual had happened but when the orders to the armies were given by two distinct trumpet blasts, Hasdrubal deduced at once that two consuls and two armies were there; confusion arose among his men. Hasdrubal had intended to take positions in the northern bank of the river Metaurus because he was not sure about the situation of his brother Hannibal. Uncertain as to

what his brother Hannibal was doing, Hasdrubal had a change of mind and decided to by-pass the Roman armies and march towards Etruria or Umbria and find out if anything had happened to Hannibal. The fear that his brother had lost made Hasdrubal retreat and the following morning he arranged his best troops, Carthaginians and veteran Spaniards facing Livius in the southern bank of the Metaurus and his Gauls facing Nero; other Spaniards and Ligurians were in the center: the battle that followed was ferocious and lengthy on Hasdrubal's right but on the left the Gauls did not move aginst Nero.

Nero decided that the real battle was on the left and moved behind the battleline and attacked the Carthaginian right wing; this outpouring of fresh legionaires made Hasdrubal's veterans fall and in panic they attempted to pass the Metaurus while Hasdrubal's right wing was collapsing. Realising that all was lost, Hasdrubal spurred his horse into the Roman lines and died, sword in hand. "A heroic gesture, says Polybius, but Hasdrubal was worth far more to the Carthaginians alive". About 10.000 Carthaginians died and that day was decisive for Carthage: when the head of Hasdrubal was delivered wrapped up in bloody cloth to Hannibal, it is alleged that he said: "There goes the fate of Carthage".

Nero's army, which had returned to their original position, sent the head of Hasdrubal to Hannibal, thus paying with scorn the Carthaginian Commander, he who had in the past buried with honours several of his contenders dying in the battlefield such as Paulus, Gracchus and Marcellus.

Hannibal was now in despair, his hope was over, and he decided to abandone Apulia and the remaining areas under his control and retired with his troops to the land of the Bruttians. Although Rome resumed a normal peaceful life Hannibal stayed four more years among the Bruttians. Out of fear the Carthaginian authorities sent re-inforcements to Hannibal in Italy and Mago in Spain: with the remains of the Spanish army Mago attacked and took Genoa, destroyed the city and attempted with gold to re-inforce his army with Gauls and Ligurians. But it was too late for Carthage.

The Romans had only one problem: in order to invade Africa they needed a leader since most Roman commanders had died or were too old to attempt it. Publius Scipio returned from Spain and was acclaimed and elected consul for the year 205 BC not without certain opposition from the senate. No one else other than Scipio would have accepted so quickly to undertake an expedition to Africa but the ancient gods were protecting him: in forty days a fleet was ready for the sea with a large number of volunteers. Thus he went to Africa in the spring of 204 BC with two legions of veterans (about 30.000 men) and 40 war vessels and landed near Utica without any resistance.

Hasdrubal, son of Gisgo, was prepared to fight for the protection of Carthage with an army of 20.000 men; 6.000 cavalry and 40 elephants recently captured by another man also named Hanno. Scipio was ready for a naval attack on the weak Carthaginian army when Syphax arrived with 50.000 infantry and 10.000 cavalry. Scipio withdrew the siege of Utica and encamped between Utica and Carthage to spend the winter of 204 BC. Scipio deceived the Carthaginians with a proposal of peace and secretly at night put to flames both the Numidian huts and later the Carthaginian camp. An attack of the Roman naval camp although undecisive allowed the Romans to capture Syphax. After several defeats such as these the Carthaginian peace party decided to ask for peace and was told the conditions but the patriotic party did not accept them and sent orders to Mago and Hannibal to return with full speed to Africa. Mago, who had just been defeated by the double Roman army was wounded but obeyed the order to embark and died during the trip back to Carthage.

Hannibal decided to comply and after putting to death his horses and the Italians who refused to follow him to Africa, he left. The Romans began to breath again at the news of Hannibal's departure and the senate conferred a grass wreath to the only general who had survived those troubled times with honour, Quintus Fabius, now 90-year-old.

In the same year the old general who had taught the Romans how to face Hannibal, died. Hannibal arrived without any problems to Leptis, the Phoenician colony, after 36 years of absence from his native Carthage. The temporary peace plans with Rome were now broken. He was intelligent enough to realise that the overall Carthaginian position was hopeless. He had defeated the Romans many times in battle but he knew how resourceful they were. The war faction in Carthage resumed hostilities and attacked a Roman convoy bringing supplies for Scipio: he interpreted this as a signal that the truce was over and renewed the war. He attacked the small Carthaginian towns in his surroundings and devastating the population and the territory came to conclude that no peace would be possibe until he and Hannibal met in battlefield.

Hannibal was now receiving orders from Carthage to go and face the enemy but he refused to do so until he felt prepared for it. He proceeded to improve his cavalry and add elephants to his forces. These, however, were new animals that needed training. His army was quite heterogenous: Spaniards from the Balearic islands, Ligurians, Bruttians, Gauls, and Africans. Hannibal was now forced to march west to meet Scipio near the place that became known as Zama. His original intentions would have been to go to Carthage but well aware that he could not feed his army and maintain his elephants there he went towards the Romans. He, who had known every part of Italy was now in North Africa unawere of the problems of its own country. Upon reaching Zama he sent some spies to gain information on the Roman army but according to Polybius they were made prisoners by Scipio and after feeding them, he sent them back to misinform Hannibal, especially about the Numidians who had joined Scipio.

Thus Hannibal sent messengers to ask Scipio for a face to face meeting to discuss terms of peace. Scipio accepted: they had been in opposite camps in at least three occasions from Ticino and Cannae and Southern Italy. Hannibal knew that the Roman tactics had changed under Scipio since his victories in Spain but they had never met personally.

Although most likely the encounter described by Livy and Polybius may not have taken place as decribed by the two historians, truthfully it may have served the two commanders as a way to measure each other. Both were highly cultivated: Hannibal spoke besides Punic, various Spanish dialects, Gallic, Greek and Latin. Scipio was educated in Latin and Greek. Their conversation took place in one of the latter languages. Hannibal, according to Livy, "offered to surrender all the lands of Sicily, Sardinia and Spain but did not mention the Western Baleares, which had been so useful to Carthage". Scipio did not accept: he gained information about Hannibal's state of mind and allowed himself more time for the arrival of Masinissa with his cavalry of 4000 men and infantry of 6.000.

The exact geographical location of Zama is unknown. It appears to have been a place between two hills with a plain in between, one of the hills had a spring for water supply, so needed, under the sun of Africa. Hannibal had no choice but to take the waterless camp. Scipio's cavalry was now superior and his legionaires were well trained. On his left wing he placed the Roman cavalry and on his right the Numidians with Massinissa. He occupied the center with his infantry. Hannibal had no choice but to start with his 80 elephants in front and behind them his infantry; the Carthaginian horses on the right facing the Roman cavalry with his left side composed of the

Numidian horses facing Massinissa. His Carthaginian and African infantry was behind. The battle began in an unfortunate fashion because the untrained elephants upon hearing the Roman trumpets panicked and began to break towards their own infantry first and stampeded towards Hannibals's Numidian cavalry. Masinissa then attacked the other Numidians facing him and both wings collapsing the Roman legionairs had to face the Carthaginian's finest veterans who were fighting ferociously the legionaires. Scipio then sounded retreat and re-aligned his legionaires in a single line to face the experienced Carthaginians also in a single line: the battle was now man to man but then the Roman cavalry and Massinisass' horsemen returned and attacked the old Hannibalic infantry: the battle was lost and the war was over.

Hannibal returned to Carthage from Hadrumetum to tell the council that there was no longer any hope by continuing the war and advised them to accept the best terms the Romans would offer for peace. Polybius says that the council accepted Hannibal's advice as "wise and sent emissaries to the Romans to inform them that they accepted the Roman conditions". Scipio demanded the surrender of all deserters, prisoners of war and slaves, all the elephants and one hundred hostages of his choice, to be delivered by him to Rome. Carthage could retain its former territory in Africa but doubled the original war indemnity that had been proposed previously, to be payed over 50 years. They had to give Massinissa control of his former kingdom but nobody demanded the surrender of Hannibal.

Historians believe that this measure was intended to keep a leader in Carthage who could fully appreciate the good terms of the surrender. There was considerable opposition in Rome to these terms which were considered quite lenient.

In Carthage they found, with the exception of the rich who had to pay the initial amount of the indemnity, the citizens supported Hannibal who proved to be an incorruptible and capable statesman in peace as he had been a leader in war. He was named Chief Magistrate of Carthage and during the next seven years he devoted himself to the affairs of his country, to modify the Constitution of Carthage and to rebuild their mercantile position. This showed how wise Scipio's decision had been. Scipio was then given the title of "Africanus", the first time that a soldier had been given a title for his victories in the field of war. He refused other honours offered to him and retired to live a life of leisure and to indulge in his passion for Greek literature.

In the meantime the Romans defeated Philip V of Macedonia, breaking the power of Greece forever. But the financial skills of Hannibal revived the Roman hatred for him. In 195 BC a commission was sent to Carthage demanding the surrender of Hannibal for allegedly supporting an enemy of Rome: Antiochus the Great, who had recently occupied Phoenicia, Palestine and Cyprus.

Cato the Elder, who had served under Scipio and also disliked him, was now consul and determined to bring Hannibal in chains back to Rome. It is unknown whether there was any correspondence between Hannibal and Antiochus as the Romans claimed. Hannibal sure that his enemies in Carthage would betray him, after receiving the emissaries from Rome and giving them proper qurters to stay, left in the evening and went to his villa near Hadrumetum from which with several manoeuvres he managed to evade the Romans and finally reached the land of his ancestors, the ancient home of the Eastern Phoenicians: Tyre. It was from here that Dido (Elissa) left to found Carthage.

Antiochus in the meantime was defeated by the Romans in 189 BC and gave up all his possesions. Hannibal, having been declared "the enemy of the Roman people" decided that it was time to move: he went secretly to the island of Crete and settled in the ancient city of Gortyna, in a mansion near a small river.

There appears to have been another encounter between Scipio and Hannibal before he left the kingdom of Antiochus. Rome had sent a mission to Ephesus, headed by Scipio, with the intentions of finding out what were the plans of Antiochus. Scipio took the opportunity to invite his former contender for a conversation and Hannibal agreed. Although there is no record of their conversation and the recounts of Livy and Plutarch are suspect and probably apocryphal, the conversation has been repeated many times after.

Talking about old times Scipio asked Hannibal whom he thought "was the greatest general in history?". Alexander the Great, Hannibal replied, "because with a small army he had defeated many greater ones and went to the most remote areas of the world". Asked once more whom he would put next? he said: Pyrrhus, the king of Epirus, for his brilliant choice of battle grounds and arrangement of his armies.

And "the third", myself, no doubt" Scipio asked laughing. And continued "What would you have said if you would have beaten me?". Hannibal responded: "Then I would have placed myself first among all commanders in history". With the exception of Alexander the Great, most historians would agree with that response.

In time the Romans came to Crete in search of pirates and other resources. Hannibal knowing that soon they would learn the name of the wealthy Carthaginian living there in retirement, he left again secretly and went to Bithynia, in the kingdom of Prusias. Finally, when the king here was forced to disclose the whereabouts of his distinguished guest and the soldiers secretly surrounded his country home, he committed suicide with his own sword; escaping from his enemies forever.

Historians have often discussed whether or not the history of the West would have been different had Hannibal defeated Scipio Africanus: the evidence suggests that most likely nothing would have been different. Hannibal had basically a Greek culture and education: he learned from a Greek tutor, spoke Greek along with Phoenician (Punic) and other Iberic languages, took along during his campaigns two Greek secretaries and even appears to have written a history in Greek, dedicated to the people of Rhodes, no longer extant. Most likely nothing would have been different, had he been the final victor. His Greek education would have allowed the influence of the great Greek thinkers of the 5th century BC to permeate the rest of the West and the end result would have been similar to what happened following his final defeat.

His friend Scipio was, however, charged by Cato before the senate with defaulting on public funds. In reply Scipio brought his books, tore them up before his accusers and asked the senators to seek for proof in the fragments. He added that his victories had given Rome not only Spain and Africa but also Asia Minor. With extreme bitterness he then left Rome, went into exile and never returned.

CHAPTER TWELVE

THE WRITERS

ZENO of KITION: (c. 360-263 BC) or 333-261 BC.

Son of Mnaseas, a rich merchant from Phoenicia. Born at Kition, he went to Athens to learn from the Cynics and later developed his own system of philosophy. He taught under the **Poikile Stoa** of the agora, thus his philosophy was named **Stoicism**. His father was a Phoenician merchant and during his travels to Athens, the chroniclers tell us, it was always his custom to bring back the newest books and writings containing Socrates' teachings for the use of his son for either education or entertainment. Thus Zeno was acquainted with the Socratic teachings before he came to Athens. During a voyage from Phoenicia to Piraeus his ship capsized with a cargo of purple and forced him to stay in Athens. There he met Cratus who became his first teacher. He also attended the lectures of Xenocrates, Polemo and Stilpo. In recognition of his learning in Athens he would say years later "I made a prosperous voyage when I suffered shipwreck". Others claim that he was already in Athens when he was told his ship wrecked to which he exclaimed "It is well done of you, O Fortune, thus to drive me to Philosophy." He had a peculiar way of life. He showed the utmost endurance and the greatest frugality. He declined most invitations to dinner and was fond of eating green figs. He would not refuse to eat little loaves and drink a little wine of good bouquet. "The truth is that in virtue and dignity, one of his contemporaries remarked, he surpassed all mankind and in happiness too, for he was ninety eight when he died and always had enjoyed good health without an ailment to the end". The Athenians held Zeno in high honor, deposited with him the key of the city and gave him a golden crown and a bronze statue.

The Athenians passed a decree about him that, in a summarised fashion, reads:

"Whereas Zeno of Kition, son of Mnaseas, has for many years been devoted to philosophy in the city and has continued to be a man of worth in all other respects, exhorting to virtue and temperance those of the youth who came to him to be taught, directing them to what is best, affording to all in his own conduct a pattern for imitation in perfect consistency with his teaching, it has seemed good to the people to bestow praise upon Zeno of Citium, son of Mnaseas, and to crown him with a golden crown according to the law, for his goodness and temperance and to build him a tomb in the Ceramicus at the public cost…"

He was all of his life in good relations with King Antigonus of Macedonia who according to the records invited him to come visit him and to "instruct the ruler of Macedonia and by guiding him in the paths of virtue he will also be training his subjects to be good men". Because of old age he declined his invitation and sent instead one of his disciples "whose mental powers are not inferior to mine, while his bodily strenght is far greater…"

Upon Zeno's death Antigonus also requested the Athenians to bury Zeno in the Ceramicus.

Here is the epitaph composed for him by Antipater of Sidon: "Here lies great Zeno, dear to Citium, who scaled high to Olympus, though…he did not toil the labors of Heracles, this was the path he found out to the stars…the way of temperance alone".

Another one by Zenodotus the Stoic, a pupil of Diogenes of Tolemais, says:

> "…………………O godlike Zeno
> with aspect grave and hoary brow serene
> yours was a manly doctrine: and by your prudence
> with much toil you found a great new school,
> chaste parent of unfearing liberty.
> And your native country was Phoenicia,
> what need to slight you? Did not Cadmus come from there
> who gave to Greece her books and art of writing?

His contemporaries and disciples described him as lean, fairly tall with a wry neck and thick legs but flabby and delicate. According to Apollonius of Tyre, one of his students, Zeno consulted the oracle to know what he should do in order to attain the best life and being told that he should acquire the complexion of the dead he proceded to study the writings of the ancient authors, in order to learn of their habits and opinions.

He wrote a number of books which have not survived. Several extant fragments of his works exist and we know of his writings from his numerous disciples who quoted him often. Some of their titles were The Republic, Of Life according to Nature, Of Emotions, Of Duty, Of Law, Of Greek Education, Of the Whole World, Pythagorean Questions, Universals, Homeric Problems, Handbook of Rhetorics, Ethics, Recollections of Crates and several others. Zeno is often quoted by his contemporaries, especially by his disciples.

"The reason why we have two ears and only one mouth is that we may listen the more and talk the less".

"Beauty he called the flower of chastity while according to others it was chastity which he called the flower of beauty."

To the question "Who is a friend?", his answer was "A second alter ego".

He and his school developed the doctrine of predestination (**heimarmene**) or "alloted destiny", the foremost obligation of man is to do his duty, regardless of what may come. Essential harmony of the world of nature with the divine world.

His doctrines range from materialistic pantheism to polytheism. Against the unchanging nature, the Stoics opposed the divine element. The divine element had its origin in pure fire which is identified with creative reason **(logos spermatikos)** by the Stoics. Orthodox Stoics denied the existence of a conscious afterlife. This was Zeno's belief.

A theocentric system of ethics was developed by Zeno's followers: the eternal laws of destiny are essentially good but man has limited capacity to comprehend them. Astrology became an integral part of Stoicism and Geminus of Tyre, disciple of Zeno, translated into Greek the Babylonian astronomical tablets during the 1st century BC.

Cleanthes of Assos, Boethus of Sidon, Apollonius of Tyre, Antipater of Sidon, Geminus of Tyre, Posidonius of Alexandria, Diogenes of Ptolemais and Zeno of Sidon were among the immediate followers of Zeno, the Phoenician from Kition. The author of the teachings of the Ecclesiastes appears to have been a Stoic.

Zeno divides Philosophy into three parts: Physics, Ethics and Logic. A simile used to describe the parts of Philosophy says that it is like an animal: Logic corresponds to the bones, Ethics to the flesh and Physics to the soul. Logic comprises Rhetoric and Dialectic. Cleanthes makes six subdivisions of Philosophy: Dialectic, Rhetoric,

Ethics, Politics, Physics and Theology. Dialectic, they say, gives the wise man the means of distinguishing between Truth and Falsehood and allows him to postulate questions and answers.

A teaching proposed by Zeno and Chrysippus was that among wise men there should be a community of wives with free choice of partners: under such circumstances we shall have equally divided, similar instincs and paternal feelings for all children. The idea, however, according to Aristotle, had already been proposed by Socrates, who advocated community of wives, children and property, a feature described by Plato in the **Laws** and criticized by Aristotle in his **Politics**.

Another Stoic doctrine called for the perpetual exercise of virtue for virtue's sake and requires of the good man to be always exercising his mind, that is to be perfect. Justice, law and correct reasoning exist by nature and not by convention. Betwen virtue and vice there is nothing and virtue is worthy on its own sake.

They reject bad conduct because nothing is really good but the morally bautiful. And that is in itself sufficient to ensure well-being: for virtue alone can raise us above everything. Their definition of love is an effort towards friendliness motivated by visible beauty and its sole end is friendship not bodily enjoyment. They consider three forms of life, contemplative, practical and rational and declare their choice for the latter because a rational being is produced by nature for contemplation and action.

The wise man may terminate his life for the sake of his country, his friends or in case of intolerable pain or incurable disease. The Stoics approve of honoring parents and family first and only after the gods.

The most universal emotions include grief, fear, desire and pleasure.

Grief and pain are considered irrational aberrations of the mind and comprise pity, envy and jealousy. **Fear** is the expectation of evil and contains in itself the sensations of terror, shame, panic and mental agony. **Desire** encompasses anger, love, hatred and resentment. The passion of love is a craving from which good men should be free, for it is an effort to gain affection before the visible presence of beauty. **Pleasure** is an irrational elation at the accruing of what seems choice-worthy while **wrath** is anger which has become malicious with displeasure in the heart.

Anger is a craving to punish someone who is perceived as having done us an undeserved injury. Malevolent joy is pleasure at another's ills. **Delight** is the propensity of the mind to a state of weakness. To be transported by delight is the melting away of virtue. Gout and arthritis are maladies of the body while love of fame and pleasure are diseases of the soul.

Zeno was philosophically a materialist but his followers eventually, under the influence of Plato, abandoned materialism. Zeno's doctrines are most important in relation to Ethics and that portion of Theology that is relevant to ethics. Stoicism is the last

Greek of all philosophic systems among the ancients: the early Stoics, disciples of Zeno, were mainly from Middle Eastern origins and the late Stoics were especially Romans. Nearly all rulers and Kings in the generations that followed Zeno adopted Stoicism as their philosophy. Although initially influenced by the Cynics, Zeno was an eclectic individual and later was especially influenced by the teachings of Socrates. Socrates represented with his way of life, the ideal of the Stoic: his attitude in his trial, his calmness before death, his plainness in matters of food and dress, his indifference in matters of bodily confort, all fitted best the doctrines of Zeno and his followers. The Stoics did not take Plato's doctrine of ideas and did reject his belief in immortality. Only later stoics accepted his ideas of the soul as immaterial.

Zeno did not accept metaphysics except when it had something to do with **Virtue**, which he considered essential to his philosophy. Zeno believed that there is no such a thing as chance but that the course of nature is determined by natural laws. He thought that the end of things will come in a cyclical manner in nature, in the form of a cosmic conflagration that will repeat itself over and over. In Stoicism the course of nature is predestined to occur to secure certain ends by natural means. These ends are to be found in the life of man and the purpose of everything is connected with the human being. All things are part of Nature and individual life is good as long as it is in harmony with Nature. **Virtue** is a will in agreement with Nature and in the life of an individual, virtue is the only good. Every man has perfect freedom when he is deprived of mundane desires. To a modern man is difficult to understand a virtuous life if nothing materialistic is obtained by it, to the Stoic of Zeno's time, the virtue in a man is the end in itself. The Stoic is not virtuous in order to do good but he does good in order to be virtuous. From Seneca, the Stoics preached universal love, an idea he took from the early Stoics. For Zeno the whole universe formed the substance of God and Mind. Destiny, God and Nature were all only one thing.

On the question if the soul survives death, Cleanthes believed that all souls survived death until the next conflagration while Chrysippus thougt only the souls of the wise survived. Stoicism influenced the thinkings of Cicero and through him became known to the Romans. Although many early Stoics believed in astrology some others later made important scientific contributions to Astronomy and Mathematics. Posidonius of Alexandria, a disciple of Zeno, maintained that there is no hell but that the soul of the wicked after death did not rise above the earth level while those of the virtuous and wise, would rise to the stellar sphere. One has to wonder if this was the basis of the idea adopted later by Christianity. Stoicism flourished in the persons of Seneca, Epictetus and Marcus Aurelius. Many of the teachings of Seneca are indistinguishable from those of Christianity; Epictectus taught that we should love our enemies and despise mundane pleasures. Marcus Aurelius doubted the existence of immortality but accepted that life in harmony with the universe is what is good. From his adopted father he followed the advice "not to fall in love with boys".

One of his maxims was

"Whatever may happen to you, it was prepared for you from all eternity".

"The City of God" by Augustine of Hippo was taken at least in part from the Meditations of Marcus Aurelius. The Stoic philosopher thinking of himself holds that happiness is contrary to Nature and worldly goods are worthless. The main importance of the Stoichs, even until modern times, has been their strenght in Ethics: Kant himself developed an ethical system quite similar to that of the Stoics. Finally the Stoics made important contributions to the doctrine of Natural law and natural rights:

"by nature all human beings are equal".

ZENO of SIDON:

This is Zeno, the Epicurean, a disciple of the former and a native of Sidon, who discovered at Gerzeh a mass of papyri from the Ptolemaic period in the early 3d century BC and who chose to adhere to the teachings of the Epicureans. He had been born about 150 BC and headed the Epicurean School at Athens. Cicero audited his lectures. Besides Philosophy he practiced Geometry with a certain degree of success. The name "Zaynun" (translation of Zeno) became very popular in Phoenicia and has been given to many children as first name although it has also survived as a family name.

ANTIPATER OF SIDON:

Born in Tyre, he excelled as an epigrammatist, influenced certain early poets of the Roman Republic and was known to Cicero and Pliny. He made the earliest extant list of the Seven Wonders of the World: The Pyramids of Egypt at Giza, the Hanging Gardens of Babylon, the statue of Zeus at Olympia, the temple of Artemis at Ephesus, the Mausoleum of Halicarnassus, the Colossus of Rhodes and the Pharos of Alexandria.

PORPHYRY OF TYRE:

This Phoenician philosopher named by birth Melek ("king"), born in in Tyre on 233 AD, became known by later writers as Porphyry ("clad in royal purple"). He went to Rome where he taught Neoplatonism until his death in 305 AD. He was a very prolific writer and published many treatrises on multiple subjects including philosophy, grammar, mathematics and even music. He is better remembered as a furious anti-Christian and one of his books on this matter was burned publicly by the Church, about a century after his death. He collected the philosophical works of his teacher Plotinus, whose name may have been forgoten were it not for the fact that Porphyry collected his works in nine books.

THALES OF MILETUS (640-562 BC) or 640-548 BC.

Of Phoenician descent, according to Herodotus, Thales was considered one of "the seven wise men" of Antiquity, as testified by Plato. Herodotus and Democritus, who greatly admired him, knew that Thales was the son of Examyas and Cleobulina, considered among the noblest of the phoenician descendants of Cadmus and Agenor. He acquired his citizenship at Miletus when he came to that town accompanied by Nileus, a friend who had been expelled from Phoenicia. He appeared to have travelled extensively through Egypt and Babylonia. After an adventure in politics he became a student of Nature. In most courses of history of philosophy Thales is mentioned as the first philosopher, but in modern times the tendency is to consider him more as a man of science than a philosopher. He propounded the doctrine that water is the universal primary substance. Modern science, over 2500 years later, tends to favor this view since the world most likely evolved out of hydrogen (according to Beadle, the Universe developed from hydrogen) which forms two thirds of water.

He seems to have been the first to study astronomy, the first to predict eclipses of the sun (he predicted the one that occurred on May

28, 585 BC) and the first to fix the solstices. He appears to have been the first to divide the year in 365 days and to name the 30th day of the month. He discovered how to calculate the distance of a ship at sea from observations using two points on land and how to estimate the height of a pyramid from the lenght of its shadow. Some writers assure us that he was the first to maintain the immortality of the soul. He was the first to learn geometry from the Egyptians and to bring it to Greece. He lived under Thrasybulus, the tyrant of Miletus, and never appeared to have married. Several legends and sayings are attributed to him: when asked why he never had any children he responded "because I love children".

Asked what is difficult, he replied "To know oneself".

To the question what is the divine? "That which has neither beginning nor end" was his response.

When asked what was the strangest thing he had ever seen, his answer was "An aged tyrant". Obviously this reflected his belief that wisdom should come with age.

He held that there was no difference between life and death. When asked "Why then, do you not die?" "Because, said he, there is no difference".

Many more legends exist about Thales but perhaps the best known was related by Aristotle in his **Politics**: "He used to be reproached for his poverty and to those who value wealth-getting Thales gave an example which is attributed to him because of his wisdom but is really of universal application. Thales, so the story goes, because of his poverty was taunted with the uselessness of philosophy; but from his knowledge of astronomy he had observed, while it was still winter, that there will be a large crop of olives later that year, thus he raised a small sum of money and paid deposits for the whole of the olive-presses in Miletus and Chios, which he hired at a low rent because nobody was competing with him. When the season arrived there was a sudden demand for a large number of presses at the same time. By letting them out on his own terms he realized a large sum of money, so proving that it is easy for philosophers to get rich if they so choose, but this is not what they care about. Thales is reported to have thus displayed his wisdom, but as a matter of fact this device of taking an opportunity to secure a monopoly is a universal principle of business..." This is further proof of his phoenician origin and behaviour and lends further support to the proponents of his descent.

Thales died at old age (some say over 90 years of age) while watching an athletic contest during the 58th Olympiad, because of heat, thirst and weakness of old age. The inscription on his tomb reads:

"Here, in a narrow tomb great Thales lies;
Yet his renown for wisdom reached the skies"

According to Apollodorus he had been born in the first year of the 35th Olympiad.

BIBLIOGRAPHY

1. W.F. Albright Yahveh and the gods of Canaan; London, Athlone; 1968.

2. W.F. Albright From the Stone Age to Christianity; 2d Edition; Garden City, NY, Doubleday Anchor, 1957.

3. W.F. Albright Archeology and the Religion of Israel. Johns Hopkins Univ. Press, Baltimore, 1946.

4. Coogan, M D Stories from Ancient Canaan, Philadelphia, Westminster, 1978.

5. Posener, G Sur les inscriptions pseudo-hieroglyphiques de Byblos Melanges de l'Universitée St. Joseph 45 (1969) pp. 225-239.

6. Albright W.F. The phoenician inscriptions of the 10th Century B.C. from Byblus. J. of the American Oriental Society, 67: 153-160, 1947.

7. Dunand, M. Le dechiffrement des écritures et des langues...Paris (1975) pp. 75-84.

8. Dunand, M. Nouvelles inscriptions pseudo-hieroglyphiques decouvertes a Byblos. Bulletin du Musée de Beyrouth 30 (1978 and 1981) pp. 51-59.

9. Dunand M. Byblia Grammata, pp. 71-138, Paris, 1945.

10. Montet, Pierre Byblos et L'Egypte Quatre Campagnes de Fouilles a Gebeil: 1921-1924. Librarie Orientalist Paul Geuthner, Paris, 1929.

11. Dhorme, E. Dechiffrement des inscriptions pseudo-hieroglyphic de Byblos SYRIA 25: pp. 1-35; (1946-48).

12. Mendenhall G. E. The syllabic inscriptions from Byblos, Beirut, American University of Beirut Press, 1985. Regenstein Ref. # PJ 3081. M. 460, 1985.

13. Florian de Ocampo. Los quatro libros primeros de la cronica general de España que recopila el maestro Florian do campo, Zamora, Libro III, chapters 7-8; 1543.

14. Giovanni Battista Ramusio Primo volume delle navigationi et viaggi nel qual si contiene la descrittione dell' Africa, Venice, 1550, 2d Edition 1554.

15. Samuel Bochart Geographie sacrae...pars altera, Chanaan, seu de coloniis et sermone Phoenicum......Caen 1646, Frankfurt 1681, et al. Pars II lib.I, chapter 37, "Phoenices in Africae parte occidentali ad Oceanum"

16. Pascal Francois Joseph Gossellin Recherches sur la Geographie systematique et positive des anciens, 4 vol., Paris 1797/8-1813,...Book I 61-102 and also (I 102-162)

17. Lipinski, Edward, (Ed.) **Studia Phoenicia**, Vol. IV, Religio Phoenicia, 1988.

18. Bonnet, C. **Studia Phoenicia** Vol. VIII.. Melqart. Cultes et Mythes de L'Heracles Tyrian dans la Mediterranee, 1988.

19. Edwards RB Kadmos, the phoenician. A study in Greek Legends...Amsterdam, 1979.

20. Contenau, G. "La civilisation phenicienne", Revised Edition, Paris, Payot. (1949).

21. Dunand, Maurice Fouilles de Byblos, vol 1 & 2 Librarie Orientaliste Paul Geuthner, Paris, 1939.

22. Dunand, Maurice Byblia Grammata-Post-scriptum. Librarie Orientaliste Paul Geuthner, Paris, 1946

23. Attridge HW, RA Oden Jr. Philo of Byblos, The Phoenician History. Introduction, Critical Text, Translation, Notes. The Catholic Biblical Quarterly Monograph, Series 9. Washington, 1981.

24. Virolleaud, Charles "L'Epopee de Keret, Roi de Sidonians..." Revue des Etudes Semitiques Vol. I pp. 6-13, 1934.

25. Virolleaud, Charles "Le dechiffrement des tablettes alphabetiques de Ras-Shamra" SYRIA 12:15-23, 1931.

26. Baurain C. Portées chronologique et geographique du terme "Phenician". In **Studia Phoenicia**, Vol. IV, Societé des études classiques, Namur, Belgium, 1986.

27. Pritchard, James B Ancient Near Eastern Texts......(Editor) 2d edition, Princeton University Press, 1955.

28. Breasted J. H. The Dawn of Conscience (Chicago, New York, 1934).

29. Pope M. H. El in the Ugaritic texts. Leiden, The Netherlands, 1955. Vol. 2, Vetus Testamentum;

30. Gray, John The Legacy of Canaan. (2d Revised Edition), Leiden, 1965. Vol 5, Vetus Testamentum.

31. Gordon, Cyrus H. Ugaritic literature. Rome, Vatican Press, 1949.

32. Lyon DG & Moore GF Studies in the history of Religions. New York, 1912. Chapter by Jastrow M. "The Liver as the Seat of the Soul", pp 143-168.

33. Kapelrud A.S. Baal in the Ras Shamra texts, Copenhagen, 1952.

34. Cassuto U. The Goddess Anath, Jerusalem, 1951.

35. Harris Z S A Grammar of the Phoenician Language, New Haven, Conn., 1936.

36. Frazer J G Adonis, Attis, Osiris (The Golden Bough, Part IV), 3d Edition, Vol. 1, London, 1919. (Condensed edition in one volume, 1926).

37. Dussaud, R. Les decouvertes de Ras Shamra (Ugarit) et L'Ancien Testament, 2d Edition, Librairie Orientalist Paul Geuthner, Paris, 1941.

38. Soyez B. Byblos et la fête des Adonies (EPRO 60), Leiden, 1977.

39. Mouterde, Rene Le Nahar-el-Kalb, Guide Archeologique, Imprimerie Catholique, Beyrouth, 1932.

40. Luckenbill, Daniel D. Ancient Records of Assyria and Babylonia, Vol II, 228, University of Chicago Press, 1927.

41. Diogenes Laertius Lives of Eminent Philosophers, Loeb Classical Library, Harvard University Press, Cambridge, 1995.

42. Diodorus Siculus The Library of History, Loeb Classical Library, Harvard University Press, Cambridge, MA & London, England, 1994.

43. Polybius The Histories (6 volumes), Loeb Classical Library, Harvard University Press, Cambridge, MA, 1979.

44. Livy History of Rome (14 volumes). Loeb Classical Library, Harvard University Press, Cambridge, MA, Reprinted in 1979.

45. Herodotus The Histories (4 volumes). Loeb Classical Library, Harvard University Press, Cambridge, MA

46. Thucydides The War of the Peloponese (4 volumes). Harvard University Press, Loeb Classical Library, Cambridge, MA.

47. Pliny, the Elder Natural History (12 volumes). Loeb Classical Library, Harvard University Press, Cambridge, MA

48. Tacitus Histories & Annals (4 volumes). Loeb Classical Library, Harvard University Press, Cambridge, MA

49. Ovid Metamorphoses (4 volumes). Loeb Classical Library, Harvard University Press, Cambridge, MA

50. Plutarch MORALIA (Vol V) Isis and Osiris, Loeb Classical Library, Harvard University Press, Cambridge, MA; 1993.

51. Plutarch MORALIA (Vol IV) Alexander Virtues, Loeb Classical Library, Harvard University Press, Cambridge, MA;

52. Plutarch LIVES (VOL. VII) Alexander and Cesar, Loeb Classical Library, Harvard University Press, Cambridge, MA. 1994.

53. Pausanias Description of Greece (5 volumes). Loeb Classical Library, Harvard University Press, 1995

54. Nonnos Dyonisiaca (2 Volumes) Loeb Classical Library, Harvard University Press, Cambridge, MA. & London, England; 1985 & 1995.

55. Fulco, WJ The Canaanite God Resep; American Oriental Society, New Haven, Conn., 1976.

56. Lipinski E. Resheph Amyklos; **Studia Phoenicia** V: 87-99, 1987.

57. Apollodorus "The Library", Loeb Classical Library, 2 volumes. Harvard University Press, Cambridge, MA & London, England.

58. Hesiod "Theogony"; The Loeb Classical Library, Harvard University Press, Cambridge, MA & London, England, 1995.

59. Dunand, Maurice "Byblos", Imprimerie Catholique, Beirut, Lebanon, 1973.

60. Du Mesnil du Buisson, R. Etudes sur les Dieux Pheniciens Herités par L'Empire Romain. Leiden, E.J. Brill, Netherlands, 1970.

61. Du Mesnil du Buisson, R. Nouvelles études sur les dieux et les mythes de Canaan; E. J. Brill, Leiden, Netherlands, 1973.

62. Albright W. F. The Phoenician inscriptions of the Tenth Century B.C. from Byblus. J. Amer. Oriental Soc. 67: 153-160, 1947.

63. Diringer, David Writing. Frederick A. Praeger, Publisher, New York, 1962.

64. Gelb, Ignace J. A Study of Writing. (Revised Second Edition) The University of Chicago Press, Chicago, London, 1963.

65. Fell, Barry America B.C. Simon & Schuster, New York, London, Sydney,...Tokyo, 1989.

66. Paulshock, Bernardine Z. Tutankhamun and his brothers, JAMA 244: 160-164, 1980.

67. Harrison RG Tutankhamun postmortem The Lancet 1: 259, 1973.

68. Arrian Anabasis of Alexander.(2 vol.) Loeb Classical Library, Harvard University Press, Cambridge, MA

69. Roland de Vaux "La Phenicie et les Peuples de la Mer"; Melanges de L'Université Saint-Joseph, 45-31, Beyrouth, pp.481-98, 1969.

70. Pettinato, Giovanni The Archives of Ebla. Doubleday & Co. Inc., Garden City, New York, 1981

71. Lipinski, Edward Dieux et deesses de l'univers phenicien et punique. **Studia Phoenicia** XIV, Leuven, Belgium, 1995; Peeters Press.

72. M. Gras, P. Rouillard, J. Teixidor L'Univers Phoenicien. Hachette, 1995

73. Drucker, Johanna The Alphabetic Labyrinth. Thames & Hudson Ltd. London, New York, 1995.

74. Euripides "The Phoenician Women", D. Greene & R. Lattimore, University of Chicago Press; Chicago & London, 1968.

75. Maalouf, Amin The Crusades through Arab Eyes. Schocken Books, New York, 1984.

76. Augustine of Hippo The City of God, 7 vol. The Loeb Classical Library. Harvard Univ. Press; Cambridge, MA & London, England.

77. Marcus Aurelius The Meditations, Grolier Enterprises Corp., Danbury, Conn. 1988.

78. Seneca, the Younger Moral Essays, 3 vol. The Loeb Classical Library. Harvard Univ. Press; Cambridge, MA & London, England.

Anthony Strong

INDEX

Abdi-Ashirta, 16, 41, 42, 43, 168

Abi-Milki, 41, 42, 43, 90

Acharbas, 381, 382

Acre, 7, 132, 372

Adonis, 27, 28, 29, 57, 59, 62, 64, 65, 66, 67, 68, 70, 71, 72, 73, 76, 81, 89, 102, 103, 110, 111, 119, 121, 124, 132, 260, 272, 475

Adonyads, 67, 68, 70, 71, 72, 73, 74, 81

Aeskulapius, 59, 61, 76, 129, 130, 133, 134, 140, 143, 264

Afqa, 65, 67, 68, 83, 110, 111, 131, 215, 216

Africa, xviii, xix, 4, 31, 56, 143, 145, 224, 256, 275, 276, 277, 283, 284, 299, 375, 383, 391, 394, 396, 397, 408, 411, 414, 419, 422, 423, 438, 440, 442, 447, 448, 450, 451, 455, 472

Afterlife, 25, 26, 170, 186, 274, 460

Agenor, xviii, 116, 266, 382, 394, 467

Ahiram epitaph, 234

Ahiram sarcophagus, 7, 11, 236

Akh – mose, 179

Akhenaten, 169, 173, 174, 176, 177

Akhetaton, 40

Akkadian, 3, 89, 157, 183, 243, 295

Akko, 133

Albright, 53, 54, 56, 166, 177, 178, 180, 236, 393, 471, 479

Aleppo, 131, 138, 141, 183

Alexander the Great, 12, 68, 91, 145, 216, 249, 453, 454

Aliyn Baal, 87

Alphabet, xviii, xix, 6, 8, 11, 12, 17, 78, 114, 115, 125, 182, 218, 220, 222, 223, 224, 225, 226, 227, 229, 230, 232, 235, 236, 246, 274, 285, 290, 291, 293, 394, 398

Althaemenes, 126

Amanus mountains, 88, 190

Amenhotep II, 168

Amenhotep III, 168

Amenhotep IV, 42, 56, 169

Amenophis II, 10, 75, 147, 149, 151, 168, 173, 174, 176

America BC, 479

Ammoneans, 61, 62

Ammon-mose, 179

Amorites, 4, 6, 70, 71, 138, 190

Amrit, 133

Amunira, 16

Amurru, 42

Anat, 7, 19, 20, 30, 60, 79, 80, 85, 90, 92, 93, 95, 96, 97, 98, 99, 100, 101, 102, 103, 104, 105, 106, 107, 132, 140, 150, 158, 163, 178, 193, 194, 195, 196, 197, 198, 199, 200, 201, 202, 203, 208, 209, 212, 214, 215, 347

Anatolia, xiii, 5, 10, 20, 89, 115, 142, 158

Anobret's sacrifice, 60

Anti-Lebanon, 3, 33, 56, 88

Antipater of Tyre, 372, 458, 460

Antoninus Liberalis, 62

Aphrodite, 61, 63, 64, 68, 69, 71, 72, 73, 75, 83, 109, 110, 111, 119, 124, 378, 406

Apollo, 22, 121, 130, 133, 152, 157, 159, 160, 219, 274, 313, 392

Apollodorus, 62, 64, 116, 120, 270, 367, 469, 478

Arabia, 261, 265

Arados (Arvad), 7, 40, 296, 298, 299, 308, 321, 354, 372

Arameans, 138, 191, 224, 230

Archimedes death, 441

Ares, 110, 118, 119

Arganthonius, 271, 397

Ariadne, 126

Aristotle, 399, 402, 461, 468

Arrian, 346, 357, 363, 364, 369, 370, 479

Artaxerxes III, 338, 364

Artemis temple, 466

Artemisia, 321, 331, 333, 335

Asherat, 17, 79, 80, 86, 92, 93, 101, 139, 194, 198, 204, 206, 208, 212, 213, 215

Asherat of the Sea, 86, 215

Ashtar, 18, 19, 20, 75, 113, 131, 132, 155, 156, 189, 190

Ashtart, 18

Ashtoreth, 139

Asia, xvii, xviii, 3, 4, 6, 43, 128, 132, 141, 178, 271, 273, 281, 288, 305, 306, 308, 309, 311, 314, 317, 321, 334, 337, 340, 343, 346, 347, 348, 349, 363, 372, 373, 376, 394, 395, 455, 507

Asia Minor, xvii, xviii, 3, 43, 141, 178, 273, 305, 309, 340, 343, 347, 372, 373, 395, 455, 507

Assyria, 4, 55, 64, 80, 91, 133, 140, 142, 190, 252, 296, 297, 298, 368, 476

Astarte, 19, 30, 58, 61, 68, 71, 73, 75, 76, 78, 79, 80, 81, 83, 84, 88, 109, 110, 112, 115, 130, 131, 134, 135, 136, 138, 139, 140, 143, 144, 147, 148, 149, 152, 155, 156, 158, 159, 166, 167, 168, 178, 189, 193, 195, 196, 208, 225, 272, 274, 292, 301, 303, 381, 392, 393

Athalia, 168

Athena, 58, 60, 118, 132, 203, 348

Athens, 68, 74, 203, 264, 306, 309, 310, 311, 314, 315, 322, 327, 328, 329, 330, 331, 332, 334, 335, 336, 340, 343, 347, 358, 387, 456, 465

Atlas, 57, 58, 280, 281, 283

Atlas mountains, 280

Aton, 16, 293

Attica, 60, 73, 121, 328, 330, 334

Aziru, 42

Baal, xvii, 6, 7, 19, 20, 44, 45, 46, 47, 48, 49, 50, 51, 52, 56, 59, 60, 66, 67, 69, 75, 76, 79, 80, 85, 87, 89, 90, 91, 92, 93, 94, 95, 96, 97, 98, 100, 102, 103, 104, 105, 107, 114, 133, 138, 139, 140, 141, 142, 143, 144, 146, 149, 158, 159, 162, 166, 178, 189, 190, 191, 192, 193, 194, 195, 196, 197, 198, 199, 202, 206, 212, 213, 214, 215, 232, 238, 272, 286, 291, 293, 297, 347, 366, 392, 418, 475

Baal Hadad, 56, 59

Baal Hammon, 146, 162

Baal of Lebanon, 114

Baal Saphon, 140

Baal Shameem, 76

Baalath, 103, 109, 149, 236

Baalbeck, 6, 7, 60, 373, 374

Baau (Night), 55

Babylon, 65, 67, 68, 69, 74, 75, 81, 82, 88, 91, 152, 249, 251, 259, 269, 299, 300, 305, 339, 342, 350, 353, 358, 361, 365, 366, 367, 368, 466

Bacchus, 24, 119, 121, 265, 267, 386

Batrun, 16, 42, 168, 373

Beirut, xiv, 3, 15, 40, 41, 42, 55, 61, 76, 90, 116, 129, 131, 134, 140, 188, 190, 215, 222, 232, 249, 255, 300, 373, 375, 387, 388, 389, 472, 478

Beroe, 121, 125

Berouth, 57

Beruna, 42, 168

Berytus, 7, 11, 12, 40, 53, 60, 88, 116, 121, 124, 226, 243, 355, 372, 373, 387, 388, 389

Bible, 102, 179, 207, 210, 226

Bochart, 396, 473

Boeotia, 22, 117, 122, 218, 219, 327, 337

Bostan-el-Sheikh, 129, 133

Botrys, 7, 168

Byblians, 2, 6, 42, 74, 226, 227

Byblos, xiv, xviii, 2, 3, 5, 6, 7, 9, 11, 12, 14, 15, 16, 17, 18, 19, 20, 23, 25, 26, 27, 29, 33, 40, 41, 42, 43, 44, 45, 52, 53, 57, 58, 60, 66, 67, 68, 70, 72, 73, 74, 75, 76, 81, 82, 88, 89, 90, 108, 109, 110, 111, 112, 113, 115, 131, 140, 141, 144, 145, 148, 153, 155, 156, 161, 168, 172, 180, 185, 186, 188, 203, 210, 212, 215, 222, 223, 226, 227, 228, 229, 230, 231, 232, 234, 235, 236, 237, 238, 241, 243, 259, 260, 261, 262, 286, 297, 298, 299, 300, 303, 305, 307, 308, 354, 372, 373, 393, 471, 472, 473, 476, 478

Cabires, 129, 131

Cadmeia, 117, 119

Cadmeians, 114

Cadmus, xvii, xviii, 21, 22, 25, 114, 117, 120, 123, 209, 218, 219, 220, 221, 260, 458, 467

Cambyses, 305, 306, 307, 308, 314

Canaan, 1, 3, 4, 5, 9, 15, 16, 32, 40, 43, 66, 80, 88, 92, 178, 188, 189, 190, 196, 202, 208, 210, 252, 395, 471, 475, 478

Canaanites, 1, 4, 6, 10, 80, 101, 102, 178, 180, 182, 189, 211, 213, 221, 260, 275, 286

Caracalla, 249, 250, 254, 387

Cartagena, 393, 394, 416, 419, 422, 441, 443

Carthage, 71, 79, 83, 110, 114, 115, 134, 137, 142, 143, 144, 146, 152, 158, 160, 161, 162, 163, 181, 187, 262, 263, 264, 276, 279, 280, 284, 289, 291, 294, 354, 355, 383, 385, 391, 392, 397, 398, 399, 400, 402, 403, 404, 406, 408, 411, 413, 414, 419, 420, 421,

422, 424, 431, 433, 439, 440, 441, 442, 444, 446, 447, 448, 449, 450, 451, 452, 453

Carthaginians, 181, 182, 246, 254, 262, 271, 275, 276, 277, 283, 307, 392, 398, 401, 403, 404, 405, 407, 408, 409, 410, 411, 412, 413, 414, 415, 416, 420, 421, 424, 425, 429, 430, 431, 432, 434, 436, 438, 439, 440, 444, 445, 446, 448, 451

Caucasus, 5, 7, 363

Cerne, 279, 280, 281

Chalcolithic, 2

Chaldean, 366, 368

Christianity, 26, 67, 83, 157, 167, 291, 464, 471

Cicero, 464, 465, 466

Cilicia, 117, 247, 309, 311, 339, 347, 350, 351

Cinyras, 62, 64, 68, 71

Cleopatra, 137, 343, 374

Colpia (Wind), 55

Contenau, 473

Corinth, 126, 343, 347

Crete, xvii, 8, 9, 114, 115, 117, 122, 126, 376, 383, 399, 453, 454

Cyprus, 52, 64, 68, 69, 71, 76, 81, 82, 110, 111, 114, 130, 134, 142, 149, 152, 156, 158, 159, 160, 188, 203, 249, 262, 273, 298, 306, 308, 309, 338, 340, 355, 357, 376, 381, 395, 452

Cyrus, 305, 306, 314, 475

Dagon, 57, 59, 62, 85, 89, 91, 92, 94, 103, 107, 149, 152, 190, 194, 196, 206, 303

Damascus, 7, 166, 167, 188, 296, 373

Danel, 213, 214

Darius, 91, 305, 308, 309, 311, 312, 314, 315, 322, 325, 334, 338, 343, 348, 350, 351, 352, 353, 357, 360, 362, 364

Dark Age, 8

Delos, 61, 116, 313

Delphi, 117, 127, 327

Demarus, 92, 138

Dhorme, 180, 472

Dido, 82, 381, 382, 383, 385, 386, 387, 453

Diodorus Siculus, 21, 114, 120, 122, 126, 220, 260, 271, 287, 344, 352, 476

Diogenes Laertius, 476

Dione (Baalath) of Byblos, 58, 60

Dionysus, 21, 22, 24, 29, 61, 118, 119, 120, 121, 122, 123, 124, 146, 260, 261, 265, 267, 269, 364

Dioscuri, 57

Dog River, 249, 250, 254, 300

Dunand M, 472

Dusk & Dawn, 29, 45, 325, 428

Ebla, 2, 3, 12, 40, 59, 61, 67, 76, 89, 91, 135, 138, 143, 144, 147, 148, 152, 171, 172, 183, 184, 186, 187, 188, 189, 190, 226, 227, 262, 480

Eblaites, 40, 183, 189

Ecbatana, 360, 365, 367

Egypt, xiii, 2, 4, 5, 6, 7, 8, 10, 14, 16, 19, 21, 23, 24, 25, 26, 27, 28, 29, 31, 33, 34, 36, 37, 41, 42, 43, 44, 46, 48, 49, 50, 51, 52, 55,

61, 67, 71, 72, 75, 80, 83, 89, 103, 109, 111, 112, 113, 115, 121, 134, 136, 144, 145, 146, 147, 149, 150, 151, 153, 156, 160, 161, 163, 169, 172, 173, 175, 178, 179, 180, 183, 186, 193, 195, 222, 231, 235, 236, 251, 252, 259, 260, 262, 275, 295, 298, 299, 300, 308, 314, 315, 338, 340, 353, 357, 360, 372, 374, 377, 378, 379, 380, 391, 395, 466, 467

Egyptians, 5, 9, 14, 15, 17, 19, 22, 25, 27, 28, 29, 31, 41, 43, 57, 91, 112, 136, 155, 161, 173, 178, 179, 191, 195, 211, 222, 226, 231, 243, 253, 257, 269, 295, 306, 314, 317, 320, 335, 395, 468

Eighteenth Dynasty, 147

Eliyin, 214

Elysian Fields, 128

Eshmun, 59, 61, 66, 75, 76, 80, 91, 115, 128, 129, 130, 131, 132, 133, 134, 139, 140, 142, 151, 152, 158, 264, 301, 303, 305, 392, 393

Euripides, 128, 366, 480

Europe, xviii, 222, 260, 279, 291, 300, 308, 311, 317, 319, 320, 323, 334, 348, 376, 388, 394, 396, 423, 507

Eusebius of Cesarea, 83

Evening Star, 19, 76, 85

Field of Reeds, 25

Fountain of Oedipus, 127

Gades (Cadiz), 77, 111, 142, 270

Ge (Earth), 57

Gebal (Byblos), 15, 17, 18, 19, 110, 111, 112, 113, 155, 233, 236, 237, 238

Genneas, 56

Genos, 55, 56

Gordon translation, 90, 180

Granada, 79, 272, 398

Greek alphabet, 125, 221

Greek language, 220

Gubal (Byblos), 109

Hadad, 7, 67, 75, 77, 88, 91, 138, 158, 251

Hadrumentum, 143, 144, 391, 398

Halicarnasus, 321

Hamilcar, 264, 383, 404, 405, 406, 407, 408, 410, 411, 412, 413, 414, 415, 416, 417, 418, 445

Hammurabi, 91, 157

Hannibal, 142, 314, 383, 385, 405, 413, 414, 415, 416, 417, 418, 419, 420, 421, 423, 424, 425, 426, 427, 428, 430, 431, 432, 433, 434, 435, 436, 437, 438, 439, 440, 441, 442, 444, 445, 446, 447, 448, 449, 450, 451, 452, 453, 454

Harmonia, 102, 118, 119, 128, 209

Hasdrubal son in law, 394

Hasdrubal son of Gisgo, 447

Hasdrubal's head, 446

Hathor-Isis, 15, 112, 241

Hebrews, 67, 89, 101, 162, 166, 179, 190, 191, 202, 226, 262, 381

Helen of Troy, 137

Heliopolis, 6, 7, 60, 70, 373

Hellas, 31, 114, 135, 136, 218, 314, 315, 317, 320, 321, 322

Hellespont, 310, 311, 317, 318, 319, 320, 328, 334, 337, 347, 348

Herakles the Thasian, 135

Herakles the Tyrian, 59

Hermes, 57, 58, 120, 123, 125, 261

Herodotus, xvii, xviii, 1, 30, 31, 63, 69, 70, 81, 82, 83, 90, 109, 114, 135, 136, 139, 160, 218, 219, 224, 260, 271, 276, 299, 305, 306, 309, 311, 312, 313, 315, 320, 324, 330, 335, 354, 376, 377, 379, 396, 467, 476

Hesiod, 62, 260, 478

Hierapolis, 75

Hiram I king of Tyre, 90, 135

Hispania, 79, 271, 272

Hittites, 3, 6, 16, 40, 41, 43, 75, 90, 175, 178, 243, 253, 295

Homer, 9, 12, 376, 379

Horus, 19, 23, 25, 27, 37, 148, 150, 151

Hurrians, 3

Hyginus, 62

Hyksos, 4, 6, 7, 35, 88, 178

Iberia, 146, 247, 271, 272, 288, 292

Iberian script, 246

Iliad, 153, 376, 379

Imhotep the physician, 171

India, xviii, 259, 270, 284, 289, 308, 363, 367

Indian Ocean, 276

Indo-European, 6, 224, 271

Io Inachus, xvii

Ionia, 114, 309, 311, 333

Ishtar, 29, 67, 69, 75, 82, 103, 189, 251

Ishtar Gate, 75

Isis, 19, 21, 23, 24, 25, 27, 28, 29, 30, 76, 103, 110, 144, 146, 477

Isles of the Blest, 128

Israel, 139, 165, 166, 168, 180, 181, 213, 239, 296, 298, 471

Ittobaal father of Jezebel, 168

Jaffa, 10, 91, 128, 188, 190

Jerusalem, 132, 167, 475

Jezebel, 89, 139, 165, 166, 167, 381

Jocasta, 120, 126, 127, 128

Julius Cesar, 374

Kabirim, 131

Kabrim, 132

Kadmos, 221, 265, 266, 473

Kadmos and Crete

    Foundation of Thebes, 117, 118, 221

    Hellas, 31, 114, 135, 136, 218, 314, 315, 317, 320, 321, 322

    Hermes, 57, 58, 120, 123, 125, 261

    Jocasta, 120, 126, 127, 128

    Karatepe, 89, 152, 158, 163, 247

    Keb, 27

    Keret (Krt), 157, 474

    Laius, 120, 126, 127, 219

    Oedipus, 120, 126, 127, 128, 219, 220

    Phoenician origin, 53, 56

    Polydorus, 118, 120, 219

Search of Europa, 135
　　　Wedding, 119, 204, 208, 209, 343
　　　Writing, 479
Khafre, 171
Khattusilis, 16
Kinnor (lyre), 71
Kronos (EL), 57, 58, 59, 60, 61, 102, 116, 191, 203, 213, 393
Kushor (Chusor), 57, 203
Labyrinth, 102, 126, 480
Lady of Baza, 79
Lady of Byblos, 15, 17, 108, 109, 110, 112, 233, 303
Lady of Elche, 79
Laius, 120, 126, 127, 219
Land of the Gods, 19
Laodicea of Canaan, 389
Lebanon, xiii, xiv, 3, 4, 14, 33, 48, 49, 56, 68, 74, 88, 100, 110, 124, 125, 131, 143, 173, 185, 199, 231, 250, 253, 255, 265, 373, 478
Legend, 136
Lesbos, 260, 310
Libya, 384
Linear A, 8
Lord of Canaan, 59
Lord of the land, 59
Lord of the Underworld, 28
Mago son of Hamilcar, 442
Mago the agronomist, 263

Maharbaal, 439

Malaga, 391, 393, 394

Male Sphinx, 20

Malta, 114, 115, 134, 144, 161, 263, 273, 393, 398

Manetho, 5, 30

Marduk, 251, 253

Mari, 4, 12, 91, 157, 184, 187, 188, 189, 190, 243

Mathos, 410, 411, 412, 413, 414

Mediterranean sea, 3, 4, 12, 56, 65, 270, 276, 296, 374, 433

Melkhart, 115

Memphis, 30, 147, 148, 149, 169, 217, 251, 298, 377, 380

Mesha king of Moab, 238

Mesopotamia, xiii, 4, 5, 55, 89, 103, 183, 185, 188, 223, 243, 295, 360, 391

Midas, 121

Miletos, 121

Mining & mines, 10, 88, 111, 271, 272, 273, 287, 288, 292, 311, 398, 416

Minos, xvii, 119, 121, 126

Minotaur, 102, 126

Misor, 57

Mnaseas, 456, 457

Monotheism, 16, 169, 170, 171, 172, 173, 176, 177, 178, 180, 202, 216

Mose, 179

Moses, 162, 178, 179, 180, 202, 216

Mott, 60

Mount Amanus, 56

Mount Athos, 311, 315

Mount Carmel, 258

Mount Kassius, 214

Murex molluscum, 1

Mylitta, 70

Myrrha, 62, 63, 64, 124

Nahar Ibrahim (Adonis River), 68, 73, 74, 83, 216

Nahar-el-Kalb, 250, 296, 476

Naiads, 63

Nebuchadrezzar, 75

Neolithic, 4, 221

Nephthys, 25, 27, 178

Neptune (Poseidon), 120, 278, 384

Nether World, 25, 26

Nile, 5, 10, 21, 23, 24, 28, 33, 123, 340, 378

Nimrud, 133

Nineteenth Dynasty, 16

Niniveh, 133, 184, 249, 252, 295, 298, 299, 360

Nonnos, 124, 142, 264, 266, 478

North Africa, 7, 8, 264, 290, 375, 381, 397, 419, 440, 449, 507

Nubia, 147, 149, 151, 161, 172, 251

Nut, 25, 27

Obeliscs Temple of, 132

Octavian, 374

Odyssey, 379

Oedipus, 120, 126, 127, 128, 219, 220

Orontes River, 389

Orpheus, 21, 22

Osiris, 20, 21, 22, 23, 24, 25, 26, 27, 28, 29, 30, 62, 66, 67, 89, 103, 111, 144, 156, 475, 477

Osorkon I, 17, 237

Ovid, 62, 63, 119, 477

P(h)oinikasta, 9

P(h)oinix, 1

P(h)oinos, 1

Palestine, 10, 59, 92, 134, 152, 179, 188, 191, 298, 308, 320, 373, 374, 452

Palmyra, 7, 59, 68, 75, 110, 156

Papyrus, 231

Papyrus of Golenicheff, 210

Paris son of Priam, 127, 318, 380

Pausanias, 117, 119, 127, 130, 132, 345, 346, 477

Pax Romana, 375

Pdry wife of Krt, 97, 98, 101, 132

Periplus of Hanno, 392

Persians, 254, 262, 296, 299, 305, 306, 307, 308, 309, 312, 314, 317, 318, 319, 320, 321, 323, 324, 325, 327, 328, 330, 333, 335, 337, 338, 339, 340, 343, 348, 349, 350, 351, 352, 353, 357, 361

Pharaohs, 14

Philo of Byblos, 3, 53, 54, 55, 64, 92, 129, 130, 138, 181, 203, 210, 220, 269, 275, 474

Phoenicia, xiii, xiv, xviii, 2, 4, 6, 7, 9, 10, 12, 14, 15, 16, 17, 19, 24, 27, 28, 33, 37, 41, 44, 55, 57, 58, 59, 60, 65, 66, 67, 68, 70, 72, 76, 79, 81, 82, 83, 89, 90, 91, 92, 102, 103, 104, 110, 111, 114, 117, 121, 123, 125, 131, 132, 133, 136, 141, 143, 144, 145, 146, 149, 160, 161, 162, 163, 165, 166, 168, 181, 187, 188, 190, 195, 203, 204, 211, 215, 220, 235, 246, 258, 259, 262, 273, 274, 285, 286, 289, 290, 293, 294, 295, 297, 298, 299, 300, 305, 308, 338, 339, 340, 353, 358, 368, 372, 373, 374, 375, 376, 379, 382, 389, 452, 456, 458, 466, 467, 473, 474, 478, 480

Phoenician

    Afterlife, 25

    Alphabet, 273, 372

    Glass, 257, 259

    Gold, 403

    Language, 475

    Literature, 90

    Philosophers, 476

    Vine, 98, 99, 100

Phoenix (brother of Kadmus), 116, 311

Plato, 461, 462, 467

Pliny the Elder, 137, 220, 277, 397

Plutarch, 22, 27, 30, 62, 66, 344, 346, 362, 364, 435, 438, 453, 477

Poiniki, 395

Polybius, 142, 160, 279, 280, 392, 394, 396, 405, 409, 411, 413, 414, 418, 421, 427, 429, 431, 433, 438, 439, 446, 449, 450, 451, 476

Pompey, 373

Porphyry of Tyre, 55

Poseidon, xviii, 60, 76, 114, 116, 121, 124, 131, 203, 214, 278, 322, 355, 394

Poseidon Society, 61, 116

Predestination, 459

Prima (Maritima)
  Secunda, 7, 375

Pseudo-hieroglyphic, 11, 223, 226, 227, 229, 230, 231, 244, 472

Ptahhotep, 171

Ptolemy, 111, 363, 364, 366, 371, 372

Punic, 8, 160, 182, 246, 247, 254, 277, 285, 286, 288, 290, 292, 293, 294, 375, 382, 391, 392, 394, 418, 450, 454

Purple dye, 1, 139, 272

Pygmalion, 64, 71, 83, 381, 382

Pyramid Texts, 26

Pyramids, 111, 112

Qabr Smun, 134

Quadesh, 178

Qudshu, 80, 148

Quintus Fabius, 430, 431, 448

Ramesses II, 3, 9, 10, 17, 148, 178, 195, 249, 250

Ramesses III, 9, 10, 148

Reshep, 18, 19, 77, 113, 131, 142, 147, 148, 151, 152, 153, 154, 156, 157, 158, 159, 160, 163, 189, 193, 272, 394

Rib-Addi, 9, 16, 41, 42, 43, 90

Rider of the Clouds, 95, 194

Roman Empire, 389

Rome, iii, 24, 76, 138, 142, 225, 247, 254, 388, 404, 405, 408, 418, 419, 420, 421, 422, 423, 425, 426, 428, 430, 431, 432, 433, 438, 439, 440, 441, 442, 444, 445, 447, 448, 451, 452, 453, 455, 466, 475, 476

Sacred prostitution, 274

Sacred tree, 264

Sacrifice human, 60, 85, 160, 161, 162, 163, 181

Salamis, 309, 328, 329, 330, 332, 334, 337

Samaria, 166

Sanchuniathon, 53, 54, 88, 129

Sappho, 66

Sarepta, 79, 133, 143, 144, 188, 294

Sargon of Akkad, 91

Schaeffer CFA, 19, 91, 223, 230

Scipio the Africanus, 392

Scripts, 7, 8, 89, 223, 224, 227, 250, 293

Sea People, 9

Seafaring, 221, 269

Semele, 21, 22, 118, 119, 120, 121, 122, 123, 260

Sennacherib, 191, 251, 269, 295, 298

Seth brother of Osiris, 22, 23, 25, 26, 27, 28, 88, 151, 177, 178

Seti I the great, 16, 75

Seven wonders, 466

Seven-year servitude, 102

Seville (Spain), xiv, 74, 76, 78

Shalim, 132

Ship building, 14

Sicily, 10, 21, 145, 264, 273, 283, 288, 393, 397, 398, 403, 404, 405, 406, 407, 409, 410, 418, 441, 444, 450

Sidon, 3, 7, 11, 12, 15, 40, 41, 42, 43, 48, 59, 61, 75, 76, 80, 91, 128, 129, 130, 131, 132, 133, 134, 139, 140, 142, 143, 144, 145, 152, 158, 160, 165, 166, 169, 188, 203, 206, 208, 223, 243, 257, 258, 259, 264, 296, 297, 298, 300, 301, 302, 303, 305, 307, 309, 318, 321, 322, 330, 339, 340, 354, 359, 372, 373, 374, 376, 379, 398, 458, 460, 465

Si-mi-nu-na, 132

Sinuhe, 33, 35, 36, 37

Skydyk, 129, 130, 132

Spain, 76, 142, 146, 158, 160, 246, 262, 264, 269, 270, 285, 288, 290, 292, 293, 317, 375, 391, 393, 395, 396, 397, 398, 415, 416, 418, 419, 422, 423, 440, 442, 443, 444, 447, 450, 455

Spendius, 410, 412, 413, 414

Stoic, 375, 458, 460, 461, 463, 464, 465

Stoicism, 456, 460, 462, 463, 464

Sumerian, 172, 183, 185, 188

Sun-god, 25, 26, 171, 176

Suppiluliumas, 175

Sur (Tyre), 471

Syria, 4, 74, 183, 185, 188, 220, 224, 258, 308, 339, 340, 360, 373, 375

Tabnit, 131, 133, 301, 303, 372

Tacitus, 221, 477

Tammuz, 65, 66, 67, 68, 89, 103, 110, 216, 290

Tannit, 79, 143, 144, 145, 146, 162, 294, 392, 393, 394

Tarshish, 289, 292, 397

Tartessus, 78, 146, 246, 270, 272, 288, 291, 294, 396

Taurus, 15, 347, 351

Tell -el- Amarna, 12, 61, 109, 168, 217

Tell -el- Mardikh, 183

Temple prostitution, 82, 83, 274

Tennes of Sidon, 340

Thales of Miletus, 467

Thasos the hero, 135, 311

Thebes, 21, 22, 31, 40, 44, 52, 117, 118, 119, 123, 125, 127, 145, 147, 149, 150, 151, 169, 170, 219, 221, 260

Theocritus, 72, 260

Thoth, 27, 30, 57, 62

Thucydides, 160, 218, 263, 477

Thuth-mose, 179

Thutmose III, 15

Thutmose IV, 174

Thyphon, 24

Tiglath-Pileser I, 296

Titanids, 58, 59, 130

Titans, 121, 122

Trade, 2, 6, 12, 17, 77, 114, 139, 185, 221, 226, 254, 258, 270, 288, 294, 295, 308, 309, 336, 340, 391, 395

Tripoli, 7, 129, 132, 253, 255, 372, 373, 397, 398

Turkey, 65, 89, 152, 188, 247

Tyre, xiv, 3, 7, 11, 12, 40, 41, 42, 43, 45, 52, 53, 55, 56, 61, 75, 76, 77, 79, 80, 82, 83, 90, 109, 116, 124, 129, 130, 131, 133, 134, 135, 136, 137, 139, 140, 141, 142, 143, 145, 159, 165, 166, 169, 190, 203, 204, 206, 208, 211, 213, 223, 243, 251, 252, 264, 265, 269, 279, 296, 297, 299, 300, 305, 308, 309, 321, 330, 353, 354, 357, 358, 359, 372, 374, 377, 381, 382, 387, 397, 398, 402, 453, 459, 460, 466

Tyrian purple, 136, 138

Ugarit (Ras Shamra), 7, 12, 18, 19, 20, 40, 43, 54, 55, 59, 60, 61, 64, 67, 75, 80, 85, 88, 89, 90, 91, 92, 96, 97, 98, 102, 113, 115, 129, 132, 135, 137, 138, 139, 140, 141, 142, 145, 149, 151, 156, 157, 158, 159, 160, 163, 180, 181, 184, 189, 190, 192, 193, 194, 196, 202, 203, 210, 211, 212, 213, 216, 223, 226, 227, 230, 243, 259, 264, 275, 475

Uranus (Heavens), 138

Uranus genitals, 59

Usoos, 56

Utica, 134, 137, 391, 410, 411, 442, 447, 448

Vaux R de, 10, 479

Vegetation god, 190

Venus, 29, 63, 76, 85, 110, 119, 144, 157, 382, 386

Virgil, 382, 383, 385

Virolleaud Ch, 54

Wen-Amon, 2, 10, 43, 44, 45, 46, 48, 49, 51, 52, 172, 210, 231, 232

Xerxes, 305, 309, 314, 315, 316, 317, 318, 319, 320, 321, 322, 323, 324, 326, 327, 329, 330, 333, 334, 335, 336, 337, 343, 366

Yahweh, 67, 180

Ypshemuabi, 262

Ytpn, 201, 202

Zakarbaal, 2, 172, 210

Zeno of Sidon, 460

Zeno the Stoic, 463

Zenodotus, 458

Zeus, xvii, xviii, 21, 22, 25, 31, 56, 58, 64, 116, 119, 120, 121, 123, 126, 128, 138, 203, 213, 260, 261, 266, 320, 376, 379, 394, 466

Zimrida, 16, 41, 42, 43

Anthony Strong

ABOUT THE AUTHOR

The author has been a university professor for over twenty years in the United States. In his early youth he was fortunate to live abroad, frequently visiting the countries bordering southern Europe, North Africa and Asia Minor. He has also traveled widely in the rest of the world. With this background, years later he began to work on the present book as a result of fortuitous encounters with people whom he had met all over these areas.

An avid reader, he has acquired a broad knowledge of the historical civilizations that shaped Western culture. Further, he has come to realize the existence of much older, forgotten and mostly ignored pre-historical people who had been at the root of what was inherited by the West through the predominant influence of the Greco-Roman civilization. This book reflects his belief that multiple events that occurred in the remote past paved the way for our civilization to develop to the point that we enjoy today.

Printed in the United Kingdom
by Lightning Source UK Ltd.
101932UKS00001B/268